RESEARCH IN MARITIME HISTORY
NO. 18

MERCHANTS AND MARINERS:
SELECTED MARITIME WRITINGS
OF DAVID M. WILLIAMS

Compiled By
Lars U. Scholl

International Maritime Economic History Association

St. John's, Newfoundland
2000

ISSN 1188-3928
ISBN 0-9681288-8-2

Back issues of *Research in Maritime History* are available:

No. 1 (1991)   David M. Williams and Andrew P. White (comps.), *A Select Bibliography of British and Irish University Theses about Maritime History, 1792-1990*

No. 2 (1992)   Lewis R. Fischer (ed.), *From Wheel House to Counting House: Essays in Maritime Business History in Honour of Professor Peter Neville Davies*

No. 3 (1992)   Lewis R. Fischer and Walter Minchinton (eds.), *People of the Northern Seas*

No. 4 (1993)   Simon Ville (ed.), *Shipbuilding in the United Kingdom in the Nineteenth Century: A Regional Approach*

No. 5 (1993)   Peter N. Davies (ed.), *The Diary of John Holt*

No. 6 (1994)   Simon P. Ville and David M. Williams (eds.), *Management, Finance and Industrial Relations in Maritime Industries: Essays in International Maritime and Business History*

No. 7 (1994)   Lewis R. Fischer (ed.), *The Market for Seamen in the Age of Sail*

No. 8 (1995)   Gordon Read and Michael Stammers (comps.), *Guide to the Records of Merseyside Maritime Museum, Volume 1*

No. 9 (1995)   Frank Broeze (ed.), *Maritime History at the Crossroads: A Critical Review of Recent Historiography*

No. 10 (1996)   Nancy Redmayne Ross (ed.), *The Diary of a Maritimer, 1816-1901: The Life and Times of Joseph Salter*

No. 11 (1997)   Faye Margaret Kert, *Prize and Prejudice: Privateering and Naval Prize in Atlantic Canada in the War of 1812*

Research in Maritime History would like to thank Memorial University of Newfoundland for its generous financial assistance in support of this volume.

Contents

Writings

Introduction

Lars U. Scholl

It was in Berne, Switzerland, that I first met David M. Williams. In late August 1986 we both attended a session on "Shipping Industries in the Nineteenth and Twentieth Centuries" during the Ninth International Congress of Economic History. The conclave, organized by Professors Keiichiro Nakagawa of Tokyo and Peter N. Davies of Liverpool, attracted about three dozen maritime historians from all over the world, including David Williams. I was a newcomer to this crowd, having only once before participated in an international conference in 1984, when I was invited to give a paper at the Fuji Conference on Business Studies in Japan.[1] I do not recollect precisely when I talked to David for the first time or about what we spoke. From hindsight, I presume I had two reasons for seeking him out. A pragmatic reason was that I felt safe at the side of a friend and colleague of Peter Davies, whom I had met two years earlier in Japan. A more sentimental reason for wanting to speak to the gentleman from Leicester had to do with a brief flirtation I had with an attractive female from that city when as a young man I visited Great Britain for the first time back in the 1960s. Thereafter, whenever Leicester was mentioned I listened attentively.

During the course of the Berne Conference David and I spent much time together, drinking coffee and smoking cigarettes during the breaks or having supper together in the evening before we crossed the magnificent bridge over the River Aare on the way to our respective hotels. When we parted at the end of the conference we were not sure when we would meet next. But one of the results of the conference was the foundation of an organization called, rather prosaically, the Maritime Economic History Group (MEHG), which later was transformed into the

---

[1]This conference resulted in the publication of Keiichiro Nakagawa and Tsunekiko Yui (eds.), *Shipping Business in the 19th and 20th Centuries; Strategy and Structure* (Tokyo, 1985).

slightly more euphonious International Maritime Economic History Association (IMEHA) at a meeting in Leuven, Belgium, in August 1990.[2]

On the initiative of Professors Lewis R. Fischer and Helge W. Nordvik, a semi-annual newsletter began publication in June 1987 to keep scholars interested in maritime economic history informed of developments in the field. The response was overwhelming. By the end of 1988 some eight hundred historians in sixty nations received copies. While this organ was well-supported, many maritime historians pointed to the need for an historical journal in which they could communicate the results of research. When approval was given in 1988 by the MEHG's Coordinating Committee to a plan to transform the newsletter into the *International Journal of Maritime History*, David Williams was among the first to be invited to join the twenty-six member Editorial Board. The first issue appeared in 1989, and the next year the MEHG became the IMEHA. At that time the founding Chair of the Editorial Board, Peter Davies, was elected the first President of the fledgling association. To replace him as Chair of the Editorial Board, his colleagues selected David Williams. As Vice-Chair, I had the opportunity to get to know him even better. Since then, with only a break between 1995 and 1999, when he was an Editor of the *IJMH*, David has served continuously as a member of the Board. He was always a pillar of strength and a dominant force in shaping an important historical journal that has provided a focus for maritime historians.

Through our mutual service on the Board we grew closer as we worked in cooperation with the secretary, Dr. Gelina Harlaftis, and other members to help develop the *IJMH* and to act as intermediaries between the Executive of the IMEHA and the editors. Board meetings were always a problem because the members were spread all over the globe, but David always seemed to have a knack for selecting the most appropriate venue. When Board members resigned, replacements had to be suggested to the Executive. Moreover, three times in the first five years new a new book review editor had to be recruited. David and I spent much time on the phone, exchanged many letters, and tried to serve the IMEHA and the journal as best we could. But it was mainly David's experience and

---

[2]Maritime Economic History Group *Newsletter*, I, No. 1 (March 1987), 1-2.

enthusiasm that surmounted the inevitable crises. And since he bore the burden of chairing the Board it was easy for Gelina and me to fulfil our duties. When he took over new responsibilities as an editor in 1994, he had given me plenty of time to gain experience to take over from him. Needless to say, he had also served as an invaluable role model.

The basis for these successful developments was laid in Norway in 1989, when we met twice and seized the opportunity to discuss important matters while attending a pre-conference for a maritime history session planned for the Tenth International Congress of Economic History to be held in Louvain, Belgium, in 1990. It was in Bergen that I heard David lecture for the first time, delivering his paper on "Bulk Passenger Freight Trades," an essay I have selected for this volume. David's masterly presentation was one of the highlights of this conference, as his lectures always were. A few weeks later we met again in Norway, this time in Stavanger where David spoke about "The Quality, Skill and Supply of Maritime Labour: Causes of Concern in Britain, 1850-1914," the final paper in this volume. If possible, David's presentation surpassed even the lecture he delivered in Bergen. The vivid and enthusiastic way he communicated the results of his research made it a performance of the highest order. When he was through, the applause from the audience was overwhelming.

From 1989 we met regularly either at conferences or at editorial meetings; as we got to know each other better, we became fast friends. This was certainly rewarding for me, and I hope it benefited the journal as well, since it enabled us to minimize the problems and to avoid the various pitfalls that always befall an enterprise of this magnitude.

In 1991 the executive of the IMEHA decided to inaugurate a new series of research publications, which came to be called "Research in Maritime History." It was a natural choice for the first volume in this series to be an important reference work compiled by David in collaboration with Andrew P. White, *A Select Bibliography of British and Irish University Theses about Maritime History, 1792-1990.*[3] The series has been phenomenally successful, and so far sixteen additional volumes have appeared, including another one co-edited by David (with Simon Ville),

---

[3]David M. Williams and Andrew P. White (comps.), *A Select Bibliography of British and Irish University Theses about Maritime History, 1792-1990* (St. John's, 1991).

Management, Finance and Industrial Relations in Maritime Industries: Essays in International Maritime and Business History.[4] This volume contained ten papers that were presented at the Eleventh International Economic History Congress in Milan in September 1994, where David and Simon P. Ville of Australian National University organized a highly stimulating session. Having just published a masterful historiographic survey of maritime history in Britain, David displayed his talents as a scholarly *conférencier* and masterly interlocutor in congenial partnership with Simon.[5] Indeed, he is quite unrivalled as an organizer. The substantial number of British and international scholars whom he recruited to lecture at the King's College seminars series in London will never forget either the organization or the friendliness that David demonstrated ten to twelve Thursday nights per year.

David was skilled not only at organization but also at orchestrating complex gatherings. Surely no one who attended the Second International Congress of Maritime History in Amsterdam in 1996 will ever forget the way he put together the major set of lectures on the "Management of Shipping Companies, Navies and Ports," which contained more than twenty papers delivered by scholars from all over the world.[6] In addition to this Herculean task, David undertook the duty of liaising with our host, the Dutch Association of Maritime History, which was celebrating its thirty-fifth anniversary. While David and the Dutch organizers put on a splendid conference, they did so under considerable stress, as temperatures in the mid-thirties wilted even the most hardly participant. His only recompense for this hard work was a drink in the garden of the Royal Yacht Club in Rotterdam.

---

[4]Simon P. Ville and David M. Williams, *Management, Finance and Industrial Relations in Maritime Industries: Essays in International Maritime and Business History* (St. John's, 1994).

[5]David M. Williams, "The Progress of Maritime History, 1953-93," *Journal of Transport History,* Third Series, XIV (1993), 126-142.

[6]A selection of these papers have been published in Paul C. van Royen, Lewis R. Fischer and David M. Williams (eds.), *Frutta di Mare: Evolution and Revolution in the Maritime World in the 19th and 20th Centuries* (Amsterdam, 1998).

In November 1998, after the tragic death of Helge Nordvik, the co-founding editor of the *IJMH*, David, Skip Fischer and I met to discuss the future of the journal. To our surprise and regret, David announced his intention to resign as an Editor.[7] Once we got over the shock, and as it became obvious that David's decision was definite, we decided to respect it on the condition that he accept the Chair's invitation to return to the Board and remain active in the affairs of the journal. David agreed, and in the summer of 1999 was re-appointed to the Editorial Board, thus maintaining his long and close involvement with the publications of the IMEHA.

When all attempts to persuade him to remain as an Editor had failed, my feeling was that this marked a significant turning point in the history of the journal that merited special attention. After more than a generation teaching economic history at Leicester University, and after almost half that long of unflagging service to the *International Journal of Maritime History*, it was clear that all of us who had benefited from his knowledge, experience, generosity and friendship owed him a special debt of gratitude. Fortunately, it did not take long to come up with an idea to honour him in ideal surroundings at a perfect moment.

In early August 2000 the Third International Maritime History Congress will be held in Esbjerg, Denmark, and a large number of maritime historians will assemble in southern Jutland. A few days after the conference closes David Williams will turn sixty. There can hardly be a better moment to present him with a gift than in the presence of his friends and at the time of his sixtieth birthday. But what would be an appropriate present? It should, I believed, be regarded as coming from that legion of maritime historians who know David and who would want to congratulate him on his birthday and thank him for his immense contributions to the profession.

The idea that I finally decided upon had its genesis in a book that I reviewed for the Canadian journal *The Northern Mariner/Le Marin du nord*. On his sixtieth birthday two former students presented Michael Salewski with a collection of his writings as a token of their esteem; this

---

[7]This is discussed in Lewis R. Fischer, "In Memoriam: Helge W. Nordvik (1943-1998); Gerald E. Panting (1927-1998)," *International Journal of Maritime History*, X, No. 1 (June 1998), vii-xii.

type of gift appealed to me.[8] Indeed, in the past two decades it is possible to detect in Germany a trend toward presenting similar collections of their own work to important scholars. While I am not certain whether this is a Teutonic speciality, I think it is an excellent way to show appreciation, and David certainly qualifies.[9] Having decided to pursue this, I asked two of his close friends to write brief essays about David, and Professors Peter N. Davies and Lewis R. Fischer have provided essays on him as a friend and as a maritime historian, respectively. The volume also includes a list of David's publications to the end of 1999. Despite every effort, it is possible that I have missed something; if so, I would like to express my regrets for the oversight.

I believed that the most appropriate place to publish this compilation was in "Research in Maritime History," a series to which David has contributed so much. It was not very difficult to persuade Lewis Fischer, the Series editor, to go along with my plan. We agreed to reprint twelve of David's papers, a limit that forced me to be extremely selective. Fortunately, when going through David's writings systematically, it became clear that there were several recurring threads; this also convinced me that the book would be more than just a compilation of essays on unrelated topics that befit his admittedly eclectic scholarly interests. In fact, it soon became apparent that his writings could be grouped chronologically so that each paper formed a chapter of a book that ranged from about 1807 to the end of the nineteenth century. Over this period there are themes that characterise David's writings: the economic (trades, deployment of the merchant fleet, and state regulation of shipping) and social (many aspects of the seaman's condition over the century). One important feature of the papers is that they always place the maritime topic in the broader context of British and international history and thus transcend the narrow boundaries too often characteristic of maritime history.

---

[8]Michael Salewski, *Die Deutschen und die See. Studien zur deutschen Marinegeschichte des 19. und 20. Jahrhunderts* (Stuttgart, 1998). The volume was compiled by Jürgen Elvert and Stefan Lippert.

[9]For example, the distinguished historian Wolfram Fischer, *Wirtschaft und Gesellschaft im Zeitalter der Industrialisierung* (Göttingen, 1972), dedicated a selections of his writings to the memory of his academic mentors Rudolf Stadelmann (1902-1949) and Walther G. Hoffmann (1903-1971).

The papers chosen here were published between 1966 and 1994.[10] The first paper in this volume, "Abolition and the Re-Deployment of the Slave Fleet, 1807-11," examines the uses to which former slaving vessels were put after Britain abolished the trade in 1807.[11] Not surprisingly, David concentrated on ships in the service of Liverpool traders. Despite a dearth of obvious sources he doggedly traced 104 of 114 former slavers between 1808 and 1811. The great majority found employment in Central and South America, or in Africa, during a period in which European trades were constricted by Napoleon's Continental System. Since all the ex-slavers had copper sheathing and were therefore less vulnerable to tropical marine pests, they were fast enough to outsail most warships and privateers. A large number of ex-slaving vessels were relatively new and provided tonnage for a variety of trades. Indeed, they were crucial to meeting the requirements of the new trades that rose to prominence in Liverpool's commerce after 1807.

One of the most obvious of these trades was cotton. The importance of this cargo to Liverpool's economic well-being in the first half of the nineteenth century has been recognised by historians since at least the 1850s.[12] A century later Eric J. Hobsbawm reminded readers that "who ever says Industrial Revolution says cotton," a quote that David built upon by noting that "whoever speaks of Britain's industrial greatness and domination of the world trade in manufactures throughout the nineteenth century speaks of cotton."[13] Between 1820 and 1850 cotton imports into

---

[10]David began his career at the University of Leicester after completing an MA thesis at the University of Liverpool under the distinguished professor of economic history – and eminent maritime historian, Francis E. Hyde. The thesis was David M. Williams, "The Function of the Merchant in Specific Liverpool Import Trades, 1820-1850" (Unpublished MA thesis, University of Liverpool, 1963).

[11]*Journal of Transport History*, New Series, III, No. 2 (September 1973), 103-115.

[12]See, for example, Thomas Ellison, *The Cotton Trade* (London, 1858); and Ellison, *The Cotton Trade of Great Britain* (London, 1886).

[13]Eric J. Hobsbawm, *Industry and Empire* (London, 1968), 40; and David M. Williams, "The Shipping of the North Atlantic Cotton Trade in the Mid-Nineteenth Century," in David Alexander and Rosemary Ommer (eds.), *Volumes Not Values:*

Liverpool rose three-fold to well over 1.5 million bales, and more than eighty percent of British cotton imports entered the UK through Merseyside. While many details of American supply and British demand had been studied closely, David noticed that information about cotton merchants was scanty, despite Sheila Marriner's important study of the Rathbones.[14]

As a result of this insight he set out in "Liverpool Merchants and the Cotton Trade, 1820-1850," the second essay in the collection, to examine "the degree of concentration prevailing in the cotton trade and by examining the changing role and function of the individual merchant."[15] By using the Customs Bills of Entry, "a source which has been surprisingly neglected by both economic and business historians," he was able to identify a group of thirty major cotton importers who by 1839 controlled about three-quarters of cotton imports.[16] Moreover, these men tended to be specialists who no longer served as "country banker, underwriter, and broker" and "no longer possessed shipowning interests."[17]

In the mid-1970s David could still claim that "for all the attention lavished on cotton both by contemporary observers and subsequent historians...the actual transporting, the shipping of cotton across the Atlantic, has never been fully examined." He decided to fill this gap in "The Shipping of the North Atlantic Cotton Trade, 1820-1850."[18] Again using the Customs Bills of Entry, he undertook a detailed analysis of cotton arrivals at Liverpool based on a pair of three-year periods, 1830-1832 and 1853-1855. In the first period four major cotton ports –

Canadian Sailing Ships and World Trades (St. John's, 1979), 305-329. The quote is on 305.

[14]Sheila Marriner, *Rathbones of Liverpool* (Liverpool, 1961).

[15]In J.R. Harris (ed.), *Liverpool and Merseyside. Essays in the Economic and Social History of the Port and its Hinterland* (London, 1969), 182-211. The quote is on 182.

[16]*Ibid.*, 184.

[17]*Ibid.*, 200.

[18]Williams, "Shipping of the North Atlantic Cotton Trade," 305.

Charleston, Savannah, New Orleans, and Mobile – accounted for roughly eighty percent of American exports. By the second period, New Orleans and Mobile had increased their exports four-fold; Charleston's shipments had risen by only twenty-five percent; and Savannah's trade had stagnated. The number of voyages per year rose from about 540 in 1830/1832 to more than 750 in 1853/1855, although the great expansion of trade was "accommodated chiefly by an increase in the size of the vessels." A striking feature in the North Atlantic cotton trade was that a majority of vessels participated only seasonally, which led him to conclude that the cotton trade was "not self-contained but was part of a much larger and complicated pattern of commodity dealing and shipping employment."[19] He called for more detailed studies of the pattern of ship movements to understand more completely the interlocking network of trade and shipping, a plea that still awaits a scholarly response.

If the North Atlantic cotton business was one of the great commodity trades between the United States and Britain, the tonnage employed was exceeded by the shipping in the colonial timber trade, a subject that David had begun to examine as early as 1966 in "Merchanting in the First Half of the Nineteenth Century: The Liverpool Timber Trade."[20] Liverpool was one of Britain's major timber ports and imports "in 1850 outstripped those of London in both volume and value."[21] The trade expanded two and one-half times between 1820 and 1850, when it demanded about 250,000 tons. The largest source of this increase was shipments from North America, which soared from 74,000 to over 200,000 tons. This shift was encouraged by high duties on European timber relative to the colonial product. David was able to identify twenty dominant importers, ten of whom "accounted for almost all the increase in both absolute and percentage terms."[22] Unlike the situation in the cotton trade, timber importers tended to own their own vessels. Indeed, between

---

[19]*Ibid.*, 323.

[20]*Business History*, VIII, No. 2 (1966), 103-121.

[21]*Ibid.*, 103.

[22]*Ibid.*, 109.

1820 and 1850 the number of major timber merchants who owned vessels rose from eleven to nineteen. The vessels they sent out were simple in design but were often in poor condition. In fact, the Select Committee on Shipwrecks of Timber Vessels revealed in 1839 that more than 280 vessels "were either wrecked or became waterlogged on voyages from Quebec, Halifax and Newfoundland" over the preceding eight years.[23] Several of the Committee's recommendations were implemented by the government in an effort to improve safety.

The chairman of the Select Committee on Shipwrecks of 1836 was James Silk Buckingham who, as David reminded us, was a "sailor, explorer and maritime reformer.[24] A most remarkable man who has received little attention from historians, he was the force behind the creation of the Select Committee that was formed out of the "special concern and deep emotion aroused by the problem of shipwreck." David argues that the desire to safeguard the lives of those in peril had a significant influence on state intervention for safety of sea in the nineteenth century. Buckingham acted fast, and within two months a report (plus 400 pages of evidence) had been produced. Although none of the recommendations were immediately adopted – he advised, for example, against the carriage of deck loads – by mid-century almost his proposals had been enacted.

In 1982 David wrote that a "major feature of state involvement with merchant shipping in the nineteenth century was that of concern over safety of life at sea." This opening sentence from "State Regulation of Merchant Shipping 1839-1914: The Bulk Carrying Trades," heralded an examination of state regulation in two of the chief bulk carrying trades, timber and grain.[25] In the 1830s, heavy losses in the timber trade, largely caused by the use of old vessels and overloading, attracted attention. Yet

---

[23]*Ibid.*, 115.

[24]David M. Williams, "James Silk Buckingham: Sailor, Explorer and Maritime Reformer," in Stephen Fisher (ed.), *Studies in British Privateering, Trading Enterprise and Seamen's Welfare, 1775-1900* (Exeter, 1987), 99-119.

[25]In Sarah Palmer and Glyndwr Williams (eds.), *Charted and Uncharted Waters* (London, 1981), 55-80.

a long time elapsed before acts in 1876 and 1880 began to regulate the carriage of timber and grain. A statistical analysis by the Royal Commission on Unseaworthy Ships revealed that grain was "one of the three most casualty-prone cargoes in terms of vessels wrecked or missing and lives lost."[26] Although the number of casualties did drop immediately, David concluded that "government legislation on unseaworthy ships and load lines, advances in marine technology, growing experience and better trained officers all helped to reduce losses of timber and grain laden vessels probably as much, if not more so, than the specific regulation of loading."[27]

In the post-Napoleonic era, colonial timber preference led to a clever customs-evasion scheme that distorted normal trading patterns. In "Customs Evasion, Colonial Preference and the British Tariff, 1829-1842," David examined the importation of Baltic timber via North America.[28] The differential between duties on foreign and colonial timber was so high that this roundabout trade could be remunerative. While merchants and shipowners profited, David argued that it was unlikely that this had any effect on consumer prices; at any rate, legislation in 1835 put an end to this indirect trade. A second case of importing foreign produce via the colonies involved coffee between 1839 and 1842. Coffee duties traditionally favoured West Indian imports. Shipping South American and Haitian coffee around the Cape of Good Hope occurred for the first time in 1838. Despite added costs, indirect importation avoided duties ranging from forty-two to fifty-two shillings per hundredweight. For three years "Cape coffee" became the largest single source of supply. In 1843, indirect imports collapsed, in part because of a shift in government policy and in part because supply outpaced consumption. Among British consumers South American coffee was unpopular largely for reasons of taste. David concluded that the most important aspect of the indirect trades

---

[26]*Ibid.*, 64.

[27]*Ibid.*, 73.

[28]In Philip L. Cottrell and Derek H. Aldcroft (eds.), *Shipping, Trade and Commerce. Essays in Memory of Ralph Davis* (Leicester, 1981), 99-116.

was "in bringing about the rejection of traditional tariff policies and the adoption of free-trade principles."[29]

The transport of people – slaves, emigrants, convicts, indentured servants and contract labour – is the focus of "Bulk Passenger Freight Trades, 1750-1870."[30] While millions of people were shipped across the Atlantic and Pacific in this period, only when special passenger vessels began to ply the oceans after the 1840s were human beings regarded as something more than bulk freight. While all the trades discussed have been well documented, they have "never been considered before as a group sharing common characteristics, nor has their collective position and influence within the evolving pattern of modern international trade and maritime activity ever been assessed."[31] Bulk passenger traffic was a constant feature of British shipping, but since human beings had to be treated differently than other cargoes, these were the first trades on which the state focussed. In 1803 the first of a series of Passenger Acts was passed; although "unrealistically optimistic," the 1803 Act "nevertheless established areas which for the next seventy years would be the subjects of intervention – overcrowding, accommodation, provisions and diet, medical facilities and sea-worthiness." Yet there was another important aspect that has not been seen in that context: "Measures regulating the slave, emigrant, and convicts trades were not simply ends in themselves but rather the fuses which ultimately fired the process of welfare reforms for seamen."[32] Sixty years later, after the inertia of *laissez-faire* had been overcome, passenger acts "could be held up by reformers as an irrefutable precedent for intervention to assist seamen, who where so vital to the nation." Perhaps David's most important contribution in this essay is in emphasising for the first time the "collective contribution and influence of the bulk freight passenger trades in shipping employment, commercial

---

[29]*Ibid.*, 112.

[30]In Lewis R. Fischer and Helge W. Nordvik (eds.), *Shipping and Trade, 1750-1950: Essays in International Maritime Economic History* (Pontefract, 1990), 43-61.

[31]*Ibid.*, 43.

[32]*Ibid.*, 60.

development and state intervention."[33] Apart from anything else, the carriage of passengers created "a new role for government."

In "Henry Mayhew and the British Seaman," a contribution to the Dartington Hall conference series organised by the University of Exeter's Department of Economic History in the mid-1980s, David turned his attention to a remarkable journalist and literary bohemian who published six lengthy letters (about 80,000 words) on seamen in the *Morning Chronicle* in 1850.[34] Henry Mayhew (1812-1878), a founding editor of *Punch*, gained mass recognition when his letters were published as *London Labour and the London Poor* in 1861-1862, albeit with his missives on "seaman afloat" and "seaman ashore" omitted. As a result, this "unique study...appears to have been little known and certainly underutilized."[35] When they were rediscovered in the 1960s and 1970s by E.P. Thompson and other labour historians, the focus was on landsmen rather than sea-based labour. Mayhew gained his knowledge by interviewing seamen or visiting their accommodations in London. These first-hand accounts were published precisely at the time when "both the shipping industry and sailors were very much a matter of public and legislative interest in 1849-1850."[36] The Merchant Shipping Bill was before the House of Commons when the letters on seamen appeared between early March and early May 1850. While Mayhew drew attention to maritime legislation, he did not advocate specific action but instead allowed seamen to voice their conviction that "government had the power to intervene and a belief that it should" to better the lot of the British sailor.[37] One recurring complaint was that the American merchant marine offered "better service than the English, better wages, better meat, better ships." The outstanding quality

---

[33]*Ibid.*, 61.

[34]In Stephen Fischer (ed.), *Lisbon as a Port Town, the British Seaman and Other Maritime Themes* (Exeter, 1988), 111-127.

[35]*Ibid.*, 111.

[36]*Ibid.*, 116.

[37]*Ibid.*, 123.

of the information supplied by Mayhew was based on "a rare insight into the seaman's attitudes and emotions" in mid-Victorian Britain.[38]

"Mid-Victorian Attitudes to Seamen and Maritime Reform: The Society for Improving the Condition of Merchant Seamen, 1867," looked at attempts to improve the health, safety and comfort of British merchant seafarers.[39] A few months before the President of the Board of Trade introduced an amendment to the Merchant Shipping Act, the Society for Improving the Condition of Merchant Seamen was founded in February 1867 by twenty-nine people connected professionally connected with the sea: MPs, naval officers, medical men, ship masters, current and ex-civil servants, clerics and humanitarian reformers. But significantly the Society included no common seamen; instead, the "impetus for reform...emanated from humanitarian, middle-class interests."[40] The Society's objectives were to collect evidence, make recommendations and publish the results of its investigation. Subcommittees inquired into health, accommodations ashore, wages, discipline and the protection of life at sea. One of its main purposes was to influence public opinion and to stir the Board of Trade into action. The Society's published *Report* provided an outstanding summary of the varied dimensions of the seaman's condition and showed "how proposed solutions to perceived problems were framed to receive general acceptance in the confused context of a society recognising the virtue of business freedom, ambivalent towards government intervention and disturbed by a humanitarian conscience."[41]

Payments in the form of "advance notes" were one way to recruit seamen for long-distance voyages in the age of sail. Although the Select Committee on Shipwrecks turned its attention in 1836 to abuses of the advance system, this practice first became a serious public issue in the 1860s and 1870s, when seamen's welfare caught the interest of social reformers. In "'Advance Notes' and the Recruitment of Maritime Labour

---

[38]*Ibid.*, 124.

[39]*International Journal of Maritime History*, III, No. 1 (June 1991), 101-126.

[40]*Ibid.*, 104.

[41]*Ibid.*, 125.

in Britain in the Nineteenth Century," David described the history and impact of the advance note in Britain, showing how it shaped market behaviour.[42] Intended "to enable them [the seamen] to pay debts contracted for board and lodging ashore while waiting employment, and for the purchase of clothes and outfit requisite for the voyage," over time "malpractice arising from the notes" became "the order of the day."[43] Seamen often fell into the clutches of dubious operators who "rendered them open to corruption and exploitation."[44] Reformers believed that advance notes were the roots of all evil among sailors and campaigned for their abolition. While this happened in 1881, since seamen expected them and owners felt it necessary to make them, the law had little effect and they were legalised again in 1889. As steam displaced sail, however, they quickly disappeared. Their importance clearly was limited to the age of sail, when they were "an essential element of hiring labour."

The final paper in this volume deals with contemporary complaints about the quality of seamen and seamanship. "The Quality, Skill and Supply of Maritime Labour: Causes of Concern in Britain, 1850-1974," received much praise from the commentator, Atle Thowsen, and the audience when it was presented at a conference in Stavanger, Norway, in 1989.[45] In three sections David examined the concern about skill (seamanship); supply and the alleged shortage of seamen; and the responses to perceptions about these problems. What came to be known as the "manning question" featured in almost every official enquiry into the merchant marine from the late 1840s to the end of the century. During these decades the transition to steam diminished the demand for seamen but increased the need for men with different qualifications. While basic sailing skills were less important on steamers, perceptions about "true

---

[42]In Lewis R. Fischer (ed.), *The Market for Seamen in the Age of Sail* (St. John's, 1994), 81-100.

[43]*Ibid.*, 82 and 87.

[44]*Ibid.*, 88.

[45]In Lewis R. Fischer, *et al.* (eds.), *The North Sea. Twelve Essays on Social History of Maritime Labour* (Stavanger, 1992), 41-58. The comments by Dr. Thowsen have been omitted in this reprint but are on 53-56 of the original.

seamanship" were still dominated "by gilded memories" of the past. "Old-fashioned seamen and seamanship may have been in short supply in 1914 but skill of a different order was very much in evidence."[46]

The controversy over supply, on the other hand, was a long-standing issue in both the navy and merchant marine. But the problem was aggravated by the growth of British trade. The navy solved its manning problem by the 1870s but the merchant service, where a steadily growing non-British presence "commanded much attention and seemed to be the clearest evidence of a supply problem," failed to follow suit. At the same time, conditions afloat were increasingly "unattractive in an age of reform and advancing standards" because "shore-based employment improved even more and because attitudes and social values changed."[47]

In reality, David argues, there was "no difficulty in meeting the labour requirements of the British mercantile marine." Contemporaries, on the other hand, were firmly convinced of both deterioration of seamanship and recruitment problems. Ye there was a striking contrast between public concern and political action: "[t]hroughout the period government was ideologically committed to the market and jealous of expenditure." David explained this by pointing out that other maritime problems "may have been seen as more pressing and commanding priority – the impact of Navigation Law Repeal, the Passenger Acts, the quality of officers, problems associated with new technology, and the ever-present issue of safety at sea which so obsessed the Victorians."[48] And again, as we have seen in previous chapters, there was the tendency to refrain from public involvement, intervention and inspection. "Much agitation, for no great reason and to no great purpose" has to be set against the decline of old-style seamen and traditional seamanship in an "era of expansion and technological advance."[49] There was no longer any room for a romantic view of the age of sail in the harsh world of twentieth-century shipping.

---

[46]*Ibid.*, 46.

[47]*Ibid.*, 47.

[48]*Ibid.*, 50.

[49]*Ibid.*, 52.

One feature common to all articles in this volume is their clarity of structure and style. The arguments are uniformly well presented and leave no doubt that the author is in full command of his subject. As well, his long and successful teaching career shines through even in his writing. Anyone who has had the privilege to hear one of David's lectures will immediately recognize the same persuasive and stimulating qualities in his written prose. This book, as readers will discover, contains a wealth of information. But at the same time, it should become a quarry of ideas and insights for a new generation of maritime scholars to mine. Some of David's best work sounds a clarion call for new approaches and deeper investigations. In some cases David has done this himself, but in others he has left the task for a new generation. Yet what is perhaps most impressive is the unity of his work considered as a whole. I see and read the papers reprinted here as chapters of a book: all I had to do was to arrange them in a logical way and have them bound in this volume.

While I cannot deny my admiration for David's work, I have no doubt that not only readers returning to these papers as old friends and newcomers coming to them fresh will share my view that David Williams is a remarkable scholar. His work demands to be studied seriously in order to gain the most benefit from *Merchants and Mariners*.

But I cannot end this brief introduction on such a formal note; rather, I would like to make a few personal remarks which, I hope will shed a little light on this special man. Working with David over such a long period has always been a pleasure because it has been so easy. Not once was there ever a disagreement that caused friction or endangered our mutual goal of promoting the study of maritime history. This is no exaggeration, for whenever I needed his help I have always known I could count on him, both as a colleague and as a friend.

Having attended so many international maritime conferences with David is, of course, only the academic side of the coin. But to understand David Williams you have to understand the human side of the man as well. While I do not want to tell tales about trivial incidents, there are a few reminiscences that show this clearly. Take, for example, a certain taxi ride from hell that David took with Peter Davies and me in Madrid in 1990. Since we were staying in hotels relatively close to each other, we shared a taxi home one night after having a few drinks with friends. While there is still some disagreement about who sat in the front seat, I will for the moment concede this "honour" to David; Peter and I by this account sat in the back. In our broken Spanish we asked the taxi driver to take us to a square near our hotels, but he soon became hopelessly lost. When he realized this, he literally went berserk. To make up for lost time, he decided to try to imitate a Formula 1 race driver (another analogy might have been to a man using a motorized vehicle to stay ahead of the bulls in Pamplona, but I do not want to push the metaphor too far). Five lanes crowded with cars and motorbikes were no barrier as he swerved in and out of traffic. Nor did red traffic signals deter him; in one memorable incident, he ran a light and continued at high speed into a roundabout, exiting on only two wheels. Neither David's Spanish nor my pitiful attempts at the language made any impression on the driver, who only slowed his frenetic pace when he saw our hotels. I survived that trip without any physical harm, although ten years later my pulse races when I recall the scene. David, of course, took the entire incident in stride.

Another incident that says something about David's aplomb occurred in Newfoundland in 1991. Having put in several days of hard work, Skip Fischer took David, Helge Nordvik and me for a ride in the countryside outside St. John's on the last day before we parted. Helge and I had inexpensive air tickets and hence had to stay a little longer, but David was to leave that evening. Helge and I stayed with Skip's wife, Ann, while Skip took David to the airport. When they arrived at the terminal, Skip began to get nervous because there was no one else there, an unusual scene an hour before the departure of a normally crowded transatlantic flight in early summer. When David checked his ticket, he discovered that his flight was supposed to be the *next* night. Never missing a beat, David responded that this course would give us all more time to spend together. When they returned home, we had a good laugh and a few drinks to celebrate this unexpected – but very welcome – reunion.

David has always displayed a "never say die" attitude, which was nowhere demonstrated as clearly as at a conference in Leiden in 1992. One of the principal organizers was Frank Broeze, who of course has been a student at the local university. On the second evening Frank took David and me to one of his favourite pubs, where he proceeded to challenge us to several games of billiards, a sport at which we soon discovered Frank had more than modest expertise. While I did my best, I soon gave up. But not David, who continued to show his competitive spirit. I would like to distort reality by reporting that eventually David emerged triumphant, but even a number of rounds of good Dutch beer could not erode Frank's skills. But the point is that David never gave up.

This, then, is David Williams – not only a superb scholar but also a good friend and a very admirable human being. Aside from Skip Fischer, it was David who was most responsible for the *festschrift* presented to Peter Davies at the First International Congress of Maritime History in Liverpool in 1992. Now, at the Third International Congress of Maritime History in Esbjerg, it is David who will be presented with a book containing a selection of his writings. This is not exactly a *festschrift*, for David has many years of productive scholarship ahead of him, but rather a token of our affection and admiration on the occasion of his sixtieth birthday. While we hope he will forgive me for preparing this volume without seeking his consent, I am certain that no one in the audience will disagree with my decision to express our common appreciation for what he has done for the profession and for what, by being who he is, he promises for the future.

David Malcolm Williams:
A Tribute from an Old Friend

Peter N. Davies

When Lars Scholl first suggested that David Williams' sixtieth birthday should be marked by the publication of a selection of his writings, I was delighted to be asked to contribute a personal appreciation. At the same time, however, several of us were a little apprehensive, for although such an undertaking may be a regular practice in Germany, this form of tribute would only be given in Britain or North America to selected scholars on their retirement. Yet despite the fact that David's career still has a long way to go, his contributions to maritime history have been so significant that it was clear that they warranted renewed recognition at an earlier stage. Once these doubts had been resolved, we all sought to portray him in the ways that we knew him best. In my case it was decided that I should outline our lengthy friendship from being fellow undergraduates and postgraduates at the University of Liverpool to our long-standing relationship in both domestic and international professional bodies and associations.

This process inevitably involved a great deal of personal reminiscence and some degree of speculation on my part without any opportunity for either discussion or correction. Nevertheless, I felt justified in describing our association in detail so that readers might judge for themselves the basis on which many of my subsequent remarks were formulated. Any errors or omissions are entirely mine, but over a period of nearly forty-two years they can, perhaps, be excused.

In the autumn of 1957 I was in my third year as a teacher at an inner-city secondary modern school in downtown Birkenhead. At this time I was principally concerned with attempting to introduce some limited aspects of British history to frequently unresponsive pupils, who were in the main anxious to join the ranks of their elders, who were already fully employed. Although relishing the challenge which this presented, it had by then dawned on me that to make any serious progress in this profession would require the possession of a degree rather than merely my existing teaching certificate. I therefore approached my local authority and was informed that I could have a leave of absence, albeit without pay. Further, as I had received some support for my previous two-year course, it would be necessary for me to pay the appropriate university fees myself.

Fortunately, by this time my commercial interests – a legacy of my former passion for motorcycle racing and which I had been developing alongside my teaching career – were generating sufficient income for me to contemplate this course of action. Accordingly, I took advice from a university administrator of my acquaintance and made an appointment to see the Head of the Department of Economics at the University of Liverpool.

My memories of the events that followed, although over forty years old, are still vivid. I was met at the door by a lovely teenager whom I soon discovered was Val Dodd, the departmental secretary, and taken to see Professor Francis Hyde. As Francis was virtually blind, Val always gave the name of the visitor at least twice so he would know who it was. This was a very useful habit which I was to encourage and benefit from in later years when Val knew the names of all our students, while I could only remember those who were either outstanding or in deep trouble! My interview went well and, after explaining to Francis my deep conviction that economic history (then part of the Department of Economics) was the key to solving all the ills of the world and that I had been teaching for three years, he agreed that I be admitted.

Thus it was that in October 1958 I joined eleven other individuals who comprised the entire intake for the BA in economics, and a further twelve who were to study for the degree of Bachelor of Commerce. At that time the Dean of the Faculty of Arts, Professor Kenneth Muir, took it upon himself to welcome each new student personally. It was while waiting outside his door that I first met David Williams.

It should not be thought that David and I immediately became bosom pals. Like most undergraduates in a strange environment, we were primarily concerned with finding our ways about and in coming to terms with the demands of our courses. Nevertheless, we increasingly found ourselves to be part of a group which included Derek Balmforth and his girlfriend, Dianne (they were later to marry) and Harvey Range. As a result our friendship gradually evolved, and the fact that we had very different backgrounds proved no barrier to this process.

I was, of course, a mature student some thirteen years older than David, and apart from my studies still had the task of directing two small but demanding companies. At the time David was aged eighteen and had come straight from home and school. I quickly learned that home was in Caernarvon, where he had spent most of his earlier existence in a very quiet and somewhat narrow environment. I also came to understand that he had been brought up in a quite conventional and close-knit family which he regarded with a great deal of affection. But there can be no doubt that he viewed his move to Liverpool as part of a welcome process that would help to liberate him from the confines of a small town.

David was clearly extremely bright and, once settled into his new surroundings, proved to be highly articulate, outgoing and popular. While he obviously found Liverpool to be very different than Caernarvon, he adapted well to living away from home for the first time, and I understood that he was able to take full advantage of the many social and recreational facilities offered by the city. Sadly, I have little real knowledge of these events as I was already fully committed elsewhere, both personally and commercially, and my time with David was mainly limited to the working day. It was only at Christmas or on other special occasions that we met in the evening.

Neither David nor I experienced many problems in our first year, but the second presented a special difficulty. This was in the form of a compulsory course in statistics that had to be passed, since failure meant either leaving the university or repeating the year and proceeding to a degree without honours. The need to avoid these drastic penalties ensured that we, like our fellow students, tended to spend more time on this single topic than on all our other subjects combined. In spite of these efforts we were still unsure on the day of the examination, and I can remember us anxiously working through examples of standard deviations right up to the last minute before we entered the hall. Fortunately, a question on this calculation duly appeared on the paper, so our academic careers were saved and we went on to third year, where we both chose to take the economic history options.

The explanation for this choice is not hard to find. While we had been taught previously by a number of very eminent economists, such as George Clayton, Norman Cunningham, Stanley Please and, particularly, G.L.S. Shackle, we had also been motivated by a very special group of economic historians. These included John Harris, Sheila Marriner, and Berwick Saul, as well as Francis Hyde, and it was their influence which led us to our chosen path. The wisdom of following their courses was then to lead to David securing a very fine Honours degree and to us both being accepted to read for MA degrees.

In the short interregnum between sitting our finals and getting our results, David and I decided to make a brief visit to Caernarvon. At the time I had access to a Triumph TR-2 sports car and this seemed like a good opportunity to enjoy a fast run. With the hood down and bright sunny weather, we felt that all was well with the world. I was then made a welcome guest by David's parents and grandmother before being shown the delights of this historic place. Meeting David's friends and seeing him at ease with them and his family gave me a fresh insight into his character and confirmed to me his very pleasant and considerate nature.

We returned to the joy of graduation, after which David, as the best student of his year, was awarded the prestigious Gladstone Memorial Scholarship. We then went our separate ways before meeting up again in October 1961 to commence our postgraduate studies. The emergence of what was to become known as the "Liverpool School of Maritime Studies," which at the time included Hyde, Marriner and Harris, encouraged us both to consider various aspects of shipping and trade. I quickly identified the Elder Dempster line as an untouched area, and when the company refused me access to its records, I was just as happy to study the life of its founder, Sir Alfred Lewis Jones. David had more difficulty in finding a topic that suited both him and Professor Hyde, who undertook the supervision of all postgraduates in his department. Eventually, however, a subject was agreed and David threw his considerable energies into a study of "The Function of the Merchant in Specific Liverpool Import Trades, 1820-1850."

Although the only formal requirement of the course was to attend Hyde's fortnightly meetings, we were also expected to take part in whatever departmental lectures and seminars happened to be arranged. As these were not that frequent, we were able to devote most of our time to our research, but in spite of this it was often difficult to find something new to say when we reported our progress to the postgraduate seminar. While somewhat critical of these arrangements at the time, in retrospect it seems that the obligation to keep repeating what we were doing and the problems that were arising was largely beneficial, and we all gained something from the comments of Hyde and our fellow postgraduates. As these included men of the calibre of Frank Neal (then studying "Investments in Liverpool Shipping, 1815-1835") and, later, Eric Taplin ("The Origins and Development of New Unionism, 1870-1910"), it will be seen that we were in excellent company. Nevertheless, tensions and strains sometimes arose, and it was at these times that David's growing diplomatic skills were used to their best advantage. Although still somewhat in awe of the great man, David had the knack of saying the right thing at the proper moment; as a result, our relations with Professor Hyde were always kept on an even keel.

The two years of our MA research were happy ones for both David and myself. But although we saw a lot of each other in the department, we seldom met in the evenings. This was only partly due to my ongoing business commitments – it was mainly a result of my preoccupation with my forthcoming marriage. This duly took place at the end of April 1962, with David very much in attendance. But this was not the only reason for our diverging paths. David's social life was a full one and when he met his future wife, Maureen Hardy, it became even fuller!

At this point in our lives, I had no expectation of a university career, and I also doubt that David had any specific plans in that direction. This situation was soon to be dramatically changed by the resignation of our Tutor in economic history. This post had been created by Professor Hyde in order to keep John Harris in the department. Harris had been recruited to assist him with his book on Blue Funnel, and as no permanent position was the available, Hyde obtained funds for a temporary post. When a full-time vacancy did occur, Harris was duly appointed, but by then the value of the tutorship was fully appreciated and it was retained. Ian Keil subsequently succeeded Harris; when he moved to a lectureship at the University of Loughborough he was in turn replaced by Barbara Wakeham. Her sudden resignation – for no known reason – meant that the department had an unexpected vacancy. After due process, Mr. D.M. Williams was officially installed as the fourth tutor.

David's appointment to the staff did not affect his status as a postgraduate, and his Master's studies continued with their customary vigour. The combination of this increasingly heavy workload and his ongoing courtship ensured that he was a busy as well as a happy man. By then a newly-married man, I was also kept fully occupied, but we maintained our regular contacts within the department. These indicated that David was enjoying his new role and that both he and others were rapidly convinced that he had a real flair for this form of teaching. As the tutorship was a three-year, non-renewable position, I was only mildly surprised when, after only twelve months, I learned that he had applied for a lectureship at the University of Leicester. What did surprise me was that he resigned from his Liverpool post before securing his new position. His confidence was, of course, fully justified – those were the days – and in October 1964 he joined Professor Ralph Davis as an assistant lecturer in Economic and Social History. At the same time, I was invited to replace him as tutor in Liverpool.

David's move to Leicester was, of course, the end of day-to-day meetings, but we kept in touch on a regular basis. Consequently, I was soon to learn of the plans for David's and Maureen's wedding to which my wife, also Maureen, and I were kindly invited. This took place at Stratford-on-Avon, the original home of the bride, and proved a most splendid and memorable occasion. Thereafter we only met at special events, such as Economic History conferences and seminars, but even these contacts tended to diminish as we were both overtaken by family responsibilities.

David's appointment at Leicester inevitably meant that his academic priorities were considerably changed. At Liverpool he was responsible for only a few students and given a great deal of support. As a result, he was able to continue with his research and to make good progress on his thesis. At Leicester, on the other hand, he was immediately given a heavy teaching load and, as his lectures proved extremely popular, this was to become a long-standing feature of his career. In spite of this distraction and the setting up of a new home, together with the subsequent arrival of a son and a daughter, David quickly completed his MA and then published a number of articles drawn from this study. These were primarily on maritime topics, but he was then to widen his scope by examining British commercial policy and trade expansion in the period from 1750 to 1850. This was followed by an investigation into the records of the Leicester Building Society, before a series of events helped to return him to his original interests in shipping and trade.

These seminal events involved the creation of the Atlantic Canada Shipping Project in 1976 and the subsequent seminar held in Newfoundland to discuss its findings. These attracted a growing number of maritime historians and economists from all over the world and, as David and I were invited to several of these sessions, we found ourselves associated with what was to become a major centre of global significance. The need to produce papers for these meetings encouraged David to rededicate his efforts on maritime topics. This trend was to be further confirmed by the opportunity to take part in the conference on "Charted and Uncharted Waters," organized at Queen Mary College, London, by Sarah Palmer and Glyn Williams, in 1981. As these lectures were soon published, they rapidly established David as a major scholar in this area. He was subsequently to play an active role in many of the domestic and international bodies that cater for maritime history.

In the early 1980s I was invited to join the International Commission for Maritime History. The British Commission was then based at the National Maritime Museum in Greenwich. At that time this was a very small but select group which included Messrs. Andrews, Annis, Bromley, Craig, Dolley, Eames, Greenhill, Minchinton, Pearsall, Ranft, Ryan, as well as Dr. Helen Wallis, with David Proctor as its secretary. This group was soon to be joined by Pat Crimmin, Gordon Jackson, Roger Knight and David Williams. The British Commission decided to organize a number of lectures on maritime topics in 1985. These were given by invited speakers at King's College, London; as they proved highly popular, it was agreed that a regular programme should be arranged each year. These attracted increasingly large audiences and a high calibre of lecturer, including David, who spoke on "The Seaman's Skill: A Matter of Victorian Concern" in February 1989. Apart from this and a number of other well received papers, David was also quickly recognized as a man of considerable administrative ability. As a result, he was elected Secretary of the British Commission in 1989 to succeed David Proctor.

By this time I had been elected Chairman of the British Commission, so David and I were to work closely together for the next six years. During this period David successfully recruited twelve speakers a year for the King's Maritime History Seminar series, as well as organizing the normal business meetings. Although these were onerous and time-consuming tasks which were undertaken with great dedication and flair, they were not sufficient to dampen David's enthusiasm. On the contrary, he was always looking for ways in which to improve the functioning of the Commission, which had previously operated on an *ad hoc* basis. Thus, he was chiefly responsible for producing a mission statement which set out its aims concisely and for revising its constitution. These advances were followed by a series of measures designed to assist the younger members of the profession. The first of these was David's proposal to establish an annual seminar for New Researchers in Maritime History. The suggestion was taken up with some enthusiasm, and the initial meeting took place at the National Maritime Museum in Greenwich in March 1993. This proved so successful that further sessions have been held every year since then; the eighth was held earlier this year at the Greenwich Maritime Institute.

Having provided a venue for young (and some not so young) scholars, David turned his attention to providing financial support for at least one new maritime historian to attend the ICMH conference that was due to be held in Montréal in August 1995. This was approved by the Commission without hesitation; not only was a young scholar enabled to take part in these meetings but it was agreed that similar provision should be made for future conferences. Further initiatives to encourage both undergraduates and established scholars were suggested by David and quickly adopted. These included the British Commission Prizes for Undergraduate Achievement in Maritime History (six per year) and an annual prize for the Best Published Article in Maritime History.

These awards have now become well-accepted parts of the British Commission's activities and serve as permanent reminders of David's concern both for his subject and for the individuals who will carry it forward. While the acceptance of his proposals undoubtedly delighted him, they paradoxically increased his workload as Secretary. Nevertheless, he continued his tenure until 1998; when he finally left office he was provided with extensive proof of the regard in which he was held by all involved in the organization he did so much to transform. Apart from the presentation of a maritime print of Liverpool and a cheque, David was subsequently elected as the group's Vice Chairman.

David's association with the British Commission was then to lead to his appointment as a member of the ICMH's international executive, a position he holds to this day. David was also active in the other international body that was specifically established to cater for the needs of maritime economic historians. This had its origins in a session on shipping and shipbuilding at the International Economic History Congress in Berne, Switzerland, in 1986. This led to the formation of the Maritime Economic History Group, which was in due course to be transformed into the International Maritime Economic History Association. From its inception David was heavily engaged in its organization, and when its newsletter evolved into the *International Journal of Maritime History*, he served as Chairman of its Editorial Board from 1990 to 1995, and then as an Editor until 1999.

It should not be thought that David's involvement with these academic bodies detracted from his other commitments. From the beginning of his career, David had always excelled as a lecturer, and with growing maturity and confidence he had become particularly incisive and entertaining. He was, therefore, in great demand at many international and domestic venues. As I was also invited to attend a number of these events, David and I developed the habit of sharing hotel rooms – a practice which gave us a higher standard of accommodation at a lower cost. While this system may have sometimes given led to raised eyebrows, we were always able to defuse any potential criticism by explaining that we both had our wives' permission to share! Thus, over the years we were to spend much time in one another's company at a variety of conferences, which included meetings at Berne, Charleston, Greenwich, Louvain, Madrid, Milan, Montréal and Piraeus, among others.

On these occasions I learned a little of the many other aspects of David's life in which I played no part. At an early stage in his career, he had been invited by the Economic History Society to join its Schools' Committee, and thereafter had always taken an active part in the wider affairs of the profession. One particular way in which this can be seen was in his long-standing role as external examiner for the degree of Social Studies at John Moores University, and in similar positions at the Universities of Exeter and Hull. Another role in which his experience was greatly appreciated was as an external advisor. Thus, both the Centre for Maritime Historical Studies at Exeter and the Centre for Port and Maritime History at Liverpool appointed him to their respective Boards of Study and Advisory Panels. David also served as Review editor for the *Journal of Transport History*, before joining its Editorial Board in 1993.

A final aspect of David's academic life in which I was only to be involved at a later stage concerned his association with the Netherlands. This developed for two separate reasons. Over the years David had been an avid collector of historic postcards and he found a ready source of these items in the Low Countries. He was thus able to make many visits on this account and these in turn facilitated contacts with colleagues with similar interests in maritime affairs. There can be no doubt that our Dutch friends developed a considerable respect for David's abilities and, at a later date, the goodwill which this engendered was to prove extremely helpful when he was engaged in helping to organize a number of joint conferences, including the British-Dutch series and the Second International Congress of Maritime History.

All of these professional and academic activities were, of course, undertaken against the background of a heavy teaching and administrative burden at the University of Leicester. They were also completed against David's concern for the welfare of his family. This was a very real priority, as both he and Maureen proved to be involved and dedicated parents. The support he received in return was then to be a significant factor in lightening the weight of his workload. As a consequence he was also able to publish the wide range of books, articles and papers which are so well described in the adjoining historiographic essay by Professor Fischer.

In spite of all these tasks and pressures, and some periods of ill-health, David is still today little changed from the cheerful and bright young school leaver I met nearly forty-two years ago. He was then, as he has remained, highly adaptable to all situations and just as comfortable with the porters as with eminent scholars. Other aspects of his character have also remained constant. A prime feature has been his willingness to help whenever asked. As a result he undertook many activities which might well have been completed by others. It is often said that one should always ask a busy man when anything needs to be done: this has literally been true in David's case, and I must confess that I fell into this trap on several occasions. Above all I found David to be a particularly kind and considerate person who was frequently prepared to sacrifice his own convenience for that of others.

One example must suffice to illustrate any number of similar instances. In September 1987 David and I were invited to participate in an

ICMH conference which was to be held in Charleston, South Carolina. At an early stage we booked flights to New York, intending to arrange internal flights to Charleston nearer the time. At this point my son Simon, a medical student then aged nineteen, found that he needed to visit Cleveland, and it was agreed that he should fly with us as far as New York. Simon then decided that it would be interesting to accompany us to Charleston and then go on to the midwest. David readily consented to this change, no doubt thinking that we would all fly to the south together. But when Simon suggested that we should travel by Greyhound bus, David even agreed to this outrageous idea. At the time neither David nor I appreciated that this would involve a road journey of more than twenty-four hours! It must be said, however, that he accepted the situation with good humour – even though he eventually decided to return to New York by air!

This gentle side of David's nature should not obscure the fact that he is a man of strong convictions and more than capable of holding his own in any debate. Now, as he approaches his sixtieth birthday, it is clear that apart from being a thoroughly pleasant individual he has also emerged as one of maritime history's leading exponents. David's long-standing interest in various aspects of nautical advertising, and his more recent concern with the development of the cruising industry, makes it certain that he will remain at the forefront of his profession. In addition to this ongoing research activity, David will undoubtedly remain in constant demand as a commentator, lecturer and after-dinner speaker at many academic venues.

This personal tribute comes from one who, like many others, has benefited immensely from David's friendship. My affectionate regard has been compounded by his sage advice and council, and I am very anxious to place on record the great debt which I and my colleagues feel we owe him. David, your contribution and kindness has been appreciated by all who know you. On behalf of the all, I wish you continuing success in what I am sure will be a splendid future.

David M. Williams and the Writing of Modern Maritime History

Lewis R. Fischer

I have never told this to David Williams, but his scholarship is the reason I decided to become a maritime historian, although I would not have used this particular term at the time. The chain of events goes something like this. As a new graduate student in the early 1970s, I was searching without a great deal of success for help in specifying the questions and methodologies for my thesis. I knew that I was interested in general terms in examining why Nova Scotia, alone among the predominantly English-speaking colonies in mainland North American, did not join the American Revolution, but I was at a loss as to how to launch the project. While the late John Bartlet Brebner's magnificent trilogy had already convinced me that it was possible to write colonial history that was relevant to scholars with broader interests, I still had a problem.[1] Because I was interested in commerce, something that was peripheral to Brebner's interests, I was searching desperately for a model to help sharpen my questions. More-over, because there were few private mercantile records extant for Nova Scotia in this period, and because the best available source for trade data was a set of shipping records (the Naval Officers' returns), none of the previous approaches seemed to fit my needs.[2] Fortunately, my thesis supervisor, Joseph Ernst, suggested that I read an essay in *Mariner's Mirror* by a young scholar at the University of Leicester. The article, of course, was David Williams' marvellous "Bulk Carriers and Timber

---

[1]John Bartlet Brebner, *New England's Outpost: Acadia before the Conquest of Canada* (New York, 1927); Brebner, *The Neutral Yankees of Nova Scotia: A Marginal Colony during the Revolutionary Years* (New York, 1937); and Brebner, *North Atlantic Triangle: The Interplay of Canada, the United States, and Great Britain* (New Haven, CT, 1945).

[2]The recognized expert on the Naval Officers' records at the time was Lawrence Harper. But while Harper discussed them in *The English Navigation Laws: A Seventeenth-Century Experiment in Social Engineering* (New York, 1964), he had never tried to base an entire study on them.

Imports: The British North American Timber Trade and the Shipping Boom of 1824-5," which taught me a good deal about the role of transatlantic shipping and its symbiotic relationship with trade. I was even more thrilled when a literature search turned up "Liverpool Merchants and the Cotton Trade, 1820-50" and especially "Merchanting in the First Half of the Nineteenth Century: The Liverpool Timber Trade" (both included in this volume). These latter essays used trade statistics in a sophisticated way and focussed on an entire merchant community, just as I knew I was going to have to do for Nova Scotia.[3] I recognized immediately that I was dealing not only with a kindred spirit but also (and more importantly) with a scholar who had already resolved many of the conceptual and method-ological conundrums that had been troubling me. In other words, right from the beginning of my career I was in a sense a student of David Williams. I am still learning from him to this day.

After devouring these three essays, I had a pretty good idea how to structure my study. Shortly thereafter, in a moment of youthful exuberance, I sat down to write a letter of thanks to David for saving me from having to re-invent the wheel. In doing a bit of research for this article, I came across this twenty-eight-year-old missive, which remains in my files to this day. While the writing is abysmally amateurish and unfocussed – not to mention highly saccharine – I do not think that I would alter the basic sentiments one iota. "Your essays have saved me an awful lot of time and effort," I wrote to him on 21 October 1972.

> In addition, they have inspired me to believe that studies
> of trade, and especially those concerned with the mer-
> chants involved in transatlantic commerce, can shed light
> on a whole host of questions that are (or ought to be) of
> central interest to economic historians...I only hope that
> I can produce something approaching the consistently
> high quality of your work.

I never sent this letter because I feared that doing so would be considered too forward for a mere graduate student. Yet anyone who knows David –

---

[3]Since a complete list of David's writings appear at the end of this volume, readers wishing full citations of his works are directed there.

and I have now known him for close to a quarter-century – will realize how foolish this fear was, for he is among the most approachable, generous and helpful of scholars, traits for which an entire generation of younger maritime historians should be grateful.

In this brief essay I would like to repay my debt to David by trying to situate his work within the body of maritime history – especially but not exclusively British maritime history – that has been produced since the Second World War. I am not going to attempt a full-blown historiography of the past half-century, for there are some excellent historiographical essays already available.[4] Instead, I am going to concentrate upon forward and backward linkages: the people who influenced David Williams as well as those who have drawn intellectual sustenance from his work. In the process, I hope to make it clear that David's place in maritime history far transcends his individual publications, for his vision of what this discipline ought to be has had a particularly significant impact on the way in which most of us think about what we do.

Let me deal with this last point first. As the list of his writings compiled by Lars Scholl attests, David has always been a most catholic scholar, with an exceedingly wide range of interests that address a plethora of intriguing questions. Taken together they demonstrate his adherence to the "broad" definition of maritime history most usually

---

[4]Readers interested in the intellectual development of British maritime history should begin with two of David's own essays, "The Progress of Maritime History, 1953-93;" and the introduction to his edited collection, *The World of Shipping*. For a sense of temporal change, they should also look at Ralph Davis, "Maritime History: Progress and Problems," in Sheila Marriner (ed.), *Business and Businessmen: Studies in Business, Economic, and Accounting History* (Liverpool, 1978), 169-197; and P.N. Davies and S. Marriner, "Recent Publications and Developments in the Study of Maritime History: A Review Article," *Journal of Transport History*, 3rd series, IX, No. 1 (March 1988), 93-108; and Sarah Palmer, *Seeing the Sea: The Maritime Dimension in History* (Greenwich, 2000). To put British developments in perspective, see the essays in John B. Hattendorf (ed.), *Ubi Sumus? The State of Naval and Maritime History* (Newport, RI, 1994); and Frank Broeze (ed.), *Maritime History at the Crossroads: A Critical Review of Recent Historiography* (St. John's, 1995).

associated with Frank Broeze.[5] But to denigrate David's role in promoting this perspective would be a serious mistake. Indeed, any impartial observer coming to his work for the first time would find in David's scholarly output a consistently compelling argument for taking the broadest possible view of what maritime history ought to comprise. I have always found it intellectually nourishing to consult David's writings for just this reason.

Nonetheless, as the title of this volume suggests, there are clearly two foci to his work: merchants and mariners. The former were the individuals who conducted trade, a subject that dominated David's writing during the first part of his career and one that remains an on-going concern. Yet by the 1980s David was becoming increasingly interested in issues relating to seamen, who were of course crucial to the carriage of goods and people across the world's seas. This latter topic, which has been illuminated by David's broad knowledge and penetrating intellect, has always been placed in the broadest possible context, thus making it both accessible and compelling reading for non-specialists as well.

When searching for the scholars who stimulated David's interest in trade and merchant behaviour, it is well to begin with those who taught him as an undergraduate and postgraduate at the University of Liverpool. Two of them were maritime business historians, Francis Hyde and Sheila Marriner.[6] These two towering scholars were the founders of the

---

[5]This definition holds that maritime history is the study of the relationship between man and the sea. It therefore includes not only shipping, shipbuilding and seafaring but also subjects such as naval history, yachting, maritime art and even cruising (his first essay on this topic will appear this autumn in *The Northern Mariner/Le Marin du nord*). The seminal work is Frank Broeze, "From the Periphery to the Mainstream: The Challenge of Australia's Maritime History," *The Great Circle*, XI, No. 1 (1989), 1-13. The implications of this approach have been worked out most clearly in Broeze, *Island Nation: A History of Australians and the Sea* (St. Leonards, NSW, 1998).

[6]The Liverpool School worked within a paradigm that generated certain common questions, especially about the profitability of the firm, and was based largely on the use of business records. See, for example, Francis E. Hyde, *Blue Funnel: A History of Alfred Holt and Co. 1865-1914* (Liverpool, 1956); Hyde with Sheila Marriner, *The Senior: John Samuel Swire 1825-1898* (Liverpool, 1967); Hyde, *Liverpool and the Mersey: An Economic History of a Port 1700-1900* (Newton Abbot, 1971); Hyde, *Cunard and the North Atlantic 1840-1973* (London, 1975); Marriner, *Rathbones of Liverpool 1845-73* (Liverpool, 1961). Peter Davies, who was a student of Hyde, is also a prominent member

"Liverpool School of Maritime History," an approach that places a special emphasis on the history of the firm, and especially on its financial records.[7] There can be little doubt that Hyde, who supervised David's MA thesis, was the person primarily responsible for attracting him to the study of maritime history. But David was never a card-carrying member of the Liverpool School, since his interests were in trade, broadly defined, and in the mercantile communities that conducted it, rather than in the operations of specific firms.

Because Francis Hyde shared his interest only to a limited extent, we need to look elsewhere for the source of inspiration for David's studies of trade.[8] On reflection it is clear that David was strongly influenced by the work of Berwick Saul, another of his mentors at Liverpool. Saul's magnificent *Studies in British Overseas Trade, 1870-1914* was concerned with the kind of seaborne commerce that David has always written about – trade that was not simply firm-based but was much broader in scope. Moreover, while Saul, like David, used descriptive statistics where appropriate, neither one of them would be classed as enthusiastic disciples of cliometrics.[9]

But it was not only Berwick Saul who served as an exemplar of David's kind of trade study. As Peter Davies points out in his "tribute" elsewhere in this volume, David obtained his first full-time post at a much earlier age than most academics. When he moved to the University of Leicester in 1964 he was a promising, if not yet fully formed, scholar. At

---

of this school. See P.N. Davies, *The Trade Makers: Elder Dempster in West Africa, 1852-1972* (London, 1973); Davies, *Sir Alfred Jones: Shipping Entrepreneur par Excellence* (London, 1978); and Davies, *Henry Tyrer: A Liverpool Shipping Agent and His Enterprise 1879-1979* (London, 1979).

[7]The "Liverpool School" is discussed perhaps most comprehensively in Lewis R. Fischer, "Peter Davies, the Liverpool School and the Writing of Maritime Business History: Shipbroking on Merseyside as a Case Study," in Lewis R. Fischer and Gordon Jackson (eds.), *Maritime Business History: The First Decade of the Davies Lectures* (forthcoming).

[8]See especially Francis Hyde, *Far Eastern Trade 1860-1914* (London, 1973); and Hyde, G.C. Allen, D.J. Morgan and W.J. Corlett, *The Import Trade of the Port of Liverpool: Future Prospects* (Liverpool, 1946).

[9]S.B. Saul, *Studies in British Overseas Trade, 1870-1914* (Liverpool, 1960).

Leicester he joined a department headed by Ralph Davis, one of the most remarkable scholars of the past five decades and surely the most important British maritime historian of the twentieth century. Davis was a direct influence on the many of the most significant maritime historians who came of age intellectually between about 1960 and 1980 – Robin Craig and Gordon Jackson, in particular – and he also played a decisive role in shaping the intellectual development of David Williams. When David arrived at Leicester, Davis' *magnum opus*, *The Rise of the English Shipping Industry in the Seventeenth and Eighteenth Centuries*, had been in print for only two years but was already being rightly acclaimed a masterpiece.[10] And Davis had begun work on the studies that would lead to the seminal pamphlet, *English Overseas Trade, 1500-1700*, and his next book, *The Rise of the Atlantic Economies*.[11] To read any of these monographs is to catch a glimpse of the path which David Williams would soon tread, examining the always symbiotic relationship between shipping and trade.

The other obvious post-Liverpool influence on David's thinking about shipping and trade was Robin Craig. It would be hard to over-estimate Craig's impact on modern maritime history, as a scholar, supervisor, motivator and *éminence grise*. Although it was as the founding editor of the pioneering journal *Maritime History* that he arguably made his greatest impact, Craig also wrote some first-rate pieces on shipping and trade, studies very much like those that David Williams was about to produce.[12] Moreover, Robin was always willing to share his knowledge and ideas, and David was quite happy to incorporate these into his world view. Over the years, Robin Craig helped David to find his scholarly voice.

---

[10]Ralph Davis, *The Rise of the English Shipping Industry in the Seventeenth and Eighteenth Centuries* (London, 1962).

[11]Ralph Davis, *English Overseas Trade, 1500-1700* (London, 1973); and Davis, *The Rise of the Atlantic Economies* (London, 1973).

[12]Craig edited four volumes of *Maritime History* between 1971 and 1974. For examples of his trade studies, see R.S. Craig, "The African Guano Trade," *Mariner's Mirror*, L, No. 1 (February 1964), 25-55; and Craig, "The Copper Ore Trade," in David Alexander and Rosemary Ommer (eds.), *Volumes Not Values: Canadian Sailing Ships and World Trades* (St. John's, 1979), 275-302.

If Hyde, Marriner, Saul, Davis and Craig were the principal influences on David's thinking about shipping and trade, his decision in the late 1970s to undertake a series of studies on the British seaman came from other sources. If the entire range are difficult at this point to discern, some are relatively clear. Part of the impetus obviously came from a careful reading of the literature and from his own experiences as a scholar. His work on the slave trade, for example, had always included a social aspect, for to study this commerce without being concerned with the humans who manned the vessels and the Africans who comprised the cargoes would have required a degree of mental compartmentalization that would always have been beyond David. But he did little else in this vein until 1979, when the Atlantic Canada Shipping Project, on whose members David was an especially important influence, invited him to present a paper on seamen in the North Atlantic trades ("Crew Size in Trans-Atlantic Trades in the Mid-Nineteenth Century"), a project that motivated him to look more carefully at British seamen during the "golden age of sail." Once he began to do that, he was soon reminded of how neglected questions of social history had been by maritime scholars.[13] Indeed, at the same conference in St. John's were Judith Fingard and Eric Sager, both of whom had come to similar conclusions and would soon produce major social histories of seamen in their own rights.[14] As David discussed the issues with these scholars, his resolve to do more in this area was doubtless reinforced.

Yet it is important to acknowledge that David's unique background conferred important comparative advantages. While the last five

---

[13]At the time, scholarly works on seafaring labour were few and far between. Knut Weibust's superb *Deep Sea Sailors: A Study in Maritime Ethnology* (Stockholm, 1969) was the standard work, but this was soon to change. For examples of early 1980s scholarship, see Sarah B. Palmer, "Seamen Ashore in Late Nineteenth-Century London: Protection from Crimps," in Paul Adam (ed.), *Seamen in Society* (2 vols., Bucharest, 1980); H. Campbell MacMurray, "'Ships' Engineers: Their Status and Position on Board, c. 1830-65," in Stephen Fisher (ed.), *West Country Maritime and Social History: Some Essays* (Exeter, 1980). In the fishery, see especially the path-breaking work by Paul Thompson, with Tony Wailey and Trevor Lummis, *Living the Fishing* (London, 1983).

[14]Judith Fingard, *Jack in Port: Sailortowns of Eastern Canada* (Toronto, 1982); and Eric W. Sager, *Seafaring Labour: The Merchant Marine of Atlantic Canada, 1820-1914* (Montréal, 1989).

chapters of this volume are all excellent examples of his interests in social history, it is the first ("Bulk Passenger Freight Trades, 1750-1870") which in some ways is the most remarkable, marrying as it does his concerns for both economic and social history. Indeed, it is in this area that his work has been undeniably seminal: he is *the* acknowledged expert on bulk passenger trades, especially during the age of sail. It is hard to imagine anyone else being able to bring a similar array of strengths to this kind of study.

An understanding of the people and ideas that influenced David only answers part of the question about his place in the contemporary world of maritime history. To appreciate the significance of his role also requires an appreciation of those scholars who have been affected decisively by his work. While it would not be feasible to discuss all of them – or, indeed, even to know with certainty who all of them are – it is possible at least to be suggestive. On the topics of shipping and trade, there is no question that the scholars associated with the Atlantic Canada Shipping Project (ACSP) at Memorial University of Newfoundland would be at the top of the list. I have already acknowledged my own indebtedness to David, both in my writings on Nova Scotia and my studies of broader issues of transatlantic trade.[15] Eric Sager and the late Gerry Panting also borrowed liberally from David's work; indeed, the entire study of the business communities in Atlantic Canada that underpinned a major part of the methodology of the ACSP was derived more than we have ever acknowledged from David's earlier essays.[16] So, too, was a

---

[15]See, for example, Lewis R. Fischer, "Revolution without Independence: The Canadian Colonies and the American Revolution, 1749-1775," in Ronald J. Hoffman, John J. McCusker, Russell R. Menard, and Peter J. Albert (eds.), *The Economy of Early America: The Revolutionary Years, 1763-1790* (Charlottesville, VA, 1988), 88-125; and Fischer, "A Bridge Across the Water: Liverpool Shipbrokers and the Transfer of Eastern Canadian Sailing Vessels, 1855-1880," *The Northern Mariner/Le Marin du nord*, III, No. 3 (July 1993), 49-59. Both of these works explicitly use David's approach to the study of merchant communities and shipping.

[16]Some examples include Eric W. Sager with Gerald E. Panting, *Maritime Capital: The Shipping Industry in Atlantic Canada, 1820-1914* (Montréal, 1990); and Lewis R. Fischer and Gerald Panting, "Harbour and Metropolis: The Shipping Industry of Saint John and the Urban Economy, 1820-1914," in Lewis R. Fischer and Eric W. Sager (eds.), *Merchant Shipping and Economic Development in Atlantic Canada* (St. John's, 1982), 137-155.

large part of the work that Helge Nordvik did on Norwegian shipowning communities, both on his own and with me.[17] Graeme Milne's forthcoming monograph on Liverpool also employs many of David's insights.[18] A number of Dutch scholars, but especially Paul van Royen, have been influenced by his approach.[19] And it is impossible to imagine that the impressive body of scholarship produced in recent years by Gelina Harlaftis would have taken the same shape in the absence of David Williams' intellectual example.[20]

While David's writings have had an impact on the writing of maritime social history, it is well to admit that those of us who lack his broad learning are unlikely to try to replicate some aspects of his work. But his pioneering approach to the examination of crews, using a combination of both quantitative and qualitative sources, has clearly affected some of us. Again, almost everyone associated with the Atlantic Canada Shipping Project has incorporated David's ideas into their work.[21]

---

[17]See, for example, Helge W. Nordvik, "Entrepreneurship and Risk-Taking in the Norwegian Shipping Industry in the Early Part of the Twentieth Century: The Case of Lauritz Kloster, Stavanger," in Lewis R. Fischer (ed.), *From Wheel House to Couting House: Essays in Maritime Business History in Honour of Professor Peter Neville Davies* (St. John's, 1992), 323-348; Lewis R. Fischer and Helge W. Nordvik, "From Broager to Bergen: The Risks and Rewards of Peter Jebsen, Shipowner, 1864-1892," *Sjøfartshistorisk Årbok, 1985* (Bergen, 1986), 37-68; and Fischer and Nordvik, "Floating Capital: Investment in the Canadian and Norwegian Merchant Marines in Comparative Perspective, 1850-1914," *Scandinavian-Canadian Studies*, III (1988), 17-42.

[18]Milne's monograph should appear in the near future from Liverpool University Press.

[19]See, for example, Paul C. van Royen, *Zeevarenden op de koopvaardijvloot omstreeks 1700* (Amsterdam, 1987).

[20]See Gelina Harlaftis, *A History of Greek-Owned Shipping: The Making of an International Tramp Fleet, 1830 to the Present Day* (London, 1996); and Harlaftis, "The Role of the Greeks in the Black Sea," in Lewis R. Fischer and Helge W. Nordvik (eds.), *Shipping and Trade, 1750-1950: Essays in International Maritime Economic History* (Pontefract, 1990), 63-95.

[21]A complete list of publications here would be extremely lengthy. But it would certainly include Sager, *Seafaring Labour*; Eric W. Sager, "Labour Productivity in the Shipping Fleets of Halifax and Yarmouth," in Rosemary Ommer and Gerry Panting (eds.),

Yrjö Kaukiainen's excellent *Sailing into Twilight* borrows from the Williams approach in its sections on maritime labour.[22] So too does a significant portion of the scholarship produced by Merja-Liisa Hinkkanen, who has written some of the best maritime social history of the past decade.[23] But what is especially heartening is to see some younger scholars draw inspiration from David's writings.[24] In the coming years, I fully expect to see this list expand dramatically.

In short, David Williams has played a pivotal role in the development of key areas of maritime history in the past three and one-half decades. Building upon the seminal work of Francis Hyde, Sheila Marriner, Berwick Saul, Ralph Davis and Robin Craig, he distilled important ideas through his own set of unique intellectual prisms before passing them on to a group of scholars who, as a group, have been some of the more prolific scholars of the past twenty years. While this would have been more than enough to secure an honoured place for most scholars, David also played a key role in moving the concept of maritime history away from the narrow definition of "ships and shipbuilding" to encompass a more diverse range of topics as well as important insights derived from economic and social history. His current project on the development of the cruising industry promises to add yet one more strand to an exceedingly impressive scholarly career. I am certain that there are many maritime historians who, like me, are looking forward with eager

---

Working Men Who Got Wet (St. John's, 1980), 155-184; Lewis R. Fischer and Helge W. Nordvik, "Norwegian *Matroser*: Seafarers and National Labour Markets in Norway, 1850-1914," *Scandinavian-Canadian Studies*, IV (1989), 58-81; Fischer and Nordvik, "Fish and Ships: The Social Structure of the Maritime Labour Force in Haugesund in the 1870s," *Sjøfartshistorisk Årbok, 1986* (Bergen, 1987), 139-170.

[22]Yrjö Kaukiainen, *Sailing into Twilight: Finnish Shipowning in an Age of Transport Revolution, 1860-1914* (Helsinki, 1991).

[23]For a sample of her work, see Merja-Liisa Hinkkanen, "When the AB was Able-Bodied No Longer: Accidents and Illnesses among Finnish Sailors in British Ports, 1882-1902," *International Journal of Maritime History*, VIII, No. 1 (June 1996), 87-104.

[24]The most recent of these is David J. Clarke, "Maryport Coasters and Coaster Men, 1855-1889," *The Northern Mariner/Le Marin du nord*, IX, No. 3 (July 1999), 23-38.

anticipation to many more years of intellectual stimulation from this most engaging of scholars.

Abolition and the Re-Deployment of the Slave Fleet, 1807-1811

The slave trade was a major branch of British overseas trade in the late eighteenth century.[1] It employed upwards of 30,000 tons of shipping and in the decade after 1796, when the trade reached a peak of activity, over a hundred vessels a year left British ports for Africa on the first leg of the triangular voyage.[2] By this date the British slave trade was dominated by Liverpool to such an extent that Liverpool sailings accounted for 1099 slave voyages out of a total of 1283 such voyages undertaken from British ports in the ten years from 1795 to 1804.[3] However, while the trade enjoyed a boom period, the forces of abolition were steadily increasing in

---

[1]The literature on the British slave trade is vast and it is not thought necessary to list here the multitude of works which trace the development of the trade in the eighteenth century. Apart however from the works referred to in subsequent footnotes, the following items are of particular relevance to this paper which is specifically concerned with shipping and the Liverpool branch of the trade: C.M. MacInnes, *England and Slavery* (1934); E. Williams, *Capitalism and Slavery* (1944); Elizabeth Donnan, *Documents Illustrative of the History of the Slave Trade to America*, vol. II, *The Eighteenth Century* (New York, 1931); D.P. Mannix and M. Cowley, *Black Cargoes, A History of the Atlantic Slave Trade 1518-1865* (1963); G.F. Dow, *Slave Ships and Slaving* (Salem, Mass., 1927); *Liverpool and Slavery. An Historical Account of the Liverpool-African Slave Trade by a genuine 'Dicky Sam'* (1884); Averil Mackenzie-Grieve, *The Last Years of the English Slave Trade, Liverpool, 1750-1807* (1941); C.N. Parkinson, *The Rise of the Port of Liverpool* (1952).

[2]This figure and that of the tonnage engaged in the trade is based on statistics contained in *Parliamentary Papers*, 1801-2(88) IV, 431-51; 1806(265) XIII, 783-96. The volume of shipping engaged in the trade caused contemporaries to argue that, next to the fisheries, the slave trade was the most valuable nursery of seamen upon which the Navy could call in time of emergency. See C. Lloyd, *The Navy and the Slave Trade, the Suppression of the African Slave Trade in the Nineteenth Century* (1949), 10.

[3]T. Troughton, *The History of Liverpool* (1810), 266.

strength and influence[4] and humanitarian interests gained their victory in May 1807 when the slave trade was abolished by Parliament. The coming of abolition, though anticipated, was a severe blow to all those with commercial interests in the slave trade. Merchants and shipowners in Liverpool looked on abolition with both alarm and despondency. Many forecast the ruination of the port[5] and a contemporary observer prophesied the demise of its shipping, declaring that "Liverpool's glorious merchant navy, whose keels penetrated into every land, and whose white sails wooed the breeze on every ocean, was to dwindle into a fishing vessel or two."[6] Such dismal predictions were soon proved false, for Liverpool's commerce increased rapidly in the first half of the nineteenth century and the cotton trade assumed an importance far in excess of that ever held by the slave trade. Nevertheless the fact remains that, in the short run, abolition checked growth and caused major problems for operators previously engaged in the Africa trade. merchants had to seek new markets and outlets for capital, shipowners had to consider the re-deployment of their vessels, and where, as was frequently the case in the slave trade, the function of merchant and shipowner was performed by the same individual, nothing short of a total redirection of resources was required. This paper seeks to examine one feature of this process of readjustment which was forced by the ending of the slave trade, namely, what became of the slave fleet after abolition, and in particular what trades ex-slave vessels were put into in the years immediately after 1807. The paper confines itself to considering vessels engaged in the Liverpool slave trade and restricts its analysis of post-abolition employment to the period 1807-1811, for after this date information becomes too patchy to allow any meaningful general conclusions to be drawn.

Before however inquiring what happened to the slave fleet after abolition it is necessary to establish that the slave fleet did exist. One

---

[4]The very high level of the trade in the opening years of the nineteenth century can be partly attributed to the expectations of planters and merchants that the trade would soon be terminated by legislative action. See P.D. Curtin, *The Atlantic Slave Trade, A Census* (Madison, Wisc., 1969), 154.

[5]*Liverpool a Few Years Since by an Old Stager* [James Aspinall], (3rd edn, 1885), 177.

[6]Quoted in G. Williams, *History of the Liverpool Privateers and Letters of Marque with an Account of the Liverpool Salve Trade* (1897), 621.

assumption made by many writers on the slave trade, and implicit in the preceding paragraphs, is that it is possible to point to a body of vessels which were regular traders on the Liverpool-Africa-West Indies route. Clearly this is an issue of vital importance, for if instead the slave trade was carried on by vessels which made occasional voyages to Africa and at other times operated in other trades, the coming of abolition would not have been particularly calamitous, for such vessels would subsequently have merely devoted more time to the alternative trades in which they had also been engaged. In actual fact, however, the very nature of the slave trade and its organization caused the trade to be to a great extent the preserve of constant traders. At the end of the eighteenth century the trade was relatively specialized in its organization and in Liverpool it was concentrated in the hands of a few large firms. While small operators and newcomers could, and did, profitably engage in the trade, successful and speedy purchases and sales of slaves in Africa and the West Indies required experience and considerable knowledge of fluctuating localized market conditions on the part of merchants and ship's masters, and therefore favoured regular and large-scale trading by merchant houses with interests in a number of vessels.[7] Furthermore, although slave ships were of no particular tonnage or rig, the fitting out of vessels for slave cargoes and the need for costly copper sheathing to prevent hull damage in tropical waters and to facilitate a speedy middle passage made it likely that operators would use the same vessels rather than make casual or haphazard use of a variety of vessels. That this was the case in the early nineteenth century is clearly evident from lists of vessels clearing from Liverpool for Africa in the years 1800-1805, which are available in parliamentary papers.[8] In each year around sixty percent of vessels sailing for Africa, and in one year as much as eighty percent of such clearances, were undertaken by vessels with previous experience of the Liverpool-Africa trade and which had made at least one slaving voyage in the previous two years. Further evidence of the existence of a body of vessels regularly, and in many cases exclusively, engaged in the slave trade can

---

[7]Good accounts of the organization of the Liverpool slave trade are contained in C.M. MacInnes, "The Slave Trade," in C.N. Parkinson, ed., *The Trade Winds* (1948), 251-277; R.B. Sheridan, "The Commercial and Financial Organization of the British Slave Trade, 1750-1807," *Economic History Review*, 2nd ser. XI (1958), 249-263.

[8]*Parliamentary Papers*, 1806(265) XIII, 783-96.

be gained from an examination of the vessels which left Liverpool for Africa in the final years of the trade, 1806 and 1807. Complete parliamentary returns are not available for these years but fortunately *Gore's Liverpool Directory for the Year 1807* contains a list of vessels clearing out of Liverpool for the coast of Africa between 1 January 1806 and 1 May 1807.[9] The list details 185 Liverpool-Africa clearances including thirty cases of vessels making two clearances in the period. It thus covers 155 different vessels. Of these 155 vessels, 114 can be classified as regular slave trading ships through having made two voyages in the trade in 1806 and 1807 or through having been engaged in the trade before 1806. Indeed, many vessels which made Africa voyages in 1806 and 1807 were making their fourth or later successive voyage in the trade and some had been regularly employed in slaving ventures for over a decade.[10] There was then in the final years of the slave trade a body of shipping, upwards of one hundred vessels, with a combined tonnage of around 30,000 tons, which was regularly engaged in the Liverpool slave trade. It should be stressed that these were vessels whose prime activity was the collection and conveyance of slaves from Africa to the West Indies. The popular view of the triangular trade as involving the successive freighting of trade goods to West Africa, slaves to the West Indies and then sugar, coffee and other tropical commodities back to Britain has little relevance for the end of the eighteenth century, for by then the majority of slave vessels returned to Britain with their remittances in the form of bills of exchange, and few carried cargoes of any significance. The carriage of West India produce was undertaken by a different set of vessels engaged

---

[9]*Gore's Liverpool Directory for the Year 1807* (1807), 97-100. As far as can be ascertained the list provides a complete record of clearances out of Liverpool for Africa in 1806 and 1807. It catalogues a total of 185 such clearances and the accuracy of this figure is confirmed by a table in Troughton, *op. cit.*, 265, which records three Liverpool-Africa clearances for 1806 and seventy-four for 1807. Moreover, although Gore's list gives no indication of its source, there is evidence to suggest that it was complied from Customs material. The list gives details for each clearance of the vessel's name, master, destination on the African coast, owners, date of sailing, tonnage, and the number of slaves which the vessel was permitted to carry, and this type of list of Africa clearances setting out precisely the same items of information appears in identical form in other nineteenth-century works on the slave trade which acknowledge Customs records as their original source. See G. Williams, *op. cit.*, 681-685; *Liverpool and Slavery...*, *op. cit.*, 120-129.

[10]This statement is based on a survey of lists of vessels sailing for Africa between 1795 and 1806 contained in *Parliamentary Papers*, 1806(265) XIII, 783-796.

in a direct trade with the West Indies and in no way did the importation of Caribbean produce depend on vessels making the triangular voyage.[11] Thus for vessels regularly engage in the Liverpool slave trade, abolition meant an end to their established field of employment and forced shipowners to consider entry into new trades or the disposal of their vessels.

The ending of the slave trade whenever it had taken place would have caused grave problems for shipowners but coming when it did in 1807, abolition occurred at a time when a series of difficulties was affecting many of Liverpool's major trades. Apart from the slave trade and the extensive coastal and Irish trades, the chief avenues of employment for Liverpool shipping on the eve of abolition in 1805 were the trade with Europe, particularly with the countries bordering the Baltic, the West India trade and the allied trade with British North America, and the United States trade, although the domination of the latter by American vessels greatly reduced its significance to Liverpool shipowners.[12] In the years after 1805 each of these trades encountered difficulties, all of which stemmed from the war with France and its repercussions on international trade. Trade with the Continent, already suffering from over a decade of disruption, was restricted further by the Berlin and Milan decrees which extended the controls of the Continental System to Northern Europe and the Baltic. Thus a major sector of Liverpool's commerce was severely damaged. Moreover, the tightening of the Continental System with its increasingly effective exclusion of British colonial produce from Europe seriously depressed the West India trade. Equally damaging in their effects on commerce were Britain's counter measures to Napoleon's strategy. The passing of the Orders in Council of 1807 and 1808 aimed at preventing the French gaining supplies via neutral carriers provoked American retaliation in the form of the Non-Importation Act of 1806 directed at British manufactures and the 1807 Embargo. While neither of these measures

---

[11]On the character of the triangular trade and the involvement of slave trade vessels in the freighting of West India produce see J.E. Merritt, "The Triangular Trade," *Business History*, III (1960), 1-7; F.E. Hyde, B.B. Parkinson and Sheila Marriner, "The Nature and Profitability of the Liverpool Salve Trade," *Economic History Review*, 2nd ser. V (1953) 369; Sheridan, *loc. cit.*, 249-254.

[12]This summary of Liverpool's commerce is based on a table appearing in Troughton, *op. cit.*, 263.

were wholly enforced, their operation and worsening diplomatic relations seriously disrupted Liverpool's trade with the United States.[13] The ending of the slave trade thus coincided with difficulties in all of Liverpool's other important trades and William Rathbone, one of the port's leading merchants, stated in 1808, "that at this time the town of Liverpool is deprived of twelve-sixteenths of that trade which she had twelve months ago."[14] This widespread depression had the effect not only of closing possible channels of employment for ex-slave vessels but also, as Liverpool business men were to testify before the Select Committee on the Orders in Council in 1812, of throwing out of employment a considerable number of vessels in other trades.[15] In such a situation the task of finding alternative employment for the vessels of the slave fleet was doubly difficult.

In these depressed conditions did the vessels of the slave fleet find employment after the completion of their final Africa voyage? Answering this question presents problems of source material, for the most obvious sources for discovering the post-abolition employment of vessels, newspapers or the Customs Bill of Entry, are either incomplete or not available. In their absence *Lloyd's Register of Shipping* is the only suitable source. *Lloyd's Registers* are of course a truly magnificent source for maritime historians providing as they do a mass of information on all vessels insured at Lloyd's, giving details of tonnage, age, rig, ownership, draught, and condition. In addition the *Registers* list the voyage which each vessel was scheduled to undertake at the time of its survey. It is this information which is valuable in this context, for by tracing the entries relating to those vessels which had been regularly employed in the slave trade in its final years through the *Registers* for 1808-1811 it is possible to gain a clear indication of the post-abolition employment of the slave fleet. Table 1 is the result of such an exercise undertaken for the 114

---

[13]Good accounts of the problems encountered by Liverpool merchants during the Napoleonic period are S.G. Checkland, "American Versus West Indian traders in Liverpool, 1793-1815," *Journal of Economic History*, XVIII (1958), 141-160; B.H. Tolley, "The Liverpool Campaign against the Order in Council and the War of 1812," in J.R.Harris, ed., *Liverpool and Merseyside* (1969), 98-146; Hyde, *op. cit.*, 35-38.

[14]*Parliamentary Papers*, 1808(119), X, 287.

[15]*Parliamentary Papers*, 1812(210) III. See the evidence of John Aspinall, John Gladstone and Joseph Poole.

vessels which made slaving voyages to Africa in 1806 and 1807 and which may be classified as regular trades.[16] The table covers 104 vessels only, the deficiency stemming from the fact that nine vessels were lost on their

Table 1
Entries in Lloyd's Register for the Years 1808, 1809, 1810 and 1811
Relating to 104 Vessels Regularly Engaged in the Slave Trade before Abolition

	1808	1809	1810	1811
Cumulative total of vessels re-surveyed since last slave voyage	14	67	80	83
Vessels listed as Liverpool-Africa on the basis of a pre-abolition survey	88	31	13	10
Vessels disappeared from registers without having been re-surveyed after abolition	-	6	11	11
Voyages listed at time of re-surveying				
Liverpool-West Indies	8	23	23	19
Other British ports-West Indies	-	2	2	4
Total of voyages to West Indies	8	25	25	23
Liverpool-South America	2	12	17	12
Other British ports to South America	-	2	4	5
Total of voyages to South America	2	14	21	17
Liverpool-Africa	-	11	10	10
Liverpool-USA	-	3	2	-
Liverpool-British North America	2	1	4	2
Liverpool-Southern Europe, the Canaries and the Azores	1	7	8	11*
Other voyages	-	3	2	3
Lying in British ports, no voyages specified at time of re-survey	1	3	1	4
No entry in register but vessel had been re-surveyed after abolition	2†	-	7	13

* Includes one voyage from a port other than Liverpool.
† Includes two vessels temporarily absent from the *Register*

---

[16]For the period under review both Underwriters' volumes and Shipowners' volumes of *Lloyd's Register of Shipping* are available. Both sets of the *Registers* were used in the compilation of Tables 1 and 2. The *Registers* have been reprinted by the Gregg Press, London.

final slaving voyage[17] and one further vessel could not be traced in the *Registers*.[18] The table shows the voyages for which ex-slave vessels were listed in *Lloyd's Registers* for the years 1808, 1809, 1810 and 1811. It is important to recognize that the table merely serves as an indicator of trends and that the figures for any one year refer to entries in the *Registers* for the years 1808, 1809, 1810 and 1811, and not to actual voyages undertaken in those years. This is because all vessels were not surveyed annually (often voyages were of more than twelve months' duration), and hence the information which time of its last survey which inevitably took place before the commencement of the year covered by the *Register*, and may in fact have taken place some years earlier. It is therefore essential in surveying the *Registers* from 1808 on to take into account only information based on surveys made after the completion of a vessel's final voyage in the slave trade, for surveys made in 1806 and 1807 would relate to the final slaving venture. This need to distinguish between pre- and post-abolition surveys is clearly shown in the second line of the table which indicates that many entries appeared in the 1808 *Register* and in subsequent issues on the basis of pre-abolition surveys. The process of re-surveying was in fact a gradual one, but most vessels however were surveyed sooner or later after 1807, thus enabling an impression of post-abolition employment to be gained.

The top line of the table which presents the cumulative total of ships re-surveyed after May 1807 shows that of the 104 vessels available for employment after the completion of their last slaving voyage, a total of sixty-seven had been re-surveyed for voyages in new trades by the time of the appearance of the 1809 *Register* in the January of that year. In other words, by the end of 1808, only a year and a half after the formal ending of the trade, and in the case of many vessels which sailed for Africa on their final slave voyage in 1807 a matter of months after their return to Liverpool, over sixty-four percent of the vessels thrown out of employment by abolition had been placed in new employment. One year later, by the close of 1809, the number of vessels re-surveyed since abolition had risen to eighty, seventy-seven percent of the slave fleet, and a further year later the figure had risen to eighty-three, that is eighty percent. It would

---

[17]*Gore's Liverpool Directory for the Year 1807*, 97-100.

[18]The absence of but one vessel from *Lloyd's Register* indicates the comprehensiveness and value of the *Registers* as a source.

appear therefore that the great majority of slave trade vessels found fresh employment, and found it relatively speedily, after abolition.

Table 2
Entries in Lloyd's Register for the Years 1808, 1809, 1810 and 1811
Relating to Voyages Undertaken by ex-Slave Vessels to the
West Indies and South America

Voyages listed at time of survey	1808	1809	1810	1811
Liverpool-West Indies (unspecified)	-	2	2	2
Liverpool-Barbados	-	2	3	2
Liverpool-Jamaica, Bahamas, Antigua or Dominica (all Free Ports of long standing being designated as such before 1793)	1	5*	3*	3†
Liverpool-Trinidad (designated as a Free Port in 1797)	3	5*	6*	4*
Liverpool-Berbice, Demerara or Surinam	1	5	5	5
Liverpool-Tobago (designated a Free Port in 1805), Martinique, or Guadeloupe	-	1	2	4*
Liverpool-St. Thomas	-	1	1	1
Liverpool-Haiti	3	4	1	-
Liverpool-Havana	-	-	2	2
Total West Indian voyages from Liverpool and other British ports	8	25	25	23
Liverpool-Monte Video	2	2	1	1
Liverpool-Bahia	-	1	2	1
Liverpool-Brazil	-	9	16*	10
London-Brazil	-	1	2	4
London-Lima	-	1	1	1
Total South American voyages from Liverpool and other British ports	2	14	21	17

* Includes one voyage from a port other than Liverpool.
† Includes two voyages from a port other than Liverpool.

In surveying the voyages undertaken by slave vessels an important feature revealed by the table is that most vessels continued to be engaged in Liverpool-based trades, that is vessels continued to use Liverpool as their home port. To some extent it is inevitable that the table should show this for vessels would naturally have returned to Liverpool after their final slave trade voyage and their first subsequent voyage would therefore be from Liverpool. Nevertheless, over the entire period covered by the table, up to the beginning of 1811, sailings from Liverpool predominated and the number of vessels which sailed from other ports were but few. Thus the vessels of the slave fleet remained a significant part of the port of Liverpool's shipping.[19] This is not to suggest however that slave vessels did not change hands in the years after abolition. Details of ownership contained in *Lloyd's Registers* are somewhat superficial but the evidence suggests that about half of the eighty-three vessels which found fresh employment did so under new owners. But whether with unchanged or new owners, the bulk of the slave fleet found employment within the framework of Liverpool's commerce.

The picture of post-abolition employment of slave vessels which emerges from table I is one of vessels entering a very limited number of trades. While it would be dangerous to attach any precise numerical significance to the actual figures presented in the table the trends of post-abolition employment are clear enough. The chief avenues of employment were the West Indies and South American trades. Also of importance were the trades with West Africa and with Southern European ports in Portugal, Spain and Malta. In contrast very few vessels found employment in the United States of British North American trades and none in the trade with Northern Europe. This pattern of employment reflects very clearly the market situation which faced Liverpool merchants and shipowners after 1807 and the important changes which occurred in the port's trade at this time. The disruptions of war which were causing such difficulties in Liverpool's trade with Northern Europe and North American and the consequent fall in the employment of vessels engaged in those trades meant that such trades offered few prospects for ex-slave vessels. Given that these trades had been major branches of Liverpool's commerce before abolition, the situation after 1807 would have been gloomy indeed for ex-slave vessels had not there developed at this time fresh outlets for Liverpool's merchanting and shipping enterprise. The new trades to appear arose ironically from the very two factors which were causing Liverpool such problems; abolition, and the long French wars. Abolition, which ended the triangular trade, led to a recognition amongst mercantile interests that West Africa possessed commercially viable products other

---

[19]In the early nineteenth century most Liverpool-owned shipping was engaged in trades sailing to and from Liverpool. See the evidence of John Bridge Aspinall, *Parliamentary Papers*, 1812(210) III, 372.

than human merchandise, and saw the first real beginnings of a direct trade between Liverpool and West Africa.[20] Vessels continued to take out to the West African coast the cargoes which had been carried on the first leg of the old slave voyage, but now these cargoes were exchanged for products such as gum, ivory and palm oil, the trade in the latter being a "commerce brilliantly improvised by Liverpool merchants after the crash of 1807."[21]

Of more significance in the short run after 1807 than the new legitimate trade to Africa was the opening of markets in the West Indies and South America. This occurred as a direct consequence of the wars with France. The naval struggle in the West Indies saw the seizure by Britain of foreign colonial possessions such as the capture from Spain in 1797 of Trinidad, which was not returned at the Peace of Amiens as other territories were. Berbice, Demerara and Surinam, all Dutch colonies under French control, were captured in 1803 and 1804, the Danish island of St. Thomas was gained in 1807, and the French islands of Mount Tobago, Martinique and Guadeloupe fell to Britain in 1804, 1809 and 1810.[22] In 1804 also the French colony of Haiti successfully declared itself independent. Apart from representing new outlets for trade, many of these islands served as convenient bases for the infiltration of Spanish colonial markets in Central and Southern American. Despite Spain's long-held policy of excluding foreigners from trade with her colonies, the last thirty years of the eighteenth century had seen a growing traffic between British Caribbean possessions and the Spanish colonies, largely through the British policy of Free Ports which encouraged and legitimized trade

---

[20] A direct trade between Liverpool and West Africa did exist before 1807 but was almost totally insignificant. In the period 1795-1805 vessels not engaged in the slave trade which cleared from Liverpool for Africa numbered only seven. See *Parliamentary Papers*, 1806(265) XIII, 783-796.

[21] J. Gallagher, "Fowell Buxton and the New African Policy, 1838-1842." *Cambridge Historical Journal*, X (1950), 38.

[22] Caribbean islands changed hands with bewildering frequency in the period of the French wars. Some guidance on this complicated subject can be gained from Sir Alan Burns, *History of the British West Indies* (2nd edn. 1965).

between specified British West Indian islands and foreign plantations.[23] Such intercourse was not ended by the state of war that existed between Britain and Spain from 1796 to 1802 and again from 1804 to 1808. The capture of Trinidad, conveniently situated close to Spanish territories, and its addition together with other islands to the list of Free Ports, greatly encouraged the illicit trade, and the alliance of Britain and Spain in the face of Napoleon's invasion of Spain in 1808 led to further breaches in practice, if not in theory, of the Spanish monopoly. Furthermore, the beginnings of revolutions against Spain the countries now comprising Bolivia, Venezuela, Argentina and Chile offered hopes of new commercial opportunities.[24] Table 2, which presents in greater detail the voyages of ex-slave vessels to the West Indies and South American, shows plainly that almost all voyages to the West Indies were to captured islands or to Free Ports which were extensively engaged in trade with Spanish colonies. It was thus the new opportunities for commerce in the West Indies rather than the traditional trade of that area which provided employment for slave vessels. As table 2 shows, the chief source of employment of Latin America was the trade to Brazil. Here again it was French activity in Europe which opened a hitherto closed market. The French invasion of Lisbon in November 1807 led to the flight, with British assistance, of the Portuguese royal family and court to Brazil. The Portuguese government now established in Rio de Janeiro opened Brazil to British trade, and the new commercial relationship between Britain and Brazil was formalized in two treaties granting concessions to Britain early in 1810. These developments gave rise to a massive trading and shipping boom in 1808, 1809 and 1810.[25] Subsequent dislocation ensured from speculative excesses, but Brazil became an important sphere of Liverpool's commerce

---

[23]Frances Armytage, *The Free Port System in the British West Indies* (1953); Dorothy B. Goebel, "British Trade to the Spanish Colonies, 1796-1823," *American Historical Review*, XIII (1938), 288-320.

[24]See Goebel, *loc. cit.*, and J. Lunch, "British Policy and Spanish America, 1738-1808," *Journal of Latin American Studies*, I (1969), 1-30.

[25]On the opening of the Brazilian trade and the boom of 1808-1810 see A.K. Manchester, *British Preeminence in Brazil. Its rise and Decline* (Chapel Hill, N.C., 1933), 69-161, and the fine contemporary accounts in J. Mawe, *Travels in the Interior of Brazil* (1812), 101-102, 322-334, and J. Luccock, *Notes on Rio de Janeiro and the Southern Parts of Brazil* (1820), 72-140.

not only as a promising market for British manufacturers but as a supplier of raw cotton[26] and as a source of employment for Liverpool vessels, particularly in the troubled period after 1807. Apart from the African, West Indian and South American trades, the only other significant areas of employment for ex-slave vessels were the Canaries and Azores, and the Mediterranean. Here the former reflected Spanish wartime relaxations while the latter consisted largely of voyages to ports, notably Malta, suitable for the infiltration of goods into the European market.[27] Thus once more it was new, albeit temporary, trades which provided employment of ex-slavers.

However, while the ending of the slave trade coincided with the appearance of new commercial outlets, the fact remains that slave ships were not the only vessels seeking employment at this time. The dislocation of Liverpool's other long-standing trades at the time of abolition had created a considerable amount of unemployed tonnage. Why then did ex-slave ship gain employment so readily? Two sets of factors can be advanced in explanation, one relating to ownership and the other to the vessels themselves. With regard to the former, owners of slave ships, who did not sell off their vessels after abolition and who were therefore seeking fresh employment for their ships, were well placed to take prompt advantage of the new trading outlets which appeared for each was of a character, or was in a part of the world, of which ex-slave operators had some knowledge or experience. Obviously merchants and shipowners previously engaged in the slave trade, with their intimate acquaintance with conditions and customs on the West African coast, were well equipped to develop the legitimate trade with Africa, which in the case of palm oil was organized on very similar lines to the slave trade.[28] Indeed, John Tobin, Jonas Bold and the Aspinall family, all leading slave traders,

---

[26]Because of the disruption to trade with the United States, Brazil quickly became an important supplier of raw cotton. Brazilian cotton represented almost twenty percent of total imports of cotton into Liverpool in 1810 and over twenty-five percent in 1811 and 1812. See the table of imports in H. Smithers. *Liverpool, Its Commerce, Statistics and Institutions* (1825), 146.

[27]Judith B. Williams, *British Commercial Policy and Trade Expansion 1750-1850* (1972), 364-7.

[28]Gallagher, *loc. cit.*, 38.

were amongst the pioneers of the trade in palm oil.[29] Similarly former slave traders with their extensive West Indian connections would be well aware of opportunities in the Caribbean area and familiar with the organization of commerce there. Again the new Spanish American trade was not totally unfamiliar and Brazil with its slave-owning plantation economy offered a market and produce almost the same as that of the British sugar islands. Past experiences thus stood ex-slave operators in good stead in relation to employing their vessels in the new trades. A more significant factor favouring the employment of slave vessels was that they were eminently suitable for the new trades. A more significant factor favouring the employment of slave vessels was that they were eminently suitable for the new trades. It is this which explains why at a time when there were general trading difficulties and a considerable amount of unemployed tonnage, slave ships put up for sale generally found purchasers, for as noted earlier around half of the salve fleet changed hands in the years immediately after 1807. The outstanding feature of the vessels of the slave trade was that they were copper sheathed. The copper sheathing of merchant vessels commenced in the last quarter of the eighteenth century and, as recent research has shown, was first taken up on any scale in the slave trade where vessels sheathed with copper were widespread by the late 1780s.[30] By the early nineteenth century the practice was almost universal in the trade: of the 104 slave vessels covered in table 1, 101 were copper sheathed.[31] The causes of the fuller adoption of copper sheathing by slave ships lay in its effect in reducing hull damage caused by marine life in the tropical waters in which the salve trade was prosecuted, and in its effect of improving sailing speeds, particularly in the "light airs" of the tropics, a significant factor given the need for a speedy middle passage and the fact that slave ships, being runners (that is, they did not sail in convoys in wartime), relied primarily on speed and

---

[29]K. Onwuka Dike, *Trade and Politics in the Niger Delta 1830-1885* (1956), 49.

[30]G. Rees, "Copper Sheathing, An Example of Technological Diffusion in the English Merchant Fleet," *Journal of Transport History*, N.S.1 (1971), 87-89. On the development of copper sheathing see J.R. Harris, "Copper and Shipping in the Eighteenth Century," *Economic History Review*, 2nd ser. XIX (1966), 550-568.

[31]Based on information contained in *Lloyd's Registers*.

their own armaments to resist capture.[32] Both of these advantages of copper sheathing had a relevance for the new trades which appeared after abolition. The key new trades to Africa, the West Indies and Latin America were all undertaken in tropical waters, and apart from the general preference for fast-sailing as opposed to slow-sailing vessels, in the troubled trading conditions of wartime with enemy privateers on the seas, speed was an important asset.[33] This was a quality which slave ships possessed. James Penny, a slave-ship captain giving evidence to a parliamentary committee in 1788, described Africa vessels as "remarkably sharp-fast sailors,"[34] and slave ships probably had a finer hull design than vessels in other trades.[35] A further feature of the slave fleet which may well have enhanced the likelihood of vessels finding employment was the varied tonnage of vessels. The shipping needs of the new trades were often for vessels of a particular size. The African trade required relatively small vessels of under 180 tons capable of sailing up coastal rivers for trading purposes,[36] but in the Brazilian trade much larger vessels of around 300-400 tons were preferred.[37] At both these extremes the slave fleet was capable of supplying vessels. While the average tonnage of the 104 vessels seeking employment was around 250 tons, twenty-six vessels were under 180 tons and a further thirty were over 300 tons. A final factor which may have favoured slave vessels was the large number of vessels which were relatively young, around half of the slave ships available for employment being less than ten years old at the time of their last slaving voyage. In a variety of ways therefore the vessels of the slave fleet possessed features

---

[32]Rees, *loc. cit.*, 90.

[33]This was particularly the case in many of the new trades where the convoy system did not operate.

[34]*Parliamentary Papers, Accounts and Papers*, 1789(629) XXIV, 40.

[35]Slave trade vessels were certainly finer than West India merchantmen which were broad in the beam and often slow sailors. See Lucy F. Horsfall, "The West India Trade," in Parkinson (ed.) *op cit.*, and Sheridan, *loc. cit.*, 252-253.

[36]The average tonnage of seventy-one vessels which cleared out of Liverpool for Africa between 1808 and 1811 was 170 tons. See *Parliamentary Papers*, 1812 (277), X, 67.

[37]Mawe, *op. cit.*, 322-323.

which made them highly suitable for employment, particularly in the new trades, after abolition.

It remains to consider that section of the slave fleet about which *Lloyd's Registers* provide no information, that is the twenty-one vessels which were not re-surveyed after 1807. By the time of the appearance of the 1811 *Register*, eleven of these vessels were no longer listed and the remaining ten which were still listed on the basis of pre-abolition surveys, all disappeared in the next few years without any of them being re-surveyed. The disappearance of ships from *Lloyd's Register* could arise from a variety of circumstances. Most obviously a vessel could be lost through shipwreck, fire or enemy action, or it could be dismantled or broken up. Alternatively a vessel could change hands and not be re-insured, be sold to foreigners, be bought into the Navy, or be put into trades such as the coast and Irish trade where it was not the practice to insure vessels. How relevant each of these possibilities is in the case of slave trade ships is difficult to ascertain. Some vessels additional to those listed as lost in *Gore's Directory* may have been lost on their final slaving voyage or soon after. Again others may have been broken up. Amongst the vessels which disappeared from the *Register* were some of consider-able age, including one of forty-five years, two over thirty years and another of twenty-five years. After abolition the owners of such vessels may well have decided in the prevailing market conditions that dismantling was the wisest course of action. On the other hands, some of the vessels which disappeared from the *Register* may well have found employment. Certainly there were vessels small enough to have been put into the Irish and coastal trade and some may have been sold off and not re-insured by their new owners. Sales to foreigners however are less likely, given the strained international situation, and the absorption of merchant vessels into the Navy other than as transports (which are listed in the *Register*) was infrequent by this time. A further possibility to consider is whether any of the vessels continued to take part in the slave trade. Information on direct Liverpool participation in the trade after 1807 is, for understandable reasons, hard to come by. The penalties for engaging in the trade, seizure of vessels and heavy fines, made slaving after 1807 a risky venture, but the lure of exceptional profits attracted a few speculators and according to Sir Reginald Coupland, "Groups were formed to fit out slave ships at continental ports and even at Liverpool and London."[38] To such operators ex-slave vessels would have been the obvious to use, but while there was some illicit trading involving Liverpool vessels[39] I have found no evidence to implicate any of the vessels which were not re-surveyed after 1807.

What happened to the vessels which were not re-surveyed after 1807 is therefore entirely conjectural, but is not unreasonable to assume that some at least gained employment. This would serve to increase the proportion of the slave fleet which gained employment in the post-abolition period. However a conclusion on the fate of the slave fleet need not rest on assumptions. The *Registers* clearly show that the great majority of slave trade vessels quickly found employment in other trades despite the apparently unfavourable market situation which prevailed after 1807. The re-deployment of slave vessels was directly associated with the appearance of new trading outlets, and of considerable significance were the special features of the vessels of the slave fleet which made them admirably suited for these new trades. Indeed it might be argued that the ability of Liverpool to respond to the new opportunities in Central and South America and Africa was greatly facilitated by the presence of a body of suitable shipping. Thus the gloomy predictions which attended abolition proved groundless. More than ever before, the ships of "Liverpool's glorious merchant navy ... penetrated into every land" and the vessels of the slave trade met the shipping requirements of trades which were to assume an important place in Liverpool's commerce in the century after 1807, and to give the port a totally different pattern of trading activities from that which it possessed during its rise to prominence in the eighteenth century.[40]

---

[38]Sir Reginald Coupland, *The British Anti-Slavery Movement* (2nd edn. 1964), 110-11.

[39]*The Times*, 27 September 1811 reported the capture of a Liverpool vessel, the *Falcon*. Quoted in Checkland, *loc. cit.*, 152.

[40]Much of the research on which this paper is based was undertaken with the aid of a grant from the Research Board, University of Leicester. I should like to thank the board for its assistance and support.

Liverpool Merchants and the Cotton Trade 1820-1850

Our knowledge of merchanting and commerce in Liverpool in the first half of the nineteenth century is surprisingly slight. Even in the case of the cotton trade, rightly by virtue of its size and importance the best documented of the port's trades, there are remarkable gaps in our understanding. The eighteenth-century origins of the trade, its dramatic expansion after 1780, the evolution of the cotton market, the emergence of the specialist broker as the lynch pin on which sales depended, and the beginnings of future trading, have all been subjects of scholarly study,[1] yet many features of the trade and its organisation still await research. One such feature is the structure and character of that section of the merchant body which imported cotton into Liverpool. Very little is known about the Liverpool cotton merchant; true the names of Cropper, Brown, Baring and Collman are familiar enough and there is Dr. Mariner's excellent study of the Rathbones and their trading operations,[2] but of the cotton merchants as a group, or as individual entrepreneurs, our information is really superficial. We do not know who the cotton merchants were or how many importers were active in the trade. Similarly, the importer's scale of operation and the reaction of the merchant body to the tremendous growth of the trade are issues of doubt. The purpose of this short paper is to remedy these deficiencies in our knowledge through a study of Liverpool's cotton merchants in the first half of the nineteenth century with particular reference to the period after 1820. The choice of the year 1820 as an

---

[1]See for example: S. Dumbell, "Early Liverpool Cotton Imports and the Organisation of the Cotton Market in the Eighteenth Century," *Economic Journal*, Vol. XXXIII (1923), pp. 362-73; S. Dumbell, "The Cotton Market in 1799," *Economic History*, Vol. I (1926-9), pp. 141-48; S. Dumbell "The Origin of Cotton Futures," *Economic History*, Vol. I (1926-29), pp. 259-67; G.W. Daniels, "The American Cotton Trade with Liverpool under the Embargo and Non-intercourse Acts," *American Historical Review*, Vol. XXI (1916), pp. 276-88; F.E. Hyde, B.B. Parkinson and S. Marriner, "The Cotton Broker and the Rise of the Liverpool Cotton Market," *Economic History Review*, 2nd series, Vol. VIII (1955), pp. 75-83.

[2]S. Marriner, *Rathbones of Liverpool* (1961).

opening date was influenced by two factors, namely, the regaining of stability in the trade following the dislocations of the war and of the immediate post-war period and the availability of source material. It is proposed to consider first the degree of concentration prevailing in the cotton trade between 1820 and 1839 and then to examine more generally the changing role and function of the individual merchant over the slightly longer period from 1820 to 1850.

The period 1820 to 1850 was one of immense expansion in the cotton trade. Within thirty years imports of cotton into Liverpool increased threefold, from under half a million bales in 1820 to well over a million and a half bales in 1850. This huge increase in imports is revealed in Table I, which shows the total receipts of cotton at Liverpool subdivided into the various sources of supply and the total imports of the country as a whole.[3] Comparing the Liverpool and the national totals, the dominance of the port in this particular trade is striking. In every year over eighty percent of the country's supplies of this vital raw material came through Liverpool and in some years such as 1837 the proportion reached ninety percent. Both sets of figures reveal an upward trend, national imports rising some 300 percent in the thirty years and Liverpool's imports by over 400 percent. Only in 1839 and 1846-1847 is there any major departure from this movement and this was entirely due to poor crops in the U.S.A., the smaller quantities imported in 1826, 1828 and 1841 being

---

[3]The absence of the Liverpool Port Books for much of the eighteenth century and the first half of the nineteenth century necessitates statistics of the port's trade being assembled from secondary sources. The sources for Table I were as follows: national figures were obtained from T. Ellison, *The Cotton Trade of Great Britain* (1886), 85, and Liverpool figures from E.J. Donnell, *Chronological and Statistical History of Cotton* (1873), *passim*. In both cases the original sources were brokers' circulars, Ellison relying on the circulars of George Holt & Co. and Donnell those of Collman & Co. As Donnell's statistics date only from 1821, figures for 1820 were obtained from H. Smithers, *Liverpool* (1825). Smithers' reputation as a statistician is to say the least, weak, but in his table of imports of cotton 1790-1823 he does obtain a high degree of accuracy. Checking his figures with others which exist for the period reveals only very slight discrepancies.

It is regrettable that the unit of measurement, bales, is not a strictly homogeneous unit, for bales from the southern states of the U.S.A. were larger and weighed more than those from Brazil. Moreover, over the peiod 1820-1850 there was a steady tendency for the average weight of all kinds of bales imported to increase. As figures, however, in pounds weight are unobtainable and impossible to construct, Table I represents the nearest approximation we have to the trend of cotton imports over this period. On the question of the size and weight of bales, J.A. Mann, *The Cotton Trade of Great Britain* (1860), 51, provides valuable information.

the result of exceedingly large imports in the preceding years which allowed unusually large stocks to be accumulated.[4] Liverpool's supplies of cotton were drawn from the U.S.A., Brazil, Egypt and the East Indies. Supplies from other sources, mainly the West Indies, the Mediterranean and later Australia fell considerably over the period and were negligible by 1850. United States' cotton dominated Liverpool's imports of cotton, averaging seventy-five percent of the total, and rose from around a quarter of a million bales to well over a million bales in the thirty-year period. Imports from Brazil enjoyed no such increase, fluctuating in absolute terms, generally between 90,000 and 160,000 bales, but declining continuously in relative terms from over thirty percent of total imports in 1820 to around ten percent in 1850. The East Indies on the other hand rose from insignificance to a figure of nearly 200,000 bales (thirteen percent) in 1850. Even more spectacular was the growth of supplies from Egypt. Imports from this source, unknown in Liverpool before 1823, represented six percent of total imports in 1850. Overall the trend was one of great expansion. Braithwaite Poole, one of the more accurate commentators on Liverpool's commerce, calculated that of the port's total trade valued at £50m. in 1850, cotton accounted for some £20m.[5]

In seeking to enquire who handled these immense amounts of cotton and how the merchant body responded and reacted to the very rapid increase in imports, the greatest problem facing the historian is that of source material. What is required is not a collection of business-house records but a comprehensive source which provides full and detailed information on the import trade of the port and on the activities of all merchants engaged in import operations. These requirements are admirably fulfilled by the Customs Bills of Entry, a source which has been surprisingly neglected by both economic and business historians. The Customs Bills of Entry were a daily publication published by the Customs' authorities for the convenience of the merchant community. Over the period 1820 to 1850 there were some slight changes in the form of presentation but the content of each daily Bill remained the same. Each

---

[4]On market movements over the period 1820-1850 see Donnell, *op. cit.* and T. Ellison, "History of Cotton Prices and Supply 1790-1862," *Exchange Magazine,* Vol. I (1862), 306-315, Vol. II (1863), 45-54.

[5]B. Poole, *The Commerce of Liverpool* (1854), 196-197. The figure of £50m. excludes imports of bullion valued at £7m. in 1850.

Bill contained a list of all vessels arriving in Liverpool and particulars of the port of registration, the tonnage, crew, master, dock, ship's agent in Liverpool, and last port of clearance, together with a full account of all merchandise carried and to whom it was consigned. Apart from these "Ships' Reports" as they were termed, summaries of imports and exports, and of articles entering and released from the bonded warehouses, appeared in every issue, as did information regarding ships entered outwards, ships cleared outwards and ships loading. It is, however, only the ships' reports which are of value in a study of merchanting for it is they which contain data on imports relating to the individual merchant.

The search for empirical evidence on concentration in the cotton trade and the changing function of the cotton merchant took the form of a detailed examination of the ships' reports for four years taken at ten-yearly intervals in the period 1820-1850. The absence of the Bills of Entry for the year 1840 necessitated the use of those for 1839.[6] For each of the years 1820, 1830, 1839 and 1850 a list was compiled of all merchants who during the year either imported cotton or acted as a ship's agent to a vessel carrying cotton as part of its cargo. The date of every appearance of these merchants in the Bills of Entry was noted, special notation being used if the reference was to cotton being imported or to a vessel carrying nothing but cotton. From the resulting lists, four in all, it was possible to see from the hundreds of merchants engaged in the trade, who were the most important. It was not at this stage possible to establish those who were importing the largest amounts of cotton (although it may often be a reasonable inference that a merchant who imported cotton on fifty occasions during a year, imported more in absolute terms than one who imported cotton on ten occasions), but an examination of the lists did reveal those importers who were of little significance in the trade. Merchants who imported cotton on fewer than five occasions during a year could be safely disregarded, for even if on each occasion the amount imported had been the entire cargo of a vessel, their annual total would

---

[6]No complete set of Liverpool Bills of Entry is available and the earliest existing volume is for the year 1819. Odd volumes between this date and 1842 are in the Customs House Library, London. A complete sequence from 1842 on is available in the Liverpool Record Office. I should like to express my gratitude to Prof. F.E. Hyde for allowing me to use the volumes for 1820 and 1839 while they were in his possession, and to Mr. R.C. Jarvis, until recently Librarian, H.M. Customs & Excise, for permission to consult the 1830 volume.

have been under one percent of the quantity imported for the port as a whole.

Table I
Receipts of Cotton at Liverpool and Total British Imports
of Cotton 1820-1850 (in Bales)

Date	U.S.A.	E.I.	Egypt	Brazil	other	Total	Total
			Liverpool				G. Britain
1820	272,574	7,668	-	161,628	16,823	458,693	571,651
21	240,257	3,273	-	70,060	54,673	367,673	491,658
22	274,832	1,613	-	67,106	95,380	439,031	533,444
23	390,914	13,684	-	84,598	58,797	557,993	688,797
24	265,413	13,863	28,170	94,460	55,722	457,628	540,092
25	419,490	15,060	71,486	140,057	82,820	728,913	820,883
26	371,143	11,573	36,767	35,765	35,366	490,614	581,950
27	579,134	12,902	12,524	93,373	30,590	728,523	894,063
28	403,255	15,076	19,636	121,586	49,367	608,920	749,552
29	422,109	17,453	22,259	128,707	39,645	630,173	746,707
1830	570,808	12,276	11,023	161,225	38,538	793,870	871,487
31	560,181	33,601	25,019	138,312	32,511	789,624	903,367
32	581,695	39,778	32,196	104,760	18,489	777,278	902,322
33	612,031	52,694	2,450	123,688	43,329	834,192	930,216
34	664,023	47,216	1,886	94,598	29,203	836,926	951,034
35	700,359	54,560	26,255	106,071	50,785	938,030	1,081,253
36	708,994	103,248	21,397	143,761	46,233	1,023,633	1,201,374
37	769,408	69,684	25,817	97,701	48,321	1,010,931	1,175,975
38	1,066,790	60,592	22,820	94,743	74,287	1,312,212	1,428,600
39	787,900	82,800	17,029	66,749	57,300	1,011,778	11,116,200
1840	1,155,270	92,643	34,594	64,035	53,984	1,400,528	1,599,500
41	843,755	153,396	35,332	101,192	28,919	1,162,584	1,344,000
42	931,612	165,026	17,340	80,662	22,620	1,217,260	1,392,800
43	1,291,807	108,729	45,649	97,004	19,679	1,562,868	1,744,100
44	1,028,811	145,165	37,551	116,333	28,018	1,355,878	1,681,600
45	1,370,455	86,888	64,127	107,051	11,549	1,640,070	1,855,700
46	933,833	49,521	60,767	77,998	10,578	1,132,694	1,243,700
47	809,809	114,730	21,712	113,747	8,099	1,068,147	1,232,700
48	1,284,689	133,168	27,840	99,467	9,948	1,555,112	1,740,000
49	1,342,771	106,127	70,117	168,046	7,070	1,694,181	1,905,400
1850	1,084,644	198,138	83,052	152,498	3,820	1,522,152	1,749,300

For all merchants who imported cotton on more than five occasions in a year (and in any marginal case where there was an element of doubt) a chart was constructed of all the references to each individual in the Bills of Entry. Each chart noted the date of the reference, the commodity or commodities imported and the quantity, the port of origin, and the name, tonnage and port of registration of the vessel. The compilation of these charts, some two hundred in all, many of which contained over one hundred references, was a lengthy procedure, but once completed a very clear picture of each merchant's activities could be seen. His scale of operation, the commodities he dealt in, the markets he traded with, and his performance of the function of ship's agents were but a few of the facts which were visible. More important still, the quantities of each commodity that the merchant imported could be totalled up and set against the port's total import of that commodity. It thus became possible to discover to what extent the cotton trade was concentrated into the hands of a group or groups of importers. This object was attained by examining the combined imports of the largest importers in each year. For each of the years studied the thirty largest importers of cotton were selected and subdivided into sub-groups of ten, the order of size being the guiding factor. The imports of each group were then added together and compared with the total imports of cotton in that year. As the degree of concentration is best expressed as a proportion of total imports, both absolute and percentage measures were used at this stage of the analysis.[7]

One further point remains to be mentioned before presenting the results of the analysis. In theory the comprehensive survey described above would account for all imports of cotton, i.e. every bale of cotton imported would be allocated to an individual merchant, but in practice such a complete breakdown was not possible. The ship's reports appearing in the Bills of Entry were made up from ship's manifests which embodied a list of the vessel's cargo and information regarding its markings and consignees. In certain cases, however, the name of the consignee did not appear; instead the phrase, "to order," or just "order." Sometimes this was because the consignee did not wish it to be known that he was importing, but more often it was because the goods were not consigned to any one in particular. The significance of this practice of consigning goods to order is that it prevents the complete division of total imports into the imports of individual merchants, for it is impossible to discover who actually purchased and thus imported goods consigned to "order" remained under twenty percent of total imports in the first three years

---

[7]For a more detailed discussion of the method followed in examining concentration see D.M. Williams, "The Function of the Merchant in Specific Liverpool Import Trades. 1820-50" (unpublished Liverpool M.A. thesis 1963), 26-35.

examined and hence is not sufficient to invalidate the survey or significantly distort the basic trends which occurred within the group of
merchants importing cotton, but in the decade after 1839 the practice of
consigning bales to "order" increased rapidly. By 1850 around sixty
percent of total imports of cotton were consigned in this manner.[8] With
over half of total cotton imports being untraceable any attempt to trace the
degree of concentration prevailing in 1850 would be futile, hence the
analysis of concentration was confined to the years 1820, 1830 and 1839.
It was, however, possible for the year 1850 to draw up a list of the leading
thirty importers which could be used for the examination of changing
merchant functions where the quantification of imports was not required.

Table II
Total Number of Importers of Cotton Subdivided by
Frequency of Import in the Years 1820, 1830 and 1839

	Total number of merchants importing on some occasion	On one occasion	On two occasions	On three to five occasions	On six and more occasions
1820	607	318	77	92	120
1830	318	153	40	47	78
1839	341	155	58	41	87

The dominant position occupied by the cotton trade in the
commerce of the port, and the importance of the Liverpool cotton trade to
the nation's industrial economy, have quite naturally led, in the past, to
the view that the majority of Liverpool's merchants devoted their
commercial energies to the importation of cotton. This view is correct
only in so far that the number of merchants who imported some cotton

---

[8]The reason why this tremendous rise in the quantity of cotton consigned to
"order" occurred is not clear. The most likely explanation is that it was linked with the
arrival of the steam packet ship on the Atlantic route which meant that for the first itme
information could travel more swiftly than goods. This situation would permit the sale of
"cotton afloat" which may have been an earlier development than has hitherto been
supposed.

during the course of any one year ran into hundreds. Table II illustrates this.

It is, plain, nevertheless, that the total figure of cotton importers gives an entirely erroneous impression, for in each year around half of them imported cotton on one occasion only, and between seventy and eighty percent of the total number of merchants fell into the category of importing on five occasions or under. Clearly the majority of these merchants were individually of little account in the trade although taken collectively they were of some importance. The information which can be drawn from Table II is limited, as the accounting unit is "occasions on which cotton was imported," and quite obviously the amount imported on any one occasion could vary from one to a thousand bales, but the table does throw some light on the nature of the trade.

Of most interest is the high number of (if the term may be used) "occasional importers of cotton," and a striking feature is the fall in the total number of merchants engaged in the trade from 607 in 1820 to 318 in 1830 and 341 in 1839. This was due to several factors. Firstly there was a larger number of small operators in business in 1820; secondly, the dominance of the U.S.A. as a supplier of cotton was by no means as great in 1820 as in 1830 and in subsequent years, and thirdly, perhaps of lesser importance, there was a change in the attitude held by Liverpool's mercantile classes towards the trade. In 1820 the growth of the cotton trade was still viewed with wonder and amazement, and even at this late date a desire to share in its prosperity prevailed in all sections of the merchant body, and amongst men not fully engaged in merchanting. An enthusiasm similar to that which the slave trade had inspired fifty years earlier, when "he could not send a bale sent a bandbox,"[9] existed until the need for specialised knowledge made apparent the futility of haphazard and amateur participation in the trade.

The degree of hypothesis which analysis based on Table II must inherently contain, prevents any definite conclusions being formulated. Concrete evidence on concentration requires the consideration of merchants in the light of actual quantities of cotton imported. Table IIIa shows the amount imported by the thirty leading importers of cotton subdivided into three groups, I, II, and III in order of size, together with the total receipt of cotton at Liverpool and the amount consigned to order.

---

[9]F.W. Wallace, *History of Liverpool* (1795), 73.

Table IIIb gives exactly the same information expressed in percentage terms.

Table IIIa
Imports of the Thirty Leading Cotton Merchants at
Liverpool in the Years 1820, 1830, and 1839 (in Bales)

	1820	1830	1839
Total receipts at Liverpool	458,693	793,870	1,011,778
Amount imported by Group I	109,272	259,156	368,595
Amount imported by Group II	48,020	105,107	153,351
Amount imported by Group III	24,794	58,385	64,228
Total imports of the thirty leading importers (Groups I, II and III)	182,086	422,648	586,174
Consigned to "order"	89,935	117,403	161,911

Table IIIb
Imports of the Thirty Leading Cotton Merchants at
Liverpool in the Years 1820, 1830, and 1839 Expressed
as a Percentage of Total Imports

	1820	1830	1839
Total receipts at Liverpool	100	100	100
Amount imported by Group I	23-82	32-64	36-44
Amount imported by Group II	10-47	13-23	15-16
Amount imported by Group III	5-40	7-35	6-35
Total imports of the thirty leading importers (Groups I, II and III)	39-69	53-22	57-95
Consigned to "order"	19-60	14-78	16-00

The tables show that in 1820 the thirty leading importers handled thirty-nine to sixty-nine percent of total imports. An examination of the appendix, which shows the imports of each individual merchant, reveals, not surprisingly, that most of the leading importers were dealing in United States' cotton. Nine members of Group I, eight of Group II and six of Group III fell into this category, the exceptions in each case importing their cotton from South America, mainly Brazil. By 1830 the imports of the thirty leading merchants had risen to form fifty-three to twenty-two percent of total imports. Group I's imports rose to 260,000 bales (thirty-two to sixty-four percent) a rise which exceeded that of Groups II and III.

Once again only one merchant in Group I was not engaged in the United States trade, and the presence of but one Brazilian merchant in each of Groups II and III, reflected the relative decline in importance of this market as a supplier of cotton; for while imports from the U.S.A. had trebled over the decade 1820-1830, the Brazilian figure had just remained constant. The year 1839 saw the upward trend of the previous decade continuing, although at a slower pace, the share of the thirty leading importers in total imports rising to 57.95 percent. Group I's imports rose to thirty-six to forty-four percent of total imports, and Group II's to 15.16 percent but Group III's share fell from 7.35 percent to 6.35 percent. In absolute terms, however, the imports of all three groups showed an increase on the 1830 figure. A survey of the markets traded with again shows the changing sources of cotton supplies, United States' merchants completely monopolising Group I while the Brazilian trade could only muster one merchant in Group II and one in Group III. Significantly one East Indian importer appeared in the ranks of Group II.

    If the entire period covered by the tables is examined, certain trends are plainly visible. Most outstanding is the fact that in the twenty years from 1820 to 1839, a period of very rapid expansion, the cotton trade became more and more concentrated into the hands of a small group of merchants. The amount handled by the thirty leading importers rose greatly in both absolute and percentage terms. Whereas they had controlled under forty percent of the trade in 1820, in 1839 their share was nearer sixty percent, a remarkably high proportion when one remembers that at this date sixteen percent of total imports were untraceable through being consigned to "order." Hence, in 1839 almost three-quarters of traceable cotton imports were handled by this small group of thirty importers. The increasing dominance of the cotton trade by a small number of importers is all the more apparent if the figures of total receipts are compared with the total imports of the leading importers. Between 1820 and 1830 total imports of cotton increased by some 345,000 bales, and between 1830 and 1839 by 218,000 bales. Imports of the thirty leading importers over the corresponding periods rose by 240,000 bales and 164,000 bales. In other words over seventy percent of the increments were being handled by the leading merchants. Table II showed that the number of merchants actually importing cotton was subject to a great decline between 1820 and 1830, and that the 1839 figure was only slightly higher than that of 1830. Thus up to 1839 the increase in imports was not met by a greater number of importers but by an expansion in the leading merchants' scale of operation. This expansion was not uniform but was geared towards the larger importers as evidenced by the increasing proportion of total imports handled by the leading thirty merchants. Even within this group of leading merchants the gap between the larger merchant and the small merchant widened. This can be seen most fully by looking at the scale of operations of individual merchants as given in the appendix to this article but it is illustrated in Table IV which compares the imports of the three largest and three smallest importers in Groups I, II and III in the years 1820, 1830 and 1839. This small sample reveals the extent to which the large importer of cotton left behind his smaller counterpart between 1820 and 1839.

Table IV
Comparison of the Imports of the Three Largest and Three
Smallest Importers in Groups I, II and III in the Years 1820,
1830 and 1839 (In Bales)

	Three Largest Importers		Three Smallest Importers	
1820	Richards A.S.	17,632	da Costa A.J.	2,258
	Brown W. & J. & Co.	12,696	Ewart, Myers & Co.	2,209
	Alston, Eason & Co.	12,219	Haworth & Co.	2,175
1830	Bolton & Ogden	40,185	Burn J.	5,179
	Brown, W. & J. & Co.	39,448	Barclay & Co.	5,081
	Alston, Finlay & Co.	26,297	Cardwell Bros.	5,043
1839	Molyneux & Witherby	53,122	Dawson, R.L.	4,657
	Brown W. & J. Co.	48,238	Gilliatt W.H. & Co.	4,569
	Humphreys & Biddle	46,018	Rushton J.	4,322

The analysis of the process of concentration in the cotton trade between 1820 and 1839 shows that while the number of merchants in any one year ran into hundreds, a large portion of the trade was handled by a small group of some thirty operators who gained increasing control as they absorbed a larger part of increased imports. Within this group, all merchants increased their scale of operation and the gap between the big importer and the small importer considerably widened. This was very marked; in 1839 the twenty leading importers accounted for over fifty-two percent of total imports, while the next leading ten importers accounted for only six percent of the total. Clearly, after 1820 the cotton trade became the preserve of large operators dealing in United States' cotton.

The merchant houses which made up the group of leading importers in each year were of varied form and origin. The greater part were Liverpool-based family firms or simple partnerships often long established in the port and engaged in the cotton trade before, sometimes long before, 1820. Firms such as Rathbones, Bolton and Ogden, Cropper & Co., Issac Lowe & Co. and Brown, Shipley & Co. were branch houses of the American firm of W. & J. Brown of Baltimore.[10] Baring Bros. was a branch of the London parent firm. A. Dennistoun & Co. had their headquarters in Glasgow, as did Rankin, Gilmour & Co., Pollock, Gilmour & Co. being the parent firm.[11] Gibbs, Bright & Co. was an associate house of Anthony Gibbs & Co. of London, and the firm of Humphreys & Biddle who were active in the late 1830s were the Liverpool agents of the American speculator Nicholas Biddle. Regrettably, the absence of merchant house records and the present level of research into Liverpool's commerce make it impossible to form any real conclusions on the composition of the port's merchant body, but it may reasonably be suggested that as the cotton trade, and particularly the United States' section of the trade, expanded and became more sophisticated in its organisation and finance, the structure of the merchant body engaged in the trade became more complex as important operators both in the United States and in London and Glasgow set up branch, associate or agency houses in Liverpool.

The absence of merchant house records also prevents any positive pronouncements being made on the nature of the import business undertaken by the leading importers in the cotton trade. Imports were made on a commission basis or on own account, but it is not wholly clear which form of business predominated or whether importers engaged in one or both forms of business. N.S. Buck in his pioneer work on the organisation of Anglo-American commerce in the first half of the nineteenth century concluded that most cotton was imported on commission by merchants acting on behalf of others but that there was a general tendency for the merchant who acted on his own account to become more

---

[10]A. Ellis, *Heir of Adventure: The Brown Shipley Story, 1810-1960* (1960), 10.

[11]J. Rankin, *A History of our Firm* (1921), p. 49 *et seq.*

important.[12] Witnesses before the Select Committee on Commerce, Manufacturers and Shipping in 1833 giving evidence on the Liverpool cotton trade stated that cotton was chiefly imported on commission but that importing on own account was increasing.[13] This was certainly the predominant form of business by the mid-century, when the coming of the steam packet and the increased speed with which market information was communicated caused a decline in consignment business generally. The conservative, cautious Rathbones found it increasingly difficult to obtain sufficient commission business from the late 1840s, for most Liverpool houses were by that date importing solely on own account. In the twenties and thirties, however, it would appear that most merchants conducted a mixed business, partly receiving consignments on a commission basis and partly on own account, the proportion of each type of business depending on the state of the market, contacts overseas, and the individual merchant's spirit of risk, commission business being safer but less profitable than business on own account.

Whatever the form of merchant house operating and whether the import business prosecuted was on own account or on a commission basis, a common feature of all cotton importers in the years after the 1820 was that their scale of operation increased. An important feature which must be considered is how this increased scale of operation affected the operator's other commercial activities; in particular, did the importer as he handled greater and greater amounts of cotton come to devote more and more of his attention to this one operation? In other words, did the large-scale importer of cotton become more specialised both in the sense of importing only cotton or importing only from certain areas, and in the sense that he came to deal specifically in import business and to cease to perform other mercantile functions such as those of exporter, broker, shipowner and ship's agent?

It is by no means an easy matter to discover whether import merchants specialised in terms of commodities dealt in or markets traded with. The use of commercial directories in this respect has long since been regarded as totally unsuitable and registers of trade associations though

---

[12]N.S. Buck, *The Development of the Organisation of the Anglo-American Trade 1800-1850* (1925), pp. 37-45.

[13]*Report from the Select Committee on Manufacturers, Commerce and Shipping,* 1833 (690) vi, Qs. 1510, 4086-122.

perhaps less unreliable are open to widespread misinterpretation as it was common practice for a merchant to belong to a variety of associations.[14] Again, there is the problem of definition; while a specialist is clearly a merchant who confines his dealings to one particular commodity or one particular market, what criteria does one use to assess specialisation?

When only a single firm is being examined and the actual records of the firm in question are available, it is possible to consider a variety of criteria before formulating the final evaluation of the degree of specialisation attended. The quantities of commodities imported from various sources, the value of criteria before formulating the final evaluation of the degree of specialisation attained. The quantities of commodities imported from various sources, the value of the several branches of the merchant's business, the amount of time and energy devoted to each, and the regularity of trade can all be taken into account. No such comprehensive examination can be made when the merchant body as a whole, or a large number of merchants is being considered. The absence of sufficiently detailed information about each merchant's activities, and the need to establish a set of common criteria necessitates judging import specialisation solely by the quantities of goods imported and the countries traded with. Even the use of this seemingly simple yardstick does, however, present some problems. Extreme cases are straightforward enough, the merchant who imported 20,000 bales of cotton and nothing else was clearly a specialist, and at the other end of the scale the merchant who in the course of a year imported 10,000 bales of cotton, 5000 tons of timber, 7000 barrels of flour and quantities of cheese, turpentine, tar, maize, wheat and sugar was equally clearly not a specialist. It is in instances where the merchant's imports do not allow a clear-cut decision to be made that difficulty arises. No common scale can be adopted to help in the balancing of the merchant's imports of one commodity against those of another, for the numerous problems involved in expressing imports in value terms, and the sheer magnitude of the task, render such compilation impracticable. In any event such an exercise would give results which were severely distorted towards more valuable commodities. Again, there is the question of whether specialisation should be assessed by balancing the merchant's imports of one commodity against his imports of any other

---

[14]For example, John Gladstone was a member of the West Indian, E. Indian, Baltic, Portugal and Brazil Associations in Liverpool at the beginning of the nineteenth century.

single commodity, or against his imports of all other commodities taken together. Even if the latter definition is accepted as being the more satisfactory of the two, the weakness of comparing quantities of one commodity against those of others still remains. The presence of this inherent difficulty results in decisions on marginal cases being in the last resort arbitrary judgments.

The examination of the degree to which the thirty leading importers of cotton specialised in importing that commodity took the form of classifying importers into one of four categories according to the degree of specialisation attained, perfect specialists, near perfect specialists, marginal specialists and non-specialists. The degrees of specialisation represented by these four classifications are as follows: perfect specialists are merchants who import one commodity to the exclusion of all others, near-perfect specialists are merchants who import more than one commodity but whose imports of cotton completely outshadow all others, marginal specialists are merchants whose imports of cotton are greater than those of any other commodity but not to the extent that these other commodities are rendered negligible, and finally, non-specialists are merchants importing a variety of commodities, no one of which is distinguishable as being more important than any other. Examples of merchants falling into each category and the classification of each of the leading importers are contained in the appendix. An overall view of the degree of specialisation attained by the thirty leading importers of cotton in the years 1820, 1830 and 1839 is depicted in Table V. If the number of specialists, (i.e. perfect specialists, near-perfect specialists and marginal specialists) is compared with the number of non-specialists in each year, two features emerge from the table. Firstly, the majority of merchants were specialising in the importing of cotton, and secondly, there was little increase or decrease in the number of specialists between 1820 and 1839. The ratio of specialists to non-specialists in the years 1820, 1830 and 1839 was twenty-four to six, and twenty-five to five respectively, and within the "specialist group" the distribution between perfect, non-perfect and marginal specialists shows no major change. It would appear then that the period 1820 to 1839, a period when the scale of operation of leading importers of cotton was increasingly rapidly, saw no movement towards specialisation in importing but rather merely the maintenance of the very high degree of specialisation which already existed in 1820.

Table V
Degree of Specialisation Attained by the Thirty Leading
Importers of Cotton of Liverpool in the Years 1820, 1830
1839

	Perfect Specialists	Near-perfect Specialists	Marginal Specialists	Non-Specialists
1820	2	13	9	6
1830	6	12	6	6
1839	6	13	6	5

As yet, no consideration has been given to specialisation by country or area traded with, as opposed to specialisation by commodity. However, an analysis of import specialisation by commodity is to a great extent an analysis by country traded with also, for the geographical sources of supply of a commodity are generally strictly limited. The specialist cotton importer must obtain his supplies from the U.S.A., Brazil, the East Indies or Egypt. If he obtains the great bulk of his supplies from one country only he must obviously be a specialist importer both in terms of commodity dealt in, *and* in terms of area traded with. Table VI shows that with insignificant exceptions importers gained their supplies almost entirely from one country only.

Table VI
Degree to Which the Thirty Leading Importers of
Cotton Obtained Their Supplies of the Commodity
From One Country Only

	1820	1830	1839
Merchants importing cotton from one country only	25	29	26
Merchants importing over 90% of cotton imports from one country only	5	1	3
Merchants importing under 90% of cotton imports from one country only	-	-	1

The conclusion that the great majority of the leading importers of cotton were specialising in their importing business in importing cotton from one source only (nearly always, as might be expected, the U.S.A.) does, however, require some qualifications. Firstly, it is worth remembering that a small number of importing houses were actually branches of merchant houses centred outside Liverpool, set up specifically to handle imports of cotton. This was true of the near-perfect specialist firm of Humphreys & Biddle which was operating in 1839, and an even better example from the same year is the perfect specialist firm of Purton, Parker & Co. which was set up to take over the business of the Liverpool branch of T. Wilson & Co., which handled cotton imports for the parent firm in London.[15] Secondly, as a study of the appendix will reveal, there was a distinct tendency for the very largest importers of cotton to be non-specialists, so that the ratio of the imports of non-specialists to those of specialist importers is not the same as the ratio of the number of non-specialists to the number of specialists. Thus the proportion of total imports of cotton handled by specialists is less than might be imaged at first sight. Thirdly, it is very important to remember that the conclusion that the majority of the leading cotton importers specialised in the importing of cotton from one area, refers to the leading cotton importers in *any one* year. The pattern of business of the individual firm was frequently changing as market conditions fluctuated and new opportunities presented themselves. Firms might at any time move from one degree of specialisation in cotton to another and occasionally switch from specialisation to non-specialisation. Such movement was constantly occurring, but in each of the representative years chosen in the period 1820 to 1839 the majority of the leading thirty importers of cotton, around eighty percent in fact, were specialising in importing cotton from one area.

In specialising in importing one commodity from one area the merchant engaging in the cotton trade in the years after 1820 had moved a far cry from the typical merchant of the eighteenth century who tended to be a general merchant with widely spread interests. The interests of the eighteenth-century merchant were diffuse not only in the sense that he traded in many commodities and with many countries, but often also in the sense that he performed a variety of mercantile functions additional to that of importing. While even in the eighteenth century men specialising in

---

[15]A. Ellis, *op. cit.*, 57.

providing well-defined services emerged in the fields of banking, insurance, shipowning and general brokerage, many merchants in the late eighteenth century remained men of many parts, importing and exporting, selling and purchasing supplies of goods, owning shares in vessels, acting as ship's agent to vessels docking in his local ports and sometimes dabbling in banking business or the underwriting of vessels and their cargoes. This is in no way to suggest that all merchants performed each of these functions, but simply that the average merchant of the eighteenth century did engage in a wide range of activities. Gradually, however, as the scale of trade increased, as commercial organisation became more intricate and as the need for specialised knowledge became more apparent, the merchant of necessity had to surrender many of the functions which had traditionally been part and parcel of his everyday business to specialist operators, and, in doing, became more of a specialist himself, restricting his dealing to a narrower range of activities. The remaining section of this paper attempts to assess how far the leading importers in the cotton trade had moved in this direction by 1820 and whether the trend towards specialisation of function continued as the importer's scale of operation expanded over the period 1820 to 1850.

In Liverpool certain functions had by 1820 been generally given up by virtually all merchants and become solely the province of specialist operators. The activity normally described as Country Banking was one such function and a similar development was apparent in the insurance field. Other functions had been surrendered wholly or partially in some trades but not all. In many import trades general brokers were taking over the business of selling produce in the Liverpool market, but this trend was most noticeable and most complete in the cotton trade, where merchants were almost completely dependent for the disposal of their imports on the specialist cotton broker, who had provided, from the turn of the century, the vital link between the Liverpool importer and Manchester manufacturing interests.[16]

In the case of other functions the break was less pronounced and is less easy to determine. For example, conclusions on the degree to which importing and exporting were combined by one merchant are impossible without a close survey of the business records of individual houses. It is to be regretted that there is no general source of information on exports

---

[16]F.E. Hyde, B.B. Parkinson and Sheila Marriner, *op. cit.*, 76-77.

such as the Bills of Entry provide for imports. I have not, however, come across any evidence to suggest that importing and exporting were becoming separate functions and I know of no example of a firm operating only in the import trade or only in the export trade. On the other hand, examples of merchants engaging in both functions are legion and it is well worth repeating the words of a Mr. A.H. Wylie (himself both an importer of cotton and an exporter of manufactured goods to the U.S.A.), who stated in evidence before the Select Committee on Commercial Distress of 1847-1848 that, "the importers of raw materials are generally exporters of manufactured goods."[17]

One group of operators engaged in the importing of cotton who most certainly dealt in imports and exports were the merchant banking houses who figured so prominently amongst the leading cotton importers throughout the period 1820 to 1850. A. Dennistoun & Co., W. & J. Brown & Co., Baring Bros. & Co., Wildes, Pickersgill & Co., Reid, Irving & Co., McAlmont Bros, and Brown Shipley & Co., were all important merchant bankers in the Anglo-American trade.[18] As such they handled imports and exports on commission and on own account and performed a host of international banking services, acting as agents, guaranteeing credit, and financing trade all over the world as well as on the Atlantic route.

Amongst the other functions undertaken by the merchant banking firms were those of ship's agent and shipowner. These are two functions which can be examined thoroughly and statistically because of the availability of fully comprehensive source material. Information on the performance of the function of ship's agent is to be gained readily from the Bills of Entry, while the Statutory Register of Merchant Shipping so fully utilised by Mr. Neal in an earlier essay provides a clear indication of shipowning interests. The function of the ship's agent, that of looking

---

[17]Quoted in N.S. Buck, *op. cit.*, 45.

[18]R.W. Hidy, "The Organisation and Function of Anglo-American Merchant Bankers, 1815-60," *Journal of Economic History*, Vol. I (1941), supplement, 53-66. For a comprehensive survey of the activities of one of these merchant banking firms see R.W. Hidy, *The House of Baring in American Trade and Finance: English Merchant Bankers at Work, 1763-1861* (1949).

after a vessel and its interests while the vessel was in port,[19] was a customary function of the eighteenth-century merchant, but by 1820 specialist ships' agents were operating in certain trades, notably the Mediterranean, Baltic, Coastal and South American trades. In other trades the function was still performed by a large number of merchants. Table VII shows that this was certainly true of the majority of importers in the cotton trade.

Table VII
Performance of the Function of Ship's Agent Amongst the
Thirty Leading Cotton Importers in the Years 1820, 1830
1839 and 1850

	Number of Merchants acting as ship's agent on some occasion	Number of merchants not acting as ship's agent
1820	24	6
1830	26	4
1839	28	2
1850	26	4

The table reveals a remarkable level of consistency; in each year more than three-quarters of the leading thirty importers acted as ship's agent on some occasion, and the proportion rose slightly between 1820 and 1839 as importers dealing in S. American cotton declined in importance in the leading group and were replaced by merchants trading with the U.S.A. Knowing that the merchant had surrendered many other functions and that specialists in the business of acting as a ship's agent had appeared in other trades, it may appear surprising that almost all the leading importers of cotton should continue to perform the function. One feature, however, which is revealed by a detailed study of the Bills of Entry, is that whenever importers in the United States' cotton trade acted as ship's agent they invariably had a heavy interest in the cargo of the vessel in question. This would suggest that the performance of the function was very closely allied to that of importing and that the leading cotton merchants looked on it as part of their operations as importers. It remains,

---

[19]See R.H. Thornton, *British Shipping* (2nd ed. 1959) 139, for an excellent description of the function of ship's agent.

nevertheless, somewhat strange that the practice should have been retained and performed so generally in the United States' trade where specialisation of function so often first appeared.

One occasion when an importer always acted as ship's agent was on the arrival in Liverpool of a vessel in which he had a personal interest as a shipowner. Shipowning was for the greater part of the eighteenth century a secondary function of the merchant. Most shipowners were merchants, and conversely most merchants were shipowners.[20] At the beginning of the nineteenth century, a slight difference between trading and shipping interests was beginning to appear,[21] and as the century progressed the specialist shipowner became increasingly more important.[22] There was not, however, and indeed never has been, a complete separation of the two functions of shipowning and importing, and in trades involving bulky low-value commodities the functions were very closely linked; the most outstanding example of this was to be found in the British North American timber trade. In the cotton trade, as Table VIII shows, the majority of the leading importers did not engage in ship owning.

The table shows that in 1820, 1830 and 1839 some two-thirds of the leading importers of cotton were without shipowning interests, and the departure from this trend in 1850 is due not to an increased desire on the part of importers of cotton to own vessels but to the fact that six of the leading importers of cotton in this year also possessed interests in the colonial timber trade where shipowning was the rule.[23] The extent of shipowning interests amongst those importers of cotton who performed the function varied enormously, but whatever the size of the holding, the merchant did not use his ships exclusively for the furtherance of his trading activities. If the information gained from the Registers of Shipping and the Ship's Reports of the Bills of Entry is brought together, it emerges that cotton importer/shipowners were neither shipping all their imports in

---

[20]R. Davis, *The Rise of the British Shipping Industry* (1962), 81.

[21]C.R. Fayle, "Shipping and Marine Insurance," in *Trade Winds*, ed. C.N. Parkinson (1948), 25.

[22]N.S.B. Gras, *Business and Capitalism* (1947), 174.

[23]D.M. Williams, "Merchanting in the First Half of the Nineteenth Century: The Liverpool Timber Trade," *Business History*, Vol. VIII (1966), 111-114.

their own vessels, nor using the vessels solely to carry their own imports. Thus whereas the function of ship's agent was clearly regarded by all cotton importers as ancillary to importing, in cases where the cotton importer possessed shipowning interests he regarded these in a different light. It seems that shipowning was held to be a business interest in itself, apart from importing, on which returns were to be made from freight charges rather than in the free carriage of imports.

Table VIII
Number of Shipowners Amongst the Thirty Leading
Importers of Cotton in the Years 1820, 1830, 1839 and 1850

	Merchants with shipowning interests	Merchants without shipowning interests
1820	9	21
1830	8	22
1839	7	23
1850	15	15

Viewing the entire range of functions which were customarily performed by the merchant of the eighteenth century it would appear that the typical importer of cotton of the first half of the nineteenth century, that is one of the leading thirty importers, was much more of a specialist. True, all merchants continued to engage in both importing and exporting and nearly all acted as ship's agent at some time in a year. Again, some as international merchant bankers conducted far-ranging financial business, but the functions of country banker, underwriter, and broker had been wholly taken over by specialist operators and the majority of importers no longer possessed shipowning interests. The majority of leading importers of cotton in the first half of the nineteenth century were relative specialists in terms of function. This stage had been reached by 1820 and the following decades saw no increase in the degree of functional specialisation. This was partly because it was already very high in 1820, and also, because specialisation had gone sufficiently far to render the merchant body capable of coping with the increasing scale and pace of the trade. Not until the laying of the Atlantic cable and the appearance of an immensely complex and sophisticated futures market was there any pressure towards a higher degree of functional specialisation amongst importers operating in the cotton trade.[24]

The conclusions reached from the foregoing examination of the Liverpool cotton trade in the first half of the nineteenth century are simple and straightforward. Between 1820 and 1850 the cotton trade was increasingly concentrated into the hands of a small group of operators who generally undertook only a narrow range of functions and who tended to specialise in their import business in the one commodity, cotton. While attention throughout this paper has focussed on one trade, and the conclusions must strictly be seen as referring only to the cotton trade, the statistical exercises undertaken and their findings do, I think, have a wider relevance. One of the greatest weaknesses of our entrepreneurial and commercial history to date had been a lack of information on merchants as a class, and there has been a dangerous tendency to try to overcome this deficiency through sweeping generalisations based on only a few case studies often of an incomplete nature. Any value which this study possesses lies not so much in its findings which tend merely to substantiate prevailing views about specialisation, but in the fact that changes in the import merchant's function and scale of operation are examined through a study of empirical evidence which relates to a large section of the merchant body. In providing statistically based evidence of concentration and specialisation in the cotton trade, the surveys of the Bills of Entry add greater plausibility to views about specialisation in other trades in the first half of the nineteenth century. At the same time they bring to light a valuable source of information which, it is hoped, may be used by other students to enlarge our understanding of merchanting and commercial practice in this period of dynamic trade expansion.

---

[24]Sir J.H. Clapham, *An Economic History of Modern Britain* (1932), Vol. II, pp. 315-16.

APPENDIX

Liverpool's Thirty Leading Importers of Cotton in the Years 1820, 1830, 1839, and 1850

Note on presentation

For the years 1820, 1830 and 1839 each importer's activities are presented in the following sequence: name, quantity of cotton imported and the area of origin [United States of America (U.S.A.), East Indies (E.I.), or South American (S.A.)]. In cases where not all imports of cotton came from one source, the area quoted refers to the area from which over ninety percent of cotton imports were obtained. In the one instance where less than ninety percent of an importer's supplies came from one area, both the areas in question are given. There then follows the percentage of total imports represented by the individual operator's imports. On the right-hand side of the page appears the degree of specialisation which the merchant is adjudged to have attained (Perfect Specialisation (P.S.), Near-perfect Specialisation (N.P.S.), Marginal Specialisation (M.S.), or Non-specialisation (N.S.)* and the other commodities (if any) handled by the importer together with their port or country of origin. Unless otherwise stated, where no quantity is given, imports are on a very small scale. *An asterisk denotes a merchant with shipowning interests and a dagger denotes an importer who performed the function of ship's agent on some occasion during the year.*

For the year 1850, the year in which it was not possible to determine the full cotton imports of individual operators, a list is given of the leading importers (of that cotton which was actually consigned to specific Liverpool merchants) indicating as above their performance of the functions of shipowner and ship's agent.

---

* A full explanation of this classification is contained in the text of the essay.

Liverpool Cotton Importers 1820

Group I	Bales	Per Cent	
†Richards, A. S.	17,632 (U.S.A.)	3.82	(M.S.) Turps, 4,474 brls - *U.S.A.* Tobacco, Tar, Rice, Flour, Apples - *U.S.A.*
†Brown, W. & J., & Co.	12,696 (U.S.A.)	2.77	(N.S.) Flour, 20,560 brls - *U.S.A.* Tobacco, 475 hds - *Virginia* Rice, Turps, Staves - *U.S.A* Ashes - *N. York, Belfast* Molasses - *Demerara*
†Alston, Eason & Co.	12,219 (U.S.A.)	2.66	(N.P.S.) Rice, Mahogany, Indio - *U.S.A* Coffee, Sugar, Ginger - *India*
*†Rathbone & Co.	11,139 (U.S.A.)	2.43	(N.S.) Turps, 4,554 brls - *N. York* Tar, 679 brls - *N. York* Ashes, 766 brls. - *N. York* Tobacco, 429 hd. - *U.S.A.* Flour, 2,179 brls - *U.S.A.*, & 1,781 brls - *Ireland* Hides, 2,632 - *M. Video* Wheat, 6,680 qrs - *Ireland, Baltic, Canada* Apples, Bark, Flaxseed, Staves- *U.S.A.* Oats, Mats, Port, Barley - *Ireland* Mahoghany, 238 lgs - *Belize* Sugar - *Demerara*
†McGregor, A., & Co.	10,587 (U.S.A.)	2.31	(M.S.) Flour, 8,557 brls. - *N. York* Staves - *N.York* Tobacco - *N. Orleans*
†Lowe, I., & Co.	10,387 (U.S.A.)	2.27	(N.P.S.) Tobacco - *N. Orleans*
Dyson Bros.	9,291 (U.S.A.)	2.03	(N.P.S.) Orchella Weed, 787 bgs- *Lisbon*
*†Cropper & Co.	9,030 (U.S.A.)	1.98	(N.S.) Flour, 14,625 brls - *U.S.A.* Flour, 211 tons - *Ireland* Tar, 1,839 brls - *N. York* Tobacco - *U.S.A.* Turps, 1,573 brls - *U.S.A.* Oats, 7,313 qrs - *Ireland* Wheat, 6,824 qrs - *Ireland* Ginger, 3,233 bgs - *Calcutta*

†Marshall, J.	8,203 (U.S.A.)	1.79	(N.P.S.) Flour, Rice - *U.S.A.*
*†Lodges & Tooth	8,088 (U.S.A.)	1.76	(M.S.) Ashes, 6,879 brls - *U.S.A.* *Canada* Tar, Turps, Apples - *U.S.A.* Rice, 350 tcs - *Charleston*

Group II

*†Duff, Finlay & Co.	5,929 (U.S.A.)	1.29	(M.S.) Sugar, 8,187 bgs - *Manilla* Sugar, 595 bxs - *Cuba* Flour - *U.S.A.* Hides, 10,763 - *Argentina, W. Indies* Timber, 305 tons - *N. Brunswick* Gum, Valonea - *Smyrna*
†King & Gracie	5,576 (U.S.A.)	1.22	(M.S.) Flour, 500 brls - *N. York* Rice, 1,000 tcs - *Savannah* Turps, 408 brls - *U.S.A.* Staves - *U.S.A.*
Otis, T.	5,138 (U.S.A.)	1.12	(N.P.S.) Ashes, 591 brls - *Canada*
†Crowder, Clough & Co.	5,081 (U.S.A.)	1.11	(M.S.) Flour, 700 brls - *U.S.A., Canada* Wheat, 3,214 bsls - *Quebec* Ashes - *Quebec* Tobacco - *Charleston* Rubber - *Brazil*
†McAdam & Co.	5,068 (U.S.A.)	1.11	(N.P.S.) Turps, 500 brls - *Boston* Ashes - N. York, *Quebec* Rice - *U.S.A.*
*†Campbell, C. & J.	5,002 (U.S.A.)	1.10	(M.S.) Hides, 5,871 - *N. York* Tobacco, 225 hds - *N. Orleans* Rice, Sago, Indigo, Saltpetre, Ginger - *Calcutta*
†Bolton & Ogden	4,622 (U.S.A.)	1.01	(N.S.) Flour, 7,468 brls - *U.S.A.* Turps, 410 brls - *N. Orleans* Tar, Apples, Bones, Rice - *U.S.A.* Sugar, Rum - *Demerara*
*†Heyworth, O.	4,518 (S.A.)	0.98	(N.P.S.) Hides, 7,292 - *Brazil* Sugar - *Bahia* Flour - *Quebec*

†Dixon & Dickson	3,558 (U.S.A.)	0.78	(N.P.S.) Fruit - *Malaga* Tobacco, Rice, Turps, Resin - *U.S.A.*
*†Earle, T. & W., & Co.	3,428 (S.A.)	0.76	(M.S.) Flaxseed, 800 tcs - *N. York* Turps, 1,648 brls - *U.S.A.* Flour - *N. York* Tobacco - *N. Orleans* Sugar, Fustic, Molasses - *Trinidad* Sugar - *Berbice*

Group III

†Wainwright & Co.	2,959 (U.S.A.)	0.65	(M.S.) Turps, 600 brls - *N. York* Rice, 321 csks - *Savannah* Flour - *N. York*
†Barber, W. & Co.	2,717 (U.S.A.)	0.58	(N.P.S.) Rice - *U.S.A.* Flour, 500 brls - *U.S.A.*
Pedra, A.M., & Co.	2,713 (S.A.)	0.58	(P.S.)
Milne, J. & A.	2,662 (U.S.A.)	0.57	(N.P.S.) Tobacco - *N. Orleans*
*†Watson, J.	2,415 (U.S.A.)	0.54	(N.P.S.) Rice, 495 tcs - *Charleston*
†Maury & Latham	2,369 (U.S.A.)	0.52	(N.S.) Tobacco, 947 hds. - *Virginia* Flour, 1,274 brls - *U.S.A.* Rice, Staves, Apples - *U.S.A.*
Roach, G., & Co.	2,317 (S.A.)	0.52	(N.P.S.) Orchella Weed - *Lisbon*
†Da Costa, A.J.	2,258 (S.A.)	0.49	(N.P.S.) Coffee, 400 bgs - *Para* Cocoa - *Para*
*†Ewart, Myers & Co.	2,209 (U.S.A.)	0.48	(N.S.) Tobacco, 434 hds - *U.S.A.* Flour, 500 brls - *Richmond* Beans, 840 qrs - *Baltic* Iron, Hemp - *St. Petersburg* Sugar - *W. Indies* Cutch, Saltpetre, Coffee - *Java*
Haworth & Co.	2,175 (S.A.)	0.47	(P.S.)

Liverpool Cotton Importers 1830

Group I	Bales	Per Cent	
†Bolton & Ogden	40,185 (U.S.A.)	5.06	(N.S.) Tar, 2072 brls - *N.York* Turps, 4.014 brls - *U.S.A.* Flour, 82,914 brls - *U.S.A.* Flaxseed, 1,150 tcs - *N. York*
†Brown, W. & J., & Co.	39,448 (U.S.A.)	4.96	(N.S.) Flour, 17,714 brls - *U.S.A.* Bark, 1,279 hds - *Philadelphia* Turps, 5,962 brls - *N. York* Tobacco, 226 hds - *Virginia* Apples, 334 brls - *N. York* Hides, 1,479 - *N. York* Linen - *Ireland, Scotland*
†Alston, Finlay & Co.	26,752 (U.S.A.)	3.37	(M.S.) Turps, 1,600 brls - *N. York* Tar, 2,340 brls - *N. York* Flour, 4,000 brls - *N. Orleans* Tobacco - *N. Orleans*
†Wainwright & Co.	26,297 (U.S.A.)	3.33	(N.S.) Maize, 29,474 bsls - *N. York* Flaxseed, 338 tcs - *N. York* Turps, 3,860 brls - *N. York* Flour, Tar - *N. York*
†Cearns & Cary	24,391 (U.S.A.)	3.07	(N.S.) Turps, 8,758 brls - *N. York* Flour, 4,331 brls - *U.S.A.* Hides, 1,059 - *U.S.A.* Ashes, Tar, Seed, Apples - *U.S.A.* Tin Plates, 2,080 bxs - *Bristol*
*Moon Bros.	24,044 (S.A.)	3.03	(N.P.S.) Butter, 1,205 frks - *Cork*
*†Cropper, Benson & Co.	23,363 (U.S.A.)	2.94	(N.S.) Sugar, 7,202 bgs - *Calcutta* Wheat, 8,299 bsls - *Baltic, Ireland* Oats, 3,851 qrs - *Ireland* Flour, 11,590 csks - *U.S.A.* Tar, Turps - *N. York* Large variety of E.I. goods - *Calcutta*
*†Taylor, A., & Co.	19,681 (U.S.A.)	2.50	(N.P.S.) Flour, 6,300 brls - *N. York* Cedar Wood, Canes, Reeds - *N. Orleans* Ashes - *Quebec* Molasses - *Demerara*
†Lowe, I., & Co.	18,285 (U.S.A.)	2.30	(N.P.S.) Rice, Nuts - *Africa*

*†Rathbone & Co.	16,530 (U.S.A.)	2.08	(N.S.) Wheat, 3,321 scks - *Dublin* Oranges & Lemons, 682 bxs - *Palermo* Flour, 6,062 brls - *U.S.A.* Wood - *Sydney* Logwood, Mahoghany - *W. Indies* Ashes - *Canada* Tobacco - *Virginia* Bran, Butter - *Ireland*

Group II

*†Tayleur, C. Son & Co.	13,400 (U.S.A.)	1.69	(N.P.S.) Hides, 22,580-*S. America* Logwood - *W. Indies* Calicoes - *Ireland*
†Collman, Lambert & Co.	12,786 (U.S.A.)	1.59	(N.P.S.) Organes & Lemons 288 chsts - *Lisbon*
†Maury & Latham	12,494 (U.S.A.)	1.57	(M.S.) Flour, 7,260 brls - *Virginia* Tobacco, 873 hds - *Virginia* Tar, Turps - *U.S.A.*
†Hagarty & Jerdein	12,187 (U.S.A.)	1.54	(M.S.) Tobacco, 492 hds - *Virginia* Flour, 3,282 brls - *U.S.A.*
*†Buchannan, Laird & Co.	10,257 (U.S.A.)	1.29	(N.P.S.) Coffee, Logwood - *W. Indies* Indigo, Sugar - *Calcutta*
†Martineau, Smith & Co.	10,196 (U.S.A.)	1.28	(P.S.)
Inglis, W.	9,185 (S.A.)	1.16	(P.S.)
†Hobson, J.	8,614 (U.S.A.)	1.09	(P.S.)
†Gordon, A.	7,997 (U.S.A.)	1.01	(N.P.S.) Calicoes - *Ireland*
*Ewart, Myers & Co.	7,991 (U.S.A.)	1.01	(M.S.) Flour, 3,000 brls - *U.S.A.* Sugar 1,000 hds - *W. Indies*

Group III

†Peck & Phelps	7,361 (U.S.A.)	0.93	(N.P.S.) Tinplates, 11,535 bxs - *S. Wales*
†Sands, Hodgson & Co.	7,270 (U.S.A.)	0.92	(M.S.) Flour, 5,018 brls - *U.S.A.* Tar, Turps - *U.S.A.*
†Thornley, T.J. &D.	6,130	0.77	(N.P.S.) Tar, Turps - *U.S.A.*
*†Heymorth & Co.	5,664 (S.A.)	0.71	(N.P.S.) Hides, 18,000 - *S. America*

†Jackson, D.	5,656 (U.S.A.)	0.71	(P.S.)
†Leech & Harrison	5,576 (U.S.A.)	0.70	(N.P.S.) Rye - *London* Indigo - *Calcutta* Fruit, Wine - *Opporto*
†Molyneux, W.E., & Co.	5,425 (U.S.A.)	0.68	(P.S.)
Burn, J.	5,179 (S.A.)	0.65	(P.S.)
†Barclay, G.	5,081 (U.S.A.)	0.64	(N.P.S.) Tobacco - *N. Orleans*
†Cardwell Bros.	5,043 (U.S.A.)	0.64	(M.S.) Flour, 7,932 brls - *U.S.A.* Cochineal, Tar, Turps, Bark - *U.S.A.*

Liverpool Cotton Importers 1839

Group I	Bales	Per Cent	
†Molyneux & Witherby	53,122 (U.S.A.)	5.25	(N.P.S.) Tea, 665 chsts - *Bristol* Flaxseed, Turps - *N. York* Ashes - *Montreal*
†Brown, W. & J., & Co.	48,238 (U.S.A.)	4.77	(N.S.) Flour, 10652 brls - *Philadelphia* Tobacco, Apples, Tar - *U.S.A.* Turps, 4,296 brls - *U.S.A.* Iron, Tinplates - *Newport*
†Humphreys & Biddle	46,018	4.55	(N.P.S.) Turps, 4,193 brls - *Philadelphia* Flour - U.S.A. Iron - *Cardiff*
†Dennistoun, A.	42,234 (U.S.A.)	4.17	(N.P.S.) Logwood - *N. Orleans*
†Roskell, Ogden & Co.	35,578 (U.S.A.)	3.52	(N.P.S.) Turps - *N. York*
†Purton, Parker & Co.	33,341 (U.S.A.)	3.29	(P.S.)

†Baring Bros.	29,000 (U.S.A.)	2.89	(N.S.) Turps, 3,064 brls - *N. York* Flour, 10,922 brls - *U.S.A., Leghorn* Wheat, 2,025 qrs - *Leghorn* Timber, 950 tons - *Canada* Tea, 3,350 chsts - *Canton* Pork, 555 brls - *Belfast* Iron, 4,173 tons - *S. Wales* Logwood, Wax, Rubber - *W. Indies* Sugar - *Calcutta* Cochineal - *Vera Cruz*
†Holford, J.	29,000 (U.S.A.)	2.87	(N.P.S.) Flour, 2,008 brls - *Baltimore* Flaxseed - *N. York* Iron - *Glasgow* Rye, Tallow - *Baltic* Wool - *Trieste*
†Reid, Irving & Co.	26,426 (U.S.A.)	2.61	(N.P.S.) Beeswax - *U.S.A.*
†Brown, Shipley & Co.	25,638 (U.S.A.)	2.54	(M.S.) Turps, 3,002 brls - *U.S.A.* Flour, 7,790 brls - *U.S.A.* Tobacco - *U.S.A.* Iron - *S. Wales*

Group II

†Todd, Jackson & Co.	24,306 (U.S.A.)	2.40	(N.P.S.) Iron, 582 tons - *S. Wales*
†Collman & Stolterfront	22,857 (U.S.A.)	2.28	(M.S.) Flour, 7,875 brls - *N. Orleans* Turps, 3,605 brls - *U.S.A.* Flaxseed - *N. York* Indigo - *Valpariso*
†Maury, J., & Sons	17,465 (U.S.A.)	1.73	(M.S.) Flour, 2,500 brls - *U.S.A.* Turps, 5,000 brls - *N. York* Tobacco, 806 hds - *U.S.A.* Flaxseed, 480 tcs - *U.S.A.*
†de Lizardi, F.	16,945 (U.S.A.)	1.67	(N.P.S.) Logwood - *U.S.A.* Iron - *Cardiff*
†Wildes, Pickersgill & Co.	15,325 (U.S.A.)	1.51	(N.S.) Timber, 20,618 tons - *Canada* Turps, 7,303 brls - *N. York* Flour, 3,187 brls - *N. York* Tar, Tea - *N. York* Ashes - *Montreal*

*†Moon Bros.	14,012 (S.A.)	1.39	(N.P.S.) Rubber, Hides - *Maranham*
*†Rathbone & Co.	12,472 (U.S.A.)	1.23	(M.S.) Tobacco, 619 hds - *Virginia* Copper Ore, 749 tons - *N. York* Oranges & Lemons, 3,057 bxs - *Palermo* Hemp - *Riga* Ashes - *Montreal* Flour, Turps - *U.S.A.*
*†Tayleur, C., Son & Co.	11,850 (U.S.A.)	1.17	(M.S.) Logwood, 620 tons - *Laguna* Wool, 4,534 bls - *S. America* Skins - *Monte Video*
*†Barton, Irlam & Co.	9,117 (E.I.)	0.91	(M.S.) Sugar, 5,887 hds - *W. Indies* Sugar, 4,895 css - *Mauritius* Pepper, Ginger, Coffee, Molasses - *W. Indies* Ginger, Indigo, Pepper, Ivory - *Bombay*
†Fountain & Price	8,912 (U.S.A.)	0.88	(P.S.)

Group III

*†McAlmont Bros.	3,507 (U.S.A.) 5,347	0.88	(N.P.S.) Rum, Sugar, Logwood- *W. Indies* Cordage - *Baltic*
†Waddington, Holt & Co.	8,510 (U.S.A.)	0.84	(N.P.S.) Turps, 1,625 brls - *N. York* Tar - *U.S.A.* Fruit - *Malaga*
†Poutz, V.	8,406 (U.S.A.)	0.83	(P.S.)
*†Mure, H., & Co.	6,675 (U.S.A.)	0.66	(N.P.S.) Iron Ore, Apples - *N. York*
†Green G., & Son	6,465 (U.S.A.)	0.64	(P.S.)
Pope A.	6,005 (U.S.A.)	0.59	(P.S.)
†Hagan, Magee & Co.	5,765 (U.S.A.)	0.57	(P.S.)
†Dawson, R.L.	4,657 (U.S.A.)	0-46	(N.S.) Turps, 1,840 brls - *U.S.A.* Flour, 1,507 brls - *Baltimore* Timber, 589 tons - *Canada* Porter - *Dublin*

*†Gilliatt, W.H., & Co.	4,569 (U.S.A.)	0.45	(N.S.) Timber, 474 tons - *Canada* Tobacco, 1,555 hds. - *U.S.A.* Tar, Turps - *U.S.A.*
Ruston, J.	4,322 (S.A.)	0.43	(N.P.S.) Rubber, Sarsparilla - *S. America*

Liverpool Cotton Importers 1850

†Dennistoun, A.

†Jackson, W. & Sons

*†Moon, W.

*†Johnston, S.

*†Rankin, Gilmour & Co.

*†Zwilchenbart, R., & Blessig

†Brown, Shipley & Co.

*†Gibbs, Bright & Co.

†McHenry, J.

†Duckworth & Williams

Melly, Romilly & Co.

†Bird, Gillian & Co.

†Baring Bros.

†Petrochino, E.

*†McAlmont Bros.

*†Fielden Bros.

†Crook, J.T.

*†Rathbone & Co.

*†Zwilchenbart, E.

Ryder & Tetley

*†Moon, E.

*†Hutchinson, R.

Rushton, J.

†Lowe, I. & Co.

†Collman & Stolterfont

*†Cater, J.W.

†Morewood Bros.

*†Holderness & Chilton

*†Toole, J.

*†Kleingender Bros.

The Shipping of the North Atlantic Cotton Trade in the Mid-Nineteenth Century

Professor Hobsbawm's famous comment that "whoever says Industrial Revolution says cotton,"[1] might be taken a stage further to observe that whoever speaks of Britain's industrial greatness and domination of world trade in manufactures throughout the nineteenth century, speaks of cotton.[2] Cotton was not merely the first industry to demonstrate the superiority of modern technology and large scale organisation, it remained Britain's chief manufacturing industry down to 1914 and cotton goods which supplanted woollens as Britain's leading export in the 1790s maintained their primacy for more than a century. Equally, to the United States, cotton was of crucial importance. It was the great staple of the South and after replacing tobacco as the country's principal export around 1815 it grew to account for well over half of United States' exports in value terms by the mid-century. Understandably therefore cotton is possessed of a vast literature, studies of the extremes of plantation and factory are numerous and the commercial organization of the cotton market on both sides of the Atlantic has been the subject of detailed examination,[3] interestingly as

---

[1]E.J. Hobsbawm, *Industry and Empire* (London, 1968), 40.

[2]The material for this paper was obtained chiefly from the Customs Bills of Entry for Liverpool which are stored in the Customs House Library in London. I am grateful to the Librarian for permission to consult the Bills and for assistance and facilities at the Customs House. I should also like to thank Dr. Phillip Cottrell of the University of Leicester and Mr. Robin Craig of University College, London, for assistance and advice at various stages of my research.

[3]See for example, N.S. Buck, *The Development of the Organisation of Anglo-American Trade* (New Haven, Conn., 1925); H.D. Woodman, *King Cotton and His Retainers: Financing and Marketing the Cotton Crop of the South, 1800-1925* (Lexington, Ky., 1968); R.W. Hidy, *The House of Baring in American Trade and Finance: English Merchant Bankers at Work, 1763-1861* (Cambridge, Mass., 1949); E.J. Perkins, *Financing Anglo-American Trade, The House of Brown* 1800-1880 (Cambridge, Mass., 1975).

early as 1858 in the British case with Thomas Ellison's *The Cotton Trade*.[4] Yet for all the attention lavished on cotton both by contemporary observers and subsequent historians, one element of cotton's spectacular nineteenth century expansion, namely the trade in raw cotton, has gone largely unconsidered. Of course the massive growth of British imports of cotton is well documented as is the development of a sophisticated market system associated with the introduction of the telegraph, but the actual transporting, the shipping of cotton across the Atlantic, has never been fully examined.[5]

This neglect is all the more surprising when one views the quite incredible growth of the trade in raw cotton. In the forty years before 1860 imports of cotton into Britain increased almost tenfold. Liverpool was the chief port of receipt, accounting throughout the period for never less than eighty percent of Britain's annual imports. Within Liverpool's imports, cotton from the U.S.A. predominated. Table 1[6] which shows imports of cotton into Liverpool from the U.S.A. reveals the dramatic expansion which occurred. The scale of cotton shipments across the North Atlantic and the nature of cotton as a bulky, though light, commodity imposed heavy demands on shipping and the aim of this paper is to examine the shipping involved in the Anglo-American cotton trade and to pose a limited number of basic questions. First, how many voyages were required to transport these vast quantities of cotton? This involves a consideration of the size of vessels, the number of ports engaged in the shipping of cotton and the extent to which cotton figured within the cargo of an individual vessel. Second, a more pertinent question not to be confused with the first, how many vessels were engaged in the trade, or to put it another way, how far was the trade conducted by vessels which made a

-----

[4]T. Ellison, *A Handbook of the Cotton Trade* (London, 1858). Of even greater value are two other works by Ellison: *The Cotton Trade of Great Britain* (London, 1886), and "History of Cotton Prices and Supply, 1790-1862," *Exchange Magazine*, 1 (1862), 306-315, 11 (1863), 45-54.

[5]Albion discussed aspects of the shipping of cotton in two books, but in neither was it the chief theme of his study. See, R.G. Albion, *The Rise of New York Port* (New York, 1939), and *Square-Riggers on Schedule* (Princeton, 1938).

[6]Both Smithers and Donnell used brokers' circulars in compiling their tables. Donnell, whose massive statistical survey appears to have been little used in the past, relied on the circulars of the firm of Collman and Co.

series of voyages freighting cotton or by vessels which participated but occasionally in the trade? Such questions embrace the issues of how far the trade possessed seasonal characteristics and the duration of voyages. Third, the paper considers two aspects of the vessels themselves, namely tonnage and the sources of shipping, that is nationality and ports of registration. Answers to these questions have been sought through a detailed analysis of cotton arrivals at Liverpool in selected periods using the Customs Bills of Entry as a source.[7] It should be stressed that this is very much a preliminary survey and one based on British sources.

Table 1
Receipts of Cotton From the United States
At Liverpool 1820-1860
(Bales)

1820	272,574	1834	664,023	1848	1,284,689
1821	240,257	1835	700,359	1849	1,342,771
1822	274,832	1836	708,994	1850	1,084,644
1823	390,914	1837	769,408	1851	1,346,505
1824	265,413	1838	1,066,790	1852	1,646,804
1825	419,490	1839	787,900	1853	1,479,731
1826	371,143	1840	1,155,270	1854	1,584,502
1827	579,134	1841	843,755	1855	1,587,799
1828	403,255	1842	931,612	1856	1,703,613
1829	422,109	1843	1,291,807	1857	1,410,122
1830	570,808	1844	1,028,811	1858	1,758,468
1831	560,181	1845	1,370,455	1859	1,958,756
1832	581,695	1846	933,833	1860	2,492,138
1833	612,031	1847	809,809		

Source: H. Smithers, *Liverpool* (Liverpool, 1825); E.J. Donnell, *Chronological and Statistical History of Cotton* (New York, 1872).

---

[7]E. Carson, "Customs Bills of Entry," *Maritime History,* 1 (1971), 176-190.

The Customs Bills of Entry were a daily publication published by the Customs for the convenience of the mercantile community. Bills relating to London appear to have commenced in the mid-seventeenth century and Bills for Bristol date from the 1770s but it was not until the nineteenth century that Bills came to be generally produced for the main outports. The earliest set of Bills for Liverpool held in the Customs Library is dated 1820 but the Library's holdings are incomplete until 1852 when a full sequence commences. The information contained in the Bills changed over time but basically they provide a full picture of the trade and shipping of the port. Each Bill commenced with "Ships Reports" which detailed the arrival of each vessel in the port, and there followed summaries of imports and exports and lists of vessels cleared for loading, loading and cleared outwards. For the purpose of this paper it is the ship's reports which are of prime importance. The reports listed the vessel's name, port of registration, master and tonnage, port of origin, dock and ship's agent in Liverpool, together with a full account of cargo and consignees. At various times the reports also listed crew size and date of sailing from the port of origin.

Table 2
Cotton Exports to Great Britain from United States' Ports

	1830-1832		1853-1855	
	Bales	%	Bales	%
New Orleans	623,631	33.67	2,453,150	50.90
Mobile	161,362	8.71	683,770	14.19
Savannah	371,004	20.03	386,848	8.03
Charleston	424,768	22.94	558,378	11.59
Virginia	63,972	3.45	500	--
Florida	---	---	43,708	0.91
New York	189,701	10.24	654,360	13.58
Others	17,421	0.94	38,899	0.80
Total	1,851,859		4,819,613	

Note: Three year periods ending 30 September. For Virginia and Florida, combined exports from ports in the state.

Source: Compiled from E.J. Donnell, *Chronological and Statistical History of Cotton* (New York, 1872).

The statistical survey embodies in this paper is based on two three-year periods, 1830-1832 and 1853-1855. The choice of periods was influenced by the availability of source material and the need to choose periods of relative stability. While the secular trend of United States exports of cotton to Liverpool was dramatically upward, annual figures could vary considerably as they did, for example, in the years 1823-1828 and 1837-1841. It was thought desirable to avoid periods of excessive fluctuation where the demands on shipping would have been very different from one year to another.[8] In Table 1 which shows receipts of United States cotton at Liverpool between 1820 and 1860 it will be observed that the years of 1830-1832 and 1853-1855 were periods of comparative stability.

The great growth in the North Atlantic cotton trade in the forty years before the Civil War was accompanied by significant changes in the position of the various ports engaged in the export of cotton to Liverpool. The focus of the trade throughout the period was the four major cotton ports of the South, Charleston in South Carolina, Savannah in Georgia, New Orleans in Louisiana and Mobile in Alabama. Originally the trade centred on Charleston and Savannah but gradually these ports were overtaken in volume of business by the old French ports of New Orleans and Mobile. New Orleans came to hold a position of overwhelming superiority. Table 2 shows exports of cotton to Britain from the major cotton ports in the two periods with which this paper is concerned. In the early 1830s the four major ports accounted for eighty-five percent of United States cotton exports to Britain and in the mid-1850s the proportion was about the same. The relative importance of the four individual ports had changed considerably, however, for while exports from New Orleans and Mobile had risen about fourfold, those of Charleston had risen by little more than a quarter and Savannah's trade had virtually stagnated. This changing pattern reflected the westward shift in the cultivation of cotton away from the Carolinas and Georgia towards the more fertile soils of Alabama, Mississippi and Louisiana, and it was this shifting pattern of cotton culture which accounted for the demise of Virginia and the rise of

---

[8]It would be interesting to discover the impact on shipping of massive fluctuations in the annual level of cotton shipments. For example, in 1827 and 1838 when shipments dramatically exceeded those of the previous year, was the additional demand for shipping met by a transfer of shipping from other branches of North Atlantic commerce or were vessels normally engaged in trades outside the North Atlantic drawn into cotton carrying?

Florida, the two minor suppliers which appear in the table. A further factor underlying the relative decline of Charleston and Savannah as cotton ports was the diversion of a considerable part of their trade in cotton to New York through the development of coastal packet services.[9] The expansion of such services and the increasingly quantities of cotton carried north explain the growing cotton exports of New York, although the importance of that port within the overall volume of United States cotton exports to Great Britain should not be over emphasized.[10]

The great quantities of cotton annually exported from the United States to Liverpool involved the employment of a large amount of shipping space. Table 3, which lists arrivals in Liverpool of vessels carrying significant amounts of cotton, indicates the level of demands made by the trade on shipping.[11] It is important to stress that the table refers simply to "arrivals" and that the amount of cotton associated with an "arrival" could vary enormously depending on the size of a vessel and the nature of its cargo. In consequence no special importance should be attached to any particular figures and when considering inter-year comparisons the different level of imports in each year should be borne in mind. Notwithstanding these qualifications the table clearly reveals the basic trends, namely that in the early 1830s the United States/Liverpool cotton trade involved over five hundred voyages per year, while in the mid-1850s around seven hundred voyages per year were involved. The issue of the tonnage of vessels engaged in carrying cotton is to be considered in a later section of this paper, but at this stage it can be observed from Table 3 that the huge increase in cotton shipped to Liverpool between the 1830s and 1850s must have been accommodated largely by an increase in the size of vessels engaged in the trade and only to a lesser extent by a growth in the number of voyages.

---

[9]Albion, *Square Riggers*, 49-76.

[10]New York's importance in the cotton trade lay not so much in its exports of cotton but rather in its role in the finance and organisation of the trade. On this see the various works listed in note 3.

[11]For the purpose of this survey a "significant amount" was defined as anything over 400 bales. By the period under review United States bales were relatively standardised and weighted around 400 lbs. On the dimensions of bales see: Albion, *New York Port*, 98; B. Poole, *The Commerce of Liverpool* (Liverpool, 1853). An examination of imports in 1832 showed that over ninety-five percent of imports were accounted for by this definition.

Table 3
Arrivals At Liverpool of Vessels Carrying
Significant Amounts of Cotton

	1830	1831	1832	1853	1854	1855
New Orleans	160	185	151	313	364	252
Savannah	115	97	113	45	46	84
Charleston	111	107	113	84	75	94
Mobile	46	59	52	73	83	76
Virginian Ports	31	19	18			
Wilmington	4	3				
Apalachiola				25	21	13
Galveston				5	4	6
New York	92	62	75	160	188	171
Philadelphia	2	5	1	1		
Boston			1	2	2	1
Baltimore		1	2	1	1	1
Total	561	538	526	709	784	698

Note: Virginia Ports are Norfolk, Richmond and Petersburg. In 1853 Apalachiola includes one vessel from Key West. Source: Compiled by the author from Customs Bills of Entry for Liverpool.

Whether a vessel transported cotton to the full extent which its size permitted depended on the proportion of its cargo space which was devoted to cotton. The number of voyages involved in transporting cotton to Liverpool each year was significantly influenced by the extent to which vessels carried cargoes consisting solely or largely of cotton, or mixed cargoes. Cotton was invariably shipped as a bulk cargo, that is in large quantities, but in the case of United States' cotton a clear distinction can be made in the period under review between the cargoes of vessels sailing from Southern ports and those of vessels sailing from New York. Southern port vessels generally carried cargoes comprised solely of cotton. An examination of arrivals of cotton carrying vessels at Liverpool in 1832 showed that eighty three percent of all vessels from Southern ports had cargoes exclusively of cotton, or cotton accompanied by such derisory amounts of reeds, staves, fustic, treenails, logwood and ballast, that to all intents and purposes they were carrying nothing but cotton.[12] In the cargoes of the remaining seventeen percent of vessels from Southern ports, cotton dominated in every case. A few vessels from New Orleans carried significant amounts of hides, and some vessels from both New Orleans and Virginia carried tobacco. Some Charleston vessels included turpentine, tar and rice in their cargoes while a number of vessels from Mobile carried copper ore taken aboard at Puerto Cabello. In the main vessels from southern ports were carrying little other than cotton, a situation which reflected the limited range and small quantities of commodities other than cotton which the South had available for trade [at this time].

In the 1850s produce entering Southern trade was more diverse. As the steamboats on the Mississippi and its tributaries opened up a vast hinterland, New Orleans had developed a quite considerable trade in foodstuffs: bacon, pork, beef, flour, maize, lard and oil. The export of pitch pine from Savannah was also beginning to expand.[13] Cargoes from New Orleans, Savannah and Charleston were certainly more mixed than before and within such cargoes cotton dominated far less. Cargoes from Mobile however continued to be comprised almost wholly of cotton as that port was almost barren of alternative cargo. Even so the proportion of Southern port cargoes which were exclusively or largely composed of cotton remained high, at seventy six percent of all cotton carrying vessels from Southern ports. Perhaps a more interesting aspect of the diversification of Southern produce was that in the 1850s a few vessels from New Orleans, Charleston and Savannah docked in Liverpool carrying no cotton, a situation almost inconceivable twenty years earlier.

Whereas cotton predominated in the cargoes of vessels from Southern ports, the reverse was the case with vessels from New York. These vessels carried mixed cargoes which reflected the varied produce of New York's hinterland and its prosperous entrepot trade. In 1832 only three of the seventy five vessels carrying cotton to Liverpool carried solely cotton and in 1855 not a single vessel out of the 171 which carried cotton had an exclusive cargo. Cotton arrived from New York in company with a wide assortment of produce: flour, wheat, ashes, turps, flaxseed, beef,

---

[12]Reeds and staves may very well have been used in the stowing of cotton cargoes. See R.W. Stevens., *On the Stowage of Ships and their Cargoes* (London, 5th, ed., 1869), 138-139.

[13]For a discussion of commodities other than cotton exported from southern ports see Albion, *Square-Riggers*, 70-73; 309-312.

pork, bacon, cheese and apples were commonly featured, and the list could be extended almost indefinitely to include the two vessels which docked in Liverpool in April 1855 with mixed cargoes of cotton and guano.

The different character of cargoes from Southern ports and those from New York explains why New York features more significantly within total arrivals than is warranted by its share of total cotton exports to Liverpool. The figures for New York apart, the arrivals from various ports bear out the relative position of the different ports engaged in the trade. In particular the growth of New Orleans' dominance is plainly shown, while the disappearance of Virginia and rise of Florida in the mid-century is also apparent. Above all the table reveals the very limited number of ports involved in the shipping of cotton, especially in the mid-1850s.

The annual number of arrivals of cotton carrying vessels at Liverpool points to the overall demands made on shipping by the North Atlantic cotton trade but does not indicate the number of vessels engaged in the trade. In general, series of figures of annual arrivals or sailings have little bearing on the number of actual vessels employed unless, in the trade under consideration, a full voyage (that is, outward and inward passages together with associated stays in port) has a duration of about a year. Many factors influence the number of vessels taking part in a specific trade but of crucial significance are those of voyage times and the existence or otherwise of seasonal characteristics in the trade. Both these features influenced the number of vessels involved, and the nature of that involvement, in the annual shipping of cotton.

Table 4 shows the number of vessels which carried cargoes of cotton to Liverpool in the periods 1830-1832 and 1853-1855. The table reveals that in the earlier period a total of 756 different vessels conveyed cotton from the U.S.A. to Liverpool on at least one occasion and that in the later period the figure was 1153. These figures of total number of vessels in each period are broken down according to the number of arrivals in Liverpool made by a vessel. This breakdown enables the pattern of vessel participation in the shipping of cotton to be considered.

The shipping of any trade can be divided into two basic categories, those of regular and occasional traders; regular traders being vessels which spend all or most of their time on a particular route or in a particular commodity trade, and occasional traders being vessels which make only a single voyage, or engage but irregularly in a particular trade

during the period under consideration. Now the working definition of a
regular trader will vary according to the trade and period being examined
and the source material available. In this study, based on arrivals of cotton
carrying vessels at Liverpool, the criterion used for assessing regular
trading can only be that of the achievement of a certain number of arrivals
at Liverpool during the three year period under review. After a survey of
the pattern of arrivals of all vessels and a consideration of the factors of
voyage time and seasonal characteristics in the trade (both to be discussed
below) it was decided to define a regular trader as a vessel which, in a
three year period made either four arrivals in Liverpool having sailed from
a Southern Cotton port, or six arrivals in Liverpool if New York was the
port of departure. The differential was introduced to take account of the
different character of the New York trade and the shorter distance
involved. Where a vessel had a mixed pattern of departures from both
New York and Southern ports, the lower requirement of four arrivals
operated. On the whole the definition was pitched on the low side to
permit vessels which made their first arrival in Liverpool late in the first
year or early in the second year of the three year periods a chance of
meeting the requirement. One further case where it was felt appropriate
to apply the classification "regular trader" was that where a vessel made
only three arrivals but made one in each year which indicated that it was
following a regular pattern of employment in which carrying cotton was
a significant part.

Such a definition is obviously open to criticism; the situation of
vessels which made five arrivals from New York is clearly marginal, and
arguably some account might have been taken of the differences in passage
length between various Southern ports and Liverpool though complexities
would have arisen where vessels made departures from both Atlantic and
Gulf ports. Again, there is the issue of vessels which during the period
under review did not attain the requirement of the definition yet which,
through their pattern of employment immediately before or after the
period, may have qualified as regular traders. This latter problem
inevitably arises unless one makes a complete survey of a very long
period, which in this case source materials do not permit. However,
whatever the weaknesses of the chosen working definition of a regular
trader, it has the virtue of simplicity and there can be little doubt that the
vessels which it excludes would be deemed "occasional traders" by any
standard. Moreover, it should be stated that the aim of the analysis is
simply to provide an informed estimate of the division of the trade

between regular and occasional trading vessels and not to state categorically which precise proportions of the trade were carried by one or the other.

Table 4
Number of Arrivals At Liverpool of Vessels
in the Cotton Trade

Number of Arrivals	1830-1832		1853-1855	
	Vessels	Arrivals	Vessels	Arrivals
1	372	372	662	662
2	164	328	248	496
3	95	285	107	321
4	51	204	54	216
5	41	205	39	195
6	15	90	18	108
7	7	49	12	84
8	8	64	8	64
9	2	18	5	45
10	1	10		
	756	1625	1153	2191

Note: "Number of Arrivals" is number made in the three year period.

Source: Compiled by the author from Customs Bills of Entry for Liverpool.

Table 5 divides the arrivals of cotton carriers at Liverpool between regular and occasional traders using the definition established above. The table reveals that in each period a relatively small number of vessels accounted for a significant proportion of total arrivals. In the period 1830-1832, 148 vessels, less than twenty percent of the total number of vessels which took part in the trade, accounted for 695 arrivals, around forty three percent of all cotton arrivals. In the mid-1850s, 158 vessels, some fourteen percent of the total, accounted for 751 arrivals (thirty four percent). The presence of such a group of regular trading vessels is in no way surprising. The cotton trade was large, long established and based on only a few ports. There was obviously scope for regular trading which brought with it clear advantages to both shippers and shipowners. Amongst vessels designated as regular traders a few stand out through their achievement of an unusually high number of arrivals in Liverpool. Most remarkable was the performance of the *Brittania* which made ten arrivals at Liverpool carrying cotton in the earlier period. The *Brittania* was a packet of the Black Ball Line and other packets were amongst those vessels which made seven or more arrivals in the earlier period. Northern packets of the Black Ball, Red Star, Blue Swallowtail and Dramatic lines featured even more strongly in the mid-century when nearly all vessels achieving seven or more arrivals were New York packets. It would appear that because of the existence of packet services, regular traders played a more significant role in the shipping of cotton from New York than was the case with cotton shipped from Southern ports. But it should not be thought that New York packets alone shipped cotton from New York or that they dominated the Northern branch of the trade. Moreover, it might be observed that while some New York packets can be described in the context of this paper as regular traders in cotton, they were first and foremost regular traders in the sense of the route they operated on rather than in the commodity they carried.[14]

The majority of vessels in the regular trading category achieved between three and six arrivals. Such vessels followed various patterns of trading. Those which made four to six arrivals at Liverpool appear either to have been engaged in a regular shuttle between Liverpool and Southern ports or to have followed the three cornered route of the cotton triangle trading but from the available material it does not appear to have been the predominate form of trading. Of the vessels designated "regular traders" which made only three arrivals, but one in each year of the period, some certainly were operating on the cotton triangle but more interestingly a significant number were engaged in a combination of the North Atlantic timber and cotton trades; undertaking a sailing from Southern ports to Liverpool, normally arriving between May and July, and then sailing for British North America. After returning to Liverpool with a cargo of timber the pattern was repeated with a further voyage in the cotton trade.

A brief but unsustained participation in the varied trading patterns followed by regular traders – Southern port shuttle, cotton triangle and cotton/timber combination – can sometimes be observed amongst vessels classified as occasional traders which made two or three arrivals; but the most noticeable feature of the occasional trader category is the presence of very large numbers of vessels which made only one arrival in Liverpool. The magnitude of the figure in each period requires some comment

---

[14]New York packets carried whatever cargo was available at the time of sailing. Cargoies were invariably mixed. See Albion, *Square-Riggers,* 307-308.

for it might be argued that it is swelled by the inclusion of vessels which either concluded their involvement in the cotton trade at the beginning of the period, or entered it at the very end. No doubt such an element of distortion is present but it is unlikely to have been very great because in each of the two periods around a third of the vessels which made only one arrival did so in the central year of the period, i.e. 1831 and 1854, and thus had an opportunity for previous or further participation in the trade. It would appear then that in each year of the two periods examined a considerable number of vessels, around one hundred in the early 1830s and two hundred in the mid-1850s, made what was for them a very occasional voyage in the cotton trade.

Table 5
"Occasional" And "Regular" Cotton Traders

Number of Arrivals	1830-1832		1853-1855	
	Vessels	Arrivals	Vessels	Arrivals
Occasional Traders				
1	372	372	662	662
2	164	328	248	496
3	64	192	67	201
4	2	8	9	36
5	6	30	9	45
	608	930	995	1440
Regular Traders				
3	31	93	40	120
4	49	196	45	180
5	35	175	30	150
6	15	90	18	108
7	7	49	12	84
8	8	64	8	64
9	2	18	5	45
10	1	10		
	148	695	158	751

Note: Number of arrivals at Liverpool from the U.S.A. in the three year period.

Source: Compiled by the author from Customs Bills of Entry for Liverpool.

A number of factors can be advanced to account for the division of cotton carrying between occasional and regular traders. Of particular significance was the fact that – the New York trade excepted[15] – the shipping of cotton from the United States was not evenly distributed throughout the year. This stemmed directly from the nature of cotton as an annual crop with definite times for planting and harvesting which imparted a seasonal character to the shipping of cotton. While variations occurred according to area and each year's weather conditions, the rhythm of cotton culture was basically that of planting around March and the commencement of picking about the middle of August. Picking continued until the turn of the year. Once picked, cotton was packed into bales and despatched to the shipping ports. The first supplies usually arrived on the coast about October and cotton continued to arrive at the ports for the next six months or so because of the prolonged picking season and the often lengthy journey from the plantations.

The commencement and duration of the shipping season was subject to some slight variation from year to year depending on the size of crop, transportation to the ports, the state of the market and a host of other influences but the season can reasonably be described as occurring from very late in the year until the early spring. Albion in his examination of the seasonal variations in the supply of cotton cargoes for northbound coastal packets stated that the season got under way in October. "By midwinter," he observed, "the movement was in full swing until it began to taper off after April."[16] My own examination of the sailing dates of cotton carriers in the 1850s (by which time such information was included in the Bills of Entry) suggests a similar pattern but with perhaps a later start, more towards late November and December, and the tailing off after May rather than April. An analysis of the sailing dates of cotton carrying vessels from Southern ports which arrived in Liverpool in 1853 and 1854 showed that in 1853 eighty five percent of vessels had sailing dates in the months of December to May. In 1854, when the season appears to have been less concentrated, December to May sailing dates accounted for seventy two percent of vessels. Sailing dates in the months of June to November were correspondingly low and in the months of July to October sailings dwindled markedly, accounting for only eleven percent of vessels

---

[15]An examination of the months of arrival in Liverpool of cotton carrying vessels from New York in the periods 1830-1832 and 1853-1855 showed no pattern of a concentration of arrivals in any particular month or season.

[16]Albion, *New York Post*, 110.

in 1854 and a mere four percent in 1853.[17] The uneven pattern of sailings from the United States was in turn duly reflected in the timing of arrivals at Liverpool which were at their highest between February and July and at a low ebb from September until the turn of the year. The presence of peak and slack periods in the shipping of cotton influenced the relative involvement of occasional and regular traders in the trade, for during the peak period the high demand for shipping drew vessels into the trade[18] while the existence of a lengthy slack period limited the number of regular traders which the trade could sustain.

The tendency for a large number of vessels to make only a single trip in the trade during the year, and that in the peak period, was reinforced by the factor of voyage length. The extent of employment a vessel can gain in a trade with a seasonal peak is greatly influenced by the relative durations of the season and a full voyage in the trade. In the cotton trade the duration of a full voyage from a Southern port comprised the total of the time spent in eastward and westward crossings of the Atlantic together with that involved in unloading and loading – turn around time – in Liverpool and the Southern port. The Bills of Entry provide useful information only on eastbound passages[19] and on turn around time in

---

[17]See Appendix 2.

[18]I have been unable to locate a suitable series of freight rates from southern ports to Liverpool but it may be assumed that freight rate movements reflected the seasonal peak and slack periods of the trade. Freights for cotton carried coastwise from southern ports to New York certainly did so. See Albion, *Square-Riggers*, 73.

[19]A survey of eastbound passage times in 1855 revealed that passage times could vary enormously but a fairly definite pattern of times emerged. Eastbound passages between New York and Liverpool, the shortest route and the one well served by regular packets, tended to be of 20 to 30 days duration. From Charleston and Savannah, passages were customarily of between 25 and 40 days. Vessels carrying cotton from New Orleans to Liverpool took between 35 and 50 days and similar times prevailed from the other Gulf port, Mobile. Such times could be improved upon, but while the scope for bettering the customary time was limited, that for exceeding it tended to the infinite. Unfavourable winds could result in passages of inordinate length. In 1855, particularly severe weather and strong easterly winds in the opening months of the year considerably extended passages: five vessels from New York took over fifty days and nineteen vessels from New Orleans and Mobile exceeded seventy days.

Liverpool[20] but a good indication of full voyage times can be obtained through an examination of the dates of arrival in Liverpool of individual regular traders. Such a survey indicated that New York packets took around three and a half to four months for a full voyage, while regular traders sailing from Charleston and Savannah, though occasionally achieving this sort of figure, normally spent around five months on a full voyage. For the more distant Gulf ports of New Orleans and Mobile, five to six and a half months was the usual duration.[21] These times applied for both the periods examined, there being no evidence to suggest any significant change in voyage times between the 1830s and the 1850s. It should be emphasized that the quoted voyage times relate to regular traders which were likely to have enjoyed some advantages through the routine nature of their business, notably those of masters familiar with the sailing routes and, more important, close associations with experienced ships' agents in Liverpool and Southern ports which would greatly facilitate a rapid turn around.

The significance of voyage duration in the cotton trade lies in the fact that with a full voyage from Southern ports to Liverpool taking from four to six months – and the shift of the trade towards the Gulf ports tended towards the longer term – it was unlikely that more than one sailing from the United States could be made during the peak period of shipping activity unless the first sailing occurred at the very outset of the shipping season. In consequence many vessels which took part in the cotton trade during the peak period did not return to a Southern port because of the diminished opportunity for obtaining a further cotton cargo.

Another factor militating against a full round voyage was that of the problem of return cargoes. Throughout the nineteenth century British exports, being principally manufactures, required a much lower volume of shipping space than that involved in the delivery of imports of bulky primary products. Moreover the predominance of New York as the chief receiving port for American imports from Europe, and the tendency for Southern needs of European goods to be met via New York, all restricted

---

[20]Turn around time in Liverpool varied enormously. Two to four weeks appears to have been the customary time. A significant influence was that of the level of activity in the port. A large number of vessels arriving at about the same time (as was often the case in the cotton trade) served to prolong turn around time. It was noticeable that in such busy periods the most rapid times were achieved by regular traders.

[21]See Appendix 1.

the possibility of obtaining cargo for a return passage to Charleston, Savannah or the Gulf ports. One witness giving evidence before the Select Committee on the Navigation Laws in 1847 went so far as to claim that all vessels which sailed from Liverpool to American ports for cotton went in ballast.[22] The Bills of Entry however record only a few instances of vessels leaving for Southern ports in ballast,[23] but it is unlikely that many sailed with a full cargo.

Thus with the exception of that section of the regular trading category which engaged in the Southern ports to Liverpool shuttle, it was not customary for vessels which carried cotton to Liverpool to return to a Southern cotton port. As mentioned earlier other regular traders followed the triangular route and thus sailed from Liverpool to New York while those which combed the timber and cotton trades left generally for Quebec. The chief destination of occasional cotton carriers leaving Liverpool was North America. As a rule American vessels, which comprised the majority of vessels, sailed either for New York, which offered the principal opportunities for the freight of goods and emigrants, or for their home ports. In the 1850s New York was by far the commonest destination as railway construction and a peak period of emigration provided ready return cargoes of iron and steerage passengers.[24] Where vessels sailed for home ports other than New York it seems that a variation of the classic cotton triangle was being followed with ports such as Baltimore, Newbury port, Philadelphia and Portland substituting for New York. Apart from the North Atlantic trades, the only other trades worthy of comment which American vessels went into, were the Mediterranean and Indian trades which featured in the 1850s. For British and colonial registered vessels, New York or ports in British North America were the common destinations though the Crimean War diverted a few to Balaclava in 1855.

It would appear then that most sailings from Southern cotton ports to Liverpool were followed by a return passage across the Atlantic but how far vessels then continued to operate on North Atlantic trade routes

---

[22]*Select Committee on the Navigation Laws*, 1847 (232) X, Qs. 1116.

[23]The few instances recorded nearly all related to regular traders operating on the Southern ports to Liverpool shuttle.

[24]See *Select Committee on Emigrant Ships*, 1854 (349) XIII.

is not clear and could only be ascertained through a survey of vessel movements from both American and European ports over a long period. This lack of knowledge of the sailing patterns of individual vessels over time needs to be borne in mind when considering the position of the large number of occasional traders in the cotton trade. Such vessels were certainly occasional traders in the context of the United States to Liverpool cotton trade but it would be dangerous to regard them all as generally operating on a tramp or transient basis. Some, perhaps most, were transients, picking up cargoes wherever they might be found and undertaking a haphazard series of voyages; others, however, may have operated in a more regular fashion within the North Atlantic while a few may even have had a further commitment to cotton through taking part in the much smaller trade in cotton between the United States and continental European ports.

In the shipping of the North Atlantic cotton trade United States vessels comprised the major element. Table 6 shows the shipping of the trade divided according to nationality. In the early 1830s United States vessels numbered 490, sixty-five percent of the total, compared with 253 British and thirteen Colonial vessels which together comprised the remaining thirty five percent. Very similar proportions prevailed in the period 1853-1855 when United States vessels numbered 738 (sixty four percent), against 326 British (twenty eight percent) and sixty-one (five percent) Colonial. Within the category of regular traders United States vessels were even more prominent accounting for seventy six percent of the category in 1830-1832 and seventy three percent in 1853-1855. The presence of such a high proportion of United States vessels in the cotton trade is not particularly surprising in view of the rise of United States shipping in the first half of the nineteenth century. Superior and cheaper shipbuilding and reputed greater operating efficiency enabled United States vessels to gain a growing hold on Atlantic trade generally and their control of the lion's share of cotton freighting was a part of this wider dominance. Two minor features of Table 6 worthy of comment are those of the modest growth of colonial vessel involvement and the appearance in the 1850s of foreign vessels, mostly German from Bremen, though a very few vessels were from Norway and Sweden. It was the repeal of the British Navigation Laws in 1849 which enabled foreign vessels to take part in the trade and in the context of protectionist shipping policies it is perhaps worth commenting that restrictions by both the British and United States government on certain trades had an influence on shipping patterns in the cotton trade. While the British Navigation Laws were in operation United States vessels could not combine the cotton and British North American timber trade; similarly United States restrictions on coastal traffic inhibited the full participation of British vessels in the cotton triangle.

Table 6
Arrivals At Liverpool by Nationality

	Regular Traders	Occasional Traders	Total
1830-1832			
American	113	377	490
British	35	218	253
Colonial		13	13
Foreign			
1853-1855			
American	115	623	738
British	35	291	326
Colonial	8	53	61
Foreign		28	28

Source: Compiled by the author from Customs Bills of Entry for Liverpool.

A full analysis of the ports of registration of vessels taking part in the cotton trade is prevented by the fact that in the early 1850s the Bills of Entry ceased to list the ports of registration of United States vessels and instead simply used the designation "American." Even so it is clear from the available evidence that were such an analysis possible it would touch on almost every Atlantic seaboard port in both Britain and America. For example, in 1830-1832 the 113 American regular traders were drawn from no less than twenty-six different ports. This multitude of ports however, conceals the true position. In fact over half the American regular traders came from just two ports, New York and Boston, which provided thirty four and twenty-four vessels respectively. Of the other ports, only Portland in Virginia and Newbury port in Massachusetts with six vessels each were of any significance.[25] Similarly, of the thirty five British regular trades in 1830-1832, twenty one were Liverpool registered and a further seven were from Belfast. Liverpool registered vessels again made up the

---

[25]Conspicuous by their absence were the cotton ports. Only one regular trader was registered at a cotton port, Mobile.

bulk of British regular traders in 1853-1855 accounting for twenty four of the thirty five vessels, and all eight colonial regular traders in the 1850s were Saint John, New Brunswick registrations. In the occasional trader category, New York, Boston and Liverpool were again the most prominent ports though their share was less overwhelming. As might be expected therefore, the leading shipowning ports on either side of the Atlantic were the chief contributors to the shipping of the cotton trade.[26]

Information on tonnages provided in the Bills of Entry enables the size of cotton carrying vessels to be examined. However, as the listed tonnages are registered tonnages certain problems arise when comparing the periods 1830-1832 and 1853-1855 because during the 1830s changes occurred in the basis of measurement. In the early period registered tonnage in both Britain and America was calculated on a similar basis, the Carpenter's Measure or Old Customs House Measurement, which continued to be applied in the United States until 1865. In Britain a new tonnage law was introduced in 1836 but the new law was wholly optional until 1855.[27] In consequence the registered tonnages for the later period are a mixture of old and new systems, but in order to permit comparisons every effort has been made to use old measure tonnages when compiling the tonnage distribution of British and Colonial vessels for 1853-1855. Some element of new measure tonnage may remain but it was not sufficient to seriously distort the distribution.

Table 7 divides the shipping of the cotton trade in the periods 1830-1832 and 1853-1855 into tonnage ranges distinguishing between regular and occasional traders and between vessels of different nationality. The picture which emerges from Table 7 is an interesting one and indeed a dramatic one. What stands out, and this is the key feature of the table, is the huge increase in the size of vessels over the two periods. Whereas in the earlier period virtually all vessels were under five hundred tons and the largest 723 tons, in the later period only ten percent of vessels were

---

[26]It might be noted also that the vessels of greatest tonnage were almost invariably New York, Boston or Liverpool registered.

[27]On the thorny issue of registered tonnage measurement see G.S. Graham, "The Ascendancy of the Sailing Ship, 1850-85," *Economic History Review*, IX, (1956-1957); R. Rice, "Measuring British Dominance of Shipbuilding in the 'Maritimes', 1787-1890," in *Ships and Shipbuilding in the North Atlantic Region* (St. John's, Newfoundland, 1978) being the proceedings of the 1977 Conference of The Atlantic Canada Shipping Project. Rice's paper cites the main literature on the issue.

below five hundred tons wile 293 vessels (twenty five percent) exceeded one thousand tons. Nine vessels were of over two thousand registered tons. The tremendous development in the size and design of sailing ships in the first half of the nineteenth century is not our prime concern here though it was clearly associated with the growth of bulk trades. What must be stressed is that it was this great increase in the size of vessels which enabled the huge expansion of the cotton trade to be accommodated. Had this increase in vessel size not occurred, the number of voyages required each year to ship cotton to Liverpool would have risen enormously. As it was, the three fold expansion of the United States to Liverpool cotton trade between the early 1830s and mid-1850s resulted in a comparatively small increase in the annual total of cotton carrying voyages, from around five hundred to around seven hundred voyages.

The material presented in Table 7 enables some assessment to be made of the tonnage profile of cotton carrying vessels in both periods and comparisons between different categories and nationalities of vessels. An examination of all vessels in 1830-1832 suggests the following picture of tonnages in the cotton trade: a typical vessel was between two hundred and four hundred tons; vessels between four hundred and five hundred tons were not infrequent, but vessels over five hundred tons were unusual. Attempting a similar appraisal for 1853-1855 is by no means so straight-forward. Whereas in the early 1830s the tonnage of a typical vessel could be defined within a fairly narrow range, in the 1850s it would appear that a typical vessel could be anything from five hundred tons to certainly one thousand tons, and arguably up to twelve hundred tons. Only above fifteen hundred tons did vessels become unusual. This situation has some bearing, albeit negative, on the interesting question of whether vessels in the cotton trade possessed any special features or characteristics. Only a detailed survey of American registers would supply the answers to this question, but the great range and variation in the tonnage of vessels engaged in the trade is apparent in both the regular and occasional trader categories. This, along with the way in which cotton carrying was combined with a variety of other trades, and the ease with which large numbers of vessels entered the trade would imply that there were no special requirements for cotton freighting. However, this is not to deny the possibility that some regular traders may have possessed certain adaptations associated with their customary cargo or their usual ports of call. Certainly very large vessels with a relatively shallow draught were built for the New Orleans trade where the bar presented problems. One feature which is detectable in

Table 7 is that the tonnage distribution of regular traders, compared with that of occasional traders, is skewed relatively more towards larger tonnages, so that the typical regular trader was likely to be of a greater tonnage than the typical cotton carrier generally. In part this reflected the general tendency for American vessels to be of greater tonnage than British, a trend which is visible when the tonnage distribution of American vessels is compared to that of British in both the regular and occasional trader categories. American vessels tended to be larger and in each period the really big vessels, over five hundred tons in the early 1830s, and over fifteen hundred tons in the mid-1850s, were well nigh exclusively American. This tendency serves to enhance the role of American shipping in the trade. Larger vessels were thus the crucial feature of the development of cotton carrying in the mid-nineteenth century, and within the shipping of the cotton trade in the more numerous and larger American vessels maintained the dominance which they had firmly established by the early 1830s.

In the mid-nineteenth century the cotton trade was one of the great commodity trades of the North Atlantic employing a volume of tonnage only exceeded by the trade in colonial timber. The nature of the cotton trade, its demands on shipping, and how these demands were met, have been examined in the preceding sections of this paper. The scale of cotton shipments from the United States to Liverpool required a large number of voyages every year though the great expansion of the trade was accommodated chiefly by an increase in the size of vessels. The shipping of the trade was drawn from the United States, Britain and the North American Colonies, but throughout the mid-century period vessels of the United States occupied a dominant position. A significant part of the freighting of cotton was undertaken by vessels operating on a regular basis but the majority of vessels which took part in the trade did so on a casual basis, partly because of seasonal characteristics in the shipping of cotton and because of the factors of voyage duration and return cargoes. It is hoped that these conclusions contribute to a better understanding of one of the North Atlantic's greatest trades.

One feature however which emerges from the examination embodies in this paper and which is most clearly demonstrated by the presence of such a large number of occasional traders, is that the cotton trade was not self-contained but was part of a much larger and complicated pattern of commodity dealings and shipping employment which made up the overall trade of the North Atlantic. All the various elements of North

Atlantic trade, each with their own particular characteristics, joined together to produce a complex interrelationship; an interrelationship which was continuously being modified by both short and longterm factors. A full appreciation of this interlocking network of trade and shipping can only be gained through a detailed study by historians in America and Europe of the pattern of ship movements in the Atlantic. Only when such a survey has been made will the role of the cotton trade in North Atlantic commerce be fully apparent.

Table 7

Tonnages of Cotton Carrying Vessels

TONNAGE	1830-1832						1853-1855							
	REGULAR			OCCASIONAL			REGULAR				OCCASIONAL			
	A	B	C	A	B	C	A	B	C	F	A	B	C	F
2000+											9			1
1900-1999											1			
1800-1899											9			
1700-1799							1				6	1		
1600-1699							5				9	2		
1500-1599							5				12			
1400-1499							4				21	3	2	1
1300-1399							13				25	12	3	
1200-1299							8	1	2		33	14	3	
1100-1199							10	1	1		48	16	3	
1000-1099							12	4	1		38	16	5	1
900-999							10	8	1		61	32	4	1
800-899							16	9	1		71	44	9	
700-799	1						10	7	1		75	38	9	1
600-699	4	1		6	1		8	3	2		77	28	5	6
500-599	9	5		11	2		7	1			69	37	3	4
400-499	23	19		41	30	3	5	1			35	17	5	4
300-399	63	9		159	92	6					13	23	1	3
200-299	13	1		149	83	3					2	7	1	4
100-199				8	9	1								2
0-99														
No data				3	1						9	1		
Total	113	35	0	377	218	13	115	35	8	0	623	291	53	28

Note: Tonnages are Registered Tonnages (Old Measure). The letters A, B, C, F at the head of the columns refer to nationality: A - American, B - British, C - Colonial and F - Foreign.

Source: Compiled by the author from Customs Bills of Entry for Liverpool.

Appendix I
Arrival Dates at Liverpool of Some Regular Traders

Britannia of New York 630 tons.
(Black Ball Line Packet)
All arrivals from New York

20. 1.1830
17. 5.1830
13. 9.1830
14. 1.1831
20. 5.1831
24. 8.1831
19.12.1831
21. 4.1832
8. 8.1832
8.12.1832

John Jay of New York 502 tons.
(Red Star Line Packet)
All arrivals from New York

20. 3.1830
23.11.1830
18. 3.1831
21. 7.1831
18.11.1831
19. 3.1832
13. 7.1832
17.11.1832

Elisabeth of Boston 386 tons.
All arrivals from Charleston

19. 3.1830
5. 7.1830
6.11.1830
29. 3.1831
5. 7.1831
18.11.1831
2. 4.1832
6. 8.1832
4.12.1832

Lady Rowena of Liverpool 399 tons.
All arrivals from Charleston

20. 3.1830
22. 7.1830
11. 1.1831
7. 6.1831
24. 9.1831
30. 1.1832
6. 6.1832
3.10.1832

Olive Branch of Boston 355 tons.
All arrivals from Savannah

11. 2.1830
28. 6.1830
27.12.1830
4. 5.1831
19. 8.1831
4. 1.1832
8. 5.1832
3. 9.1832

London of Whitehaven 351 tons.
All arrivals from New Orleans unless
stated

26. 2.1830
7. 7.1830
25. 2.1831
29. 7.1831 Mobile
3. 1.1832
14. 6.1832
17.12.1832

Hermitage of Portland A.S. 332 tons.
All arrivals from New Orleans

20. 3.1830
23. 8.1830
28. 2.1831
8. 8.1831
6. 4.1832

Columbia of New York 1050 tons.
(Black Ball Line Packet)
All arrivals from New York

4. 1.1853
13. 5.1853
13. 9.1853
12. 1.1854
9. 5.1854
13. 9.1854
8. 1.1855
18. 5.1855
1.10.1855

Caroline of Charleston 782 tons.
All arrivals from Charleston

25. 7.1853
14. 1.1854
12. 6.1854
28. 2.1855
14. 6.1855

Kitty Cordes of Liverpool 849 tons.
All arrivals from Mobile

31. 1.1853
7. 7.1853
19. 1.1854
3. 7.1854
26. 2.1855
27. 6.1855

William Neilson of Liverpool 427 tons.
All arrivals from New Orleans unless
stated

13. 3.1830
24. 8.1830
16. 3.1831
12. 8.1831
31. 5.1832 Mobile

Universe of New York 1432 tons.
All arrivals from New York

3. 2.1853
11. 6.1853
14.10.1853
7. 2.1854
19. 7.1854
1.12.1854
19. 4.1855
23. 8.1855

Wateree American 680 tons.
All arrivals from Charleston

4. 3.1854
17. 8.1854
27. 2.1855
16. 7.1855
26.12.1855

Sisters of Liverpool 851 tons.
All arrivals from Mobile

22. 3.1853
27. 8.1853
31. 3.1854
11. 9.1854
7. 3.1855
5.10.1855

Magistrate of Liverpool 519 tons.
All arrivals from New Orleans

Otseouthe of Bath 1300 tons.
All arrivals from New Orleans unless
stated

24. 2.1853	25. 2.1853
16. 7.1853	6. 8.1853
16. 1.1854	11. 1.1854 New York
17. 8.1854	17. 7.1854
27. 2.1855	1. 3.1855
28. 7.1855	17. 9.1855

Source: Compiled by the author from Customs Bills of Entry for Liverpool.

Appendix II
Month of Departure from Southern Ports of the United States
of Cotton Carrying Vessels which Arrived in Liverpool
in 1853 and 1854

Month	Vessels	
	1853	1854
January	88	48
February	68	54
March	62	109
April	87	73
May	59	74
June	42	51
July	28	33
August	7	15
September	2	7
October	3	9
November	8	43
December	71	43
No data	20	34
Total	545	593

Note: Southern ports include New Orleans, Charleston, Savannah, Mobile, Apalachiola, Galveston and Key West.

Source: Compiled by the author from Customs Bills of Entry for Liverpool.

Merchanting in the First Half of the Nineteenth Century: The Liverpool Timber Trade[1]

Our knowledge of the commercial history of Liverpool before 1850, apart from a few very general studies, is confined to one commodity. The majesty of "King Cotton" and Liverpool's dominance of the trade which was so vital to the nation's industrial well-being, has fascinated present-day historians just as it did contemporary commentators. This pre-occupation with cotton, though understandable, has however given rise to a very one-sided picture of Liverpool's commerce. The purpose of this paper is to redress the balance in some degree through a study of Liverpool's timber trade during the first half of the nineteenth century.

Timber became a commodity of national importance during this period, not merely because of the increased demands of the expanding home economy, but because the trade mirrored many of the country's commercial problems. The question of timber duties was an important feature in the struggle for Free Trade; the large number of ships engaged in the import of timber became a highly relevant issue in the eighteen thirties and forties when the shipping industry was suffering from over-capacity, and the increased Governmental concern about the safety and condition of ships, was a direct result of heavy losses in the shipping of timber where old, unseaworthy vessels were often grossly overloaded. Furthermore, the timber trade was closely linked with the emigrant trade, vessels returning to N. America providing a cheap form of transport for the poorer class of emigrant.[2]

Liverpool was one of Britain's major timber ports, her imports of the commodity in 1850 outstripped those of London in both volume and

---

[1]I am indebted to Prof. F.E. Hyde for generous advice and assistance in my early research on the timber trade, and to Dr. J.R. Harris, Dr. H.J. Dyos and Dr. R.B. Outhwaite for reading and commenting on the article in draft.

[2]H.I. Cowan, *British Emigration to British North America*, Revised Edition (1961), 144-171. See also M.L. Hanson, *The Immigrant in American History*, (1942), 156-160; O. Handlin, *Boston's Immigrants* (1959), 50.

value,[3] and represented over ten percent of the national value,[4] a surprisingly large proportion when one considers that ports and creeks along the whole length of the coast imported timber for local consumption. Within the commerce of the port itself, timber was of vital importance. In terms of volume,[5] it was the most important import apart from cotton and corn and a large portion of Liverpool's registered shipping was engaged in this trade. It is proposed to examine the trade in this sequence: early origins and growth; statistical evidence of growth; the timber merchants; shipping; market organisation.

Timber was one of Liverpool's earliest imports; together with corn it formed a large part of the port's commerce in the sixteenth and seventeenth centuries. Such imports were usually of native growth and were shipped coastwise, the bulky nature of the commodity and the inefficiency of internal communications favouring this means of transport. In the eighteenth century Liverpool began to import foreign timber and became the chief west coast importer of Baltic supplies, principally because of her ability to furnish salt as a return cargo.[6] Liverpool's imports from North America increased slowly throughout the second half of the century, but remained of local significance as the British timber trade was based almost entirely on European supplies. According to a Board of Trade official giving evidence before the Select Committee on Timber Duties in 1835, imports of colonial timber throughout the decade ending 1802 never exceeded one per cent of Britain's total imports.[7] In view of this it was not unnatural that the east coast ports and London should have the overwhelming influence in the trade.

The real stimulus to expansion came towards the end of the Napoleonic period, when the French successes before 1809, together with the extension of the Continental System, aroused fears in government circles that Britain might be cut off from her all-important supplies of

---

[3]T. Baines, *History of Liverpool*, (1852), 745.

[4]B. Poole, *The Commerce of Liverpool*, (1854), 9.

[5]Ibid., 196.

[6]H.S.K. Kent, "The Anglo-Norwegian Timber Trade in the Eighteenth Century," *Economic History Review*, 2nd series VIII (1955), 70.

[7]*Report from the Select Committee on Timber Duties*, 1835 (519) XIX, Q.11.

timber and naval stores from North East Europe. As the Report of the Select Committee on Foreign Trade of 1821 expressed it, "at that time the course of events placed our relations with the Northern states (from whose territories our supplies of timber as well as for domestic as for naval purposes had been chiefly derived) in a situation which gave rise to well founded apprehension lest the resources in that quarter might entirely cease to be available for the demands of this country."[8]

For such reasons the government embarked upon a policy of encouraging North American colonial timber production. By an Act of 1809, a virtual exemption from duty was granted to timber imported from Canada, and additions were made to the duties on European timber. A year later, in 1810, these duties were doubled and further increases followed: by 1819 European timber paid a duty of 655 per load while colonial timber paid, at most, only a nominal sum.[9] The effect of these measures was to work a swift transformation in the trade. Colonial timber, which occupied a position of complete insignificance before 1800, came to represent over sixty percent of total imports in the years 1808-1812 and gained an even larger share of the trade in the decades that followed.[10] Liverpool was naturally favoured by this development; she already possessed more knowledge and experience of the North American market than her competitors, and the transferance of the main source of supply from the Baltic to this sector gave her a marked advantage over London and Hull. Thomas Baines, writing in 1852, correctly observed that "no place in Great Britain has gained so much from the progress of these colonies (Canada) as the port of Liverpool."[11] After the termination of the war, the duties were maintained and came under heavy attack, not only from importers of European timber whose businesses were adversely affected, but also from Free Traders who regarded the duties as vestiges

---

[8]*Report from the Select Committee on the Foreign Trade of the Country*, 1821 (186), VI.

[9]J.H. Clapham, *An Economic History of Modern Britain* (2nd ed. 1930), I, 237.

[10]*Select Committee on Timber Duties*, 1835 (519) XIX, Q. 11.

[11]T. Baines, op.cit., 697.

of the old Colonial System.[12] Indeed the timber duties have been described by one authority as the "silent partners of the Corn Laws."[13]

The retention of timber duties was one of the main considerations of the Select Committee on Foreign Trade of 1821 which reported in favour of maintaining the duties. Reliance on a single supplier, the Committee felt, could give rise to exploitation as well as possibly leading to strategic difficulties, and the importance of the timber trade in providing employment for shipping, at a time when that industry was suffering from post-war over-capacity, was also recognized.[14] Moreover, there were fiscal considerations; it has been estimated that between 1820 and 1840 the annual revenue gained from timber duties never fell below one million pounds.[15] The Committee nevertheless recommended some relaxation of the duties, which it regarded as excessive, and in 1821 slight modifications were made. A duty of 10s. per load was placed on colonial timber, and the foreign rate was reduced by some eighteen percent to 55s. However, even if the difference in freight charges is taken into account, this still left colonial timber with a preference of 30s. per load. Duties remained at this level until 1843, after which date they were successively reduced, but the preference remained until 1860 and duties were not removed completely until 1866.[16]

The imposition and maintenance of duties favourable to the North American colonies and the position of Liverpool on the Atlantic seaboard were in no little way responsible for the continued growth of the port's timber trade, but perhaps the main factor favouring expansion was the relative cheapness of North American timber compared with that from the

---

[12]It is interesting to note however that in the twenties Huskisson, a Liverpool M.P., although an ardent Free Trader, made no reference to the duties on timber in his campaign for tariff reform! See J. Potter, "The British Timber Duties," *Economica*, New Series XXII (1955), 122.

[13]R.G. Albion, *Forests and Sea Power*, (1926), 401, quoted in J. Potter, op.cit., 122. See also on the subject D.L. Burn, "Canada and the Repeal of the Corn Laws," *Cambridge Historical Journal*, II (1928), 252-272.

[14]*Select Committee on Foreign Trade*, 1821 (186) vi, 6.

[15]J. Potter, op.cit., 123.

[16]Ibid. 124.

Baltic. This was, admittedly, due in part to the preferential duties, but also to Canada's natural advantage of extensive virgin forests. While the cheapness of Canadian timber was not denied, fierce controversy raged over whether it was of an inferior quality. Witnesses before the Select Committees of 1821, 1833 and 1835 expressed widely divergent views on this question, but the opinion most commonly held was that Baltic timber was superior only for purposes where special strength and durability were required. Masts and spars were an exception, the North American produce being favoured for its size and freedom from knots. Criticism that Canadian timber was subject to dry rot, fungoid growths and decay came invariably from prejudiced Baltic merchants,[17] and Liverpool's North American merchants, no doubt equally prejudiced, discounted such criticism and pointed to the increasing demand for colonial timber. Giving evidence before the Select Committee of 1821, William Smith stated that Canadian timber was used for a variety of purposes, including packing cases, the interior of buildings and ship repairs. He concluded that the "timber of North American colonies, with the exception of beams and for other purposes where great strength is required, is in general use in the county of Lancashire."[18] John Hamilton, another Liverpool timber importer, who owned over 3000 acres of forest in Canada, echoed these views,[19] and Barton Haigh, a joiner and house carpenter of Liverpool, testified before the same committee that he had successfully used Canadian timber for such durable purposes as warehouse floors.[20] The quality of colonial timber was still a controversial issue fourteen years later when the Select Committee on Timber Duties sat, but by then American timber was becoming more widely accepted. John Miller, a partner of Cannon, Miller & Co., one of Liverpool's leading timber houses, stated in evidence that "estimation of American timber is much increasing,"[21] and the continued

---

[17]*Select Committee on Foreign Trade*, 1821 (186) VI, see for example evidence of Sir Robert Seppings, 14, and that of Alexander Copeland, 20.

[18]Ibid., 52.

[19]Ibid., 71.

[20]Ibid., 83.

[21]*Select Committee on Timber Duties*, 1835 (519) XIX, Q. 4641.

growth of North American timber imports into Liverpool is perhaps itself
indicative that its quality was not in doubt.

    One of the inescapable weaknesses of any study of Liverpool's
commerce before 1850 is the inability to examine the rise of the port or
any particular trade in terms of imports and exports. Customs documents,
in particular the Port Books which are normally such a mine of information, are not available for Liverpool after 1737 owing to the destruction
of Customs House records and the deficiencies of the P.R.O. series.[22] The
search for a substitute set of figures of timber imports is fraught with a
number of difficulties. Theoretically it would be possible to total up the
individual shipments as they appear in the Bills of Entry,[23] but because of
the wide variety of woods and the complete lack of uniformity amongst
units of measurement, the end product of such a survey would be well-
nigh useless. The only practical solution is to add up the tonnage of the
vessels which brought timber into the port. Fortunately the majority of
such vessels carried only timber; in relatively few cases was timber
imported in vessels carrying cargoes of assorted goods and where this does
occur judicious use of multipliers allows the weight of the timber to be
calculated.[24]

    Table I is the result of such an exercise, the years chosen being
1820, 1830, 1839 and 1850, (the absence of Bills of Entry for 1840

---

[22]This shortcoming is only partially remedied by resort to secondary source
material such as Merchant's Handbills, Brokers' Circulars, and contemporary histories and
commercial directories which give annual figures for some commodities. Timber
unfortunately is not covered in this way.

[23]The Customs Bills of Entry were published daily by the Customs Authorities
for the convenience of the merchant community. Each Bill contained "ships reports" which
gave particulars of all vessels arriving at Liverpool, and the port of origin, and a full
account of all merchandise carried and to whom it was consigned. The earliest volume of
Liverpool Bills of Entry in existence is that for the year 1819. Odd volumes between this
date and 1842 are in the Customs House Library, London. A complete sequence from 1842
on is available in the Liverpool Record Office.
    I should like to express my gratitude to Prof. F.E. Hyde for allowing me to use
the volumes for 1820 and 1839 while they were in his possession, and to Mr. R.C. Jarvis,
the Customs House Librarian, for permission to consult the 1830 volume.

[24]The multipliers used were obtained from S.N. Syder, "The Effect of the
Abolition of the Slave Trade on Liverpool's Commerce," unpublished Liverpool M.A.
Thesis, 1951, Appendix I.

enforces an irregular sequence). It is not suggested that the figures are one hundred percent accurate, for vessels often carried cargoes in excess of their registered tonnage,[25] particularly in the 'twenties and 'thirties when deck cargoes were common. In addition, timber of native growth brought to Liverpool by canal and coastal shipping has been excluded. The figures however are much more than an estimate; a tonnage figure of North American timber imported in 1820 quoted by a witness before the Select Committee of 1821[26], shows a difference of under five percent from the calculated equivalent, and the total figure for 1850 is only only percent below that quoted by Braithwaite Poole, a contemporary statistician who used Customs material.[27] Perhaps a realistic estimate would be that the figures are about five percent below the actual figure.

IMPORTS OF TIMBER INTO LIVERPOOL

Table I
1820-1850 (figures in tons)

	N. America	Baltic	Fancy Woods	Total
1820	73,781	15,462	3,031	92,274
1830	97,321	13,944	6,886	118,151
1839	153,962	18,131	10,629	182,722
1850	203,683	14,941	30,808	249,432

Table I reveals that Liverpool's timber trade expanded some two and a half times between 1820 and 1850. The trade was predominantly in North American timber;[28] in 1820 imports from North America, principally in deals, red and yellow pine, fir, oak, elm and staves, totalled

---

[25]B. Poole, op.cit., 10.

[26]*Select Committee on Foreign Trade*, 1821 (186) VI, 53.

[27]B. Poole, op.cit., 10-11.

[28]The term "N. American" refers to timber imported from Canada. Not all such imports however were of colonial grown timber; as much as one third of Liverpool's total imports of timber from Canada was United States grown timber exported via Canada to avoid the heavy duties on foreign timber. See *Select Committee on Foreign Trade*, 1821 (186) vi, 66.

73,781 tons and were over four times as great as imports from the Baltic. Between 1820 and 1850 the gap between imports from the two sources widened. North European timber imports remained virtually constant throughout the period, but American imports enjoyed a 250 percent increase, rising to over 200,000 tons. Imports of fancy woods, used mainly for furniture and interior decoration, also underwent a steady growth. By 1850, imports of boxwood from Smyrna and the Levant, cedar and maple from the U.S.A., and teak, greenheart, mahogany and other woods from South America, Africa and the East Indies totalled over 30,000 tons and represented ten percent of Liverpool's total receipts.

The rapid expansion of timber imports into Liverpool naturally affected the composition of that section of the port's merchant body which was engaged in handling the commodity. An increase in imports must either be met by an increase in the individual merchant's scale of operation, or by an inflow of merchants into the trade, or by a combination of both these trends. In the case in question the years 1820-1850 saw a great expansion in both absolute and percentage terms in the quantity of timber handled by the leading merchants of the trade. This development is shown in Tables IIA and IIB which give the quantity of timber imported by the twenty leading importers, sub-divided into two groups of ten according to size, compared with the total receipts at the port in the years 1820, 1830, 1839 and 1850.[29] Table IIA is in absolute terms and Table IIB in percentage terms. A full breakdown of these tables giving a summary of the import operations of each individual is contained in the appendix.

---

[29]Tables IIA and IIB are the result of a survey of the Customs Bills of Entry. In each of the years 1820, 1830, 1839 and 1850 a list was compiled of all merchants who on some occasion during the year imported a cargo of timber. For every such merchant a chart of all references to him was constructed showing commodities and quantities imported, ports of origin, and full particulars of the freighting vessel. It was thus possible to total up an individual's imports of timber during the year and to determine the twenty leading timber importers of the port. These twenty importers were then divided into two equal groups according to their scale of import and the combined imports of each group expressed as a percentage of total imports. The bottom line of the table refers to cases in the Bills of Entry in which timber was imported but no merchant was named as consignee, instead the word "order."

For a fuller description of the methodology of this survey see my unpublished M.A. thesis, "The Function of the Merchant in Specific Liverpool Import Trades, 1820-50" (Liverpool 1963).

Table IIa
Imports of the Twenty Leading Timber Merchants at
Liverpool in the Years 1820, 1830, 1839 and 1850 (in tons)

	1820	1830	1839	1850
Total Receipts at Liverpool	92,274	118,151	182,772	249,432
Amount Imported by Group I	25,017	53,545	118,960	112,702
Amount Imported by Group II	14,695	20,538	26,201	28,350
Total Imports of Twenty Leading Importers (Groups I and II)	39,712	74,083	145,161	141,052
Consigned to Order	negligible	8,073	10,309	29,530

Table IIb
Imports of the Twenty Leading Timber Merchants at
Liverpool Expressed as a Percentage of Total Imports
in 1820, 1830, 1839 and 1850

	1820	1830	1839	1850
Total Receipts at Liverpool	100	100	100	100
Amount Imported by Group I	27.12	45.30	65.14	46.00
Amount Imported by Group II	15.93	17.37	14.33	11.56
Total Imports of Twenty Leading Importers (Groups I and II)	43.05	62.67	79.47	57.56
Consigned to Order	*negligible*	6.83	5.64	11.43

The tables show that between 1820 and 1839, the leading timber importers handled an increasing share of Liverpool's growing timber imports, the proportion rising from 43.05 percent in 1820 to almost eighty percent in 1839. In absolute terms the amount imported rose by over one hundred thousand tons, an increase which outstripped the increase in total receipts over the same period. Within this group of twenty importers, it can be seen that it was Group I, the ten leading merchants, who accounted for almost all the increase in both absolute and percentage terms. In other words, up to 1839, the growth in imports did not call forth an increase in the number of merchants importing timber, but instead resulted in a doubling of the amount imported by the ten leading merchants in absolute terms in both 1830 and 1839.

The high degree of concentration prevailing in 1839 was not maintained in 1850, for the tables reveal that the proportion of total receipts handled by the leading importers fell from 79.5 percent to under sixty percent. The importance of this fall should not however be over-emphasised as it is exaggerated by two factors. First, the quantity handled remained virtually constant in absolute terms, the drop in percentage terms being the result of an overall increase in receipts of timber. A considerable part of this increase, 20,000 tons out of 65,000 tons in fact, was of tropical timber, a branch of the trade in which the leading merchants, being all North American men, were not concerned. Secondly there was an increase in the quantity of Canadian timber consigned to "order."[30] Much of this timber was no doubt eventually handled by the leading merchants. These factors account for much of the decline in the proportion of total imports handled by the leading merchants, and while a slight fall may have occurred between 1839 and 1850, the conclusion that must be reached for the period as a whole, is that the great increase in timber imports was met by an expansion in the individual merchant's scale of operation, resulting in a growing proportion of the trade being concentrated in the hands of the twenty leading importers.

The increase in the merchant's scale of operation is clearly visible from an examination of the appendix. In 1820 the most important importer of timber, J. & H. Cummings, handled a mere 3564 tons (3.85 percent of total imports) and only one other merchant exceeded 3000 tons. Ten years later, all ten merchants in Group I imported over this amount and the greatest, Duncan Gibb, imported 13,000 tons (eleven percent). In 1839, five merchants each imported more than 10,000 tons, and the three largest, Gibbs, Bright & Co. (24,568 tons), Wildes, Pickersgill & Co. (20,618 tons) and Cannon Miller & Co. (16,459 tons), accounted for one third of Liverpool's total imports of timber. In 1850, the three greatest importers, Cannon, Miller & Co., Gibbs, Bright & Co., and Sharples, Jones & Co., again all exceeded 15,000 tons, although their share of total receipts, for reasons mentioned earlier, fell from a third to a quarter. The

---

[30]This increase in the quantity of produce consigned to "order" was not peculiar to the timber trade. It occurred also, on a much larger scale, in the cotton trade during this period.

presence of eleven merchants with imports upward of 5000 tons in 1850 clearly indicates the individual merchant's increasing imports.

Another feature which emerges from the appendix is the degree to which importers of timber specialized in importing the one commodity. The length of this paper forbids any detailed analysis of this aspect of Liverpool's timber merchants, but it is evident from the tables of leading importers that most merchants did specialize. In each of the years studied, no fewer than fifteen of the leading twenty merchants specialized to a greater or lesser extent in the importing of timber. This tendency to specialize was much more pronounced in the timber trade than in any other of Liverpool's trades, and it was by no means unusual to find importers handling nothing other than timber. This was true of ten of the leading importers in 1839, and in the same year five merchants fell only just short of this category, i.e. the quantities of other commodities handled by them were negligible. Thus in the first half of the nineteenth century Liverpool's expanding timber trade was falling more and more into the hands of a relatively small group of importers, most of whom specialized in importing the one commodity, timber from North America.

The structure of the merchant houses which imported timber was that of the one-man enterprise or simple partnership. Most firms were in business on their own account and while a small amount of commission work was engaged in by a few, there is no question of firms being solely commission merchants. This situation contrasts strongly with the Baltic trade where nearly all importers were operating on a commission basis.[31] Some Liverpool houses did, however, act as agents for firms in other parts of the country. Duncan Gibb performed this function for Pollock, Gilmour & Co. of Glasgow before 1835[32] and other merchants no doubt undertook similar contract work. The majority of firms importing timber were based in Liverpool but a few were branches of businesses which had their headquarters in other ports; Rankin, Gilmour & Co. was a branch house of Pollock, Gilmour & Co.[33] and Gibbs, Bright & Co. was an associate

---

[31] Select *Committee on Timber Duties*, 1835 (519) XIX, Q. 248.

[32] J. Rankin, *A History of Our Firm*, (1921) 130.

[33] Ibid.

house of Anthony Gibbs & Co. of London.[34] In one or two cases, North American firms set up houses in Liverpool specifically to handle their interests. Two such firms were J. & C. Bulley & Co. of Newfoundland who established Job, Bulley & Co.[35] and the firm of Frostes of Quebec which was the parent house of Joseph Froste who was active in Liverpool in the late 'twenties and 'thirties. More often, links between Liverpool and Canada were in the reverse direction, Liverpool firms having branch houses and business interests in the colonies. John Hamilton has already been mentioned as an example of a merchant with landowning interests in Canada, and William Sharples, who owned a lumber establishment in Quebec, also fell into this category.[36] Rankin, Gilmour & Co., though not strictly a Liverpool firm, had branch houses in Miramichi, St. John's, Restigouche, and Bathurst besides Quebec, where their lumber yard was valued at £20,000.[37] Businesses as highly integrated as these were of course exceptional but all merchants importing timber at Liverpool, unlike their counterparts in other trades, performed a number of functions, allied to and yet additional to that of importing. The nature of the commodity they dealt in and the unsophisticated structure of the timber market combined to enable the average timber merchant to own ships and to engage actively in the marketing of his cargo, as well as acting as an importer. It was this feature, together with the unusual degree of import specialization, and the importer's growing scale of operation, that made Liverpool's timber merchants such a distinctive section of the port's merchant body.

In Liverpool the importing of timber and the owning of ships were closely connected. Though between 1820 and 1850 the general tendency in commerce, was for importing and shipowning to become increasingly separate functions,[38] a growing number of the merchants who figured amongst Liverpool's leading timber importers were also ship owners. The

---

[34]I am indebted to Dr. W.M. Mathew for this information.

[35]R.B. Job, *John Job's Family 1730-1953* (1953) 25 et seq.

[36]*Select Committee on Timber Duties*, 1835 (519) XIX, Q. 2211.

[37]Ibid., Q. 2057.

[38]N.S.B. Gras, *Business and Capitalism* (1974) 174.

main reason for this departure from the normal trend was that the timber trade was one of the few trades where the interests of the merchant as an importer and a shipowner coincided. Professor Davis, writing of the eighteenth century, has shown that links between merchanting and shipowning tended to be closer in trades involving bulk commodities and that the great London timber merchants had extensive, though not exclusive, shipowning interests.[39] In view of this it is not surprising to find that the Liverpool timber merchants, who had huge quantities of timber to be transported over a single route, should have had shipowning interests. Table III depicts the twenty leading importers of timber divided into shipowners and non-shipowners in the years 1820, 1830, 1839 and 1850.

Table III
Performance of the Function of Shipowning Among Liverpool's Twenty Leading Importers of Timber in the Years 1820, 1830, 1839 and 1850

	Shipowners	*Non-shipowners*
1820	11	9
1830	16	4
1839	13	7
1850	19	1

The table shows that over the period 1820-1850 the number of timber merchants possessing shipowning interests increased. In 1820 only eleven out of the twenty leading importers had shipowning interests, but by 1850 the figure had reached nineteen. The key factor in this development was the growth in the imports of the individual merchant which increased the advantages to be gained from owning the means of transportation. Of lesser importance was the decline in the number of Baltic merchants amongst the leading twenty importers from three in 1820 to none in 1850. This is significant in that imports from the Baltic countries, with the exception of Russia, were largely carried in foreign vessels,[40] whereas the Canadian timber trade, partly because of the protection of the

---

[39]R. Davis, *The Rise of the English Shipping Industry* (1962) 91-96.

[40]*Select Committee on Foreign Trade*, 1821 (186) VI, 57. See also *Select Committee on Timber Duties*, 1835 (519) XIX, Q. 524.

Navigation Laws, was wholly in the hands of the British and Colonial vessels.[41]

One contemporary explanation for the presence of so many importers with shipowning interests in the timber trade, was that shipowners moved into the trade in order to find employment for their vessels. John Bainbridge, a general merchant who traded both with the U.S.A. and also with the colonies in North America, expressed this view before the Select Committee of 1821: "A great deal of the trade has been carried on by owners of ships and not by mercantile men connected with the colonies. They were obliged to have a recourse to the trade with the colonies to keep their ships and seamen in subsistence."[42] Similar arguments were advanced in the early 'thirties, as Henry Warburton, a London timber merchant, observed "It is a very common thing for shipowners to turn importers of timber with a view to finding employment for their vessels when freights are low."[43] This type of over-capacity argument may well have held true for shipowners of the smaller ports but it is not applicable to Liverpool's timber importers. In almost every case Liverpool merchants were importers before they moved into shipping, and the fact that many importers extended their shipping interests in the 'thirties and 'forties shows clearly that they were not shipowners engaging in the trade in order to utilize idle vessels, but rather importers moving into shipping as the trade and their own individual imports increased.[44]

The extent of the timber merchants' shipping interests varied greatly from one operator to another. At one extreme the firm of Brown, Fernie & Co. held a mere eight shares in one vessel, at the other, Duncan Gibb had interests in as many as fifty-five vessels. It would be pointless to determine the average holding, but it may be said that the shipping interests of merchants engaged in the timber trade were far more extensive than those of merchant shipowners in other trades, and in addition timber-

---

[41]*Select Committee on Timber Duties*, 1835 (519) XIX, Q. 3666.

[42]*Select Committee on Foreign Trade*, 1821 (186) VI, 46.

[43]*Select Committee on Timber Duties*, 1835 (519) XIX, Q. 5150.

[44]Excess capacity in shipping is nevertheless relevant in so far that it resulted in low prices which no doubt served as an incentive for Liverpool timber merchants to move into shipowning.

carrying vessels tended to be of a greater tonnage.[45] Another feature worthy of note is that most merchants held their interests in the form of the outright ownership of entire vessels; it was unusual for a merchant to own a few sixty-fourth shares in a number of vessels. On aggregate, of a total of at least 465 vessels in which leading timber merchants had shareholdings between 1820 and 1856, 356 were owned outright by one individual or partnership.[46] This trend towards a position of one owner to one vessel clearly indicates that the timber merchant was moving into shipping simply to facilitate transporting his own imports, for with complete ownership and no partners to consider he could act solely in his own interests.

There were four leading merchant shipowners engaged in the Liverpool timber trade. Duncan Gibb had shares in at least fifty-five vessels between 1820 and 1850, forty-five of which he owned outright, Gibbs, Bright & Co. had twenty-six vessels between 1841 and 1850, Holderness & Chilton had interests in twenty-three ships and Cannon, Miller & Co. owned twenty-seven vessels outright and had shares in six others. Other merchants who had interests in more than ten vessels included Anderson, Garrow & Co., Dempsey Pickard, Dempsey Frost, Fairclough & Frost, Fielden Bros. Thomas Froste, Allen & Anderson, Job, Bulley & Co. (later Job Bros.), Pryde & Jones, Rankin, Gilmour & Co., T. Roy, William Sharples, and Smith, Forsyth & Co. (later W. Smith & Son).[47]

The principal use to which timber merchants put their vessels was to transport their own imports of timber, but it was seldom that a merchant carried all of his imports in his own ships, for the trade was seasonal and entailed the carrying of vast quantities of wood across the Atlantic during the early summer and early winter.[48] Some merchants also used their vessels in other trades; Rankin, Gilmour & Co., Gibbs, Bright & Co., and McAlmont Bros., who did not specialize exclusively in timber, freighted

---

[45]*Select Committee on Foreign Trade*, 1821 (186) vi, 117-20, 148.

[46]See my thesis, op.cit., 82. Figures have been adjusted to cover timber merchants only.

[47]Ibid., Appendix IV, li - lxvii.

[48]*Select Committee on Foreign Trade*, 1821, (186) vi, 95-97.

their own imports of cotton and other commodities; other more specialized merchants chartered out their vessels or engaged in the U.S.A. carrying trade during the spring and winter. This use of timber vessels outside the timber trade militates against the charge that ships used in the timber trade were (because of size and fitness) unsuitable for the carriage of any other commodity. A further purpose served by timber vessels was the transporting of emigrants on the return voyage to North America. Timber vessels provided a cheap passage for the poorer classes of emigrants and it was claimed that any injury to the timber trade would act as a serious check to emigration.[49]

Criticism of the age of vessels used in the timber trade was widespread in the first half of the nineteenth century. It was generally accepted that the timber fleet was composed of old West Indian and East Indian vessels unfit for any other trade.[50] One witness before the Select Committee of Timber Duties, not a Liverpool shipowner, admitted with amazing frankness that if the timber trade were destroyed he would get rid of his ships as fast as he could and be satisfied with the first loss. Only "some" of the seven vessels he owned were fit for other trades, and five of them, were if not for the timber trade, would have been sold for breaking up.[51] Many old vessels were certainly used in the trade. Timber as a cargo has the characteristic of buoyancy and, though bulky, it did not necessitate vessels of any special design, and adaptations (such as large raft ports at the head and stern of the vessel to facilitate loading and discharging) were not essential.[52] Even so, by no means all timber vessels were old. Merchants often purchased colonial-built timber carriers which were sold in Liverpool after one crossing of the Atlantic[53] and some

---

[49]*Select Committee on Timber Duties*, 1835 (519) xix, Q. 2349.

[50]Ibid., Qs. 1645-57, see also *Report from the Select Committee on Manufactures, Commerce and Shipping*, 1833 (690) vi, Q. 3485 and *Select Committee on Foreign Trade*, 1821 (186) vi, 122.

[51]*Select Committee on Timber Duties*, 1835 (519) XIX, Qs. 3795-3797.

[52]Ibid., Q. 5155.

[53]*Select Committee on Foreign Trade* 1821 (186) vi, 55. See also *First Report from the Select Committee on Navigation Laws*, 1847 (232) X, Q. 659.

Liverpool importers, notably Duncan Gibb, and Gibbs, Bright & Co., ordered new vessels direct from Canadian yards.[54]

However, concern over the condition of ships engaging in the timber trade was not groundless. Between 1820 and 1840 an increasing number of vessels were lost, so much so that, following questions in the House of Commons, Parliament in 1839 appointed a Select Committee to Enquire into Shipwrecks of Timber Vessels.[55] The Committee's report reveals the severity of the problem. In the eight years from 1832 to 1839 over two hundred and eighty vessels were either wrecked or became water-logged on voyages from Quebec, Halifax and Newfoundland,[56] and the minutes of evidence contain horrifying accounts of suicide, madness, murder and cannibalism on waterlogged vessels.[57] The primary cause of these heavy losses was not the age of vessels, but the "improper stowage of ships by carrying heavy loads of timber upon deck... which renders them top heavy and liable to upset."[58] The Committee recommended the prohibition of deck loads, a measure which had been proposed by members of Liverpool's British North American Association.[59] This recommendation was accepted by the government and in 1840 the first of a series of acts relating to the safety of shipping was passed.

Timber-laden vessels, like all other ships docking at Liverpool, required the services of a ship's agent to look after the vessel while it was in port. Most vessels employed specialist operators who supervised docking and unloading, repairs and refitting, chartering, loading and re-stocking for the outward voyage, and who performed numerous other

---

[54]F.W. Wallace, *Wooden Ships and Iron Men*, (no date), 42; see also *Select Committee on Manufactures, Commerce and Shipping*, 1833 (690) vi, Q. 8877.

[55]J. Potter, op.cit., 132.

[56]*Report from the Select Committee of Shipwrecks of Timber Vessels*, 1839 (333) ix, 79. Appendix I.

[57]Ibid., Q. 976.

[58]Ibid., V.

[59]Ibid., 63-64.

duties in the course of safeguarding the vessel and its interests.[60] The timber trade however did not rely on the services of such operators; instead the merchant whose imports were involved usually performed the function himself. The interests of the vessel while it was in Liverpool, were invariably the interests of the timber importer also, for in addition to being the consignee for the whole cargo and often the owner of the vessel, the merchant was directly involved in the marketing of his imports.

Timber once unloaded, if not imported on contract or sold by public auction at the quayside, was stored in the timber merchant's yard to await sale. The market organization of the timber trade by comparison with other trades was both simple and unsophisticated. The great bulk of imports were sold "ex ship," for the difficulties of grading timber made sales "to arrive" and other speculative refinements unfeasible.[61] A timber market, in the sense of a cotton market or corn market where business was transacted through skilled brokers and dealers, did not exist. Timber was sold either by dockside auction or, more commonly, by private treaty from the importer's own timber yard.[62]

Timber was imported into Liverpool both for local and for inland consumption. Locally, importers sold to wholesalers who, in turn, sold to consumers, but also acted as retailers themselves, selling directly to the more important Liverpool builders and cabinet makers. The major portion of Liverpool's imports, however, was consumed outside the port. In 1850 between three-quarters and four-fifths of total imports were forwarded inland. The port served an area of some hundred miles radius and towns as far east as Bradford, Huddersfield and Leeds were supplied with American timber.[63] Distribution from Liverpool was effected by the Leeds-Liverpool, Ellesmere and Bridgewater canals, and, after 1840, by railway.[64] The main figure in this branch of the trade was the inland timber dealer who travelled to Liverpool to attend the auctions or to

---

[60]For an excellent description of the function of ship's agent see R.H. Thornton, *British Shipping* (1939) 144-147.

[61]J.H. Clapham, op.cit., II, 321.

[62]Ibid., 322.

[63]B. Poole, op.cit., 12.

[64]Ibid., 10-11.

inspect timber at the importer's yard and to take advantage of the relative cheapness of timber at the port;[65] Liverpool was Britain's chief market for high quality American timber and in furniture and fancy woods was of international repute, merchants coming from as far afield as France, Germany and Italy to purchase their supplies.[66]

The organization of sales in the Liverpool timber market thus followed a broad pattern of importer, local wholesaler or inland dealer, and retailer. There was no question of the appearance of the specialist timber broker buying and selling on behalf of other people. In a trade where purchases could not be satisfactorily made by sample or description but only by personal inspection, the function of such men would have been largely superfluous. The absence of the broker raises the question of the role of the importer as a provider of credit. Contemporary literature relating to the timber trade provides no positive evidence to suggest that there was a highly developed system of credit in the Liverpool market. There can be little doubt that the regular purchasers received credit terms, but it is impossible to assess what proportion of the trade was conducted on this basis. No firm credit link, however, existed between importer and dealer, and it is certain that the relatively young Liverpool market did not possess a financial framework comparable to the longer-established Baltic timber market at London.[67]

The first half of the nineteenth century saw the emergence and consolidation of the timber trade as one of the leading sectors of Liverpool's commerce. The trade underwent an expansion second only to that of cotton, and Liverpool's timber merchants came to occupy an important and unique position within the port's merchant community. The pattern of development in the timber trade was contrary to the general trend of nineteenth century business development which resulted in many of the functions the merchant had customarily performed being taken over,

---

[65]On reason for the cheapness of timber at Liverpool was the use of the string measure instead of the calliper for the measurement of timber. The string measure tended to undermeasure and thus favoured the purchaser. For a comparison of the two measures see *Select Committee on Timber Duties*, 1835 (519) XIX, Qs. 2886, 5049-5050. See also B. Latham, *Timber, Its Development and Distribution* (1957) 54.

[66]E. Chaloner, *Remarks on the St. Domingo Mahoghany Trade* (1837) 15.

[67]*Select Committee on Timber Duties*, 1835 (519) XIX, Qs. 5098 et seq.; see also H.S.K. Kent, op cit.

especially in the field of marketing, by specialist operators. The timber merchant not only retained his function of selling but also expanded the scope of his activities, building up large vertically-integrated businesses through moving backward into shipping and lumbering. The power of this small group of entrepreneurs, many of whom owned forest land and lumber establishments, imported vast quantities of timber in their own vessels and who supervised the handling, storing and selling of timber in Liverpool, and in particular their ability to influence prices, must, in the absence of merchant house records, remain a matter for conjecture. Nevertheless, there can be little doubt that successful entry into the trade by newcomers must have become increasingly difficult. The most telling comment which can be made about the activities of established timber importers, and one which sums up the progress and state of the timber trade in 1850, is perhaps that of a contemporary observer who spoke of twenty men styled as timber merchants "all of whom have recently amassed fortunes."[68]

---

[68]B. Poole, op.cit., 9.

APPENDIX

Liverpool's Twenty Leading Importers of Timber in the Years 1820, 1830, 1839 and 1850

Note on presentation: each merchant's activities are presented in the following sequence: name, quantity of timber imported, area of origin (Canada (C) or Baltic (B) and percentage of total imports. On the right hand side of the page are given the other commodities (if any) handled by the merchant together with their port or country of origin. Unless otherwise stated, where no quantity is given, imports are on a very small scale.

An asterisk denotes a merchant with shipowning interests.

LIVERPOOL TIMBER IMPORTERS—1820

GROUP I	Tons	Per cent	
*Cummings, J. & H.	3,564 (C)	3.85	OIL - HALIFAX MAHOGHANY, DYE-WOODS - HONDURAS
Crossfield, E.M.	3,156 (C)	3.42	
*Smith, Forsyth & Co.	2,770 (C)	3.00	WHEAT, 21,856 bshls—QUEBEC FLOUR, 682 brls—QUEBEC COTTON, 1,995 bls, APPLES—U.S.A. OIL, ASHES—CANADA COFFEE—ST. DOMINGO
Wilmot, A.C.	2,566 (C)	2.78	
*McIver, W.	2,416 (C)	2.62	
*Leigh, J. & Co.	2,389 (B)	2.60	WHEAT, MATS, TAR, PEAS—BALTIC
Hamilton, J. & R.	2,250 (C)	2.45	ASHES—QUEBEC

*Job, Bulley & Co.	2,082 (C)	2.26	WHEAT—QUEBEC OIL, SKINS—NEWFOUND-LAND SUGAR—BAHIA RUM—DEMERARA CAMWOOD—U.S.A., BAHIA
*Wood & Watson	1,911 (C)	2.07	COTTON—U.S.A., BAHIA TIMBER—BERBICE
*Neuman, C.W. & Co.	1,911 (B)	2.07	WHEAT (large quantity) BARK, MATS, FLAX, MADDERS, SEED—BAL-TIC, RUSSIA, NETHER-LANDS

GROUP II

Leddon, W.	1,874 (C)	2.02	
Brown, S. & Co.	1,665 (C)	1.80	SUGAR—PERNAMBUCCO
*Stokes, W.S.	1,634 (C)	1.77	ASHES—QUEBEC
Parr, J.	1,496 (C)	1.61	
Henderson & Sands	1,449 (C)	1.57	WHEAT, LINSEED —QUEBEC
Langton, W. & T.	1,375 (B)	1.49	OATS, 2,200 qrs—RUSSIA TALLOW 900 brls—BAL-TIC, RUSSIA BARLEY, WHEAT, FLAX, ASHES, HEMP, MATS—BALTIC
*Sharples, W.	1,340 (C)	1.45	
*Dempsey, J.	1,324 (C)	1.44	MAHOGHANY 275 lgs— HONDURAS
Dixon, Waln & Co.	1,310 (C)	1.44	COTTON—U.S.A. TAL-LOW 431 csks—LEGHORN HEMP—ST. PETERS-BURGH
*Nelson, E.	1,230 (C)	1.34	

Liverpool Timber Importers—1830

Group I	Tons	Percent	
*Gibb, D.	13,002 (C)	11.0	COTTON, 1539 bls—U.S.A. FLOUR 1845 brls—N. YORK, MONTREAL WHEAT 9550 bsls—MONTREAL ASHES 689 brls —MONTREAL MAHOGHANY, LOGWOOD—HONDURAS PORK—N. YORK, IRELAND RUM—DEMERARA SUGAR, TEAK, EBONY, GROCERIES—INDIA SALT—LISBON
*Fairclough, W. & Co.	6,006 (C)	5.08	TOBACCO—VIRGINIA
*Brown, Swainson & Co.	5,874 (C)	4.97	OIL, ASHES—HALIFAX TOBACCO—N. YORK WOOD—PORTUGAL COFFEE—JAMAICA
*Sharples, W.	5,123 (C)	4.33	
*Cannon, Miller & Co.	4,705 (C)	3.98	TIMBER—SAVANNAH, IRELAND
*Smith, W. & Sons	4,689 (C)	3.97	COTTON, 2341 bls—U.S.A. FLOUR 2806 brls—N. YORK, MONTREAL WHEAT, ASHES, APPLES—QUEBEC
*Neuman, C.W. & Sons	3,838 (B)	3.24	WHEAT, 6553 qrs—BALTIC FLAX, OATS, PEAS, MATS, BARK, HEMP, FLOUR—BALTIC, RUSSIA

*Glen, G. & Co.	3,639 (C)	3.08	MOLASSES, 656 cks—-DEMERARA FUSTIC 340 tons—SAVANNAH
Thomas, J.W.	3,448 (C)	2.92	TEAK 370 ps.—SIERRA LEONE
*Gibbs, Bright & Co.	3,221 (C)	2.73	MAHOGANY 164 ps.—HONDURAS SUGAR, COFFEE—JAMAICA BARK—BAHIA. CALICOES—DUBLIN OIL, WOOL, MERCURY —-SPAIN, PORTUGAL

Group II

Gibsone, J.W.	2,722 (B)	2.30	WHEAT, 1653 qrs—BALTIC TAR, 2130 brls—BALTIC BARLEY, OATS, PEAS—BALTIC
*Challinor, C.	2,560 (C)	2.17	CHINA CLAY—CORNWALL WHEAT, ONIONS—SPAIN
Mure, J.	2,468 (C)	2.00	COTTON—BERBICE
*Buchanan, D.	2,139 (C)	1.81	TEAK 354 logs—S. LEONE MAHOGHANY 115 logs—HONDURAS TAR, CLOVERSEED—U.S.A.
*Dempsey, Pickard & Co.	2,163 (C)	1.83	COTTON 740 bls—U.S.A.
*Roy, T.	1,803 (C)	1.53	COTTON—U.S.A. COFFEE, COCOA—TRINIDAD
*Froste, J.	1,778 (C)	1.50	ASHES 502 brls, FLOUR—QUEBEC
*Chaloner, E.	1,775 (C)	1.50	MAHOGHANY 301 logs—HONDURAS
*Parlane, A.	1,642 (C)	1.38	
*Barber, J.	1,488 (C)	1.26	

Liverpool Timber Importers—1839

Group I

*Gibbs, Bright & Co.	24,568 (C)	13.44	COTTON, 1253 bls— U.S.A. SUGAR, MOLASSES— BARBADOS TEAK 474 tons—S. LEONE COOPER 264 tons, WOOL 1822 bls—PERU INDIGO, BARK, SARSA- PARILLA—PERU CEDAR —MOBILE, STEEL— GENOA
Wildes, Pickersgill & Co.	20,618 (C)	11.28	COTTON, 15,325 bls— U.S.A. BARK, TEA—U.S.A. TURPS, 7303 brls—N. YORK FLOUR, 3187 brls—N. YORK TAR, 1,665 brls—N. YORK ASHES—MONTREAL
*Cannon, Miller & Co.	15,459 (C)	8.46	COTTON, 1027 bls—U.S.A.
*Anderson, Garrow & Co.	11,765 (C)	6.47	HIDES 2804—MONTE- VIDEO
*Sharples, W.	10,640 (C)	5.82	PITCH PINE—CHARLES- TON
*Rankin, Gilmour & Co.	9,235 (C)	5.09	
*Gibb, D.	8,741 (C)	4.78	TURPS, 574 brls—U.S.A.
*Chaloner & Houghton	7,771 (C)	4.24	MAHOGHANY, LOGWOOD—HONDURAS
*Holderness & Chilton	5,521 (C)	3.02	
*Houghton, Smith & Co.	4,642 (C)	2.54	

Group II

*Fairclough & Frost	4,137 (C)	2.27	TEA, PINE—U.S.A.
Rigby, R.	4,136 (C)	2.27	

Gibstone, Whitehead & Co.	3,497 (B)	1.92	TAR, 8482 brls—BALTIC HAMS, PORK, PEAS—DANZIG
*Neuman & Engel	2,923 (B)	1.62	BARLEY, 7010 qrs—BALTIC PEAS, 8659 scks—BALTIC WHEAT, 29,849 scks— BALTIC OATS, 2231 qrs, RYE 3383 qrs—BALTIC BEER, SPIRITS, FLAX, BEANS—BALTIC COTTON, TOBACCO-U.S.A.
Blundell, Falk & Co.	2,596 (B)	1.37	TAR, 2321 brls—BALTIC BEANS, 2050 qrs—NANTES BARLEY, 2200 qrs, FLAX, PEAS—NANTES, BALTIC
*Dempsey, Frost & Co.	2,465 (C)	1.35	
*Tisdale, C.W.	2,086 (C)	1.15	
Hudson, J.	1,995 (C)	1.08	
Amey, J.B.	1,600 (C)	0.90	COTTON—U.S.A. FLAX—BALTIC
Duncan & Ewing	806 (C)	0.40	

Liverpool Timber Importers—1850

Group I	Tons	Percent	
*Cannon, Miller & Co.	20,269 (C)	8.28	COTTON, 2176 bls—U.S.A. LARD, 1215 brls—U.S.A. PIG IRON, 261 tons—ST. JOHNS TEAK, 659 logs—BURMA FURS—HALIFAX PINE—SAVANNAH

*Gibbs, Bright & Co.	19,791 (C)	8.08	COTTON, 13,525 bls—U.S.A. MOLASSEES, COFFEE, STAVES—U.S.A. COPPER, GUANO 4150 tons—CALLAO TURPS 2,638 brls—U.S.A ROSIN, 2429 brls—U.S.A SUGAR, 1090 hds—U.S.A MAIZE, WHEAT— ALEXANDRIA
*Sharples, Jones & Co.	16,188 (C)	6.61	STAVES—U.S.A.
*Rankin, Gilmour & Co.	9,946 (C)	4.16	COTTON 18,766 bls—U.S.A. FLOUR, 4734 brls—U.S.A. SUGAR 7072 cs—MAURITIUS
*Cannon, D. & Sons	9,634 (C)	3.93	COTTON, 7498 bls.—U.S.A., INDIA
*James & Morrow	9,267 (C)	3.78	
*de Wolf, J.S.	9,028 (C)	3.68	STAVES, COTTON 1020 bls—U.S.A. LOGWOOD 185 tons—AUX CAYES
*Dempsey, Frost & Co.	7,156 (C)	2.92	PINE—SAVANNAH
*Holderness & Chilton	5,761 (C)	2.35	COTTON, 4147 bls—U.S.A. MAIZE, 6000 qrs—U.S.A FLOUR, 3263 brls—U.S.A. WHEAT, 4220 qrs—U.S.A., DANZIG
*Pryde & Jones	5,666 (C)	2.31	MAIZE—TRIESTE

Group II

*Gibb, D.	5,104 (C)	2.08	SAPANWOOD, SUGAR 9668 bgs—MANILLA PALM OIL 661 pns— AFRICA LOGWOOD 480 tons— BERBICE BARWOOD 820 tons— PONGUA
*Froste, T.	3,776 (C)	1.54	FLOUR 1757 scks— ROUEN, EU COTTON, PINE, RICE, STAVES— U.S.A.
*Houghton & Smith	3,313 (C)	1.35	
*Fielden Bros.	3,100 (C)	1.27	COTTON, 9154 bls— U.S.A. FLOUR 11,127 brls. RICE 678 brls—U.S.A. TURPS 3493 brls—- U.S.A MAIZE 27049 scks— U.S.A. STAVES (large quantity)— U.S.A.
Douglas & Westcott	2,928 (C)	1.19	OAK—SAVANNAH FLOUR—MONTREAL
*Graves, S. & R.	2,747 (C)	1.12	PINE—SAVANNAH LOGWOOD, 132 tons— BLACK RIVER
*Spurr, J. de W. & Co.	2,334 (C)	0.95	
*Brown, Fernie & Co.	2,005 (C)	0.82	COTTON, CHEESE, LARD—U.S.A.
*McAlmont Bros.	1,851 (C)	0.70	COTTON 9282 bgs—S. AMERICA SUGAR, 11390 bgs— BRAZIL MAIZE 5593 bgs—- U.S.A. LOGWOOD 1000 tons-- BRAZIL
*Garnock, Bibby & Co.	1,192 (C)	0.48	

James Silk Buckingham:
Sailor, Explorer and Maritime Reformer

This paper arises out of a research interest in the field of state involvement with shipping, in particular government intervention in the early Victorian period. It was this interest which prompted an examination of the Select Committee on Shipwrecks of 1836 of which James Silk Buckingham was Chairman.[1] This alone would make Buckingham a figure of interest; however, for Buckingham, the chairmanship of this important Committee was but one episode in a full and varied career. Buckingham, a Cornishman by birth, led an exceptional life. Indeed, the diversity of his talents, interests and activities and his participation in many of the major issues and events of his time were such that Buckingham can well be regarded as one of the most remarkable men of the first half of the nineteenth century. The title of this paper which describes Buckingham as sailor, explorer and maritime reformer is highly selective: to reflect fully the breadth of his ability one would have to add author, linguist, journalist, lecturer and politician, for in all these roles he was a significant figure. Despite his wide-ranging impressive talents and an amazing career, Buckingham has been poorly served by historians. But one biography has appeared, some fifty years ago, and that sadly is little known.

The purpose of this paper is twofold. First, to provide a brief outline of Buckingham's life and career, and second, to focus on his role and contribution in the matter of state regulation and safety at sea through his involvement with the Select Committee on Shipwrecks. Like Buckingham himself, the Committee of 1836 has hardly gained the attention it deserves. Looked at in the context of the late 1830s this neglect of the 1836 enquiry is perhaps understandable; the Committee was set up at the fag-end of a parliamentary session, it lasted for less than a month, and its recommendations were ignored by government. However, viewed over a longer perspective in the context of state involvement in merchant

---

[1]Select Committee on the Causes of Shipwrecks, *British Parliamentary Papers* (*BPP*), 1836, XVII.

109

shipping during the nineteenth century, the 1836 Committee appears in a wholly more positive light and deserves to be seen as an important milestone in the process which was to make, by the end of the Victorian era, merchant shipping one of the most regulated sectors of economic activity and the merchant seaman the most legislated for group within the labour force. With such an interpretation Buckingham's close involvement with the 1836 Committee assumes a special significance.

To say the James Silk Buckingham led a full life is something of an understatement. The lives of most men of mark, especially those who attain the psalmists' span of three score years and ten, are usually prefaced and concluded with the relatively quiet years of early childhood and retirement, but Buckingham's life was eventful from almost its start and certainly to its finish. At risk of simplifying what was a very complex career, one can view Buckingham's life as falling roughly into three phases. The first, up to Buckingham's twenty-fourth year, can be summarised as the Falmouth/Atlantic phase; the second, the period between the ages twenty-four and forty-six, can be termed the oriental phase; while the third, from 1832 to his death in 1855, aged sixty-nine, may be viewed as Buckingham's reformist and campaigning period.[2]

Buckingham was born at Flushing near Falmouth in 1786. The earliest influences on his life were certainly maritime. In his own words he was born "in a house which was literally washed by the sea" with steps from the dwelling direct to a mooring, and his family was a seafaring one with his father retired from the merchant service. Falmouth, of course, was a focus of shipping activity with its fleet of Post Office mail packets, and in the late eighteenth century, the stationing of two frigate squadrons

---

[2]Information on Buckingham's life was drawn chiefly from his own writings which were extensive. An appendix to this paper which lists his major works indicates the range and scale of his output and in itself provides a summary of his travels and wide interests. Particular use was made of Buckingham's autobiography which he was working on at the time of his death. Only two of the projected four volumes appeared. *Autobiography of James Silk Buckingham including his voyages, travels, adventures, speculations, successes and failures, faithfully and frankly narrated* (London, Longman, Brown, Green and Longmans, 1855). Other words consulted included: *Biographical sketch of James Silk Buckingham from "Lives of the Illustrious"* (London, Partridge and Oakey, 1853); *A Falmouth resident* (S.E. Gay); *Falmouth and Flushing a hundred years ago* (Falmouth, Earle, 1895). Ralph E. Turner, *James Silk Buckingham 1786-1855: A Social Biography* (London, Williams & Norgate, 1934) is the sole retrospective biography to have been written.

under Warren and Pellew, the latter being a family friend of the Buckinghams. Buckingham's early education was at a school in Plymouth and at a Naval Academy at Falmouth where he learnt navigation. At the age of nine his parents permitted him to ship in the packet *Lady Harriet* of which Buckingham's brother-in-law was sailing master. Two voyages to Lisbon passed uneventually, but on the third, in 1796, the vessel was captured off Finistere by a French corvette and before he was ten Buckingham was a prisoner of war at Corunna. A friendship with his Spanish gaoler's daughter slightly eased the privations of six months starving confinement, but he was then with other prisoners marched hundred of miles through Spain and Portugal. Abandoned by their guards en route, the party eventually reached Lisbon just when the victorious Jervis was sailing up the Tagus. After hiding from the British navy's press gangs Buckingham eventually returned to Falmouth in a British packet commanded by a family friend. Several years ashore followed when he worked in a nautical instrument shop at Devonport during which time he read very widely, but at the age of fifteen, frustrated with sedentary employment, he volunteered for the Royal Navy. The brutalities of that service, especially flogging, soon disillusioned him and without actually sailing under the colours he deserted and returned home. A brief period in a solicitor's office came to nought but Buckingham was not inactive, courting, and marrying in 1806, Miss Elizabeth Jennings of Penrhyn. An unsuccessful venture in establishing a nautical instrument and chart depot at Falmouth left him severely impoverished and led to his return to sea. Initially, with a relation of his wife, a West Indiaman captain, and later acting as captain/supercargo in his own right, he performed between 1807 and 1810 several voyages to the Caribbean and North and South America. In 1810, following disagreements with his shipowner masters, allegedly over his refusal to take part in an insurance fraud, he changed his sphere of operation from the Atlantic to the Mediterranean. At this time he appears to have severed his connections with Falmouth.

The years between 1810 and 1830 were a period when the countries of the Middle and Far East were the focus of Buckingham's activities. After leaving Falmouth Buckingham worked for a London merchant house as master/agent throughout the Mediterranean. During this time he became proficient in many languages including Arabic. Hopes of his operating on his own account in Malta were thwarted by plague and quarantine, and 1813 saw Buckingham in Egypt as guest of the British Consul General. Through the latter he gained the friendship of Mehemet

Ali, the ruling Pasha. 1813 and 1814 were years of travelling and exploring in Egypt and the Upper Nile valley where he suffered the distress of temporary blindness and the attack of brigands who left him naked in the desert.

Arriving back in Cairo, Buckingham was commissioned by the Pasha and Anglo-Egyptian merchants to undertake a hydrographical survey of a Red Sea route to India. Shortly after his arrival in Bombay he was required to leave on the technicality of not possessing the licence of the East India Company to operate within its geographical sphere of influence. This incident marked the beginnings of a clash between Buckingham and the East India Company which was to last twenty years and involve several official inquiries. However, in 1814, frustrated by the Company, Buckingham made the return voyage to Egypt completing his mission enabling new hydrographical charts to be compiled of the Red Sea coasts.

Back in Egypt Buckingham was appointed a formal representative of the Pasha and thus exempt from the East India Company's licence requirements he set out again for India, this time overland. A twelve-month journey through Lebanon and Persia with extensive travelling in the Holy Land saw him arrive at the port of Bashir. There he joined an East India Company expedition against Persian Gulf pirates acting in the capacity of Arabic interpreter before ultimately arriving in Bombay. (Some of these travels were written up in his *Travels in Palestine*, first published in 1821.) In Bombay he took shop for several months as captain in the service of the Iman of Muscat until that worthy directed him to Zanzibar on a slaving venture whereupon Buckingham resigned his commission thus foregoing substantial financial prospects. This high-minded decision, together with the recognition of Buckingham's obvious varied talents by the Governor, Warren Hastings, led to an invitation to him to establish and edit a newspaper in India. This he did and the paper, under the title of the *Calcutta Journal*, initially twice weekly, and later daily, was an immediate success and, shortly, highly profitable. Buckingham used his paper as a means of propagating his own views on such as free trade, free settlement in India and a free press. Such liberal principles aroused considerable hostility. When Hastings returned to England his replacement, John Adams, prompted by local opposition, ordered Buckingham, without trial or defence, to leave Calcutta. Efforts by Buckingham to avert this failed, leaving him in considerable debt, and he and his wife, who had just joined him after ten years' separation, were required to return to England. The Buckingham Case became something of a "cause celebre" with massive publicity, public meetings and two Select Committees of the House of Commons which recommended compensation. Such, however, was the strength of East India Company influence that his claims were rejected and he was not even permitted to return to India to wind up his affairs. The complicated details of the case are beyond the scope of this paper though it should be observed that the injustice suffered by Buckingham was such that yet a further Select Committee enquired into the case in 1834.

It speaks volumes for Buckingham's character that he did not succumb to the hardship, injustice and disappointment that he had experienced. Far from it, between 1824 and 1832 (when he was to embark on a new career as an M.P.), Buckingham's life was a positive frenzy of activity. Writing and lecturing were his principal activities. He produced a further four volumes on his Middle Eastern travels, and in the field of journalism he founded the *Oriental Herald and Colonial Review* (1824-1829) in which he pursued the objectives he had previously prosecuted in the *Calcutta Journal*). Most of all he wrote and campaigned against the East India Company's monopoly, advocating free trade with India and China. Also in journalistic vein he founded, in 1827, *The Sphynx*, a political paper, and a year later *The Athenaeum*, a literary and scientific journal. Simultaneous with these literary endeavours he embarked on a series of lecture tours, lecturing on his experience of oriental lands and campaigning against the Company monopoly. A near contemporary comment claims he addressed one million persons in four years.

A consequence of such activity was that Buckingham became a well known figure, and one of recognised liberal principles at a time when "reform" was very much the spirit of the age. It was this public recognition which led Buckingham to be invited by the city of Sheffield to stand as a candidate in the election for the first reformed Parliament of 1832. Buckingham accepted and was successfully returned. The first six years or so of the final phase of Buckingham's career saw him as an active reformist parliamentarian. A contemporary account observed that "he took his full share of labour in all the great questions of humanity, and of moral and social improvement brought before parliament." As ever his opposition to the monopoly of the East India Company and no doubt gained a special satisfaction when the Company's charter was not renewed in 1834. Less successful, however, was his continued prosecution of his personal claims against the Company. A further Select Committee, whose members included Russell, Peel, Althorp and the young Gladstone, to investigate his case in 1834 did conclude that "compensation ought to be made to Mr. Buckingham." But instead of recommending a specific sum of compensation it left this to the discretion of the Company, which proceeded to ignore the Committee's findings. Socially, Buckingham revealed an awareness of the problems of life in the new growing towns with his Bill aimed at providing for parks, museums and libraries. Such proposals were linked with the issue of temperance which Buckingham came increasingly to advocate. In 1834 he acted as Chairman of the Select Committee on Drunkenness, and in 1835 he became President of the British Teetotal Temperance Society. Buckingham's other great area of parliamentary activity was maritime reform. He was a strong supporter of the abolition of flogging and impressment and, as will be shortly indicated, an active and influential promoter of means to improve safety at sea.

Few of Buckingham's parliamentary endeavours gained immediate success, and it is likely that a sense of frustration, coupled with some personal bitterness, let alone the financial strains emanating from the failure of his compensation claims, led to his resignation of his seat in 1836. Almost immediately, in response to invitations, he embarked on a lecture tour of North America and he spent the next three years, 1838-1840, so employed. He travelled all over the sub-continent and four works comprising nine volumes published in the early 1840s and described his experiences. Returning to England he continued his lecturing activity. In 1841-1842 he toured Britain as a lecturer for the Anti-Corn Law League of which he had been a founder member six years earlier. Temperance became Buckingham's chief interest in his later years, and he held high office in various temperance societies. Even so, he continued to have other interests: in 1844 he founded the British and Foreign Institute in London and in 1848 he attended the World Peace congress in Brussels. Travels in Western Europe and Italy were the subject of further volumes, and he re-emphasised his social concern with a major work on *National evils and practical remedies, with a plan for a Model Town* in which he summarised his social and political philosophy. Financial insecurity dogged his later life and it was his relatively impoverished condition, together with a recognition of his immense contribution in many fields, which saw him being granted a Civil List pension of £200 per annum in 1851. Active to the end – he was advocating prohibition in 1853 – he died in London in

1855 in the midst of writing his memoirs. Regrettably only two of his four projected volumes were complete at the time of his death.

Such then was the life of James Silk Buckingham: by any standards full and quite remarkable. Scarcely less remarkable is neglect of Buckingham's life and activities by generations of historians. Only one biography has ever appeared, in 1934, by Ralph Turner, an American scholar with a somewhat unusual style. This absence of study and research is hard to explain; it can hardly be said that Buckingham is not an interesting subject, nor can the excuse of the lack of any collection of Buckingham's personal papers hold water given the nature and immense volume of Buckingham's published works. Perhaps the fact that Buckingham was never an outstanding figure for any length of time in any one field is a partial explanation; perhaps also the very fullness, versatility and length of Buckingham's career has made him too daunting a prospect for would-be biographers.

The Select Committee on Shipwrecks of 1836, of which Buckingham was chairman, owed its origin to the general growth of reformist and humanitarian feeling which characterised the 1830s and 1840s and the special concern and deep emotion aroused by the problem of shipwreck.[3] The high drama of disaster at sea with its connotations of man's frailty in the face of the elements held a peculiar, almost morbid, fascination for the Victorians (witness the near canonisation of Grace Darling and later Plimsoll). This desire to safeguard the lives of those in peril on the sea may arguably have been the chief influence underlying much of the state's intervention for safety at sea in the nineteenth century. However the impetus for Parliament's first investigation of safety at sea came not so much from the strength of general feeling but rather the drive and persistence of one individual, James Silk Buckingham. The Committee of 1836, which was to prove of considerable significance in the field of state intervention in shipping, was in its instigation, proceedings and recommendations the child of Buckingham. Certainly that the Select Committee was established was solely due to his initiative and persistence.

---

[3]In the 1830s there was growing interest and concern in the problem of shipwreck as a result of the widespread reporting of a number of major disasters. For example, the *Amphitrite*, a female convict ship, wrecked off Boulogne with the loss of 136 lives covered in *The Times* on 4, 5, 6, 9, 25, 26 September 1833, or the *Francis Spaight*, where the vessel being dismasted and waterlogged the crew had resorted to cannibalism. See *The Times*, 22 June, 14 July 1836.

In March 1836 Buckingham gave notice of his intention to present a motion for a Select Committee, but pressure of parliamentary business led to it being twice deferred.[4] His motion was ultimately presented on 14 June. Lord John Russell for the administration and unsympathetic, expressing Board of Trade opposition and pleading the lateness of the session, the full parliamentary schedule and the difficulty of finding sufficient members to serve. Buckingham, however, appears to have anticipated such a reply for he responded that he had already approached and gained the approval of seventeen members who were willing to serve. Russell, his prevarication exposed, conceded with the proviso that the Committee merely reported the evidence.[5] This condition Buckingham accepted, but later chose to ignore.

Having achieved his aim of a Committee, Buckingham immediately set to work. Within three days the Committee set for its preliminary meeting, and two days later it began hearing evidence. Between 1 July and 5 August it held twelve such sessions.[6] Two further meetings were held to draw up the report which was presented to Parliament and ordered to be printed with the evidence on 15 August. The Committee's proceedings thus comprised a short period of immense activity; within two months of appointment, its report of eleven pages and some 400 pages of evidence was available. It is worth stressing the speed of the Committee's proceedings for this was highly significant in two ways. First, it reflected efficient, and, though this is conjectural, prior organisation on Buckingham's part; and secondly, the rushed nature of the Committee no doubt enabled Buckingham as chairman to exert considerable influence on both proceedings and the report. Indeed, Turner, Buckingham's biographer, suggests that it was Buckingham who composed and wrote up the report.

The Committee's report comprised three sections: the first, which examined the extent of losses at sea; the second, which listed the principal causes of shipwreck; and the third, which considered remedies, proposed or suggested. In its first section the Committee, using returns supplied by

---

[4]*Mirror of Parliament*, 2nd sess. I, 805, 25 March 1836; II, 1320, 3 May 1836.

[5]*Mirror of Parliament*, 2nd sess. II, 1897, 14 June 1836.

[6]The Committee heard evidence from thirty-three witnesses. These provided information relative to some fifteen major ports from all round the coast of Britain.

Lloyds, examined the extent of losses comparing the three years 1816-1818 with 1833-1835. Drawing on these returns and having made assumptions regarding crew size and average values of cargoes, it demonstrated a substantial increase in vessels, lives and property lost in the second period. The Committee showed considerable perception in its appreciation of the wider implications of shipping losses. It noted that though property might be insured "it is not the less absolutely lost to the nation and its cost is paid for by the British public" and it further observed that the loss of life was attended by "pecuniary burthens to the British public which had to support widows and orphans left destitute."

Having established the dimensions of the problem the Committee turned its attention to the principal causes of shipwrecks concentrating on those causes which appeared "susceptible of removal or diminution" as opposed to those associated with storm and natural nautical hazards. The Committee laid much stress on deficiencies in ship design and construction which it believed had been adversely influenced by the official system of tonnage measurement and Lloyd's system of classification. These systems of measurement and classification were the subject of much debate in the 1820s and 1830s, hence the Committee's interest. Both systems were in fact modified in 1834, but the Committee, while welcoming such changes, emphasised the weaknesses of the old systems and the need for further positive reforms. The operation of the old system of tonnage measurement, together with the heavy duties levied on tonnage, was claimed to have induced shipowners to build vessels of such forms as would combine a small nominal measured tonnage with large actual carrying capacity. Such qualities could only be obtained by some sacrifice of speed, buoyancy and power which, coupled with the tendency to build flat-bottomed vessels to accommodate shoal harbours, all contributed to reduce the sailing qualities of British vessels and limit their manoeuverability in difficult and dangerous conditions.

The criticism of Lloyd's system of classification was somewhat more complex. Underwriters at Lloyd's categorised vessels into various classes. How a ship was classified materially influenced such matters as its cargo, freight and insurance, first class vessels being more favoured than second class. Between 1798 and 1834 the criteria used at Lloyd's for classification were not those of construction, soundness and strength, but solely those of age and place of building, and it was on these criteria that a vessel was placed in the first class for a period of six to a maximum of twelve years. This system was criticised by the Committee on a number of counts: it was alleged that shipowners were encouraged to build cheap, shoddy vessels with little thought for long term durability; further, it was said that the tendency to build replacements for vessels whose first class status had expired led to overcapacity, hence excessive competition. Such competition encouraged overloading and the foregoing of repairs thus impairing safety. The competitive situation was further heightened by foreign shippers who enjoyed lower shipbuilding and operating costs.

Apart from criticising the systems of classification, the Committee also queried the principle of marine insurance which, they thought, had a tendency to induce a lack of care in the construction and operation of vessels. The Committee also indicted masters and ships' officers for incompetence, citing evidence of appalling ineptitude and utter ignorance of navigational skill and techniques. Drunkenness, it was felt, was a further cause of disaster and the better record of United States' "temperance vessels" was held up as an example. Two final causes of wreck which perhaps implied less criticism of owners and master were those of imperfections of charts and the lack of harbours of refuge on certain stretches of the British coast. Such, then, was the Committee's assessment of the causes of shipwreck.

It will be recalled that when Russell had reluctantly agreed to the appointment of the Select Committee he had stipulated that it should merely report the evidence, i.e., there was no suggestion that the Committee should make recommendations. Strictly speaking therefore, the Committee completed its brief in its opening two sections which examined the extent and causes of shipwreck. Buckingham, however, intended the Committee to serve a more positive role – he favoured state intervention and he had definite ideas about the type of action required. His views were presented in the third section of the report, headed *Remedies, Proposed or Suggested*, a use of words enabling lip service to Russell's proviso of merely reporting the evidence.

The remedies proposed comprised an extensive programme of reforms implying great growth of state intervention in merchant shipping. First and foremost the report proposed the establishment in London of a Merchantile Marine Board comprising representatives of the royal and merchant navies, shipowners and shipbuilders, and technical and legal authorities. This Board was to be empowered under the sanction and authority of Parliament to direct, supervise and regulate the affairs of the merchantile marine of the United Kingdom. In particular the Board was to pursue the following primary objectives:

a.   the codification of maritime law;
b.   the better classification of ships;
c.   the examination of officers;
d.   the establishment of registry offices, saving banks, asylums and nautical schools for seamen;
e.   the institution of courts of inquiry into shipwrecks;
f.   the formation of tribunals to settle disputes between owners;
g.   more vaguely, the promotion of maritime improvement and the collection of data on the building, surveying and equipping of vessels.

The establishment of a Merchantile Marine Board with its clearly defined programme of objectives was the key-stone of the Committee's proposals. Apart from this, however, the Committee also pointed to five further areas for direct action by government. These included the reduction of duties and taxes on shipping; international negotiations to secure arrangements for dealing with wrecked vessels, cargoes and crews; and the encouragement of research into ship design and rescue apparatus. Less grandiose, but more specific, recommendations were those of the prevention of deck loading (a major cause of shipwreck in the timber carrying trade)[7] and, in a slightly more bizarre vein, the cessation of the rum ration in the Royal Navy as an example to encourage sobriety on merchant ships - an over-optimistic proposition, no doubt emanating from Buckingham's lofty temperance.

Two further paragraphs completed the report: one drawing attention to the disturbing rise of United States' shipping competition and the other suggesting legislative action in the next parliamentary session. It is worth emphasising the scope of these varied recommendations. Overall they made up a most comprehensive package of shipping reform and government intervention. Buckingham's view of a merchantile marine operating under an extensive system of controls and positive encouragement was ambitious indeed for the mid-1830s.

Presented to parliament in the mid-summer, at the end of the parliamentary session, there was no chance of any action being taken on

---

[7]The practice of deck loading was a major area of investigation by a further Select Committee which examined shipwrecks in the 1830s. See Select Committee on Shipwrecks of Timber Ships, *BPP*, 1839, IX.

the report in 1836. Early in 1837 in the new session Buckingham sponsored a bill to carry out the 1836 proposals. Though not without support, the bill was defeated at its second reading. Not surprisingly its opponents protested that "it touched on things which were not susceptible to legislative regulation;" phrases such as "legislative monstrosity" were bandied, and Labouchere described it as a "vexatious interference with the shipping interest of the country."[8] Thus, no action was taken on the report, and Buckingham resigned soon afterwards and appears to have taken no further part in campaigning for maritime reform. Parliament then shelved the 1836 Committee's report and most historians since appear to have done likewise.

And yet a detailed perusal of the statute book in the mid-century reveals that almost all the proposals of the Committee of 1836 were ultimately acted upon.[9] A brief examination of the main features of the 1836 proposals and mid-century legislation demonstrates clearly how Buckingham's programme anticipated subsequent government action:

1836 proposals	**Subsequent legislation of action**
1. The formation of a Merchantile Marine Board	While a Board of the composition suggested was not set up, in 1850 the Marine Department of the Board of Trade was created. This served many of the functions envisaged of the proposed Board.[10]

---

[8]*Mirror of Parliament*, 3rd sess. I, 551-560, 9 March 1837; II, 965-966, 12 April 1837; III, 1737-1738, 7 June 1837.

[9]A useful summary of mid-nineteenth century maritime legislation is to be found in the Report to the President of the Board of Trade on Recent Legislation concerning Merchant Ships and Seamen, *BPP*, 1876, LXVI, 333.

[10]13 & 14 Vic c93.

1836 proposals	Subsequent legislation of action
2. The codification of maritime law	This was undertaken in the Merchant Shipping Act of 1854 and further revised in subsequent Acts in 1869, 1870, 1871 and 1872 by the introduction of Consolidation Bills.[11]
3. The better classification of ships	This aim was advanced through the private agencies of Lloyd's, the Liverpool Register, and overseas by the Bureaux Veritas.
4. The examination of officers	A system of examination of masters and mates was introduced by the Mercantile Marine Act of 1850 and a further Act in 1862 extended the system of examination and certification to engineers in merchant ships.[12]
5. The establishment of registry offices and welfare provisions for seamen	Registry offices were attempted under the 1850 Act and Seamen's Savings Banks were founded under a special Act in 1856. Less progress, however, was made in the matter of homes and asylums where the closure of Greenwich Hospital was a retrograde step.[13]
6. The setting up of Courts of Enquiry into shipwrecks	This was covered by the 1850 and 1854 Acts. The Board of Trade commenced its Wreck Register and the provision of annual statements from the early 1850s.[14]

---

[11] 17 & 18 Vic c104; 32 & 33 Vic c11; 34 & 35 Vic c110.

[12] 13 & 14 Vi c93; 25 & 26 Vic c63.

[13] 13 & 14 Vic c93; 19 & 20 Vic c41.

[14] 13 & 14 Vic c93; 17 & 18 Vic c104. Details of the compilation of the Wreck Register are contained in Royal Commission on Unseaworthy Ships, *BPP*, 1873, XXXVI, q. 222a.

1836 proposals	Subsequent legislation of action
7. The establishment of tribunals to settle disputes	This purpose was served by Acts in 1844, 1854 and 1862.[15]

Of other recommendations: taxes on shipping were reduced by free trade measures and Acts in 1853,1860 and 1861 reducing local charges, light dues and tolls;[16] deck loading was limited in 1839, the first of a series of loading regulations on bulk cargo trades;[17] some action was taken encouraging ship design and rescue apparatus; and even temperance was furthered by severe penalties for drunkenness amongst officers by acts of 1850, 1854, and 1862.[18]

In the longer term then it would appear that the measures advocated by Buckingham were adopted by government in the mid-century. Buckingham's view of a mercantile marine operating under an extensive system of controls and positive encouragement aimed at promoting greater safety and enhanced efficiency was in great measure put into effect. True, Buckingham's central feature of a Mercantile Marine Board was not established, but his role was in part fulfilled by the Marine Department of the Board of Trade which exercised much of the directing, supervisory and regulatory functions which Buckingham had envisaged, even if it did not always assume the positive stance he had hoped for.[19] Subsequent legislation thus vindicated Buckingham's proposals.

In tracing the similarities between the proposals of 1836 and mid-century legislation it would be wrong to imply that the 1836 proposals served as a blue-print for government action in merchant shipping matters; there is no evidence to suggest that ministers or officials viewed the proposals as a programme or plan to be generally pursued. State

---

[15]7 & 8 Vic c112; 17 & 18 Vic c104; 25 & 26 Vic c63.

[16]16 & 17 Vic c129; 24 & 25 Vic c47.

[17]2 & 3 Vic c44; 3 & 4 Vic c36.

[18]13 & 14 Vic c93; 17 & 18 Vic c104; 25 & 26 Vic c63.

[19]On the establishment and working of the Marine Department of the Board of Trade, see P.G. Parkhurst, *Ships of Peace*, (New Malden, 1962), I, 129-170.

intervention in the mid-century was not conceived of in overall terms, the pattern of government intervention was built up step by step on a piecemeal and sometimes haphazard fashion. The prevailing belief in the minimum of state interference in the market, for want of a better phrase, *laissez-faire* ideology, decreed that state intervention was gradual, one measure at a time. Indeed, given the prevailing philosophy, Buckingham's 1836 proposals were seeking too much, altogether, too soon. Moreover, given the political climate of the time, Buckingham failed to distinguish between what was socially and economically desirable and what was politically possible. Thus Buckingham's reforms failed as a programme. However the individual proposals he advocated were in isolation acceptable, and were, in time, almost all, acted upon.

Of course the attainment of legislation on each particular issue depended on different circumstances, fresh pressures and often further enquiries, notably another general enquiry into shipwrecks in 1843 which reiterated many of Buckingham's suggestions,[20] but regularly, interested parties drew attention to the 1836 proposals as evidence supportive of their case. Buckingham's proposals can thus be looked on as a starting point for much of the mercantile marine legislation of the mid-century and as an amazingly farsighted overall statement of measures to be taken.

For such reasons Buckingham might justly be said to be as deserving as Plimsoll of the accolade of "the Sailor's friend" and to be recognised for his much wider vision of the relationship between the state and the merchant service. In assessing Buckingham's contribution to maritime reform the adjective "remarkable" is as appropriate as it is for his career generally.

---

[20]Select Committee on Shipwrecks, *BPP*, 1843, IX.

APPENDIX

Principal Published Works of James Silk Buckingham
(place of publication London, unless otherwise stated)

(a)   *Works on travel*

Travels in Palestine, through the countries of Bashan and Gilead, east of the River Jordan (Longman & Co., 1821).

Travels among the Arab tribes inhabiting the countries east of Syria and Palestine (Longman & Co., 1825).

Travels in Mesopotamia, 2 vols. (Henry Colburn, 1827).

Travels in Assyria, Media and Persia (Henry Colburn, 1829).

America, historical, statistic and descriptive, 3 vols. (Fisher, Son & Co., 1841).

The Slave States of America, 2 vols. (Fisher, Son & Co., 1842).

The Eastern and Western States of America, 3 vols (Fisher, Son & Co., 1842).

Canada, Nova Scotia, New Brunswick and the other British provinces in North America (Fisher, Son & Co., 1843).

Belgium, the Rhine, Switzerland, and Holland. An autumnal tour, 2 vols. (Peter Jackson, 1845?).

France, Piedmont, Italy, Lombardy, the Tyrol and Bavaria. An autumnal tour (Peter Jackson, 1848).

(b)   *Social and political works*

Evils and remedies of the present system of popular elections (Simpkin, Marshall & Co., 1841).

Plan of an improved income tax and real free trade (Ridgway, 1845).

National evils and practical remedies, with a plan for a model town (Peter Jackson, 1849).

An earnest plea for the reign of temperance and peace, as conducive to the prosperity of nations; submitted to the visitors of the Great Exhibition (Peter Jackson, 1851).

Plan for the future government of India (Partridge, Oakey & Co., 1853).

Examination of the principal questions connected with national education (Partridge, Oakey & Co., 1854).

History and progress of the temperance reformation in Great Britain and other countries of the globe (Partridge, Oakey & Co., 1854).

Proposed plan of a new reform bill to purify and extend the suffrage (Partridge, Oakey & Co., 1854).

The coming era of practical reform not "looming in the distance" but "nigh at hand." A new series of tracts for the times (Partridge, Oakey & Co., 1854).

(c)   Autobiography

Autobiography of James Silk Buckingham, including his voyage, travels, adventures, speculations, successes and failures, faithfully and frankly narrated (Longman, Brown, Green and Longmans, 1855).

(d)   Periodicals and newspapers founded and edited by Buckingham

The Calcutta Journal (founded Calcutta 1818).

The Oriental Herald and Colonial Review (founded London 1824).

The Sphynx (founded London 1827).

The Athenaeum (founded London 1828).

The Parliamentary Review and Family Magazine (founded London 1833).

Transactions of the British and Foreign Institute (founded London 1845).

A contemporary estimate in 1853 suggested that Buckingham had published "upwards of 100 volumes, averaging at least 500 pages each; in addition to which, Mr. Buckingham has issued at various times, between forty and fifty pamphlets, on various topics of the day." (*Biographical Sketch, op. cit.*).

State Regulation of Merchant Shipping 1839-1914: The Bulk Carrying Trades[1]

A major feature of state involvement with merchant shipping in the nineteenth century was that of concern over the safety of life at sea. In the mid-century, with the exception of the Passenger Acts which regulated the carriage of emigrants,[2] such concern assumed the form of investigative rather than legislative action. The Select Committee on Shipwrecks of 1836 which undertook a lengthy and detailed examination of the problem of shipwreck and loss of life at sea was the first of a series of such investigations which added up to over a dozen Select Committees and Royal Commissions in a fifty-year period. On a more permanent basis the establishment of the Marine Department of the Board of Trade in 1850[3] with powers of inquiry into cases of shipwreck and the more accurate compilation of the Wreck Register from 1856 provided a regular flow of information on casualty and loss in the British mercantile marine.[4] From the late 1860s the issue of maritime safety gained a fresh impetus with the campaigns of Hall and Plimsoll, and in the seventies concern was

[1]I should like to thank Phillip Cottrell who kindly read through an early draft of this paper. I also gratefully acknowledge the receipt of grants from the Research Board of the University of Leicester.

[2]On the Passenger Acts see O. Macdonagh, *A Pattern of Government Growth 1800-60* (1961).

[3]P.G. Parkhurst, *Ships of Peace* (New Malden, 1962), I, 129-170; R. Proughty, *The Transformation of the Board of Trade, 1830-1855* (1957).

[4]Details of the compilation of the Wreck Register are contained in *Royal Commission on Unseaworthy Ships*, *PP* (1873), XXXVI, q 222a.

translated into positive action in the form of the well-known legislation on unseaworthy ships and load lines.[5]

Less well known, however, is that both before and during the 1870s, government found it necessary to make special provision for certain bulk trades. In the nineteenth century, "volumes not values" were the essence of increasing ocean transport throughout the world and the expansion of British registered shipping was based on the long distance freighting of bulk commodities, notably before 1850 timber and cotton and later coal, mineral ores, fertilisers and grain.[6] Two aspects of this development attracted notice of government. First, the sheer number of vessels engaged in the bulk trades which ensured that in any investigation or statistics of wrecks, vessels carrying, say, timber or grain, featured prominently. Contemporary analysis by trade of the Wreck Register in the 1860s made this abundantly clear. Secondly associated with the increase in vessel size which took place from the 1830s, there occurred a huge growth in the size of individual shipments. This led to the development of new bulk loading and stowage practices which while embodying obvious economic advantages brought with them their own special safety hazards. Hence the early years of the bulk trades were attended by shipping losses, always costly, often tragic, and sometimes spectacular in their enormity or horror. It was the occurrence of such losses in a period when the state was coming to accept some responsibility for the safeguarding of life at sea which gave rise to a growing interest in the problems of bulk cargoes and led, in turn, to pressure on government, official investigation and attempts to regulate the bulk trades over and above those general policies aimed at merchant shipping as a whole.

This paper examines the course and nature of state regulation in two of the chief bulk carrying trades, the timber and grain trades. In the timber trade the problem was that of deck cargoes which government first attempted to regulate in 1839 and which was to prove a contentious issue for much of the nineteenth century. In the grain trade the problem which

---

[5]On the load line controversy of the 1870s see G. Alderman, "Samuel Plimsoll and the Shipping Interest," *Maritime History*, I (1971); D. Masters, *The Plimsoll Mark* (1955); N. Upham, *The Load Line - A Hallmark of Safety* (1978).

[6]D. Alexander & Rosemary Ommer, eds., *Volumes Not Values: Canadian Sailing Ships and World Trades* (St. John's, Newfoundland, 1979), contains a collection of essays on the development of bulk trades in the nineteenth century.

became a focus of concern from the 1860s was that of bulk cargoes shifting and causing instability. It must be said that, while ultimately accepting responsibility for regulating loading practice, government showed itself less than willing to involve itself in the problems of these two trades. *Laissez-faire* ideology is only a partial explanation of this unwillingness to intervene. A further delaying influence was the appreciation of those in authority that it was one thing to accept a commitment but another to fulfil it effectively. And so it proved. It was easy enough to recognise that an evil existed and that corrective action was necessary, but there were very real difficulties in defining a problem and assessing its extent, framing appropriate controls, ensuring administration and enforcement, and in overcoming the resistance of operators intent on maximising returns. In these respects the difficulties of government in its endeavours to regulate the bulk trades were similar to those experienced in other area of state intervention in the nineteenth century, both in shipping and in the wider context. However, the nature of the ocean shipping business intensified these difficulties by giving them a further dimension, forcing government to consider problems and actions in international rather than purely British terms. Eventually by the 1880s a body of regulations controlled many aspects of loading in both the timber and the grain trades, but the attainment of such controls had proved a lengthy and frustrating process and one characterised by no little trial and error.

Official concern with the problems of bulk cargo trades was first manifested in the 1830s when heavy losses in the timber trade attracted attention. The timber trade with its preferential duty system was already at this time a focus of interest and was the subject of a Select Committee in 1835.[7] This Committee heard considerable evidence on the employment of old and inferior vessels in the trade, and the safety of timber carrying vessels was examined in a more general context by the Select Committee on the Causes of Shipwreck which sat in the following year. Popular concern was also aroused by the publicity given to appalling cases of losses in the timber trade where the crews of waterlogged vessels, forced to take to the masts, resorted to cannibalism and the drinking of human blood. Such reports led the government in 1839 to set up a Select

---

[7]*Select Committee on the Timber Duties*, PP (1835), XIX.

Committee to inquire into Shipwrecks of Timber Ships, the first example of an investigation of safety and losses in a specific trade.

The Select Committee of 1839 had as its brief shipwrecks in the timber trade generally. The Committee, however, chose to concentrate on the North Atlantic branch of the trade which employed only British vessels and where the larger size of vessels employed and the greater danger of a longer voyage over less frequently crossed seas heightened the potential scale and horror of casualty. Evidence presented to the Committee on causes of losses stressed three major factors: the dangers of late autumn and winter North Atlantic passages, the character of vessels in the trade, and the practice of deck loading. An analysis of vessels lost undertaken by the Committee however revealed as large a proportion of good and A.1. vessels lost as old and inferior, and the Committee thus concluded that "loss was occasioned by other causes than the frailty of the vessels themselves." Hence the Committee reported, stressing "the almost unanimous opinion of every witness examined" that "the prime cause of all the mischief had been in the improper over-stowage of the ships, by carrying heavy loads of timber upon deck."[8] The evidence presented certainly painted a grim picture of the dangers of excessive deck loads. Most serious was that deck loads made vessels top heavy and liable to upset or to be thrown on their beam ends in heavy seas. Deck loads made vessels less manageable, impeded crews in the working of the ship and inhibited access to provisions and water in the dreadful event of the vessel becoming waterlogged. Heavy deck loads were also alleged to result in the greater wear and tear of vessels; loosening fastenings, opening seams and breaking beams. No doubt the crucial element in all these charges was the size of a deck load, its weight in relation to total cargo and ballast, and how securely it was fastened, but the Committee found it particularly significant that some marine insurers, notably North of England clubs, fixed limits on deck loads. Furthermore they imposed almost prohibitive additional premiums if deck cargoes were carried on vessels sailing from America after 1 October. Having taken all the evidence into account, the Committee recommended "that no deck loads should be suffered to be carried on any timber laden vessel from North America and that every

---

[8]*Select Committee on Shipwrecks of Timber Ships, PP* (1839), IX, iii-v.

inducement should be given to promoting a fair and efficient survey of every ship in the merchant service."[9]

In this latter sweeping proposal the Committee was some years ahead of its time, but in recommending prohibition on deck loads it was in fact re-stressing the view of the 1836 Committee on Shipwrecks which had suggested "the prevention of the practice of carrying any portion of the ship's cargoes on deck."[10] While the legislature steered well clear of any scheme of compulsory survey it did take action on deck loads, passing a temporary Act in 1839 which declared it unlawful for any timber carrying vessel clearing from British North America between 1 September and 1 May to carry a deck cargo.[11] Masters were required to procure a certificate form the customs Clearing Officer that all cargo was below deck, and there were penalties for infringement. A proviso permitted store spars for the vessel's use to be carried on deck and allowed cargo to be brought on deck in the event of leaks or damage. This temporary Act was made permanent in 1840.[12] The impact of these measures was favourably reported on by the Select Committee on Shipwrecks of 1843 which received comparative figures of losses before and after the legislation of 1839-40. It accordingly recommended to further extension of the prohibitory clauses against deck loading.[13] In the event no action was taken but the law was re-enacted in the Customs Consolidation Act of 1853.

The controls on deck loads seem to have worked effectively in the 1840s. The regulations themselves appeared to contain little ambiguity and gave rise to little resentment as all shippers were equally affected. However, from the early 1850s, shippers' compliance with the law ceased as the lifting of protectionist restrictions affecting the timber trade, namely the repeal of the Navigation Acts and later the ending of the differential duties on foreign timber, significantly changed the market in which British shippers were operating. Faced as they were from 1850 with the entry of

---

[9]*Ibid*, v.

[10]*Select Committee on the Causes of Shipwrecks*, *PP* (1836), XVII, ix.

[11]2 & 3 Vict., c44.

[12]3 & 4 Vict., c36.

[13]*Select Committee on the Causes of Shipwrecks*, *PP* (1843), IX, iii.

United States' vessels not subject to restrictions on deck loads, British shippers, as a means of competing, turned to evasion of the regulations.[14] The proviso permitting store spars to be carried on deck began to be abused but the real scope of evasion lay in the problem of defining what was a deck and hence a deck load. Evasion at first took the form of stowing timber in the poop, often of large dimensions in timber trade vessels, being specially constructed for the carriage of stores on the westbound passage when emigrants were carried. Following complaints from the Liverpool Underwriters Association in 1853 the Board of Trade issued an order to customs officers in North America to forbid this use of the poop. This brought angry remonstrations from shipowners and colonial interests who argued that the poop was measured in tonnage as part of cargo carrying capacity, that the practice was long-standing and brought important freight returns, and that foreign vessels in the timber trade bore no such restrictions. To add to the Board of Trade's problems, colonial customs officers queried whether the order preventing the carriage of goods in poops extended to goods other than wood. The matter was complicated still further by an even more blatant form of evasion; this took the form of connecting the poop with a construction at the other end of the vessel by a temporary deck, called a spar deck, by which practice deck cargo was allegedly stowed below deck. After consulting its nautical advisers, the Board of Trade adjudged poop and spar deck cargoes illegal and it accordingly instructed the customs to issue an order forbidding timber or other goods to be carried in this way. Such was the strength of feeling in British North America however, that the colonial customs was unwilling to try and endorse the order. In a test case in 1854, that of the *David G. Fleming* which sailed from British North America, ostensibly without a customs clearance, carrying 3290 deals in her poop, the Board of Trade instituted a prosecution, but this failed as did others subsequently instituted. This unsatisfactory situation was compounded in March 1860 when the differential duties on foreign timber were repealed. Until this date vessels needed a colonial clearance to ensure that their timber cargoes were admissible at the lower rate of duty, but once there was no advantage to be so gained there was a real possibility that vessels would chose to clear from a United States port (for example, from neighbouring Maine

---

[14]On the operation of the restrictions on deck loads 1839-1862, and in particular the development of evasion from 1850, see *R.C. on Unseaworthy Ships, PP*, 1873 (XXXVI), qq 223-238.

rather than New Brunswick) and hence be legally free from all restrictions on deck loads which applied only to vessels clearing from ports in British North America. This practice became common from 1860.

Thus by 1860 the situation regarding the deck load requirements was a confused one. Some vessels, by clearing from United States ports, avoided any liability under the regulations, others were alleged to be taking on deck cargoes after gaining customs clearance. Some shippers were exploiting the proviso concerning store spars to carry rough and heavy timber while poop and spar deck cargoes were being regularly carried as the Board of Trade's order had proved unenforceable. Moreover, the equity and legality of this order was increasingly questioned as it was pointed out that the poop was included in measures calculating tonnage and that poop and spar deck cargoes were regularly and legitimately carried in non-British North American trades. There was resentment too of the competition of regulation-free foreign shipping about which it appeared nothing could be done. Again, a body of opinion was developing in Canada which favoured allowing limited deck cargoes in place of prohibition and reducing the time period when restraints were imposed. By 1860 then the deck load laws were inoperative if not effectively a dead letter, and were a source of grievance to merchants and shipowners. Colonial customs officials who both disliked the law and felt that they had been inadequately supported by the Board of Trade were advocating change, and there were indications that such bodies as Lloyds and the Liverpool Underwriters Association were less inclined to restrict deck loads than in the past. Eventually, following a deputation from the St. John Chamber of Commerce, led by the leading shipowner Mr. Rankin, the laws on timber deck loads were repealed in the Merchant Shipping Act of 1862.[15]

The repeal of 1862 marked the end of the first phase of attempts to control timber deck loads. It proved to be but a temporary setback however, and in the late 1860s, with the growth of interest in the general problem of overloading, the debate over the issue resumed and took on a fresh complexity. Previously the matter had been primarily one of safety in the timber trade, but now discussion broadened to embrace deck cargoes generally, the question of deck cargo space and tonnage measurement and new proposals that all deck cargoes should be the subject of

---

[15]25 & 26 Vict., c63.

report to Customs before sailing. The complex nature of the debate was further heightened by it being conducted within the wider framework of the load line and unseaworthy ships controversy.

Fresh complaints about timber deck loads were made to the Board of Trade in 1868 by its counterpart in Quebec and the Salvage Association.[16] The Board's response was that it was now considering the legal aspects of deck loads in a broader context on the grounds that the exclusion from tonnage dues of cargoes carried on deck was unfair between one shipowner and another and encouraged dangerous practices, of which spar deck timber cargoes were a prime example. To limit the competitive advantage of shipowners who carried deck cargoes it was therefore proposed in the Merchant Shipping Bill of 1869 that deck cargo space should be taken into account when the gross tonnage of a vessel was being calculated, although the method whereby this was to be achieved was, to say the least, haphazard.[17] The 1869 Bill was not passed but the clauses concerning deck cargo and tonnage were again introduced into the Merchant Shipping Bill of 1870. Strong protests were made by shipping companies engaged in the Irish cattle trade where animals were regularly carried on deck. Such cargoes, it was claimed, in no way represented overloading; moreover, the deck was thought to be the best place for cattle on short voyages. Attention was also drawn to the good safety record of the trade. These protests combined with others concerning deck loads in the cotton trade, the carriage of large machines, the dangers of stowing substances like petroleum below deck and the impossibility of preventing deck cargoes on small coasting steamers, were to prove the obstacle to all attempts at the general prohibition of deck cargoes. Faced with such opposition, the Board of Trade reluctantly withdrew its proposal of imposing tonnage dues on deck cargo.[18]

In 1873 three important developments occurred. First, Plimsoll began to include deck loads in the campaign. *Our Seamen* which was published at the beginning of the year denounced the "desperately

---

[16]*R.C. on Unseaworthy Ships*, *PP*, 1873 (XXXVI), q 239.

[17]*Ibid*. Shipowners when registering their vessels were required to state whether they intended to have cargo carried on deck or not. If the intention was to carry deck cargo an additional ten percent was to be added to the vessel's gross tonnage.

[18]*Ibid*, q241.

dangerous practice of deck loading" as one of the "sources of disaster,"[19] and Plimsoll's new bill for compulsory survey and a load line included provisions forbidding the carrying of all deck loads to and from British ports between 1 September and 1 May and requiring masters to submit a declaration that all cargo was below deck to the Customs Clearing Officer.[20] The bill was to be defeated as was his bill, with similar deck load provisions, of the following year,[21] but Plimsoll's pressure contributed to the second major development, the appointment of the Royal Commission on Unseaworthy Ships which was to sit in 1873 and 1874. Deck cargoes were one of the Commission's chief areas of investigation and Thomas Farrar, Permanent Secretary of the Board of Trade, provided a detailed *resumé* of the experience of the previous forty years. The evidence delivered to the Commission is a major source of information on deck loads. Aspects considered were those of the wide extent of the practice in the timber and other trades, insurance, and the dangers of winter voyages; and while opinion on what action government should take ranged from prohibition, through limiting and/or seasonal restrictions to no regulation whatsoever, there was general agreement that regulation if applied to British vessels alone would be detrimental to their competitive position *vis à vis* foreign shipping. The third significant development which occurred shortly after the Royal Commission began to hear evidence, and was itself considered by the Commission, was that of action by the Canadian Parliament to regulate deck loading. Informed opinion in Canada in the 1850s and 1860s had never been anti-regulation as such, rather it had advocated reasonable limitation in place of the ineffective and inoperable prohibition which prevailed down to 1862. In 1860, William Smith, then Controller of Customs at St. John, New Brunswick, and later to become Principal Permanent Officer of the Dominion Government's Marine Department, persuasively argued for such an approach in a lengthy

---

[19]S. Plimsoll, *Our Seamen, an Appeal* (1873), 34.

[20]*PP* (1873), V, 125. Plimsoll's bill aroused considerable concern in Canada where the Parliament of Canada had but recently passed its own law on deck loads. See correspondence on the issue in *PP*, 1873 (XLIV), 47 *et seq.*

[21]*PP* (1874), V, 21.

memorandum to the Board of Trade.[22] Over a decade later his proposals formed the basis of the Canadian government's Act of 1873 which was introduced following the failure of the British government to make any progress on the issue in 1869 and 1870. The Act limited deck cargoes on any vessel sailing from Canadian ports between 1 October and 16 March. It permitted deck cargo up to a height of 3 ft. only and forbade the carrying of any unsawn timber other than dressed store spars. Certificates of compliance with the law had to be gained from Customs before clearance.[23]

Despite the evidence presented to it and the example of the Canadian Parliament, the Royal Commission declined to make any positive recommendation on deck loads. In its final report of July 1874, the Commission, while accepting the dangers of deck cargoes, observed: "but a merchant ship is a machine employed for earning freight and we are of the opinion that it would be unwise for the legislature absolutely to prohibit deck cargoes, except in the special case of the timber trade." However there was no firm recommendation other than that masters should record details of all deck cargo in the ship's log and provide a copy for Customs Officers.[24]

This basically meaningless proposal was included in the new Tory government's Bill to Amend the Merchant Shipping Acts of February 1875 which gained its first reading on the same day as Plimsoll's fresh bill which sought amongst other proposals to ban deck loads altogether on British vessels.[25] In the event neither bill was to gain the Royal Assent but the withdrawal of the government's bill in July was to occasion Plimsoll's famous Commons outburst when before departing the Chamber he shook his fist at Disraeli. The widespread indignation following the government's action forced the government to bring in a stop-gap Unseaworthy Ships Bill but while the debate on this measure included much discussion

---

[22]Smith's letter is reprinted as an appendix in *R.C. on Unseaworthy Ships*, *PP*, 1873, (XXXVI), 451-454.

[23]*Ibid*, 492. Appendix No XVI contains the terms of the Canadian Act of 1873.

[24]*R.C. on Unseaworthy Ships*, *PP* (1874), XXXIV, vii.

[25]*PP* (1985), IV, 33, 97.

on deck cargoes an attempted amendment to bain deck cargoes was defeated[26] and the Bill was enacted with no reference to the issue.

The temporary nature of the 1875 Act ensured new government proposals in the following year. On deck cargoes these merely reiterated the provision for depositing log entries with Customs together with the re-introduction of the 1869/70 proposals for the inclusion of the space occupied by deck cargo in tonnage measurement. Needless to say, such provisions seemed less than adequate to Plimsoll and his supporters who again had pressed their own Bill containing clauses prohibiting deck loads. Immediately a campaign was mounted for more effective action on deck loads and on 1 May, when its bill was in Committee, the government capitulated, introducing a new clause relating to timber deck loads.[27] This closely followed the Canadian legislation of 1873 limiting deck cargoes on "any ship, British or foreign, arriving at a port in the United Kingdom which has sailed from any port ... after first day of October or before sixteenth March." The most significant feature of this provision was the inclusion of foreign, and hence, Baltic vessels. Previously government had always been wary of placing restrictions on foreign vessels and had used as an excuse for non-intervention the difficulty of controlling loading in foreign ports. Such problems of supervision were now overcome by assessing loading arrangements on arrival in Britain, and representations from the Swedish and Norwegian government were politely rejected.[28] After amendments clarifying dates and specifying permissible timber cargo the new clause was enacted in the Merchant Shipping Amendment Act of 1876. This prevented any ship, British or foreign, arriving between 1 November and 16 April from carrying heavy wood goods on deck other than store spars, and limited cargoes of deals to a heigh of 3 ft. above deck. Customs officials were to inspect all timber laden vessels on arrival before unloading commenced.[29]

---

[26]*Parl Debates*, 3rd ser, ccxxvi, 157-160, 28 July 1875; 422-426, 2 Aug. 1875.

[27]*Parl Debates*, 3rd ser, ccxxvii, 171-182, 10 Feb. 1876; 428-466; 17 Feb. 1876; ccxxviii, 1590-1622, 1779-1803, 1921-1943, 24 & 27 April, 1 May 1876.

[28]*Representation from Swedish and Norwegian Government ... PP* (1876), LXVI, 93.

[29]39 & 40 Vict.., c80.

The Act of 1876 laid down the basic principles regulating deck cargo in the timber trade down to World War I. Essentially it was something of a compromise for it gave legal sanction to timber deck loads, albeit limited, and the Act shirked the issues of an absolute prohibition and of deck cargo space in tonnage measurement, another provision of the Act, reduced some of the incentive to carry deck cargoes. Final attempts by Plimsoll in 1890-1892 to introduce a general prohibition of deck cargoes met with no success[30] and the terms of the 1875 Act were re-enacted in the Merchant Shipping Act of 1894 and, with slight modification, in the Merchant Shipping Act of 1906.[31]

The grain trade, like the timber trade, was a longstanding trade which underwent enormous expansion in the nineteenth century. British imports of grain, drawn chiefly from North America and Russia, increased rapidly from the late 1860s. Grain was shipped either in sacks or bags or in bulk. Stowage in bulk brought with it danger in the form of cargoes shifting and causing instability, making vessels liable to listing or foundering. Such dangers increased with the growth in size of individual shipments and with the development of new methods of loading from shoots or elevators. These new methods enormously facilitated and speeded up loading – it was reported that cargoes which had previously taken a week or ten days to load could be loaded in a day – but speed was incompatible with careful loading and cargo was often not so well trimmed.[32] The dangers of cargo shifting could be alleviated by careful attention to stowage and in particular the use of boards and bulkheads to limit shifting. Robert White Stevens in his bible *On the Stowage of Ships* provided instructions detailing "strong bulkheads, good shifting board," and he also included copies of certain North American underwriters' conditions of insurance.[33] Sadly such attention to stowage was not universal practice and a combination of ignorance, inexperience and often

---

[30]*Parl Debates*, 3rd ser, cccxivi, 1245, 9 July 1890; cccxiix, 115, 1200, 26 Nov. 1890 & 27 Jan. 1891; 4th ser, i, 169, 10 Feb. 1892; v, 1215, 15 June 1892. Plimsoll's proposals aroused considerable concern in Canada. See correspondence in *PP*, 1890-1891 (LVI), 11 *et seq*.

[31]57 & 58 Vict., c60; 6 Edw 7, c48.

[32]*R.C. on Unseaworthy Ships*, *PP* 1873 (XXXVI), qq 12876-12879.

[33]R.W. Stevens, *On the Stowage of Ships*, 5th ed (1869), 200, 22407.

no doubt negligence in pursuit of a speedy turn-around gave rise to heavy casualties in the grain trade in the late 1860s and early 1870s. Losses were especially severe in the Russian trade and prompted the Consul at Odessa to report with regret the lack of controls in the overloading and stowage of grain vessels.[34]

The problem of grain ships received considerable attention from the Royal Commission on Unseaworthy Ships of 1873-1874. One witness declared that "grain in bulk is the most dangerous of all cargoes" and a further ten witnesses gave evidence on the problem of shifting cargoes.[35] A statistical analysis, compiled by the Board of Trade, of vessels wrecked and missing in the years 1860-1862 and 1870-1872 classified according to trade, revealed grain as one of the three most casualty-prone cargoes in terms of vessels wrecked or missing and lives lost.[36] Even more telling was evidence that action was already being taken at North American ports to control grain cargoes. In New York, the Board of Underwriters operated a code of practice and supervision which had to be adhered to, if vessels and cargoes were to be insured, while at Montreal, as early as 1871, an Act of the Canadian Parliament for the appointment of a Port Warden had listed amongst the Warden's duties the supervision of grain cargoes and stipulated that Customs clearance was not to be granted to grain vessels without a Port Warden's certificate.[37] Such evidence however did not convince the Commission of the need for government action. In its final report the Commission observed, "Grain cargoes are attended with danger to life, and require exceptional care. The rapid mode lately adopted for loading the grain ships adds to the danger. There are however well known precautions tending to diminish this danger, but the application of these will be best left to the responsibility of the shipowner and the practical knowledge of the captain."[38]

---

[34]*PP* (1872), LIII, 50.

[35]*R.C. on Unseaworthy Ships, PP* (1873), XXXVI, qq 673-676; see in particular the evidence of John Glover, qq 12876-12999.

[36]*Ibid*, 779, 790. Appendices, Tables E & L.

[37]*Ibid*, see evidence of Glover, also qq 13483-13486. For details of regulations in Canada and at New York see *PP* (1873), LXVII, 139.

[38]*R.C. on Unseaworthy Ships, PP* (1874), XXXIV, 3.

Not surprisingly in the light of such recommendations, published in July 1874, no action on grain cargoes was taken by the government; nor did any action seem likely in the immediate future. The Commission's recommendation was in accord with the *laissez-faire* views of Farrar at the Board of Trade who had in the past publicly stated that "they (the shipowners) must look to self interest, and not to Government regulation, as the great element of the safety of life on board ship."[39] In fairness to Farrar it must be said that in 1873-1875 there were far bigger issues to consider than that of regulating grain ships, and a change of government in 1874 added a further complication. Thus there appeared little prospect of action on grain cargoes in February 1875 when the government introduced its Bill to Amend the Merchant Shipping Acts. The bill contained nothing on grain cargoes and although Plimsoll drew attention to the success of Canadian regulations[40] no relevant changes were made when the bill was amended in Committee in April. Yet in August, the first British legislation concerning grain cargoes was to appear on the statute book. The circumstances which brought this about had a certain dramatic quality.

The impetus for action came initially from the Committee of Lloyds. In April 1875 the Committee wrote to Lord Tenterden at the Foreign Office suggesting that the adoption of rules for grain loading (such as in force at Montreal and New York) by Black Sea ports would save both shipping and lives.[41] The Committee compared the serious losses in the Black Sea trade at the turn of 1874-1875 with the better record of Atlantic grain shipping, and observed that it would be in Russia's interest to enforce regulations as the current situation was forcing up Black Sea freights and premiums. Tenterden passed the letter on to the Board of Trade enquiring whether the British Ambassador in St. Petersburg should make representations on the matter. Some two and a half months elapsed before the Board responded. Farrar, in his reply, while acknowledging the problem, counselled non-intervention. He claimed that the Board had not yet got copies of the Montreal or New York regulations – claim which

---

[39] *Journal of the Society of Arts*, XIV (1865-6), 254.

[40] *Parl Debates*, 3rd ser. CCXXIII, 539-544, 8 April 1875.

[41] For the important correspondence between the Committee of Lloyds, the Foreign Office and the Board of Trade, see *PP* 1875 (LXVII), 149 *et seq*.

with the most charitable interpretation can only be viewed as an admission of ignorance and inefficiency. He advised against involving the Russian government, observing that a dangerous precedent would be set if foreign governments were invited to legislate or make regulations for British shipping, and he pointed to the problems of regulating shipping, an international activity, and the implications for competition of special regulations on British ships. Farrar concluded, in accordance with his long-held opinion, that "underwriters and shipowners might do much without Government interference," and he reported that the Board was in communication with Lloyds on the matter. Tenterden conveyed these views to the Secretary of Lloyds in a letter dated 17 July. The Secretary responded strongly to Farrar's suggestion that the issue was one for underwriters and shipowners. In an interesting statement of Lloyds' position, he observed, "the province of underwriters is not to lead, but to follow, the course of trade; for the machinery by which commerce is carried on is independent of their control or consent." Commenting on regulations imposed in North America, Lloyds remarked that in Montreal where "Government interference prevails, the rules are absolute and general and thus far more effective than in New York where the control of the board of Underwriters is limited only to the ships they handle." In a final retort, directed at Farrar, the Secretary, speaking for Lloyds' Committee stated, "they consider these subjects are directly coming under the legitimate interference of Governments; and that by them alone they can be effectively dealt with."

These exchanges between the Committee of Lloyds and the Board of Trade, albeit using the Foreign Office as an intermediary, with both parties vigorously maintaining the other's responsibility, held out little hope for regulatory action. But events were to take a significant turn. The date of Lloyds' final letter had been 21 July. On the very next day the government announced its withdrawal of the Merchant Shipping Bill. Such was the outcry that within days, on 28 July, the temporary Unseaworthy Ships Bill was presented. At its second reading the bill was fiercely attacked for its omission of the deck load and grain cargo issues.[42] The government prevaricated briefly but so severe was the pressure that it recognised that concessions were required, and 30 July saw Farrar writing to Lloyds requesting their opinion of an amendment to the bill relating to

---

[42]*Parl Debates*, 3rd ser. CCXXVI, 225-267, 30 July 1875.

grain cargoes. The essence of the amendment was that no grain cargo should be carried on a British ship "unless ... in bags, sacks or barrels, or thoroughly secured from shifting by boards, bulkheads or otherwise." An indication of the Board's panic is gained from Farrar's request that Lloyds answer "by tomorrow morning, if possible." Lloyds' prompt reply (from the Assistant Secretary who tartly remarked that the Committee only met on Wednesdays) was not enthusiastic, observing that effective action could only be taken at the loading port and that all shipments, not merely those in British vessels, should be covered. Nevertheless, an amendment along the lines outlined in Farrar's letter was proceeded with and the bill gained the royal assent on 13 August.[43]

Any hopes entertained by the government, and the Board in particular, that the issue of grain cargoes had been dealt with and that campaigning interests had been appeased, were soon dashed. The grain cargo clause of the 1875 Act, hurried measure that it was, merely stated what should be done, and no consideration had been given as to how the intentions of the Act were to be achieved. On 11 October Plimsoll complained to the Foreign Office that no authority or instructions had been issued to consuls at grain loading ports to employ "outdoor associates" to see the law was observed, and worse was to come when Plimsoll embarked on a tour of Black Sea ports.[44] Writing from Odessa, Plimsoll complained that all consuls could do was to show masters the act and request compliance. He urged that consular authorities should employ loading surveyors. The Foreign Office referred the matter to the Board of Trade who despatched telegrams to consuls authorising them "to engage some competent person" (at a cost of not more than £2 per ship), to enable them to report whether provisions were being complied with. The Board communicated this to Plimsoll observing that the 1875 Act gave consuls no power to control loading and that the official circular on the Act merely required consuls to report on the stowage of cargo. Plimsoll in the meantime, now at Nicoliaev, had written requesting that board of Trade officials inspect all vessels arriving in British ports but the Board replied that it saw objections to such a procedure. Plimsoll's reply, dated Constantinople 2 December, denounced the Board's instructions to consuls

---

[43]38 & 39 Vict., c 88.

[44]For the correspondence between Plimsoll, the Foreign Office and the Board of Trade see *PP* 1876 (LXVI), 99 *et seq*.

as "miserable, wretched and impotent" and his hatred of Farrar and other Board officials was made clear when he wrote of a "model utterance of ignorance seated in the chair of authority, too proud to consult with men having the requisite knowledge and too tenacious of power to admit any want to ability. It is a feeble attempt to seem to do something which in fact does nothing." He proceeded to say that he had made arrangements to appoint "my own agents at a large number of ports" who would ask consuls to set up a Naval court if shifting boards were thought to be inadequate. At this the Board appears to have climbed down for on 13 December they issued instructions to district officers to inspect any grain laden ship which appeared to be listing or in a distressed condition on arrival in Britain. New detailed instructions were also issued to consuls at grain shipping ports. These instructions made a distinction between ports where vessels were loaded under local regulation or underwriter supervision (that is, Canadian or United States ports) and ports where no regulation prevailed. At the former the duties of consuls were nominal but at the latter consuls were to appoint surveyors and to act in a supervisory capacity. This distinction made within months of the introduction of official regulations was to feature prominently in subsequent legislative intervention. Some justification of this approach emerges from returns by consuls to the Board early in 1876, for consuls at United States ports reported that local underwriters rules were more stringent than the 1875 Act's requirements, while from German and Russian ports there were pleas of the difficulty of appointing "trustworthy surveyors" and the problem of surveying large numbers of vessels at the opening of the shipping season.[45]

The limitations and temporary nature of the 1875 Act ensured renewed consideration of the issue in the following parliamentary session. In February 1876 Plimsoll and others brought in their bill which included provisions banning deck loads and regulating grain cargoes. The latter proposed that one-quarter of the cargo be in sacks of bags which should be stowed on top of the bulk grain. It also stipulated the dimensions and fastenings of shifting boards. But this Bill stood little chance for the government introduced its own new Merchant Shipping Bill.[46] On grain cargoes this merely re-introduced the provision of the 1875 Act and

---

[45]*Ibid*, Abstract of returns from Consuls ...

[46]*PP* (1876), V, 53, 129.

Adderley presenting the bill spoke with some satisfaction of the Board of Trade's instructions to consuls, and the provisions for employing surveyors, submitting reports and inspecting grain ships on arrival in Britain.[47] Plimsoll pressed in his own proposals but they were criticised as being too rigid and not taking account of the variety of stowage practices being operated.[48] In the event the Merchant Shipping Act of 1876 re-stated the provisions of the previous year with only minor modifications raising fines and defining liability.

Expectations that the 1876 Act would reduce casualties in the grain trade were soon proved to be ill-founded. The number of vessels lost in 1877-80 exceeded that of the three previous years and the number of lives lost showed no improvement either.[49] Moreover, the Act proved inoperable. The attempt to appoint surveyors to assist consuls at Black Sea ports was given up in December 1877,[50] and early in the 1880 the Board of Trade came to an agreement with shipowners not to prosecute under the Act where it could be shown that reasonable precautions had been taken.[51] At this negation of duty Plimsoll immediately introduced a bill requiring all grain to be carried in bags, thereby prohibiting bulk storage.[52] Lord Sandon, Adderley's successor at the Board, passed the matter on to a Select Committee,[53] but a political crisis and an election led the Committee to meet but once to recommend a fresh committee in the next parliament. In the meantime the Board of Trade circulated a very detailed question-naire to colonial officials and consuls at seventeen grain loading ports

---

[47]*Parl Debates*, 3rd ser. ccxxvii, 171-2, 10 Feb. 1876.

[48]*Ibid.*, ccxxix, 1582, 24 April 1876. Plimsoll's proposals were criticised for not taking account of the use of iron bulkheads, stowage in layers or bins, or grain stowed with other cargo.

[49]*R.C. on Loss of Life at Sea*, PP (1884-1885), XXXV, 579. Appendix E, compiled from the Wreck Register.

[50]*Parl Debates*, 3rd ser, ccxiviii, 614, 17 July 1879.

[51]*Shipping and Mercantile Gazette*, 17 Jan. 1880, 5.

[52]*PP* (1880), V, 229.

[53]*Select Committee on Recent Founderings of ships laden with grain, coal and other heavy or bulky cargoes*, PP (1880), XI, 545.

enquiring as to practice and regulations, compulsory or voluntary, at their ports. Replies confirmed earlier reports; compliance with official regulations at Canadian ports, observance of underwriters' rules at United States ports, and no regulation of any sort at Black Sea or Baltic ports.[54]

In 1880 the Liberals on their return to power recognised the need for action and introduced a Bill to Amend the Merchant Shipping Act and the regulations on grain cargoes. Simultaneously they set up a new Select Committee to examine the problems of the bulk trades.[55] The Committee's recommendations revealed a certain ambivalence towards further intervention but the outcome was a specific Act to provide for the Safe Carriage of Grain Cargoes, a crucial Act as it established the principles whereby grain cargoes were to be regulated down to 1914.[56] The terms of the Act owed much to Plimsoll's 1876 proposals and drew on the Board of Trade's experience in operating the regulations of 1875/6. The Act laid down detailed instructions for grain cargoes carried in British ships from North America or the Mediterranean insisting that at least one quarter of the cargo be carried in bags and the bulk cargoes should be protected from shifting by a longitudinal bulkhead or well secured shifting boards. Masters were required to submit notices of cargo and stowage details to consuls or customs officials on sailing. However the Act gave the board of Trade the power to exempt from the operation of the specific instructions vessels which had submitted and gained approval of special plans of loading, and vessels which were loaded in accordance with rules approved by the Board. From December 1880 the board issued a series of Official Notices[57] approving the rules of various underwriters associations, sometimes insisting on extra safeguards, and it also commenced scrutinising plans of loading in respect of named vessels; by early 1885 some 400 vessels had been exempted in this manner.[58] By these means the Board limited its obligations to supervise actual loading at many ports and

---

[54]For details of the questionnaire and returns see *PP* (1880), LXV, 269 *et seq.*

[55]*Select Committee on loss of British ships since the Merchant Shipping Act 1873*, *PP* (1880), XI. The Committee concentrated on losses to ships laden with grain.

[56]43 & 44 Vict., c43.

[57]*PP* (1880), LXV, 269; (1881), LXXXII, 179 *et seq.*

[58]*R.C. on Loss of Life at Sea*, *PP* (1884-1885), XXXV, qq 167-173.

avoided the problems and expense of establishing a system of inspection. At most North American ports the Board relied on the local enforcement of official port regulations or approved underwriters' rules. Elsewhere, in the Mediterranean and Black Sea trade only vessels without loading arrangements required on the spot supervision by appointed surveyors. Even so, in all ports masters had to submit details of cargo, and the Board's officials had the power to inspect any vessel on her arrival at a British port.

The Act of 1880 and the Board of Trade's exercise of the discretionary powers granted to it was to be the state's solution to the problem of safeguarding grain laden vessels. In subsequent years the Board issued further Official Orders chiefly giving approval to new underwriters rules and it continued its vetting of vessels' loading plans at the request of shipowners. The terms of the Act were confirmed in the consolidating 1894 Merchant Shipping Amendment Act. The system which evolved in the last twenty years of the century thus represented a compromise between state interference and self-regulation by shipowners and underwriters. This compromise approach was continued in the final pre-war enactment on grain cargoes, the Merchant Shipping Act of 1906.[59] This extended the provisions of the 1880 Act to foreign vessels as well as British vessels, but, as Lloyd George implied on presenting the bill, "the intention was to ensure that foreign vessels observed the spirit rather than the specific details of the regulations. It is not our idea to impose our regulations on foreign ships."[60] Providing foreign vessels took precautions similar to those adopted in British vessels, the government and the Board were satisfied.

In examining the pattern of government regulation of loading in the timber and grain trades, we can see that the outstanding feature is the apparent reluctance of government, and even more so, the Board of Trade, to intervene or to act decisively. Prompt action was taken following the Select Committee of 1839 when perhaps special feelings motivated

---

[59]6 Edw 7, c48.

[60]*Parl Debates*, 4th ser. cliv, 240, 20 March 1906.

ministers and officials,[61] but thereafter the record is one of delay and procrastination. More direct and more timely action in the early 1850s might well have prevented the prohibition on deck loads from falling into disuse, and though fresh regulatory measures were promised after the repeal of 1862 nothing was forthcoming. In the late 1860s and 1870s when there was a flood of evidence on the dangers of bulk cargoes the attitude of the Board of Trade was, to say the least, dilatory. Even after the introduction of regulations in 1875-1876 the spur of Plimsoll's criticism was needed before the Board of Trade made any real attempt to fulfil its new obligations. In some measure it can be argued that official reluctance in the 1870s was the result of the focus of activity in the far greater issue of general maritime safety, and the same might be said of the early 1850s when the important Merchant Shipping Act of 1854 was under consideration. Again at that time the Marine Department was but newly formed and relatively inexperienced. However, the overriding impression is that of an unwillingness on the part of government to involve itself with the special problems of the bulk trades.

There can be no doubt that underlying this reluctance to take action was the widespread adherence to *laissez-faire* ideology. For the greater part of the nineteenth century the prevailing philosophy favoured leaving matters to the free competitive market and opposed on principle the extension of state intervention. A strong commitment to such principles clearly influenced the thinking of many ministers and also the recommendations of investigate committees and commissions. A constant theme was that the shipowner was the only agency which could really do something about safety problems,[62] though as the century progressed there was an increasing tendency to stress the obligations of the shipowner as much as his capability. Significantly the strongest commitment to a *laissez-faire* approach to shipping matters was to be found at the Board of Trade. The views of the Permanent Secretary, Farrar, have already been

---

[61]Throughout the 1830s the Whigs and certain free trade officials at the Board of Trade had engaged in a long struggle with the shipping interests of the British North American timber trade. See Lucy Brown, *The Board of Trade and the Free Trade Movement 1830-42* (1958); A.R.M. Lower, *Great Britain's Woodyard. British America and the Timber Trade, 1763-1867* (Montreal, 1973).

[62]See, for example, the speech of the Chancellor of the Exchequer, *Parl Debates*, 3rd ser, ccxxxi, 238-242, 30 July 1875.

referred to, and Thomas Gray, the Assistant Secretary for the Marine Department, has been described as "personifying the philosophy of administrative *laissez-faire*."[63] An extract from a speech by Gray in 1866 provides the clearest indication of this: "There can be no question that Government interference is not only unnecessary but may really become vicious if it attempts to attain an end by official inspection and supervision that can be better attained by the development of free and healthy competition, and by the self interest and emulation of the trader."[64]

Yet it would be wrong to suggest that ideological reasons alone influenced the attitude of government. There were also more practical considerations. Often the nature and extent of problems were by no means clear. What constituted excessive loading or dangerous stowage practices were debatable issues disputed between shipowners, and the proportion of losses attributable to timber deck loads and shifting grain cargoes could not be ascertained. More particularly, the problems of framing appropriate regulations (brought home by the experience with deck loads in the 1850s), and securing effective administration and enforcement, all counselled a cautious approach. Chief among such considerations was that shipping was an international business; hence regulation to be effective had to apply not simply to activity at British ports but also at ports overseas. This was especially so where import trades were the object of control, for action against vessels on arrival at British ports was a negative approach, serving to punish breakers of the law rather than to ensure observance, and did nothing for seamen lost on improperly stowed vessels which never reached British shores. Moreover proceedings against vessels on arrival proved a limited deterrent as Courts were often reluctant to penalise masters who had successfully and safely completed voyages.[65] The need for action at overseas ports, and the obvious difficulties of enforcement that this would involve, hardly encouraged an enthusiastic approach to intervention. Most difficult of all was the problem that any regulations imposed on British shipping would damage its competitive

---

[63]Alderman, "Plimsoll and the Shipping Interest," 78.

[64]*Journal of the Society of Arts*, XIV (1863-6), 239.

[65]*R.C. on Unseaworthy Ships*, *PP* (1873), XXXVI, q 238; *Parl Debates*, 3rd ser, ccxxvi, 245, 250, 30 July 1875.

position.[66] Henry Fry, a Canadian authority on shipping summarised the dilemma, "At bottom the trouble is that, if any nation from motives, religious, moral or philanthropic, puts restrictions upon the way in which her own traders and manufacturers may carry on their work, then other nations that care for no such motives, but only for the pursuit of gain by the shortest road to it, will have a tremendous advantage."[67] The solution according to Fry was to pass laws applying to foreign vessels as well as British, or to impose differential duties on goods carried in foreign vessels or to negotiate with foreign nations to gain agreement. None of these alternatives held any appeal to government; the dream of internationally agreed regulations could be dismissed as totally unrealistic in the 1870s,[68] and the prospects of unilaterally trying to impose regulations on foreign vessels or introducing differential duties reminiscent of the Navigation Laws were not ones which those in authority wished to consider.[69]

The reluctance of government to take action led to the initiative for regulation coming from elsewhere. In the crucial period of the 1870s, pressure and proposals for regulation came from Plimsoll's addition to the issue of the bulk trades to his general campaign for safeguarding merchant shipping. Ultimately action was forced upon the government, and forced upon it in difficult circumstances. The important initial regulations in the grain trade in 1875 and the re-introduction of controls on deck loads in 1876 were both the result of amendments to government bills and were hurried and less than satisfactory measures. Thus the Board of Trade which had been unwilling to accept responsibility for regulating loading in the bulk trades found itself required to operate regulations introduced

---

[66]It is significant that regulation, in the form of the prohibition on winter voyage deck loads, was most effective and least objected to between 1839 and 1849 when the Navigation Laws protected British shipowners from foreign competition.

[67]From an article in the *Montreal Gazette* enclosed in *Papers and Correspondence with the Government of Canada*, *PP* (1876), LXVI, 295.

[68]Almost forty years later in 1916 an official committee considering deck cargoes was to be found expressing the hope that "every endeavour should be made to get international agreement." *Report of the Committee to advise on the load line*, *PP* (1916), XII, 623.

[69]*PP* (1876), LXVI, 295. See Farrar's comments on Fry's article criticising his suggestions as "fraught with mischief."

with insufficient forethought. The Board faced difficulties both in the wording of the law and in its capacity for inspection and enforcement. While the terms of the clauses on timber deck loading were clear enough, the regulations on grain loading of 1875-1876 were vague and needed supplementing with Official Notices until the 1880 Act laid down more specific requirements. Securing the observance of regulations posed even greater problems. The Board's approach was to try and ensure checks at both ports of loading and arrival. At ports in Britain timber and grain carrying vessels were inspected on arrival by Customs of Board officials. At overseas ports of loading British masters had to provide details of cargo for Customs or Consular officials but in the matter of inspection and supervision of loading the Board's coverage was less complete. Wherever possible the board relied on other agencies to ensure satisfactory loading, notably on the offices of Port Wardens and underwriters' agents for timber and grain cargoes from North America. For Mediterranean and Black Sea grain cargoes the Board, afer some early difficulties, appointed its own surveyors, but limited the need for actual supervision through its system of approving vessels loading plans. The latter provided some coverage of Baltic grain cargoes but generally the Board relied on its checks on arrival in the case of timber and grain cargoes from the Baltic which employed only limited numbers of British vessels. By these means a measure of supervision of loading was accomplished. Overall the Board's response to the duties thrust upon it was to endeavour to gain observance of regulations with the minimum of direct interference. The Board tried to limit its own involvement and expenditure and to rely on the good sense of shipowners and underwriters. Only when self regulation was not forthcoming did the Board directly interfere, and only when blatant disregard of the law took place did the Board institute proceedings to invoke the penalties provided by the law.

It remains to consider whether the regulations introduced from the mid-1870s achieved their desired intent of reducing maritime casualty and loss of life. Only a statistical series of losses due to deck loads or shifting grain cargoes together with data of the volume of shipping engaged in each trade would provide a definite answer to this question. Regrettably such statistics are not available. Certain annual figures of casualty and loss by trade (though not always comparable over time) can be obtained from the *Wreck Abstracts* but they do not distinguish between the causes of loss. Nor can scrutiny of Board of Trade inquiries provide an answer for in the case of vessels missing (increasingly a major contributor to live lost) the cause of disaster remained a matter for sad speculation. The impression gained from the available statistics, some of which appear as an appendix, is that of no real fall in the level of casualty in the decade or so after the mid-1870s when intervention commenced; indeed, there were some years of exceptionally heavy losses, notably 1877 in the grain trade and 1882 in both trades. However, over the longer period down to 1910 there was an encouraging diminution of losses. It seems reasonable to suppose that an element of this improvement came from the operation of government regulations on loading in the bulk trades, but the precise contribution of such regulation cannot be distinguished from that of other factors which served to bring about the reduction in losses in the timber and grain trades and in overall maritime casualty. General government legislation on unseaworthy ships and load lines, advances in marine technology, growing experience and better trained officers all helped to reduce losses of timber and grain laden vessels probably as much, if not more so, than the specific regulation on loading.

The lack of any precise quantitative assessment of the impact of bulk trade regulations on safety levels should not be allowed to obscure the significance of such intervention. The regulations on timber and grain cargoes involved the shipping of two of Britain's chief import trades. They reflected the need for specific as well as general intervention in pursuit of maritime safety, and the pattern of development of controls on deck loads and grain cargoes mirrored the attitudes, pressures and responses of the wider debate on the intervention of government in the field of merchant shipping in the nineteenth century. It is something of a tribute to Britain's bulk trade regulations that, at the Washington International Marine Conference in 1890, a Committee set up to consider the establishment of a permanent International Maritime Commission observed, "some controls similar to the Merchant Shipping Act 1876 and the Merchant Shipping (Carriage of Grain) Act 1880 ought to be international."[70] Forty years were to elapse, however, before there was some international agreement on timber deck cargoes, and it was not until after the Second World War

---

[70]*International Marine Conference (Washington)*, *PP* (1890), LXXXII, Summary of Protocols.

that the shipping of grain became the subject of international maritime regulation.[71]

---

[71]Following the second and third International Conventions for the Safety of Life at Sea of 1929 and 1948.

APPENDIX

Table 1

Lives lost due to sea casualty* in Timber and Grain-laden ships belonging to the United Kingdom and British possessions abroad, all voyages** 1875-1884 (years ending 30 June)

	TIMBER	GRAIN
1875	133	307
1876	172	232
1877	140	551
1878	70	308
1879	126	412
1880	89	352
1881	198	277
1882	294	563
1883	80	299
1884	216	175

*   All forms of sea casualty except collisions.
**   All voyages to and from British ports and between foreign or colonial ports.

Source: *Royal Commission on Loss of Life at Sea, PP* 1884-1885, XXXV, 574, Appendix C.

Table 2A

Losses* of United Kingdom registered vessels carrying timber
and grain 1885-1910 (years ending 30 June)

| | TIMBER | | | | | | GRAIN | | | | | |
| | Sail | | Steam | | Total | | Sail | | Steam | | Total | |
	Vsls	Tons	Vsls	Tons	Vsls	Tons	Vsls	Tons	Vsls	Tons	Vsls	Tons
1885	28	10,592	2	942	30	11,534	16	8,010	19	20,193	35	28,203
86	14	5,614	2	1,933	16	10,547	19	8,588	9	7,026	28	15,614
87	28	17,870	2	2,008	30	19,878	24	11,179	10	8,874	34	20,053
88	17	17,610	4	3,051	31	15,661	16	9,903	16	15,362	32	25,265
89	16	11,498	6	4,621	22	16,119	11	5,967	16	15,312	27	21,279
90		3,172	4	1,874	15	10,046	8	3,248	11	12,384	19	15,632
91	12	7,079	9	8,854	21	15,933	16	7,854	9	7,285	25	15,139
92	14	10,727	8	6,726	22	17,453	11	3,545	9	10,451	20	13,996
93	11	6,944	4	2,468	15	9,412	14	13,226	10	9,491	24	22,717
94	11	4,686	4	2,063	15	6,749	14	5,518	21	21,953	35	27,471
95	12	7,358	5	4,296	17	11,654	12	4,562	6	5,476	18	10,038
96	8	1,012	6	7,407	14	11,419	12	9,355	11	15,783	23	25,138
97	10	5,493	2	2,004	12	10,497	8	3,319	12	18,347	20	21,666
98	3	1,767	6	7,337	9	9,104	8	555	13	14,986	18	15,541
99	5	718	5	6,445	10	7,163	10	3,827	13	16,397	23	20,224
1900	8	3,603	9	12,255	17	15,858	2	115	2	4,070	4	4,185
01	3	1,917	2	2,549	5	4,466	10	7,285	4	6,181	14	13,472
02	5	621	·	·	5	621	5	3,140	3	3,407	8	6,547
03	6	2,716	4	3,968	10	6,144	8	5,959	6	5,182	14	11,141
04	5	1,009	1	1,002	6	2,011	4	3,769	5	9,478	9	13,247
05	4	2,064	6	9,109	10	11,173	6	8,071	10	19,122	16	27,193
06	5	3,359	2	2,898	9	11,566	4	1,868	5	9,698	9	11,566
07	4	1,446	4	7,591	8	9,037	4	4,086	3	5,415	7	9,501
08	3	167	3	5,687	6	5,854	3	2,196	3	4,817	6	7,013
09	1	760	1	1,061	2	1,821	2	2,124	4	9,776	6	11,900
10	1	270	3	4,568	4	4,838	2	1,831	3	5,599	5	7,430

* Covers vessels totally lost only, on all voyages to and from British ports and between foreign or colonial ports.

Source: *Abstracts of Shipping Casualties* ... published annually, *PP*, 1887-1911.

Table 2B

Lives lost by sea casualties* to United Kingdom registered vessels
carrying timber and grain 1885-1910 (years ending 30 June)

	TIMBER			GRAIN		
	Sail	**Steam**	**Total**	**Sail**	**Steam**	**Total**
1885	47	8	55	77	128	205
86	41	-	41	113	5	118
87	78	-	78	102	91	193
88	47	20	67	50	117	167
89	7	1	8	67	53	120
90	46	4	50	37	44	81
91	17	32	49	66	27	93
92	33	-	33	31	75	106
93	33	1	34	101	54	155
94	28	-	28	30	122	152
95	33	3	36	48	3	51
96	36	2	38	50	68	118
97	34	8	42	8	119	127
98	3	-	3	8	76	84
99	10	26	36	41	104	145
1900	16	94	110	4	25	29
1	1	2	3	23	-	23
2	5	-	5	-	33	33
3	7	35	42	7	16	23
4	-	-	-	29	20	49
5	-	50	50	48	38	86
6	4	-	4	30	1	31
7	-	3	3	6	35	41
8	3	4	7	20	26	46
9	-	2	2	21	40	61
10	1	3	4	11	4	15

* Covers all forms of sea casualty on all voyages to and from British ports and
between foreign or colonial ports.

Source: *Abstracts of Shipping Casualties* ... published annually, *PP*, 1887-1911.

Customs Evasion, Colonial Preference and the British Tariff, 1829-1842[1]

Colonial preference occupied an important position in the British tariff of the first half of the nineteenth century. Over fifty classes of goods involved preferential duties, including many of the leading commodities of Britain's import trade and the vast majority of foodstuffs and raw materials on which duties were levied.[2] Colonial preference was also closely associated with the revenue, for, in the late 1830s, seven of the eight principal revenue-earning duties involved varying rates favouring colonial products.[3] For such reasons colonial preference was of crucial importance in the controversy over free trade and it became a major issue in the battle over tariff policy in the post-Napoleonic period.[4] In their opposition to colonial preference free-traders were attacking the general principle of differential duties. Attention, however, was focussed on the duties on only a few commodities, namely timber, sugar and coffee. This concentration arose partly from the fact that these commodities were important items of trade and also because they were in some measure representative of classes of imports and hence served almost as test cases; for example, the sugar and coffee duties involved the issue of preferences for the entire range of West Indian produce and tropical foodstuffs

---

[1]I should like to thank R.B. Outhwaite and P.L. Cottrell who kindly read through early drafts of this paper. I also gratefully acknowledge the receipt of grants from the Research Board of the University of Leicester.

[2]Based upon a survey of a statement of the British tariff drawn up by James Deacon Hume (Joint Secretary to the Board of Trade, 1828-40) which appears in J.R. McCulloch, *A Dictionary, Practical, Theoretical, and Historical, of Commerce and Commercial Navigation* (2nd edn, 1834), 1113-1135.

[3]*Select Committee on Import Duties*, PP 1840, V, Appendix I.

[4]Particularly after 1826 when Huskisson's relaxation of the century-old prohibition on imports of manufactured silks effectively overthrew the principle of protection for British industry.

generally, while the timber duties were symbolic of the high duties imposed on many raw materials. More especially the duties on timber, sugar and coffee directly concerned the influential shipowning and West Indian interests who possessed sufficient political power to offer serious resistance to any attempt to modify their favoured position. In the vast literature on Britain's relationship with her colonies in the first half of the nineteenth century much has been written on the changing flow of trade, new attitudes towards the colonies, the breakdown of the old colonial system and colonial preference issues within the free trade struggle. Yet in all these studies little consideration has been given to the subject of customs evasion which led to some strange distortions of normal trading patterns and which occupied a significant place in the dispute over colonial preference in the period.

A general feature of all systems of preferential duties is that compared with a single uniform duty they open up the possibility of customs evasion. The very fact that different rates of duty are charged on identical commodities purely on the basis of their country of origin or port of clearance is a real encouragement to deceit for some, particularly if the wording of customs regulations contains the slightest element of ambiguity. Furthermore, the special function of a preferential duty, that of favouring one source of supply as opposed to another, makes it more susceptible to movements in the market forces than a simple uniform duty which is serving straightforward revenue and protection functions. The intensity with which a fixed non-ad valorem duty falls on a commodity fluctuates with changes in the market. The degree to which a duty weights on a commodity goes up or down as the price of the commodity falls or rises. Both uniform duties and preferential duties are affected in this way by market movements but in the case of preferential duties changes in supply and demand schedules have the additional effect of altering the extent of the differential between the preferred commodity and that which is not favoured. Hence, a general fall in the price of a commodity tends to enlarge the extent of the preference and vice versa. Even greater distortions in the preference occur if movements are not uniform throughout the market and the position of one source of supply changes relative to that of other sources. If, for example, in a country receiving a preference, supply schedules contract and force costs and prices up while elsewhere costs fall or remain constant, the extent of the preference is effectively diminished, and the reverse would occur were the favoured country to gain some new economies in supply. Thus, while at the time of imposition the scaling of duties may be such as to prohibit any likelihood of customs evasion, over a period of time movements in the market may seriously distort the preference and create circumstances where evasion is a feasible proposition. Such a situation developed in the timber and coffee duties between 1829 and 1842 and combined with the imprecise nature of customs regulations to permit two spectacular cases of customs evasion to occur. In both trades evasion took the form of importing foreign produce via a colonial possession to avoid payment of duties. In the timber trade this involved taking Baltic timber across the Atlantic to British North America and then shipping it back to Britain; in the coffee trade, coffee, particularly from South America, was dispatched to the Cape of Good Hope and then re-shipped to Britain. This paper examines the extent and character of these two strange forms of trade and considers the significance of customs evasion in the struggle over colonial preference.

Between 1809 and 1860 the importation of timber into Britain was governed by a system of preferential duties introduced during the Napoleonic war to safeguard timber supplies by encouraging the expansion of the North American colonial timber trade. Following the report of a Select Committee on Foreign Trade in 1821[5] the duties were reorganized and the duty on foreign timber was reduced from 65s. to 55s. per load and colonial timber, previously virtually duty-free, became liable to a duty of 10s. per load.[6] However, these changes, while reducing the differential, still left colonial timber with a preference of 45s. per load. European timber nevertheless continued to be used in the British market because of its reputedly better quality and finish but demand for it was checked by the high duty.[7] In such circumstances any form of customs evasion which reduced the heavy burden of duty imposed on Baltic timber was bound to appear an attractive proposition.

---

[5]On the early years of the timber duties see R.G. Albion, *Forests and Sea Power, the Timber Problem of the Royal Navy 1652-1862* (Cambridge, Mass., 1926).

[6]1 & 2 Geo. IV, c. 37, 84. The duties quoted in the text refer to hewn timber. Similar preferences applied to deals (sawn timber).

[7]Between 1814 and 1833 imports of European timber, while declining rapidly as a proportion of total imports of timber, remained roughly constant in absolute terms at around 120,000 loads per annum. See *SC on the Timber Duties*, PP 1835, XIX, QQ. 11-13.

The importing of European timber via North America, or as it was termed, "taking timber by the round,"[8] in order to take advantage of the lower rate of duty levied on colonial timber provided one such opportunity, but the prosecution of the venture depended first, on its legality, and second, on the additional costs involved. Strangely enough, as a result of a series of amendments to customs regulations in the late 1820s, the practice of importing Baltic timber via the North American colonies – which had been impossible under the terms of the 1821 Act – became legally possible in 1829. The 1821 Act had stated that the preferred duty rates were to be charged only upon timber, which was "the growth of the colonies" and this definition was retained when the laws of customs were consolidated in 1825.[9] However, because some of the timber exported from the colonies was procured from the border areas of Canada and the United States and thus might well be of foreign growth, amendments were made in the regulations in 1826 and 1827 stating that such timber "be deemed on importation into the United Kingdom, the produce of some British possession."[10] A further amendment in 1829 extended this provision and introduced such an element of vagueness into the regulations that the "importing of timber by the round" became permissible.[11] This in itself was not sufficient to give rise to the practice which was obviously only feasible commercially if the total costs of importing European timber via North America at the lower rate of duty were less than the costs of direct importation from the Baltic with the normal duty payments. In other words, if the indirect trade was to be profitable, the additional costs of importing one load of Baltic timber via North America had to be well under the preference of 45s. per load. For most of the 1820s freights were too high to allow any profit to be made on a circuitous voyage. Freights were rising until 1825 but thereafter they slumped. Quebec-London freights, which in mid-1825 stood at 63s. per load, had fallen to 40s. by 1830 and freights for Halifax and Pictou followed a similar trend. Baltic freights also fell heavily; Danzig freights were as high as 34s. in 1825 but

---

[8]*Ibid.*, Q. 1001.

[9]6 Geo. IV, c111.

[10]7 Geo. IV, c. 48; 7 & 8 Geo. IV, c. 56.

[11]10 Geo. IV, c. 43.

were down to 20s. in 1831, while the rate from Memel touched 34s. in 1825 but was around 21s. in 1820.[12] Thus by the end of the 1820s North American and Baltic freights were at a low level and still falling. In part this fall reflected the secular trend of freights throughout the world which was downward in the second quarter of the nineteenth century,[13] but it was also due to excess capacity and fierce competition in both the Baltic and colonial timber trades.[14] The effect of the fall in freights on the timber trade and on the relative duties borne by colonial and foreign timber was, as John Deacon Hume observed, "such that the amount of protection intended to be the difference between a near trade and a distant one was in fact overstated."[15] However, while the fall in freights exaggerated the preference in favour of colonial timber it also opened up the possibility of the circuitous route. At the level of freights prevailing in 1829-1830, the additional costs of an indirect voyage could all be covered and still leave a saving compared with a direct Baltic voyage.

The first indirect voyages occurred in 1829 when at least two vessels from Memel sailed across the Atlantic to Halifax and returned to land their cargoes at Irish ports.[16] In the following six years an increasing number of vessels undertook the roundabout trip. Parliamentary returns list five occurrences of indirect voyages before January 1831 and a further

---

[12]For information on colonial and Baltic freights in the 1820s, see SC *on the Timber Duties*, PP 1835, XIX, QQ. 3782; 5107-5108.

[13]D.C. North, "Ocean freight rates and economic development 1750-1913," *Journal of Economic History*, XVIII (1958), 541-542.

[14]In the Baltic trade, foreign competitors, apparently working on lower cost schedules than British shipping, were forcing down rates. In the North American timber trade, traditionally the last refugee of old vessels, there was fierce competition as the trade was flooded by old East and West Indiamen, unemployed ex-wartime transports and a vast number of cheaply built colonial vessels hastily constructed in the short-lived shipping boom of 1825. See SC *on the Timber Duties*, 1835, XIX, QQ. 1329-1341; 1780; 2832-2842; 3955-3970.

[15]*Ibid*. Q. 136.

[16]*Hansard*, n.s., xxiv, 14 (8 April 1830).

five in 1831 and 1832.[17] It would appear that up to this time merchants still regarded the practice as somewhat irregular[18] but when the government, which as early at 1830 had promised legislation to forbid the trade,[19] took no action, more merchants began to engage in the indirect trade. The incentive to do so increased as freights continued to fall making the practice more remunerative. Quebec freights between 1832 and 1835 ranged from 37s. to 41s. per load, and for the lower ports of New Brunswick, rates stood at 33s. to 35s. Baltic freights showed similar falls: the Danzig rate stood at 17s. to 18s. in 1834-1835[20] and Memel freights as low as 16s. were reported in 1833.[21] In 1833 over twenty vessels shipped timber via the roundabout route and in 1834 over a dozen vessels undertook circuitous voyages.[22] In 1835, despite uncertainty regarding imminent government action, a large number of vessels were chartered for the round trip, and at least nine were chartered to take cargoes from Russia via Halifax to London alone, although in the end all these came direct in the normal manner.[23]

While the official statistics show clearly that the practice was by no means confined to isolated cases, there is reason to believe that the figures underestimate the extent of the roundabout trade. As early as 1831 a writer described the practice as "notorious"[24] and although the official

---

[17]*Quantity and Description of Timber shipped from Europe to America, and thence imported into the United Kingdom*, PP 1830-1831, X, 473.

[18]*SC on the Timber Duties*, PP 1835, XIX, Q. 1009.

[19]J. Potter "The British Timber Duties, 1815-60," *Economica*, n.s., xxiii (1955), 131.

[20]On freights in the 1830s see *SC on the Timber Duties*, PP 1835, XIX, QQ. 3782; 3886-3890; 5107-5108.

[21]*The Times*, 21 March 1833.

[22]*Quantity of timber shipped from North of Europe to North America, and thence to Ports in the United Kingdom*, PP 1834, XLIX, 691; 1835, XLVIII, 585.

[23]*SC on the Timber Duties*, PP 1835, XIX , QQ. 397; 1016-1019.

[24]Sir A. Malet, *The Canadas* (1831), 12-13.

returns list only two cargoes of Norwegian timber as having been shipped by the round it is likely that numbers were considerably higher.[25] Moreover, the returns refer only to vessels carrying Baltic timber and make no mention of another variation of the indirect trade: that of vessels laden with timber of United States' growth sailing up to a British North American port to gain a certificate of colonial origin. Such cargoes were shipped to London via Halifax,[26] and valuable pitch pine from Charleston was imported into Liverpool in a similar fashion.[27] Furthermore, the published figures list no cases of cargoes of timber brought direct from the Baltic to Britain, placed in bond, and subsequently re-exported to the colonies from whence they were finally imported at the colonial duty.[28] While the true extent of the practice can never be determined, it is certain that it was more widespread than the official returns suggest.

The practice of importing timber by the indirect route was examined by the Select Committee on the Timber Duties of 1835, and the Committee's minutes of evidence give a detailed picture of the operation and its costs.[29] The procedure followed was described by Robert Carter, a partner in the ship-brokerage firm of Carter & Bonus: "She, a vessel, had to load her cargo at Danzig or Memel, and carry it to Halifax or some other port in the North American colonies, and there land it; then take it

---

[25]It is not unreasonable to suspect that Norwegian sawn timber, which was more severely burdened by the duties on deals than any other variety of European timber, would have been shipped across the Atlantic in some quantity.

[26]*SC on the Timber Duties,* PP 1835, XIX, QQ. 305-306.

[27]*Ibid.,* QQ. 2775-2778. The importing of United States timber as colonial produce was, of course, nothing new since vast quantities of timber cut on United States soil had been carried over the frontier to be exported from colonial ports for years, but this had been regarded as inevitable and was in no way such an obvious flaunting of customs regulations as the indirect shipping method. See *SC on Foreign Trade,* PP 1821, VI, 11; 41.

[28]This certainly occurred; a correspondent to *The Times,* 21 August 1833 recounted an instance of such a procedure involving a cargo of 19,000 Baltic staves being re-exported to Quebec and then re-imported with a resultant duty saving of £586.

[29]Numerous witnesses before the Committee provided information on the costs and profitability of the indirect trade. See *SC on the Timber Duties,* PP 1835, XIX, QQ. 193-195; 1000-1007; 3894-3898; 3905-3931; 4825-4829.

on board again, and bring it to a port in the United Kingdom."[30] The costs involved therefore were those of the freight for the roundabout voyage plus the handling costs of unloading and reloading at a colonial port. The freight charges for the round voyage, according to a number of witnesses, were 55-7s. per load inclusive of handling costs. Additional insurance charges were about 1s. per load. The total costs of importing timber by the round, therefore, discounting loading charges in the Baltic and unloading charges at a British port which would be the same whether the vessel came by the direct or indirect route, were approximately 55s. freight, 1s. insurance plus the colonial duty of 10s., equalling in all 66s. per load. If the timber had been brought direct, say from Danzig, the freight would have been 18s., insurance 3d. and duty 55s., making a total of 73s. 3d. per load. Robert Carter calculated the difference between the indirect and direct route at 6s. 9d. per load, and John Astle, a Dublin merchant who claimed to have pioneered the round voyage, said he gained about 7s. per load. Other witnesses also agreed on this figure, but there were a few claims of higher profits.[31] In general it would seem that the saving was around 7s. per load: however, this saving was never assured, for there was always the danger of timber being lost or damaged through the additional loading and unloading.[32] While there can be no doubt that the circuitous voyage produced a profit, it is difficult to decide whether or not the practice resulted in a maximization of profits. Contemporaries realized that the longer duration of the round voyage tied up capital and meant a loss of interest which had to be discounted, but no-one enquired if the profit made on one indirect voyage was greater than the combined profits which could have been made on two direct Baltic trips in the same period. If, as so many Baltic merchants pleaded, there was scant profit in the regular European trade, the indirect route must have appeared highly attractive. Certainly the indirect trade provided a welcome relief to some shipowners with vessels in the Baltic trade who were feeling the pinch of

---

[30]*Ibid.*, Q. 3894. More detailed information on the ports involved in the indirect trade can be gained from the official returns cited earlier; PP 1830-1831, X, 473; 1834, XLIX, 691; 1835, XLVIII, 585.

[31]Notably by Henry Warburton who suggested a figure of 13s. per load. See *Hansard*, n.s., xxiv, 14-15 (8 April 1830).

[32]*SC on the Timber Duties*, PP 1835, XIX, Q. 4828.

foreign competition,[33] for the roundabout route offered easier employment since the Navigation Laws restricted the practice to British vessels.[34] Merchants and shipowners engaged in trade with the Baltic were not the only operators to participate in the indirect trade. Dealers in colonial timber with long-established contacts in Halifax and other colonial ports saw an opportunity of making an easy profit[35] and even a number of Canadian merchants took part in the trade and actively encouraged Baltic timber to cross the Atlantic.[36] Other, more far-sighted colonists, however, recognized that the practice exposed and jeopardized their preferential position and protested strongly, urging the government take speedy action.[37]

Though merchants and shipowners who took part in the indirect importation of timber found the venture profitable, it is doubtful whether consumers gained any benefit. As the great bulk of European timber was imported over the regular route, indirect importation is unlikely to have had much influence on prices.[38] Moreover, it may be assumed that operators practising the evasion were interested chiefly in enhancing their profit margins rather than in reducing prices. Even so, on a local scale, in small ports handling only a few European timber cargoes annually, the arrival of one or two vessels by the indirect route could alter the market and institute a fall in prices, and there are examples of such developments

---

[33]*Ibid.*, Q. 3905.

[34]*Ibid.*, QQ. 10000; 1020. Indeed, the view was actually expressed that the indirect trade was beneficial to British shipping. See *SC on Manufactures, Commerce and Shhipping*, PP 1833, VI, Q. 3628.

[35]*SC on the Timber Duties*, PP 1835, XIX, Q. 1780.

[36]"Reciprocity and Preference in Canada," *The Economist*, 18 March 1911, quoted in E. Porritt, *The Fiscal and Diplomatic Freedom of the British Overseas Dominions* (1922), 25.

[37]*Montreal Gazette*, 12 September 1833, quoted in H.A. Innis and A.R.M. Lower, *Select Documents in Canadian Economic History 1783-1855* (Toronto, 1933), 332.

[38]Whatever the actual number of cargoes shipped via the indirect route it is unlikely that they represented more than a small proportion of total imports of European timber which amounted to over a 1000 cargoes per annum in the late 1830s. See *Return of the number of Timber Laden ships*, PP 1846, XLV, 403.

occurring in Irish ports.[39] At a national level, however, the indirect trade can have had but a marginal effect on timber prices which showed no definite trend, upward or downward, during the period 1829-1835.[40]

Of all the strange features of the roundabout trade one of the most surprising is that it was allowed to continue for so long. The practice commenced in 1829 but it was not until 1835 that action was taken to prohibit it, despite the fact that the government was aware of the indirect trade from its very outset[41] and that the trade became the subject of Commons questions as early as April 1830.[42] The long delay in government intervention is best understood if one examines the position of the Tory and Whig governments of the period. The Tory government which was in office in 1829-1830 took no action on the indirect trade as it doubted whether the practice was commercially feasible, an understandable view given that only a few vessels had undertaken the roundabout voyage at that time. The position of the Whigs who held power almost continuously between 1830 and 1835 was somewhat more complex. Influenced as they were by Parnellite ideas on finance, the Whigs assumed office with plans for tariff reform, and their first budget in 1831 included proposals for reducing the preference given to colonial timber from 45s. to 30s. per load, a move which would have ended the practice of indirect importation. Opposition to the budget, particularly over the issue of the timber duties, was fierce, however, and although Althorp, the Chancellor, made concessions, the budget was rejected and the government defeated

---

[39]*SC on the Timber Duties*, PP 1835, XIX, QQ. 4923-5016, the evidence of Alexander Deane of Cork. Similar developments probably occurred in the small English ports of Gloucester, St. Ives and Padstow which all received cargoes imported via the indirect route.

[40]*Ibid.*, Appendix 11, 415-417.

[41]*Ibid.*, Q. 3904. In fact the practice was brought to the attention of the government before it had actually commenced, for the merchants who conceived of the evasion consulted the Board of Trade as to the precise wording of customs regulations before embarking on the venture.

[42]*Hansard*, n.s., xxiv, 14-15 (8 April 1830).

thus permitting the continuation of the indirect trade.[43] The situation which evolved after 1831 was that the Whigs refrained from taking specific action on the indirect trade as they still hoped to proceed with their programme of changes in the timber duties.[44] In fact, some of the more avid free-traders amongst the Whigs saw the evasion as an opportunity to introduce a reduction in the timber preference. However, the budget defeat of 1831 had shown the strength of colonial and shipowning opposition and the Whigs therefore proceeded cautiously, choosing to ignore the direct trade while they waited for an opportune moment to resume their attack on the preference. Thus, when in 1832 the indirect trade was raised in Commons questions, Poulett Thomson, the Vice-President of the Board of Trade, merely replied that, "it was not the intention of the government to interfere at present," and the government persisted in this attitude for the next two years whenever the issue was raised.[45] During Peel's brief first ministry action was at last taken. In march 1835 a bill was drawn up "to provide for the better collection of the duties on wood the produce of places in Europe," and given its first reading early in April,[46] but two days later Peel's government fell. On their return to office, the Whigs, still anxious to modify the preference, chose not to proceed immediately with the bill and instead referred it to a Select Committee on the Timber Duties which they appointed in June 1835. After due deliberation the Committee reported and recommended a reduction of 15s. in the duty on foreign timber, but such was the political situation that the Whigs took no action

---

[43]On the budget of 1831 and the issue of the timber duties in the 1830s, see Lucy Brown, *The Board of Trade and the Free-Trade Movement 1830-42* (1958), 5-50; A.R.M. Lower, *Great Britain's Woodyard. British America and the Timber Trade, 1763-1867* (Montreal, 1973).

[44]Strangely, and perhaps on purpose, when the Acts relating to the timber duties were repealed and consolidated in 1833 (3 & 4 Will. IV, c. 50 and 56) the Whigs did not avail themselves of the opportunity to close the loophole permitting the indirect trade. This omission, to say the least, was viewed with suspicion by colonial timber trade interests. See *Report from the Select Committee on the Timber Duties (NOT Ordered by the House of Commons to be printed)* (1836), 45-47. This item was a cleverly-written pamphlet satirically attacking the proceedings and findings of the 1835 Committee.

[45]*Hansard*, 3rd ser., x, 1232 (7 March 1832); xxiv, 394 (12 June 1834).

[46]On the bill and its progress see *Hansard,* 3rd ser., xxvii, 213-218 (24 March 1835); PP 1835, IV, 526-9; *House of Commons Journals,* xc (1835), 201 (6 April 1835).

on the preference. The bill designed to prohibit evasion was, however, proceeded with and the resulting Act[47] made it clear that the duties scheduled as payable on foreign timber were to be paid even though it was imported from British possessions in North America, thus putting an end to the indirect trade.

Within three years of the ending of the indirect trade in timber there occurred another spectacular case of customs evasion which again embodied the importing of foreign via a colonial possession. This new indirect trade which took place between 1838 and 1842 involved coffee and, as in the case of timber, it arose because of the nature and wording of customs regulations and changes in supply and demand schedules which distorted the differentials contained in the duty system. The duties on coffee which prevailed in the early nineteenth century embodied a long-standing preference for West Indian coffee.[48] This preference was maintained when the duties were revised in 1819[49] and in 1825-1826 when the duties were halved and amendments made in the duties levied on coffee imported from the East Indies. The new duty schedule incorporated four different rates of duty: on West Indian colonial coffee, 56s. per cwt; on coffee imported from Sierra Leone or from any British possession within the limits of the East Indian Company's charter, 84s. from any other place within the limits of the charter, 112s.; and all other coffee, 140s. per cwt.[50]

Despite the event of the West Indian preference which was such as to totally exclude all other coffees, the duty system aroused no great controversy before 1830. Free-traders naturally regarded the duties unfavourably and the preference was jealously denounced by East Indian

---

[47]5 & 6 Will. IV, c. 40.

[48]For an account of the origins of the West India preference which dated from 1732 see B. Moseley, *A Treatise on Coffee* (2nd edn, 1785), xiii-xviii.

[49]No specific study of the coffee duties has yet been undertaken but much information on the duties is contained in L.J. Ragatz, *The Fall of the Planter Class in the British Caribbean, 1763-1833* (New York, 1928; reprinted 1963).

[50]6 Geo. IV, c. 13; 6 Geo. IV, c. 104; 7 Geo. IV, c.48.

interests, but generally opposition was slight.[51] The British demand for coffee fell short of the West Indian supply, so the exclusion of other coffees was of no major significance. In the early 1830s, however, the position changed when the West Indies' ability to supply the British market diminished, partly because of a growing demand in Britain[52] but principally because West Indian production of coffee began to decline, the immediate cause being the abolition of slavery in 1834.[53] Falling West Indian exports of coffee caused a deficiency of supply in Britain which resulted in rising prices. Between 1830 and 1834 the price of British plantation coffee doubled, reversing the downward trend of the late 1820s.[54] This situation, which was common to all West Indian commodities including the chief export, sugar, gave rise to mounting pressure in Britain for government action to relieve the position by relaxing the West Indian monopoly. The government, however, felt that some consideration should be given to the problems of West Indian planters and it therefore rejected appeals to modify the duties on the principal article of discussion,

---

[51]For examples of East India interests' opposition to the West India preference see *Report of a Committee of the Liverpool East India Association appointed to take into Consideration the Restrictions on the East India Trade* (1822); Z. Macauley, *East and West India Sugar; or a refutation of the claims of the West India colonists* (1823).

[52]The demand for coffee in Britain grew rapidly in the 1820s. The main factor was falling prices, as a result of the reductions in duty of 1825-1826, but the growth of working-class coffee houses and temperance society publicity promoting coffee was also important.

[53]The decay of West Indian plantation agriculture had, of course, far deeper roots. See Ragatz, *op. cit.* Statistical series showing the decline of West Indian production after emancipation are contained in Gisela Eisner, *Jamaica 1830-1930. A Study in Economic Growth* (1961).

[54]Prices of West Indian coffee in the late 1820s and early 1830s were as follows: *Prices per cwt of superior British plantation coffee in bond in the first quarter of each year* (in shillings)

1827	58-105	1830	42-83	1833	75- 94	1836	96-120
1828	48 - 88	1831	46- 84	1834	87-112	1837	106-117
1829	50 - 88	1832	88-100	1835	81-124	1838	88-125

Source: T. Tooke, *History of Prices and the State of the Circulation 1793-1837* (1838), II, 399.

sugar, but as a concession to East Indian interests it agreed to equalize the duties on all coffee.[55] From September 1835 coffee which was the produce of any British possession was charged a duty of 56s. per cwt. Foreign coffee, however, remained liable for the duties laid down in 1825-1826.[56]

This new system of duties, now based on colonial preference rather than a West Indian preference, did little to improve the situation in the domestic market. British plantations in the East increased their production and exports to Britain, but they could not do so sufficiently rapidly to compensate for declining exports from the West Indies which fell steadily from 1836, and total imports of colonial coffee in the years after 1834 were consistently below the annual average of similar imports in the first four years of the decade.[57] Supply therefore continued to fall short of demand and the price rise was not checked.[58] Rising prices had a variety of effects; they led to an increase in the adulteration of coffee and provoked demands for an equalization of duties on foreign and colonial coffee. More important, in this context, high prices had the effect of permitting the importation of foreign coffee previously priced out of the British market by high duties. In the late 1820s and early 1830s the pre-duty price of foreign coffee was roughly equal to that of West Indian coffee, being around 40-50s. per cwt, but it had no chance of sales in Britain given the duty preference of 84s. enjoyed by West Indian coffee. In the late 1830s however, while the price of West Indian coffee rose rapidly, the price of foreign coffee on the world market remained constant

---

[55]On the clash between East and West India interests over preferential duties in the 1830s, see E. Williams, "Laissez faire, sugar and slavery," *Political Science Quarterly*. LVIII (1943), 67-85.

[56]5 & 6 Will. IV, c. 66.

[57]Imports of coffee from British colonial plantations between 1831 and 1834 averaged around 30,000,000 lb per year. In the six years from 1835 to 1840 they averaged around 25,000,000 lb and were as low as 20,292,723 lb in 1835. Imports of coffee from the British West Indies, which in 1832 stood at 24,673,920 lb, declined to 15,577,888 lb in 1837 and 9,303,984 lb in 1842. See *Quantities of Coffee imported from the British West Indies...in each year, 1831 to 1848*, PP 1849, L, 479.

[58]Prices of colonial coffee did not really start to fall until 1842. See Tooke, *op. cit.*, II, 399; and *idem, History of Prices 1839-47* (1848), 426.

or fell slightly.[59] Thus although still paying the additional duty of 84s. the gap between the selling prices of foreign and colonial coffees in the British market narrowed, particularly towards the end of the decade when West Indian coffee was approaching 100s. per cwt. In theory, West Indian coffee would hold an advantage over foreign coffee until its price exceeded that of foreign coffee by 84s., but in practice the point at which price equality, or near-equality, was reached was far lower than this. The duty system laid down in 1825-1826 and revised in 1835 provided for a reduced rate of duty on foreign coffee if it was imported from places within the limits of the East India Company's charter. Such coffee was charged 84s. per cwt, little more than half the duty normally charged on foreign coffee and a rate which reduced the preference enjoyed by colonial coffee from 84s. to 28s. per cwt. In a normal market situation even this preference would have been prohibitive, but in that of the late 1830s when there were wide discrepancies between the price of foreign and colonial coffee this was an obstacle which could be overcome., Consequently, the practice arose of importing coffee via ports located within the East India Company's charter limits. G.R. Porter in his *Progress of the Nation* described this situation well,

> and the price was by this virtual monopoly sustained so high that it became worth the while of merchants to send coffee, the growth of foreign plantations, and which was liable to pay a consumption duty of 1s. 3d. per lb., to the Cape of Good Hope for re-shipment to this country, by which expensive ceremony it became entitled to admission at the modified rate of 9d. per lb. or 28s. per cwt. beyond that exacted on coffee the growth of British possessions, the difference in the market price being more than equal to this in addition to all the charges of the outward and homeward voyages.[60]

---

[59] *Ibid.*, II, 388. See also *SC on Import Duties*, PP 1840, V. QQ. 1343-6; 1751.

[60] G.R. Porter , *The Progress of the Nation* (2nd edn, 1847), 560.

The indirect importation of coffee began in the late 1830s. It is possible that a few indirect shipments were made in 1836 and 1837,[61] but Joseph Hume claimed that the practice was "discovered" in 1838[62] and the first recorded case occurred in the February of that year.[63] The form taken by the practice varied. There were cases of Dutch East Indian coffee, particularly from Java, being shipped to Britain via Singapore and India,[64] but the bulk of coffee involved in the round about trade was of South American origin which was shipped first to the Cape of Good Hope, the most westerly British possession within the charter limits, and from there imported into Britain. Coffee arrived at the Cape for transhipment from a variety of destinations. John McGregor in evidence before the Select Committee on Import Duties in 1840 claimed that, "57 out of every 100 lbs. imported into England by way of the Cape was carried in the first instance to that colony from Brazil; 8 from Cuba; 12 I think are sent from England of foreign coffee to the Cape to be reimported into England; 6 I think from Java, and 6 or 8 sent out from Holland...and the remainder from other countries."[65] Official returns of trade at the Cape fully bear out this statement.[66] Importing foreign coffee via the Cape inevitably involved higher costs than direct importation. These were the extra freight charges and insurance premiums and handling and commission costs, for to be admitted into Britain at the lower rate of duty cargoes of coffee had to be

---

[61]Statements implying that the indirect trade commenced before 1838 appear in "Consumption of food in the United Kingdom," *Edinburgh Review*, IC (1854), 608-615.

[62]*Hansard*, 3rd ser., LVIII, 388 (13 May 1841).

[63]*Account of all Coffee imported into the United Kingdom from the Cape of Good Hope*. PP 1839, XLVI, 45. This return was reproduced in full in *The Times*, 2 November 1839.

[64]Imports of foreign coffee via Singapore were as high as 6,910,422 lb in 1840. The traffic, however, never reached the proportions of the Cape trade and it gained little publicity because it did not involve the spectacular re-routing of cargoes. See *Quantity of Coffee Imported into the United Kingdom, 1840, 1841, 1842 and 1843*, PP 1844, XLV, 25.

[65]*SC on Import Duties*, PP 1840, V, Q. 888.

[66]*Duties imposed in the Colony; Number and Tonnage of Vessels arriving at and departing from the Colony; Imports and Exports, 1835-1844*, PP 1847, XXXVII, 125-146.

unloaded and reloaded at the Cape or, as it was termed in the trade, "colonized."[67] Despite these numerous items, the additional costs of an indirect voyage were not excessive, for coffee was a commodity of relatively high value in relation to its bulk. Several witnesses before the Select Committee of 1840 commented on the costs of indirect importation. John Moore and Charles Saunders, two Liverpool merchants, assessed the additional costs for Brazilian coffee at between 4s. and 5s. 6d. per cwt, and Richard Shiel, also of Liverpool, put the additional cost of shipping Haitian coffee to London via the Cape at 6s. 6d.[68] Much higher costs, estimated at 13s. 7d., were, however, incurred if coffee was sent out from Europe to the Cape.[69] Even so, whatever the extra costs, indirect importation meant an immense saving of duty, ranging from 42s. to 52s. per cwt.

The practice of importing coffee via the Cape lasted for only a few years but at its peak it was prosecuted on a gigantic scale. Table 8 shows the trade in coffee at the Cape. In 1835 the trade was non-existent and in 1836 and 1837 it was of no significance, but in 1838 the price of coffee in Britain reached a level which made importation at the 84s. rate a worthwhile proposition. The trade grew rapidly and in 1839 and 1840 assumed phenomenal heights which gave rise to unprecedented activity at the Cape.[70] Table 9, which shows imports of coffee from the Cape in relation to the total coffee trade of the United Kingdom, reveals the dominant position held by Cape coffee in 1839, 1840 and 1841. In these years the Cape became the largest single source of supply, accounting for over one-third of total imports in 1839 and 1840 and over one-quarter in 1841. In 1840 imports from the Cape amounted to 27,882,978 lbs, and were responsible for the rise of total imports to 70,250,766 lbs, a

---

[67]*SC on Import Duties*, PP 1840, V, Q. 1745.

[68]*Ibid.*, QQ. 1746; 1271.

[69]Porter, *op. cit.*, 561.

[70]The indirect trade had an immense effect on the overall trade of the Cape of Good Hope. Four-yearly averages of imports at the Cape were as follows: 1832-1836, £508,550; 1837-1841, £1,019,188; 1842-1846, £837,661. Exports for the corresponding years were, £340,204; £619,808; £419,516. See J.T. Danson, "Some particulars of the Commercial progress of the colonial dependencies...1827-46," *Journal of the Statistical Society*, XII (1849), 388-389.

staggering increase given that in the previous 15 years total imports had averaged around 40,000,000 lbs.[71] 1840 represented the peak of the indirect trade; it fell away rapidly from 1841 and by 1843 the Cape had ceased to be an exporter of coffee to Britain.

Table 8
Trade in coffee at the Cape of Good Hope, 1835-1843 (lbs)

Year	Imports	Exports to U.K.
1835	568,176	-
1836	1,212,736	31,360
1837	1,213,296	148,176
1838	3,405,808	859,152
1839	22,071,504	19,672,352
1840	33,745,824	34,175,008
1841	2,924,432	3,931,200
1842	4,143,552	1,538,880
1843	2,366,000	1,538,880

Source: PP, 1847, XXXVII, 125-146.

Note: The slight overall discrepancy between imports of coffee from the Cape of Good Hope and exports of coffee from the Cape to the U.K. (Table 8) in the period 1838-1843 may be due to some coffee, originally bound for the U.K., being re-routed when it was realized that sales prospects in Britain were not what had been envisaged.

The spectacular rise and fall of the indirect trade in coffee was largely determined by two factors: the condition of the market in Britain and the nature of government policy. The rapid growth of the trade in 1839 and 1840 stemmed from the high price of coffee in Britain and the enthusiastic, indeed speculative, response of merchants to what was an entirely new trade, the importing of foreign coffee for the domestic

---

[71]Calculated from tables in J.R. McCulloch, *op. cit.* (new edn, 1869), 327.

market.[72] A further cause of the trade's expansion was the absence of government action. The Whig administration of the late 1830s found itself placed in something of a dilemma by the indirect trade. On the one hand, the importing of coffee via the Cape was within the letter of the law; it served to alleviate the shortage of coffee in the British market and, ironically, it substantially increased the total revenue obtained from the duties on coffee.[73]

Table 9
U.K. Imports and Consumption of Coffee, 1838-1843 (lbs)

Year	Total Imports	Total Retained for Consumption in U.K.	Imports of Cape of Good Hope Coffee	Consumption of Cape of Good Hope Coffee
1838	39,932,279	25,765,673	506,874	not available
1839	41,003,316	26,789,945	15,125,957	not available
1840	70,250,766	28,664,341	27,882,978	9,628,094
1841	43,317,762	28,370,857	11,633,259	7,441,576
1842	41,441,414	28,519,646	1,572,027	6,149,489
1843	38,912,469	29,979,404	540	2,098,650

Sources: All figures for the years 1840, 1841, 1842 and 1843 are taken from PP, 1844, XLV, 25, and *Amount of the Quantities of Coffee retained for Home Consumption* ... 1820-1843, PP, 1844, XLV, 27. Figures of total consumption for 1838 are from J.R. McCulloch, *A Dictionary, Practical, Theoretical and Historical, of Commerce and Commercial Navigation* (new edn, 1869), 327. The figure for imports from the Cape in 1838 is taken from W. Waterson, *A Cyclopedia of Commerce* (1843), 168, and the similar figure for 1839 is compiled from statistics contained in PP, 1839, XLVI, 45, and *Amount Imported into the United Kingdom from the Cape of Good Hope* ... 1840, PP, 1840, XLIV, 23.

---

[72]Particularly enthusiastic were export merchants trading to South America who for years had experienced difficulties in obtaining return cargoes because of the prohibitory duties on Brazilian produce. See *SC on Import Duties*, PP 1840, V, QQ. 1325-1334; 1815-1836; 1972-2008.

[73]The indirect trade meant that foreign coffee, which previously would not have entered Britain and paid duty, now did so. In consequence the total revenue obtained from the coffee duties rose dramatically. Annual figures were as follows: 1837, £696,645; 1838m £685,082; 1839, £779,115; 1840, £921,551; 1841, £887,747; 1842, £768,886; 1843, £697,376. See McCulloch, *op. cit.* (1869), 327.

On the other hand, it was an open flaunting of the intentions of the preference system involving a blatant evasion of the full duty payment on foreign coffee and hence a matter which could not be ignored. There were two ways in which the government could have acted. It could have legislated specifically to prohibit the Cape trade, but this was unattractive given the market situation and would have strengthened the colonial monopoly which the Whigs had no desire to favour. The alternative course was to reduce the preference given to colonial coffee and thereby render importation via the Cape unnecessary. Such action was seriously considered by the Whigs and they tentatively announced proposals for overall reductions in the duties in July 1840.[74] Administrative and budgetary difficulties, however, caused them to abandon their plans and in the following year they unsuccessfully concentrated their efforts on the timber and sugar duties. Thus the Whigs, while suffering some embarrassment from the evasion, allowed the indirect trade to continue unchecked from 1838 to 1841.[75] The collapse of the indirect trade was similarly due to government policy and the market situation in Britain. The trade came to an abrupt end in 1842 when the duty changes of Peel's first budget removed the circumstances which had given rise to indirect importation, but the trade was in fact on the decline from late 1840, for the business of taking coffee to the Cape slumped heavily in 1841 as table 8 shows. The explanation of the trade's decline about 1840 lies in the consumption figures contained in table 9. The figures of total imports and total consumption perhaps require some clarification for at first glance they appear to belie earlier statements of a shortage of coffee in Britain in the 1830s. The reason why imports appear greatly in excess of consumption is that the figures of total imports refer to all coffee which was landed and warehoused in bond at ports in Britain, and thus includes large quantities of foreign coffee brought direct to Britain for re-export purposes. Total imports, therefore, are in no way synonymous with the supply of coffee in Britain, which up to the late 1830s was restricted by the duty system to colonial coffee. However, because of the indirect trade the potential supply of coffee in the British market increased from 1838. The response of demand to this increase in supply is shown in the figures of total

---

[74]*Hansard,* 3rd ser., LV, 1073-1074 (29 July 1840).

[75]For a description of the Whigs difficulties in the late 1830s see Brown, *op. cit.,* 57-74.

consumption and consumption of Cape coffee. Both figures indicate increased consumption but not the growth that might have been expected, given that demand for coffee had been rising steadily from the early 1820s and that supply, previously restricted, expanded from 1838. While total consumption rose between 1838 and 1843, it did so but slowly, and although quantities of Cape coffee entered the British market for consumption there was a considerable gap between imports and consumption of Cape coffee. Two main factors can be advanced for the slow growth of total consumption: the persistence of high prices,[76] and more particularly, the growth of adulteration which began to occur on a massive scale.[77] In the case of Cape coffee an additional factor served to curb sales opportunities, namely that South American coffee, the chief type of coffee imported via the Cape, was for reasons of taste and quality unpopular with British consumers.[78] In consequence, Cape coffee did not achieve the sales in Britain envisaged by importers. This is clear from the figures of consumption of Cape coffee. Figures relating specifically to coffee imported via the Cape are unfortunately not available for 1838 and 1839, but figures of the total amount of coffee imported at the 84s. duty in these years indicate that of 24,000,000 lbs imported at that rate (and of this figure Cape coffee accounted for 15,500,000 lbs), only 12,000,000 lbs were consumed.[79] In retrospect, it might be observed that this was a sign of an over-supply of Cape coffee, but contemporaries apparently failed to recognize this trend and in 1840 the trade reached startling proportions with 27,882,978 lbs of Cape coffee being imported. Only 9,628,049 lbs, however, were entered for home consumption. At this point parties interested in the Cape trade began to realize that views on sales opportunities had been grossly exaggerated. Charles Saunders admitted that by mid-1840 large quantities of Cape coffee could not find a market and that merchants were obliged to re-export, and he went so far as to claim that sending coffee via the

---

[76]Imports of coffee via the Cape which were only possible because of the high level of prices in the British market could not serve to bring prices down though they did prevent prices from rising any further.

[77]On adulteration see P.L. Simmonds, *Coffee as it is, and as it ought to be* (1850).

[78]*SC on Import Duties,* PP 1840, V.QQ. 1776-1786.

[79]*Hansard*, 3rd ser., LVIII, 37 (7 May 1841).

Cape was a losing concern.[80] It would appear that this view was shared by
other operators for, as observed earlier, little coffee was sent to the Cape
for re-shipment purposes after 1840 and the indirect trade declined
rapidly. Imports of coffee into Britain from the Cape remained considerable in 1841 at 11,633,259 lb. but this was simply a consequence of the
heavy shipments of coffee to the Cape in 1840, and in 1842 imports were
down to a mere 1,572,027 lb. Any likelihood of the trade lingering on at
even this minor level disappeared when the budget of 1842 introduced a
new system of duties on coffee. This replaced the old duty system which
had incorporated four different rates of duty with a new system which
specified two duties only; a duty of 37s. 4d. per cwt on coffee "of and
from British possessions" and a duty of 74s. 3d. on coffee "of and from
foreign countries."[81] Two years later in 1844 the duty on foreign coffee
was reduced to 56s. per cwt.[82] These changes, which slashed the
preference given to colonial coffee, removed the root cause of the indirect
trade.

The indirect trade in coffee was therefore of brief duration and it
was attended by much over-optimism and speculation which led to perhaps
as much as two-fifths of the coffee imported via the Cape for the British
market being eventually re-exported. Even so the trade was of immense
importance; by any standards it was undertaken on a gigantic scale, and
it had a significant effect on the market for coffee in Britain. In the four
years 1839-1842, of some 112,000,000 lb of coffee consumed in Britain,
around 32,000,000 lb was coffee which had evaded fully duty payment
and had, moreover, been imported from a country which itself produced
not an ounce of coffee.

The history of the indirect trades in timber and coffee is of interest
as an example of how changes in the incidence of preferential duties could
divert the normal pattern of trade, on a modest scale but for a number of
years in the case of the indirect trade in timber, and on a massive scale for
three years in that of coffee. At the same time these two instances of
customs evasion bear testimony to the opportunism of British merchants
who were quick to recognize and take advantage of distorted customs

---

[80]*SC on Import Duties*, PP 1840, V, QQ. 1780-1781.

[81]5 & 6 Vict., c. 47.

[82]7 & 8 Vict., c16.

schedules. More important, however, is the role of the indirect trades in the struggle over free trade, for evasion served to embarrass the government and customs authorities and gave free-traders a fresh means of attacking the preferential tariff system. In the debate in Parliament over the British tariff the indirect trades were highly significant. The round-about trade in timber was a regular subject of Commons questions between 1830 and 1835[83] and the importing of coffee via the Cape was a frequently raised issue in debates over colonial preference in the early 1840s.[84] Again, the indirect trades played an important part in the two major parliamentary enquiries into the British tariff undertaken during the period. The evasion of duty by Baltic timber was a key factor in the establishment of the Select Committee on the Timber Duties of 1835, and in both this committee and the more influential Select Committee on Import Duties of 1840, free-trade interests, who by skilful manoeuvring enjoyed a dominant position, cleverly utilized evidence on indirect trading and evasion to produce the findings they desired. In asking parliamentary questions and using material on the circuitous trades presented to official enquiries, and outside Parliament by referring to the matter in pamphlets and letters to the press,[85] free-traders were availing themselves of the opportunities provided by customs evasion to support their claims for a reduction and eventual removal of preferential duties. For, in a variety of ways, the indirect trades pointed to weaknesses in the British tariff system, strengthening old criticisms and raising fresh doubts, and above all, exposing deficiencies in such a spectacular and absurd fashion that they could not fail to make an impression. The trades in timber and coffee indicated loopholes in customs regulations and showed that the prevailing duties were not entirely serving the purposes they were designed for; those of favouring colonial suppliers and raising revenue. Furthermore, they publicized the long-advanced argument that British exporters to South

---

[83]*Hansard*, n.s., xxiv, 14-15 (8 April 1830); 3rd ser., x, 1232 (7 March 1832); 3rd ser., xxiv, 394 (12 June 1834); 3rd ser., xxvii, 215 (24 March 1835).

[84]See, for example, the numerous references in the famous eight-day debate on the surgar duties in 1841: *Hansard*, 3rd ser., LVIII, 16-673 (7-18 May 1841).

[85]One particular letter deserves a mention. A correspondent to *The Times*, 22 November 1833, described how the government had unwittingly granted official contract for Baltic timber to a merchant whose ability to under-bid his competitors lay in his participation in the indirect trade with its duty savings.

America were often unable to fund return cargoes because of colonial preference duties, for indirect importation was a means of overcoming such a handicap. More particularly, the indirect trades cast doubts on the nature of preferential duties, for they drew attention to the way in which the existing duty system upset the natural flows of trade by excluding cheap foreign coffee at a time when coffee in the British market was growing more expensive, and burdening Baltic timber, a commodity much in demand, with an excessive level of duty.

The weight of such criticisms was enhanced by the inability of supporters of the preference system to explain away the indirect trades and effectively reply to the charges of free-traders. There were half-hearted claims that the indirect trade in timber showed the distressed state of British shipping and the lengths to which shipowners would go to get cargoes,[86] that the occurrence of the trade had been grossly and maliciously exaggerated,[87] and that the Whig administration, with its free-trade sympathies, permitted the trade to continue on purpose when prompt amending legislation would have quickly ended evasion.[88] In the case of coffee, the issue of the morality of consuming Brazilian coffee was raised in the contemporary controversy over slave-grown produce, and the massive importation via the Cape could be explained as solely due to a short run deficiency of supply in the British market although, in general, preference interests chose to remain silent on the matter. These, however, were poor counter-arguments which served only to reveal the weakness of the protectionist colonial case. For to all but the interested parties of shipowners and importers of colonial timber, West Indian and East India coffee growers and importers, the indirect trades in timber and coffee demonstrated the inherent weaknesses of differential duties, the excessive character of the preference given to colonial timber and coffee, and brought into question the principle of colonial preference. Such feelings were reinforced by disclosures, at this time, of further examples of customs evasion associated with colonial preference. Several witnesses before the Select Committee of 1840 recounted that the Cape of Good Hope served as a centre for the "colonizing" of other articles besides

---

[86]H. Bliss, *On the Timber Trade* (1831), 25-26.

[87]*Report...on the Timber Duties (NOT ordered...to be printed)*, 45.

[88]*Ibid.*, 44-47.

coffee, notably spices,[89] and the Committee also discovered that advantage of differential duties had been taken in the fancy wood branch of the timber trade where the importing of foreign mahogany via a colonial possession was common practice until expressly prohibited by the government in the mid-1830s.[90] Henry Labouchere, President of the Board of Trade, alleged in 1840 that "the great proportion of potash imported from Canadian harbours came originally from the United States,[91] and there were contemporary claims that foreign sugar, as well as coffee, was being imported via the Cape."[92]

Customs evasion thus helped to shape opinion and was a significant factor contributing to the changing attitude to colonial preference which became evident in the late 1830s. It was by no means the only influence at work; the overall market situation in timber, coffee and sugar was of crucial importance, as were the wider general acceptance of free-trade views and the shift in economic and political power from old colonial and shipping interests to industrial and new commercial groups, but changing attitudes were promoted by the publicity which stemmed from the spectacular character of customs evasion. Indeed, an indication of the impact the indirect trades had on contemporaries, can be gained from the fact that, years after evasion had ceased and when the commercial system had been liberalized, free-traders writing in appreciation of new policies often made reference to the indirect trades. The trades in timber and coffee were held up as prime examples of the absurdity of old regulations and the abuses, distortions of trade, and waste of resources to which they gave rise.[93] But customs evasion did more to foster the advance

---

[89]*SC on Import Duties*, PP 1840, V, QQ. 890-891. For statistics of the indirect trade in spices between 1835 and 1843 and for figures which suggest a similar trade in tea, see the returns of Cape of Good Hope trade contained in PP 1847, XXXVII, 125-146.

[90]*SC on Import Duties*, PP 1840, V, Q. 1290.

[91]*Hansard*, 3rd ser., LIV, 518 (22 May 1840).

[92]*Letter of James M'Queen, Esq. to Lord Melbourne on the Statistics of Agriculture and Manufactures* (1839), 30.

[93]See for example: McCulloch, *op. cit.* (new edn, 1856), 1308; Porter, *op. cit.*, 558-561; D. Buchanan, *Inquiry into the Taxation and Commercial Policy of Great Britain* (1844), 151-153; H. Dunckley, *The Charter of the Nations* (1854), 126-127;

of free trade than simply contributing to changed attitudes. The indirect trades in timber and coffee forced government to consider taking action on two key preferential duties. The open disregard of tariff law and embarrassment arising from evasion could be check only by legislation, either specifically to prohibit indirect trading or to reduce the extent of the preference. Both Whig and Tory governments chose the latter course. Only after a budget defeat and a grudging acceptance of the strength of opposition a further three years later did the Whigs abandon their hopes of reforming the timber duties and resort to specific legislation, and their reaction to the indirect trade in coffee was to propose an overall reduction in the duties, although again their weak political position frustrated their plans. No such difficulties faced Peel in 1842 and he was able to introduce successfully his free-trade budget, which has as its main features reductions in colonial preference duties and a new sliding-scale of duties for corn. Of all the changes in preferences, those in the duties on coffee and timber were of prime importance, for they involved real changes in principle.[94] Significantly, the reduction in the preference given to colonial timber, from 45s. to 29s. per load, was almost exactly that recommended by the Select Committee of 1835, and in his speech introducing the main tariff changes, Gladstone explained the new duties on coffee in terms of the indirect trade and concluded, "Thus, by the proposed reduction and equalization of the duties on foreign coffee it would be needless to send coffee half around the world in order to save a small amount of duty."[95] It is perhaps worth recalling in this context that in another crucial aspect of the struggle for free trade – the silk duties – large-scale smuggling was one of the chief reasons underlying Huskisson's decision in 1826 to relax the century-old policy of total protection for the British silk industry.[96] If this is taken in conjunction with the role of the indirect trades in reforming

---

"Consumption of Food in the United Kingdom," *Edinburgh Review,* IC (1854), 610-611.

[94]On the budget of 1842 see Brown, *op. cit.,* 229-231.

[95]*Hansard,* 3rd ser., LXIII, 522 (13 May 1842).

[96]See Huskisson's speech in the debate on duty changes, *Cobbett's Parliamentary,* n.s., XIV, 797 (23 February 1826). There can be no doubt that the highly-organized character and scale of the contraband trade in French manufactured silks was a signficant influence on government policy. On smuggling see McCulloch, *op. cit.* (1869 edn), 1281; *SC on the Silk Trade,* 1831-1832, XIX.

the timber and coffee duties, a case can be advanced for ascribing much greater importance than has been usual in the past to the ineffectiveness of tariff regulations and customs enforcement as influential factors in bringing about the rejection of traditional tariff policies and the adoption of free-trade principles.

Bulk Passenger Freight Trades, 1750-1870[1]

"Bulk passenger freight trades" is an ugly phrase but it serves as a useful collective to describe a number of trades which were of considerable importance in the period 1750-1870. All involved the transport of people – slaves, emigrants, convicts, indentured servants and contract labour. The scale of the principal trades and their essential roles in peopling new worlds has ensured the attention of generations of historians. In terms of the literature of individual trades, the slave trade has no rival and the emigrant and convict trades are also well-documented.[2] On closer inspection, however, the initial impression of an overwhelming volume of research, of a field fully-explored, is not wholly correct. Most notably, for all the quantitative manipulation of recent years, statistics of the volumes of people moved are far from certain; whereas the shipping aspects, in terms of full records of clearances, vessels and tonnages, represent major lacunae.

This paper does not seek to remedy such deficiencies; rather its aim is to present an overall appraisal. Such a general survey might appear superfluous, yet the broad sweep may serve a useful purpose. Much past research has been compartmentalised, the product of historians focussing on specialised themes – medical, demographic, naval and administrative, to name but a few. More especially, these trades have never before been considered as a group sharing common characteristics, nor has their collective position and influence within the evolving pattern of modern international trade and maritime activity ever been assessed.

[1]I am indebted to the Research Board, University of Leicester, for a grant in aid of research. I am also in the debt of my colleague, Dr. Phillip Cottrell, for his constructive criticism of an earlier draft of this paper.

[2]The volume of material consulted and, even more, the volume of material relevant to this paper is enormous. Most of the individual bulk passenger trades have an extensive literature. In a general paper such as this, to cite every reference would result in an excess of notes. In consequence footnotes are confined to a brief listing of the important studies on each trade, references to major research issues, and the attribution of quotations.

The focus of study here is British involvement in the bulk passenger trades, although some reference is made to other participating nations. This concentration, in part, reflects the weight of research, but more so, the fact that Britain was by far the leading exponent of bulk freight passenger trading. In the slave trade of the second half of the eighteenth century, Britain was the leading participant and in the transportation of convicts, she was second only to Portugal. Again, down to the mid-nineteenth century, Britain, together with Ireland, was the chief source of emigrants to North America and the sole supplier to Australia. Britain also pioneered the trade in contract labour. One further business involving passengers was trooping, in which Britain was heavily engaged during the war-torn century before 1815. Brief reference will be made to this, but trooping, organised by Navy Board officials, was primarily a service matter.[3]

This paper comprises four sections. It looks first at some of the common characteristics of these trades, thereby justifying the title and approach of the paper. Second, it reviews the scale and pattern of growth in the eighteenth and nineteenth centuries. Third, it examines the special operational and organisational problems presented by the shipping of human cargoes. Fourth, the paper assesses the importance of the trades, considering their position in the complex pattern of international shipping movements; their tendencies towards specialisation; and their role in shaping attitudes towards state intervention in the maritime field. Throughout, the paper's examination is couched in terms of sail. Steam, which made its appearance in the passenger trades at the end of the period, was to transform voyage patterns and problems, through its dramatic impact on length of passage.

Any definition of the terms "bulk cargo" or "bulk freight trades," which are regularly used in association with commodity trades, usually makes reference to three characteristics. First, they are prosecuted on a large scale; second, they involve the transport of bulky, relatively low-value produce; and third, cargoes are customarily carried by the shipload. Two of these features are clearly applicable to the trades under review. Most, and certainly the slave, convict and emigrant trades, were undertaken on a large scale. Although sometimes other cargo was carried,

---

[3]Much research is still to be done on trooping. A model for future study is David Syrett, *Shipping and the American War 1775-83. A Study of British Transport Organisation* (London, 1970).

almost invariably the body of passengers comprised the major element of the voyage's freight. But there the comparison would seem to end, for the remaining feature, that of involving bulky low-value produce would appear inapplicable. To equate human passengers with cargo would seem impossible and unacceptable. Yet it would be wrong to translate the twentieth century image of the passenger to an earlier context. In the trades discussed in this paper, passengers were not regarded as individuals, but rather simply as cargo in either (or both) the collective or unitary sense.

A variety of evidence can be adduced in support of this assertion. The use of the term "parcels of slaves;" a description of westbound timber vessels as "export[ing] emigrants pretty much as a kind of ballast;" or Herman Melville's comment on "emigrants stowed away like bales of cotton"[4] are examples of this view of humans as mere freight. And sometimes as freight of an inferior kind; Friedrich Kapp, a New York State Commissioner for Emigration, noted that shippers viewed emigrants as less than a box of goods "and handled with less care, as they did not break, nor, if injured, required to be paid for."[5] Indeed, re-enforcing the notion of humans as cargo is the fact that shippers' indifference towards their passengers was mitigated only by monetary considerations–in particular, the timing of receipts. Hence the well-being and fate of those whose passage money was paid on embarkation was of less consequence than those whose returns were only realised on delivery.

Such an inhumane, depersonalised approach prevailed for various reasons. A partial explanation reposed in racial and moral views, which saw black slaves as an inferior sub-species and convicts as having forfeited civil rights through social an moral failings. "Draining the Nation of its offensive Rubbish" was how a pamphleteer of 1731 depicted transportation.[6] Nor was the white voluntary emigrant held in high esteem; a Liverpool passage broker described his clients as "the offscourings of the

---

[4]*Chamber's Edinburgh Journal*, 7 June 1851; Herman Melville, *Redburn: His First Voyage* (London, 1849).

[5]Friedrich Kapp, *Immigration and the Commissioners of Emigration of the State of New York* (New York, 1870).

[6]Quoted in A. Roger Ekirch, "Bound for America: A Profile of British Convicts transported to the Colonies, 1718-1775," *William and Mary Quarterly*, Third Series, XLII (1985), 184.

human race."[7] Though this was an extreme view, most were branded with the stigma of poverty. As Samuel Sidney observed of emigrants embarking at Liverpool, "emigrants are not to be compared to other persons; they are an exception; they are the most helpless people in the world."[8] This quotation points to another explanation of the casual attitude to the bulk passcngcr, namcly his inability to protest against harsh treatment. Passengers were powerless because they were either captives, such as slaves or convicts; near-captives, such as indentured and contract labour; or simply poor, like the majority of emigrants – lacking status and bargaining strength. This vulnerability of passengers contributed to their relegation to the status of cargo. To this can be added a further influence: that passengers, from a shipper's point of view, were not an easy cargo. Passengers presented problems; in some trades they were a cargo of last resort and, hence, to masters in particular, an irritant and source of resentment.

The phrase "bulk passenger freight trades" thus serves to describe the character of, and to group together, a variety of trades. In a later section other common aspects in the areas of operation and organisation will be examined. But in this present context, two features merit comment as reflecting the forlorn condition of passengers which fostered the cargo approach. First, most passengers travelled with little or no luggage or possessions. This lack of baggage, with its implication of severing all links with the past, points to the second aspect: that bulk freight passenger trades were one-way, "outward only," and carried one-voyage passengers. To brokers, shipowners, masters and crews, such passengers were simply "cargo," and in their numbers, a bulk freight.

The origins of the bulk passenger trades lie in Europe's discovery of the Americas and the speedy establishment of settlements. The need in these new colonial territories for labour led to a flow of people from the Old World. Many of these passengers, such as slaves and servants, were involuntary; of the others, far more were pushed than pulled. Nevertheless, the outcome was the peopling of new lands, the expansion of primary production and the development of new shipping trades.

First and greatest of the bulk passenger trades before the mid-nineteenth century was the Atlantic slave trade, which in a sense was set

---

[7]*Letter to Lieutenant Low, R.N., ...by a Passage Broker* (Liverpool, 1838).

[8]Quoted in Terry Coleman, *Passage to America* (London, 1972), 61.

apart because of its non-European, African dimension and the need to purchase the cargo.[9] Yet, other than these differences, its practices and problems were common with those of the other trades. The slave trade existed from the fifteenth to nineteenth centuries. English participation dates from 1562, but it remained desultory for a century until the establishment of British colonies in the Caribbean. Thereafter the trade expanded; from around 1750 it was the largest single national branch of the trade, accounting for some fifty percent of slaves carried, effectively double that of the other major participants, France and Portugal. Over the period 1701-1810 it is estimated that the English trade exported nearly 2.5 million slaves from Africa, two-thirds of this total in the years after 1750. Shipping data is available in abundance only from around 1770, but in the period 1730-1760 clearances from Britain to West Africa averaged some eighty vessels per year. From mid-century, rapid growth ensued; average annual clearances in the early 1770s exceeded 150. The American War of Independence, which closed mainland markets, was a severe check, but recovery was swift and by 1783 clearances numbered 145. War from 1793 only caused disruptions in odd years, so that from 1790 to abolition in 1807, annual clearances averaged 130, representing around thirty thousand tons of shipping. Over the eighteenth century the ports participating in the trade changed. London enjoyed a monopoly until 1698. From the 1720s Bristol became the leading English slaving port. Liverpool took over in the 1740s and dominated until abolition in 1807. By the turn of the century, Liverpool clearances amounted to over one hundred vessels per year. With over seventy percent of the British trade, Liverpool enjoyed a high prominence both nationally and internationally.

The transportation of convicts to the Americas began within years of the discovery of the "New World." Spain, however, never undertook the practice on any scale, in contrast with Portugal which throughout its colonial history dispatched criminals abroad. In Britain, transportation was

---

[9]Major studies of the slave trade are: Philip D. Curtin, *The Atlantic Slave Trade: A Census* (Madison, Wis., 1969); Stanley L. Engerman and Eugene D. Genovese (eds.), *Race and Slavery in the Western Hemisphere: Quantitative Studies* (Princeton, 1975); Roger Anstey and P.E.H. Hair (eds.), *Liverpool, the African Slave Trade, and Abolition,* Historic Society of Lancashire and Cheshire, Occasional Series No. 2 (1976); Henry A. Gemery and Jan S. Hogendorn (eds.), *The Uncommon Market: Essays in the Economic History of the Atlantic Slave Trade* (New York, 1979); Herbert S. Klein, *The Middle Passage* (Princeton, 1978); David Eltis, *Economic Growth and the Ending of the Transatlantic Slave Trade* (Oxford, 1987).

first authorised in 1597 and the shipping of convicts began in the seventeenth century. Nonetheless, it only really developed after the Transportation Act of 1717. which introduced transportation as a common legal sentence. Details of the trade's shipping are sparse but between 1718 and 1776 around fifty thousand convicts were transported, two-thirds from England and Wales and the remainder from Ireland.[10] Almost all went to the mainland colonies but a few were landed in the Caribbean. How many vessels were engaged is unclear, but the leading Bristol convict contractors–Stevenson, Randolph & Cheston–in business between 1768 and 1775, appear to have averaged some seventy-five convicts per voyage, although most of their vessels carried cargo as well. Even so, using this figure as a divisor would suggest some five hundred voyages in the fifty-seven year period of the trade.[11] London was the chief port, with Bristol a good second. Dublin dominated the substantial Irish traffic. Alongside this flow of convicts were further trades in tied, if not captive, passengers. Indentured servants, perhaps more significant in the seventeenth century, and "redemptionists," bound to servitude unless on arrival their fare was redeemed by borrowing or payment by relatives or friends, represented a significant proportion of immigrants to colonial America. Between 1700 and 1775, of an estimated 250-300,000 immigrants, some twenty percent were redemptioners.[12]

With American independence, Australia became the new dumping ground for convicts. The First Fleet of 1788 opened an eighty-year period of transportation from Britain to Australia. In this time 158,702 persons

---

[10]On convict transportation to the American colonies see Abbot E. Smith, *Colonists in Bondage: White Servitude and Convict Labour in America, 1607-1776* (Chapel Hill, N.C., 1947); Richard B. Morris, *Government and Labour in Early America* (New York, 1946); A. Roger Ekirch, *Bound for America: The Transportation of British Convicts to the Colonies, 1718-1775* (New York, 1987).

[11]Kenneth Morgan, "The Organization of the Convict Trade to Maryland: Stevenson, Randolph & Cheston, 1768-1775," *William and Mary Quarterly*, Third Series, XLII (1985), 201-227.

[12]R.C. Simmons, *The American Colonies: From Settlement to Independence* (New York, 1976), 174-205; Peter Wilson Coldham (ed.), *Bonded Passengers to America* (Baltimore, 1983).

were landed in the colony, the outcome of some 850 voyages.[13] The chief ports of departure in England were in the south. As hulks often served for pre-transportation assembly, Portsmouth and Thames ports, drawing on the hulks at Deptford and Woolwich, featured prominently. Ireland, as a major source of transportees, was served by Cork, Dublin and Waterford. The trade developed slowly; before 1800 only forty-two transports sailed and wartime pressures maintained this low level. But from 1815 the trade grew rapidly. It peaked between 1831 and 1835, when 133 vessels landed 26,731 convicts. Before 1840, New South Wales was the principal recipient. Then Van Diemen's Land, which had received its first shipment in 1812, took over until 1853; thereafter, the focus of the dwindling trade was Western Australia.

Knowledge of the shipping aspects of the Australian convict trade is remarkably full. Famine replaces feast, however, when one turns to the emigrant trades. Only after 1815 are there any official figures of numbers of persons involved and accurate shipping data is not available until even later. One might expect that with the Passenger Acts relevant returns would have been assembled, but the Inspectorate was not formed until the mid-1830s and the published material is very patchy. No series exist until the 1850s and then not always in the most useful form. In consequence numbers of emigrants must serve as an index of the trade, supplemented by such shipping material as is available.

The emigrant trade to North America is the one constant feature within bulk passenger trading in the period under review. Quantitative assessment of the trade before 1820 is based on extrapolations of fragmentary material. Leaving aside the seventeenth century, between 1700 and 1775, some 250-300,000 people entered the colonies. Semi-official estimates of immigration from Independence to 1819 suggest a further quarter-million.[14] Thereafter, one is on firmer ground with official

---

[13]On transportation to Australia, major studies include A.G.L. Shaw, *Convicts and the Colonies* (London, 1966); Charles Bateson, *The Convict Ships* (Second edition, Glasgow, 1969); Robert Hughes, *The Fatal Shore* (London, 1987).

[14]Pre-1775 emigration to the American colonies is summarised in Simmons, *The American Colonies;* see also M. Campbell, "English Emigration on the Eve of the American Revolution," *American Historical Review*, LXI (1955-56), 1-20. Statistical data on later emigration is to be found in United States, Department of Commerce, Bureau of the Census, *Historical Statistics of the United States from Colonial Times to 1970* (Washington, D.C., 1975), 97-106.

U.S. statistics: from 1820 to 1845, over one million entered the United States. Then an explosion occurred: in the decade 1845-1855, some three million immigrated, and the trade continued at a high level until the Civil War. Subsequent vast increases and changes in sources of supply of migrants are outside the remit of this paper. What must be emphasised here is that, from the seventeenth century to 1860, Britain and Ireland were by far the principal suppliers, accounting for some two-thirds of emigrants. Germany largely accounted for the remainder.[15]

Assessing the implications for shipping of this two hundred year flood of people is a cause of embarrassment, since appropriate data are effectively absent. It would appear that a significant proportion of all vessels sailing to the colonies must have carried emigrants. After independence, perhaps a smaller proportion did so, but from the 1830s emigration became a serious business in its own right. In the boom decade, clearances of emigrant vessels from Liverpool averaged over five hundred annually, with perhaps a further fifty departures from Ireland. In the colonial era, however, Bristol, London and Plymouth had been the chief departure ports. A further change after 1787 was in the nationality of the vessels involved. United States vessels came to dominate Anglo-American trade. In the 1840s and 1850s, American vessels accounted for two-thirds of emigrant ship clearances.[16]

In contrast, emigration to the British North American colonies was reserved to British vessels until 1849 by the Navigation Acts. Emigration to the colonies only really got underway following the Napoleonic wars, when duty changes on timber both provided a stimulus to colonial development and led to a ready means of shipping emigrants in westbound timber trade vessels. Down to the mid-1830s, British emigration to the colonies slightly exceeded that to the U.S.A., particularly in 1830-1835, when it amounted to some 240,000. After this the United States shot ahead, but the colonies shared in the boom of the 1840s and 1850s,

---

[15]On post-Napoleonic emigration to the U.S., see Coleman, *Passage to America*; Cecil Woodham-Smith, *The Great Hunger* (London, 1962); Oliver MacDonagh, *A Pattern of Government Growth 1800-60* (London, 1961).

[16]On U.S. shipping dominance, see David M. Williams, "The Rise of United States Merchant Shipping on the North Atlantic, 1800-1850s: The British Perception and Response;" in Clark G. Reynolds (ed.), *Global Crossroads and the American Seas* (Missoula, Montana, 1988).

reaching record levels. Between 1815 and 1835 emigrants totalled four hundred thousand; between 1836 and 1860, almost eight hundred thousand. As with the nineteenth century emigrant trade to the U.S., Liverpool was supreme, although Irish and Scottish ports made some contribution.[17] Emigration to Australia was on an altogether smaller scale until mid-century. Between 1788 and 1830 there were but fourteen thousand free (as opposed to convict) emigrants. With the introduction of the assisted passage scheme, numbers increased. In 1831-1840, free immigrants totalled sixty-five thousand and in the next decade, 108,000. Gold fever raised the figure to a spectacular 601,000 in 1851-1860. Again Liverpool was the chief port, but Southampton and Plymouth enjoyed a useful share of the trade.[18]

Rather ironically, at the end of the period being examined, under the Passenger Acts of 1852 and 1855, some official shipping statistics were published.[19] Belated though they may be, they provide a glimpse of the scale of the trade at its peak in 1851-1854, when over three hundred thousand persons annually emigrated from British ports. In 1853, passenger ships totalled 524 British (354,140 tons) and 460 foreign (479,736 tons). Combined, this amounts to 964 vessels of 833,876 tons. In 1854, total clearances were 893 vessels of 835,073 tons. These figures represent a huge volume of shipping, almost entirely said. While it is true that this was the apogee, even in 1859, when emigrant numbers had fallen to the levels of the early 1840s, vessels clearing under the Acts numbered 435 (527,683 tons).

This review of the principal bulk passenger trades commenced with the slave trade, unique in its extra-European dimension and in its freighting of coloured labour. Possessing similar characteristics was the final trade to develop in the period, the transport of contract or "native" labour from India to Mauritius and the West Indies. The first act authorising such emigration was passed in 1839. A bounty system initially

---

[17]On emigration to British North America, see Helen I. Cowan, *British Emigration to British North America* (Revised edition, London, 1961).

[18]On emigration to Australia, see R.B. Madgwick, *Immigration into Eastern Australia, 1788-1851* (London, 1937); Helen R Woolcock, *Rights of Passage: Emigration to Australia in the Nineteenth Century* (London, 1986).

[19]Great Britain, Parliament, House of Commons, *Parliamentary Papers (BPP)*, "Returns of Passenger Ships," LX (1860), 1-9.

applied as an incentive to shippers but from 1843 the substantial trade was conducted by Emigration Officers. Between 1843 and 1865 Mauritius received 331,603 persons, conveyed in 1149 vessels. Shipping data are not available for the West Indies trade but in the same period British Guiana received 53,246 East Indian migrants; Trinidad, 29,254; and Jamaica, 9,195. All these migrants, over four hundred thousand of them, were carried in British vessels. The West Indies also gained labour from another source, China. The "coolie" trade to Guiana and Trinidad commenced around 1860 and was formalised with the placement of an Emigration Officer in Canton in 1863. Fourteen thousand coolies had been shipped by 1865.[20]

The brief survey undertaken above reveals that bulk passenger trading was a constant feature of British shipping activity from the early eighteenth century until beyond the mid-nineteenth century. Viewing the period as a whole, some general observations can be made on the course and character of trading. Three turning points are perhaps visible: the American revolution; the period of the French wars; and the middle of the century. The first ended transportation to the Americas and provided the first spur to the development of Australia. Less permanently, the revolution checked the slave and emigrant trades, although hostilities generated high trooping activity. Similar checks and stimuli accompanied the French wars, but the chief development of this period, albeit for reasons unconnected with the conflict, was the abolition of the slave trade. Partly as a result of these turn-of-the-century changes, a distinction can be made between bulk passenger trades in the eighteenth and nineteenth centuries. Until the late 1780s, the range of activity, though solely in an Atlantic context, was greater than in the period after 1815, when trades were confined to transportation and emigrants. These trades were to dominate the period down to the late 1840s; from this date transportation declined but Irish famine coupled with a rash of gold discoveries pushed emigration to unprecedented heights. In the fifties, the Crimean war brought much trooping; as well, a new trade in contract labour developed.

Two further distinctions between eighteenth and nineteenth century trades can be noted. First, from the turn-of-the-century, all bulk passenger trades came to be regulated. The causes and nature of regulation

---

[20]*BPP*, 25th General Report of the Colonial Land and Emigration Commissioners, XVII (1865), 17-90. On the contract labour trade, see H. Tinker, *A New System of Slavery* (Oxford, 1974).

are to be considered later, as will the ineffectiveness of early intervention. Even so, after 1800 passenger trades operated in an atmosphere of concern and scrutiny. Second, there was in the early nineteenth century a dramatic increase in the size of vessels. The ships operating on the Atlantic and Australian routes after the French wars were chiefly over four hundred tons, which represents a doubling in size compared with the typical passenger vessel of the eighteenth century, an increase which had significant implications for the cargo numbers and conditions.

The demand for shipping large numbers of people overseas, while offering enormous opportunities for business and profit, posed formidable problems of organisation and operation, totally different from those encountered with commodity cargoes. Passengers, voluntary or involuntary, could not be stored or stowed; they required servicing in terms of essential human needs and they were perishable, though this quality was not always of consequence. The parties responsible for such organisation varied. In the slave trade the master, with or without a supercargo, had all the duties of acquiring, assembling, transporting and disposing of a cargo. In the convict trade to America, private contractors, often shipowners, took delivery of batches of convicts and then assumed full responsibility for the Atlantic crossing and sale in the colonies. Transportation to Australia with the First Fleet was the work of the Royal Navy, with charters made through London shipbrokers; soon, however, government adopted a system of private contracts in which one contractor furnished vessels, crews, clothing and provisions. But unlike the earlier trade to the American colonies, government retained a supervisory role through Navy Agents and, from 1817, Surgeon Superintendents, who accompanied shipments. In the Atlantic emigrant trade until the early 1800s owners and masters were the organisers but as the trade expanded to massive proportions emigration brokers – sometimes shipowners – emerged as key figures.

The problems of operation and organisation facing such parties can be categorised, and best examined, in terms of the time at which they were encountered – whether before, during or after the voyage. Preparatory to sailing, the major tasks were to assemble the cargo, to make ready the vessel, and to secure provisions. Gathering together a large number of people at a given place, in some instances for a given date, was a significant matter in view of demurrage costs. In the case of transporting convicts or conveying troops abroad, the problem was that of government or its agencies and not that of the shipper, whose responsibility was

confined to providing a vessel according to contract. Where business was
not of a public or official nature, however, as in the slave and emigrant
trades, there was an assembly problem. This was most clearly evident in
the slave trade. The time spent acquiring a slave cargo was crucial – as
one writer comments, "from the start of the venture, entrepreneurs had to
take account of the fact that the financial outcome depended not only on
the immediate profits but on the length of time capital had been locked up
in the voyage."[21] Irrespective of the time and money equation, delays in
Africa increased the very real and potentially calamitous possibility of
crews succumbing to the treacherous climate. These factors, which
militated against overly large ships, may well have influenced a tendency
to an optimum size of vessel; they certainly explain the shift over time
along the African coast toward more easterly and southerly destinations
where supplies of slaves were more readily obtained.

Emigrants, unlike convicts and slaves, were voluntary passengers.
In the eighteenth and early nineteenth century, prospective emigrants
negotiated directly with shippers. From the 1830s, when mass emigration
developed, the scale of business and the potential for exploitation were
such as to generate intermediaries, emigration agents or brokers, who
undertook to organise and supply passenger cargoes. The growth from the
1820s of the pre-paid system contributed to the systematisation of the
trade. In the case of assisted emigration to Australia after 1831, and the
famine and crisis emigrations of the 1840s and 1850s, agents became the
norm, though timber trade vessels to British North America still operated
an opportunist trade. From the late 1840s, when U.S. packet lines, losing
cabin trade to steamers, moved into the steerage trade, the business
became highly-organised.[22] First sailing, and then steam, ship companies
established networks of agencies – no longer merely in response to
demand, but to actively promote emigration through advertising and cheap
fares.

If over time the business of assembling cargo moved towards an
outside agency, the shipper was still left with much to do in the way of
accommodation and provisions before passengers came aboard. Accommodation fittings were invariably temporary – for steerage accommodation

---

[21]B.K. Drake, "The Liverpool-African Voyage c. 1790-1807: Commercial
Problems," in Anstey and Hair (eds.), *Liverpool*, 229-231.

[22]Robert G. Albion, *Square-Riggers on Schedule* (Princeton, 1938), 247-273.

outward was the cargo hold on the return. The knocking together of berths and, in some instances, installing stagings, additional decks, privies and cooking facilities, appears to have been a simple matter of little inconvenience or cost. In some cases the requirements were more substantial; thus convict ships in the Australian trade after 1817 were required to have three apartments with heavy doors, separated by iron railings, so that different classes of prisoners could be segregated. Such modifications were clearly more costly and may have become semi-permanent in vessels which were employed in transportation for a number of years, but they were not so expensive as to inhibit many vessels from making a single voyage in the trade. Navy transports may also have retained appropriate fixtures for their period of service. In general, though, passenger fittings were crudely assembled and removed immediately on arrival. Only in the mid-nineteenth century, when some shipowners became committed to the emigrant trade, were vessels adapted on a permanent basis with iron stanchions for berths and grates on upper decks for cooking.

The provisioning of vessels with food and water presented shippers with an equation of conflicting variables. Passengers represented income, provisions represented cost. Again provisions, most obviously water, took up space which could have been utilised for more passengers or, in some trades, cargo. Length of passage was the great imponderable, since unfavourable winds or unforseen accidents could prolong a voyage to the point of disaster. In some trades these decisions were taken for the shipper. The provisioning of soldiers in transit was fixed by schedule; from the time of the First Fleet, compliance with a scale of provisions was demanded of contractors even to the extent of using Osbridge's machine for "sweetening" water; and the earliest Passenger Act, that of 1803, laid down details of food and water to be supplied. The adequacy of contractual obligations and the effective enforcement of passenger legislation may be questioned, but the setting of basic minimums removed the onus of decision from the shipper. Observance of the letter, though seldom the spirit, formalised provisioning for most bulk passenger operators in the nineteenth century.

Eighteenth century shippers did not possess such obligatory guidelines, but participants in the slave, servant, redemptioner and American colonial convict trades over time came to recognize the incentive of being able to present, at market, live and healthy produce. For slave traders this meant some long-term planning of provisions, for while water and fruit could be obtained in Africa or, if need be, at Atlantic islands *en route*, long-lasting salted provisions for cargo and, more particularly the crew, had to be laid in at the commencement of the voyage. Even so, ignorance, parsimony, and misfortune accounted for appalling incidents in all trades.

Once the chaotic process of embarkation had been completed and the voyage was underway, problems of health, organisation and order presented themselves. Health was the most crucial. Initial sea-sickness was of no consequence, but longer term problems, such as illness and contagious disease, were more serious. Overcrowding and unhygienic conditions posed high risks. "Floating pesthouses" was one description of nineteenth-century emigrant vessels. Added to this were special problems with which some passengers embarked. Slaves, for example, suffered from a quite traumatic experience; convicts were often already debilitated from months in goal and hulks; and emigrants, poor at all times, but in the 1840s starving refugees from famine, were high risks for illness and infection. On virtually every voyage sickness was endemic and some deaths the rule. Far worse could happen and all the bulk passenger trades can provide examples of disasters, extreme suffering and heavy casualty. Levels of mortality and factors bearing on this phenomenon have fascinated demographers and historians. A huge research literature exists.[23]

How masters responded to the health threat varied between trades and individuals. Indifference and ignorance regularly meant that some matters were left entirely to chance. In other instances, brutality and sometimes sadism compounded natural hazards. Such traits of character apart, the crucial determinants of whether consideration was given to the

---

[23]The following items represent some of the recent contributions to the debate on passenger mortality: James C. Riley, "Mortality on Long-Distance Voyages in the Eighteenth Century," *Journal of Economic History*, XLI (1981), 651-656; Raymond L. Cohn, "Deaths of Slaves in the Middle Passage," *Journal of Economic History*, XLV (1985), 685-692; Cohn, "Mortality on Immigrant Voyages to New York, 1836-1853," *Journal of Economic History*, XLIV (1984), 289-300; David Eltis, "Free and Coerced Transatlantic Migrations: Some Comparisons," *American Historical Review*, LXXXVIII (1983), 251-280; Eltis, "Mortality and Voyage Length in the Middle Passage: New Evidence for the Nineteenth Century," *Journal of Economic History*, XLI (1984), 301-308; Farley Grubb, "Morbidity and Mortality on the North Atlantic Passage: Eighteenth-Century German Immigration," *Journal of Interdisciplinary History*, XVII (1987), 565-585. See also two unpublished papers by John McDonald and Ralph Shlomowitz: "Mortality on Convict Voyages to Australia, 1788-1868" (1987); and "Mortality on Immigrant Voyages to Australia, 1838-1892" (1988).

physical well-being of passengers were those of the market costs and returns. Where the supply of passengers was plentiful and the shipper was paid in advance, the situation was probably at its worst; to take precautionary measures was simply to incur extra costs, while greed heightened the ever present tendency to carry an excess of passengers. The early slave trade and much emigrant traffic bear this out. However, if receipts came only after delivery, there was incentive to safeguard cargo. Dead slaves, servants, redemptioners and convicts brought no return and, in the first three instances, unhealthy stock fetched a lower price. Moreover, slaves until sold represented a debit item in the venture's accounts and the purchase price in Africa rose dramatically in the eighteenth century. As with provisions and water, in some trades government contracts or legislation contained clauses aimed at checking health risks. Inadequate enforcement meant, however, that shipboard conditions fell short of paper requirements.

The overall problem of health was the outcome of many influences – over-crowding, ill-ventilated accommodation, repetitive and poor diets, unsanitary conditions, lack of exercise, and no medical provisions. Depending on inclination and incentive, some action could be taken to deal with each aspect. The obvious expedient to ease overcrowding was to carry fewer passengers relative to vessel size. From the late eighteenth century, controls along such lines came into being, but evidence suggests that in the slave trade, even before regulation, some operators had recognised that overloading could be counter-productive. The problem of ventilation was one which offered no real solution, as a fetid, corrupt atmosphere was the inevitable outcome of the confinement of hundreds of persons below deck. Beyond removing hatches when weather permitted, a rudimentary approach was additional port holes, which often admitted as much water as air. More imaginative were attempts to use wind sails to enhance circulation. If tried at all, any approach was bound to fail in the face of the appalling sanitary problem; the common feature of bulk freight passenger vessels was that they were recognisable by their smell. On the specific aspect of sanitation, little information exists; perhaps contemporary "decency" inhibited discussion. There are odd references to privies on deck and "utensils" and chamber pots below; these probably represented the limits of provision. Squalid, filthy conditions were the general order, particularly if the master's attitude or inclement weather prevented access to the deck. The same factors influenced the possibility of exercise and recourse to fresh air, the lack of both contributing to debilitation.

A deficient diet contributed to the debility of passengers but the nature of shipboard food, other than its cost and storage, aroused no concern. Dietary science was unknown; anyway, bread/biscuit and salt provisions were the standard fare of all seafarers. Food could, however, present organisational problems through difficulties of preparation in bad weather, inadequate cooking facilities for emigrants, or in the African trade, slaves refusing or being unable to eat unfamiliar fare. Recognition of the health problems was shown in the voluntary shipping of surgeons in some slave vessels and the insistence on the same in government contract work and emigrant legislation. The power given to Surgeon Superintendents in the convict trade reflected the special demands of the long voyage. That trade apart, ship's surgeons do not appear to have made much impact; the post seems to have represented the nadir of professional success, the refuge of the half-trained, incompetent and unfit. For much of the period, medical understanding of infection and hygiene offered little guidance; yet the late eighteenth century slave trade saw some use of fumigation, wine and vinegar as disinfectants, and citrus as an anti-scorbutic. These practices were to be adopted more effectively in the convict trade.

For many masters the health aspect was perhaps only a problem if it reached such proportions as to threaten cargo and crew. They may well have regarded maintaining order as of greater consequence, seeing possible dangers in being outnumbered by their cargo and problems in crew/passenger contacts. To guard against the former, firearms were carried and occasionally used, though the danger of passenger uprising was probably only real in the slave trade. Convicts were seen as potentially mutinous but they posed little threat; often they were already institutionalised and certainly aware of the brutal retribution exacted for any infringement of rules, as were troops. Floggings, cramping boxes, double ironing and confinement in "black holes" were but the formalised means of punishing defiance.

Violent revolt was the extreme form of disorder, although it was extremely rare. Masters of emigrant vessels merely had to contend with grumblings, discontent and quarrelling between passengers themselves, all easily suppressed by the heavy hand. The passenger trades did, however, present one aspect liable to disrupt the normal order of a merchant vessel: a female presence. Here again evidence is patchy and sometimes smacks of salacious reportage, but there were incidents of rape on slave vessels, of seamen demolishing bulkheads to consort with female convicts, and of seamen "taking wives." Again, there was the infamous case of the *Lady Juliana*, whose passage to Australia represented the progress of a floating brothel. Widespread immorality was alleged to prevail amongst passengers, and sometimes crews, especially on emigrant ships where unsegregated, indiscriminate berthing and the total lack of privacy incited coarseness and promiscuity. Reaction to this sexual problem varied from acceptance as inevitable, to attempts to curb it, to violent punishment of guilty crew members. Unless prejudicial to order, the behaviour of passengers among themselves was generally ignored.

Masters no doubt arrived at their destination with a sense of relief and delight at the prospect of getting rid of a troublesome and risky cargo. For some, especially in the emigrant, Australian convict and contract labour trades, their involvement terminated once the cargo was discharged. Latterly, though, many port of entry authorities required inspection before disembarkation. In other trades – slaves, convicts to the American colonies and sometimes servants – cargo value had to be realised by sale, either through agents or by public auction. Regardless, once passengers were disposed of, the attention of shippers turned to the return voyage. Usually a freight was carried, as many passenger trades had a complimentary relationship with a commodity trade. Where such relationships were weak, masters had to weigh the cost of delay in acquiring cargo against the advantage of an earlier homeward run. In the slave trade, many favoured the quick turn-around.

In essence, the response of shippers and masters to the peculiar problems which arose in bulk freight passenger trading was entirely pragmatic. When the condition of their cargo had a bearing on profitability, then, insofar as it was possible, they would take steps to guard against or alleviate those circumstances and conditions which threatened returns. This attitude similarly governed their response when contractual obligations or legislation required them to meet prescribed standards; such requirements would be ignored, evaded or observed minimally. The suffering of passengers was quite irrelevant. After all, passenger freighting was, pure and simple, an economic business.

The position of the bulk freight passenger trades in the wider context of maritime history is one of considerable importance. At the most general level it could be argued that the development of the Americas was dependent on labour from Europe and Africa. It follows that the stimulus to shipping which stemmed from the expansion of the Atlantic economy was the outcome of those trades which transported the vital infusion of population. And this stimulus comprised not just a hugh expansion of activity; it was also one of technological and organisational advance, since the Atlantic was the forcing ground of maritime change. Putting aside, however, this broadest of macro views of world shipping history, the bulk passenger trades in a number of more specific areas can be seen to have had a particular significance, notably in the matrix of international shipping movements, the development of specialisation and in the field of government intervention in shipping.

Until the later nineteenth century most international trade and shipping movements were bilateral. A vessel would sail from its base port to a destination and from thence would return back to its port of first departure. There were exceptions to this; the slave trade is the prime example and other triangular trades also existed.[24] But the general pattern was two-sided. The relationship in terms of importance and cargo volume between outward and inward legs was seldom even, one leg being the prime and the other secondary. The role occupied by bulk freight passenger trades varied.

In the past commentators have laid emphasis on the secondary role. Trade between Europe and the outside world in the eighteenth and nineteenth centuries was characterised by an imbalance. Europe's imports of primary produce demanded shipping space far in excess of that required by her lighter exports, chiefly manufactures. Because of this many vessels left Europe partially or fully in ballast. In such an analysis passenger trades are viewed very much in a supportive role. They were a back cargo, a bonus freight for vessels which were sailing for given destinations anyway, the classic example being westward vessels in the colonial timber trade. Much of trans-Atlantic voluntary emigration may have fallen into this category of passengers replacing ballast, though a firm judgement on trades in the colonial period could only be made through detailed examination of cargoes on east and westbound legs. This situation was clearly reversed, however, from the 1840s when emigration became a trade in its own right.

---

[24]Other multilateral trades in the eighteenth and early nineteenth centuries included England, New England and the West Indies; and England, Newfoundland and Portugal. See Walter E. Minchinton, "The Triangular Trade Re-Visited" in Gemery and Hogendorn (eds.), *The Uncommon Market*, 351-352. In the nineteenth century, the "cotton triangle," involving southern U.S. ports, Liverpool, and New York developed; see Albion, *Square-Riggers*.

In other trades the passenger leg occupied a far from secondary position. Shipping to·or from west Africa revolved round the slave trade down to 1807. Two-way trade with Africa, that is a direct African trade, was minimal. Nor by the mid-eighteenth century was the slave trade dependent on, or essential to, the freighting of Caribbean produce. By-passing the controversy over triangularity, it is apparent that many slave vessels returned empty or with limited cargo. Sugar, the great West Indian staple, was chiefly carried by the "sugar fleet," wide-bellied than freighters which were quite different than the fast, sharp vessels favoured in the slave trade. If the slave trade was a trade in its own right, so too was convict transportation to Australia and, from its introduction to around 1850, the assisted passage trade. In the 1840s, the major ship-owner Duncan Dunbar claimed that the colonies seldom offered paying return freight; many of his vessels returned to England via Calcutta, having taken on cargo there.[25] By the 1850s vessels carrying such passengers may have returned direct with wool cargoes, but beyond doubt, the outward leg was the initial determinant Anglo-Australian trade. Likewise the trades in contract labour: it was hardly in pursuit of a return cargo that vessels made the long voyage outward from India to Mauritius and the West Indies.

Thus while some passenger trades fulfilled a secondary role, taking up unutilized capacity on existing routes, others represented the principal leg in their voyage pattern and their creation and development stimulated and broadened world shipping activity. Yet whether in a secondary or primary role, it was customary for a passenger trade to have, either at the outset or developed over time, a complimentary relationship with a commodity trade. This ensured the fuller utilisation of capacity on individual trade routes in that cargo was carried both outward and inward. Accordingly, early passenger trades to colonial America were linked with tobacco, timber and forest products; the slave trade with sugar and other Caribbean produce; emigration to the U.S. with cotton and to British North America with timber; and trades to Australia ultimately with wool and copper ore. Two significant implications, albeit both needing fuller investigation, stem from this passenger/commodity relationship. First, that the carriage of passengers likely led to reductions in freight rates on commodities; second, there was not only a fuller employment of vessel

---

[25]Quoted in John Bach, *A Maritime History of Australia* (London, 1976), 60.

capacity but also more active employment for a greater part of the year. This promoted port and ancillary supply trades and, while most primary product and passenger trades had a seasonal aspect, these tended to complement each other, thus promoting a regular round of activity. All in all, the bulk freight passenger trades were a significant dimension of the increasingly complex matrix of world trade and shipping, deserving of a higher profile than perhaps accorded in the past.

The emergence in the eighteenth and nineteenth centuries of a wider and more integrated pattern of international shipping movements was linked to a more sophisticated approach to the organisation of commerce. In the broadest sense this meant more decisions being required of shippers and, as these became more complicated, the specialisation of function and the rise of intermediaries. These developments, general throughout merchanting, shipping and finance, are apparent in the passenger grades. Part III of this paper indicated the variety of problems facing shippers and how, from around the turn of the century, agents, sub-agents, contractors and brokers came to play increasingly significant roles. This growth of specialisation and function is an aspect requiring much further research. So too are the issues of specialisation among shipowners and in the use of vessels. There is much evidence that some shipowners specialised in the passenger trades. The slave, Australian convict and emigrant trades all offer examples. Likewise, these trades provide evidence of the specialist usage of vessels; of vessels making a series of voyages in the same trade. How far the passenger trades were the preserve of "regular" or "occasional" traders awaits full examination, but this was the case in the slave and Australian convict trades and in emigration to the U.S.A. in mid-century. One further question remains: how far did passenger trades call forth "specialist" vessels, that is vessels of a particular tonnage, hull shape, rig and interior fittings. At present, only in the slave trade can the answer be tentatively affirmative.[26]

An area where the bulk passenger trades were of special significance was that of state intervention in shipping in the fields of safety and welfare. Passenger traffic provided such an impetus in two ways. First, it intensified the inherent dangers of trans-ocean sea travel--those of shortages of water and provisions, as well as the danger of disease. The

---

[26]See my forthcoming study "The Shipping of the British Slave Trade in its Final Years, 1798-1807."

carriage of large numbers of people in confined, unhygienic accommodation heightened both these risks and led to massive tragedies. Deplorable conditions and large scale calamity do not, however, in themselves necessitate official intervention. Rather, it is the publicity which pushes government to act. It was the publicity associated with passenger trade disaster which was the second, and arguably, the key influence; the scale of loss if, say, an emigrant vessels foundered, or if disease struck, was such as to attract widespread attention.

Disasters possess a morbid fascination and, outside of war, famine and plague, before 1840 maritime disaster had a unique publicity quotient. No other form of transport casualty could match its potential scale or dramatic nature. And while mortal danger was accepted as an inevitable risk of the sailor's lot, the tribulations of passengers aroused greater concern. Moreover, there was the "dependent" dimension. Passengers included wives and children: the influence of contemporary views on morality and femininity, and the poignant image of mothers clutching children, should not be underestimated as factors arousing public opinion and prompting reform. In consequence, it was in the bulk passenger trades that measures on welfare and safety were first undertaken. As a result of action for passengers, provisions safeguarding seamen came into being, albeit much later.

The first such action occurred in 1788 when humanitarianism and concern over the morality of slavery led to Dolbens Act.[27] In an effort to reduce mortality by relieving overcrowding, this act regulated the number of slaves to be carried according to tonnage. Eleven years later came an attempt to relate numbers to the physical dimensions of vessels. The effectiveness of such measures is debatable but what is significant is that a precedent was established. This precedent was drawn upon by the 1803 Select Committee on Emigration, which compared the requirements for slaves with the lack of provisions for emigrants. The outcome, in the same year, was the first of a series of Passenger Acts.[28] The first act, remark-

---

[27]Dolbens Act is reprinted in Elizabeth Donnan (comp.), *Documents Illustrative of the History of the Slave Trade to America* (Washington, D.C., 1930-1935), II, 589-590.

[28]The authoritative survey of the Passenger Acts is Macdonagh, *A Pattern of Growth*. Between the Passenger Act of 1803 and that of 1855, there were a dozen acts and amendments in 1817, 1823, 1825, 1827, 1828, 1835, 1842, 1847, 1848, 1849, 1851 and 1852.

ably detailed and unrealistically optimistic, specified terms of one passenger to every two tons of clear space, a daily issue of specified rations, the daily airing of bedding, weekly fumigation of accommodation, and medical provision in the forms of qualified surgeons and medical chests on all vessels with over fifty passengers. Masters also were required to enter bonds for seaworthiness. To ensure observance, Customs Officers, JPs, and, on the high seas, Navy Officers, had the right of inspection. Such extravagant terms doomed the act to failure, but it nevertheless established the areas which for the next seventy years would be the subjects of intervention – overcrowding, accommodation, provisions and diet, medical facilities and seaworthiness.

To examine the thirteen further Passenger Acts passed before 1855 would be superfluous. There is of course Oliver MacDonagh's seminal survey; more particularly, the crucial point is not the precise detail of individual acts, for they were often unenforceable and of little impact before the 1850s. Rather, what is important, is that passenger legislation laid down a schedule; it specified areas of action. But only in emigrant trades. For the vast mass of vessels afloat the Passenger Acts did not apply and their specific terms were totally irrelevant. Yet, in a much more basic sense, they were very relevant. The particular problems of the bulk passenger trades were special because of their scale, not their form. In form, the problems were those which had affected seafarers almost from time immemorial. Hence, measures regulating the slave, emigrant and convict trades were not simply ends in themselves but rather the fuses which ultimately fired the process of welfare reforms for seamen.

For the first sixty years or so of the nineteenth century, *laissez-faire* ideology and an obsession with contracts and discipline determined a negative response to the sailor's lot. But by the mid-century, mounting concern over the quality and supply of seamen, together with contemporary interest in health and morality, led to a consideration of seamen's welfare and safety. It could be said that passenger measures provided examples of possible reform, but much more significant was that early action towards passengers – inferior like slaves, undeserving like convicts, or of scant consequence like emigrants – could be held up by reformers as an irrefutable precedent for intervention to assist seamen, who were so vital to the nation. Thus, the Merchant Shipping Act of 1867 contained health requirements relating to anti-scorbutics and medical stores and laid down specifications for accommodation and sanitation. Around the same time recommendations concerning diet were scheduled and the 1870s saw the first moves to legislate for seaworthiness. Like the early Passenger Acts these initial measures were far from satisfactory, but once the principle was on the statute books, in time more effective provisions would ensue. By the turn-of-the-century, and certainly after the Merchant Shipping Act of 1906, sailors' conditions were considerably improved. By initiation, example and precedent, the government's assumed obligations to the bulk passenger trades led to wider reform.

Individually, the importance of each of the bulk freight passenger trades has been recognised in the past. The roles, including the shipping aspect, of the slave trade in the African, Caribbean, and American experience; the emigrant trade to exporting European and recipient American nations; and the convict and free passenger trades which founded Australia, have been accepted and widely researched. Far less fully appreciated has been their collective role. This paper has emphasised the collective contribution and influence of the bulk freight passenger trades in shipping employment, commercial development and state intervention. The collective dimension of this paper, however, has not strayed beyond national, or British, confines. If, to Britain's considerable participation is added that of other nations, notably France and Portugal in the slave trade, Portugal in convict transportation, Germany in the emigrant trade and the lesser involvement of many other countries including the Netherlands, Denmark, Norway, Sweden, Spain and the U.S.A., it is evident that the bulk passenger trades, taken together, occupy a position of enormous significance in international maritime development. Freighting passengers underlay expansion, organisational advance and a new role for government.

Henry Mayhew and the British Seaman

Contemporary studies of the life and position of the British seaman in the nineteenth century are remarkably rare. If one excludes material contained in Parliamentary Papers concerned with legislative proposals and action, the material available is thin indeed for most of the century. There are, of course, numerous accounts of the sailor's lot in books aimed at juvenile readers; again there is the literature associated with various seamen's mission movements; but such accounts of the hard but wholesome life of jolly Jack Tar or alternatively of rough innocents exposed to the moral perils of the sea have little to offer in the way of serious study. More meaningful material is to be found in Thomas Brassey's *British Seamen*[1] or Frank Bullen's work, published at the turn of the century, *Men of the Merchant Service*.[2] And, published in the twentieth century, there are books such as those of Runciman, looking back to the days of sail.[3] All such works, however, cover only the latter part of the Victorian era. This paper is concerned with a unique study of the British seaman in the mid-century which in the past appears to have been little known and certainly underutilized.

The study in question took the form of a collection of letters on seamen, part of a much longer series on labour in London, written by Henry Mayhew, which appeared in the daily newspaper, the *Morning Chronicle*, in 1850.[4] Lest the idea of letters in a newspaper appears insubstantial, it must be pointed out that each letter occupied some six full columns and averaged 10,000 words. There were six letters on seamen

---

[1]Thomas Brassey, *British Seamen* (Longmans, Green, and Co., 1877).

[2]Frank T. Bullen, *The Men of the Merchant Service* (Murray, 1900).

[3]Sir Walter Runciman, *Before the Mast and After* (Fisher Unwin, 1924): *Collier Brigs and Their Sailors* (Fisher Unwin, 1926); *The Shellback's Progress in the Nineteenth Century* (Walter Scott, 1904).

[4]The entire series of letters in the *Morning Chronicle* comprised eighty-two in all, published between 19 October 1849 and 12 December 1850.

comprising a study of around 80,000 words in all.[5] If the letters are impressive in length, so too are they in their breadth of coverage. Three letters concerned themselves with the "seaman afloat" – broken down into fourteen foreign trades, in steamships, and four coastal trades. The other three letters examined the life of the "seaman ashore" with detailed accounts of better boarding houses, the worst boarding houses, and charitable institutions. Many of the letters, particularly those on the seaman afloat, were heavily embellished with statistics examining such features as the growth of trade, shipping, the number of men in the service, and the commerce of the port of London.[6] All of which adds up to a comprehensive study, one which it is hardly possible to do justice to in a short survey. This paper, therefore, concentrates on a limited number of aspects. Initially, it is perhaps desirable to say a few words about Henry Mayhew and his life and work generally, and then to enquire why his work on seamen has been ignored in the past. Following this it is proposed to look at the letters themselves and to pose the following four questions. First, why did Mayhew write them, why did he include seamen in his survey? Second, what was Mayhew's technique and what is so special about the letters for historians? Third, what sort of material is covered in the letters? And finally, what special issues, worthy of further discussion, arise from the letters?

Henry Mayhew was born in 1812, the son of a London solicitor.[7] He was educated at Westminister School until, aged fifteen, he absconded allegedly to avoid a flogging for revising his Greek grammar during Abbey service. His father then sent him to sea and he served a year with the East India Company making one voyage to Calcutta. He then entered his father's practice, but soon tired of the law and embarked on a literary/bohemian career which he was to follow until his death in 1878. Looked at dispassionately, Mayhew's adult life was one of under-

---

[5]The letters on seamen were numbered and dated as follows: XL, 7 March 1850; XLI, 11 March 1850; XL II, 14 March 1850; XLVI, 3 April 1850; XLVII, 11 April 1850; XLVIII, 19 April 1850; L, 2 May 1850; LI, 9 May 1850.

[6]Mayhew's statistics were largely drawn from the contemporary works of George R. Porter, John R. McCulloch, and official returns contained in Parliamentary Papers.

[7]Biographical details of Mayhew's life are surprisingly thin. The best account is to be found in John L. Bradley's introduction to the World's Classics, *Selections from London Labour and the London Poor* (Oxford University Press, 1965)

achievement. A domineering father, a temperament capable of bursts of enthusiasm inevitably followed by lengthy periods of lassitude, and an indifference to financial matters – counsel at his bankruptcy hearing in 1846 described him as "too sanguine in his hopes, and somewhat irregular in his accounts,"[8] all combined to shape a career which never fulfilled his immense potential. True, he enjoyed a considerable literary output and he was a founder editor of *Punch*, but only one work from his pen gained him real public recognition. The work in question, *London Labour and the London Poor,* which eventually appeared in book form in four volumes in 1861-1862, itself had a chequered history.[9] Its basis was the series of newspaper letters of 1849-1850, and it then appeared as a serial in weekly parts in the early 1850s before ultimately, a decade later, appearing in a bound format. Mayhew's work on labour aroused tremendous contemporary interest because of its scale and the vividness of its revelations to a "respectable" audience of the life, work and suffering of a class of the population never before so openly written about. This was the real world of Dickens' characters sympathetically yet faithfully described and reported as E.P. Thompson observes, "by an accomplished journalist with a sharp eye for detail and character."[10] Mayhew's work thus seized the public's interest in his own time. Subsequently it has been of continual interest to historians, particularly since Eileen Yeo's study of Mayhew as a systematic empirical investigator. Yeo has championed Mayhew's work, observing that his "attempts at economic and sociological analysis entitle him to an important place in the history of social investigation."[11]

It might well be asked why, if Mayhew has for so long been a respected commentator, his work on seamen is so little known and certainly so little appreciated. The answer is simply that it has been inaccessible. Whereas many of Mayhew's *Morning Chronicle* letters were incorporated into his *London Labour and the London Poor*, some of the original letters, including those on seamen, were never reprinted. They

---

[8]Quoted by Thompson, in Edward P. Thompson and Eileen Yeo, *The Unknown Mayhew* (Penguin, 1971), 18.

[9]Henry Mayhew, *London Labour and the London Poor,* 4 vols (1861-1862).

[10]Thompson and Yeo, *Unknown Mayhew*, cover notes.

[11]*Ibid.,* 56-57.

thus existed only in their original format as newspaper articles, and newspapers being ephemeral, and the binding up of back issues a limited practice undertaken by only a few institutions, Mayhew's work on seamen virtually disappeared from sight. Once the contemporary interest aroused as the letters appeared in the press had blown over, attention focused only on those elements of Mayhew's work which were available in an accessible and bound format.[12] This was the case for virtually a century until the 1960s when there was a growth of interest in Mayhew's wider writings arising from scholars in the field of Victorian literature examining the common experience of Dickens, Trollope, Kingsley and Mayhew, and historians active in the burgeoning fields of urban studies and the new social history. Fresh research saw scholars looking beyond *London Labour and the London Poor* back to the original *Morning Chronicle* articles which were enthusiastically rediscovered and recognised for the unique social survey they comprised. The work of Humphreys,[13] Thompson[14] and Yeo in providing a proper recognition of Mayhew's importance deserves more attention than can be afforded here; however, an outcome of their work was the publication of two collections of extracts from the *Morning Chronicle*.[15] Both concentrated on reprinting those letters which did not subsequently appear in *London Labour and the London Poor*, but such was the sheer volume of the letters that neither collection attempted to reprint all previously unpublished letters. Both collections included extracts from the letters on seamen, indeed there was some overlapping, but the extracts together only covered some thirty-five percent of Mayhew's work on seamen. Yet though modern reprints have reproduced a portion of the seaman letters, they have done little more than bring them to light for the

---

[12]An examination of the *British Union – Catalogue of Periodicals* reveals that only the British, Bodleian and Cambridge University Librarian hold copies of the *Morning Chronicle* containing Mayhew's "Letters."

[13]Anne Humphreys, *Travels into the Poor Man's Country: The Work of Henry Mayhew* (University of Georgia Press, Athens, 1977).

[14]Edward P. Thompson, "The Political Education of Henry Mayhew," *Victorian Studies,* XI (1967); see also Gertrude Himmelfarb, "Mayhew's Poor: A Problem of Identity," *Victorian Studies*, XIV (1971).

[15]Anne Humphreys, ed., *Voices of the Poor* (Frank Cass, 1971); Thompson and Yeo, *Unknown Mayhew.*

scholars involved had their focus of interest elsewhere, being concerned with industrial workers, the pattern of labour, the urban population, in all of which seamen, however incorrectly, are not customarily featured.

So much for the background of Mayhew's study; to turn to the letters themselves. First, what is so special about Mayhew's letters on seamen? To begin with, an observation made at the outset must be repeated, and it bears reiteration, namely that Mayhew's study is unique. To my knowledge there is nothing in the nineteenth century of comparable length or depth. Nor of the objectivity; it is worth emphasizing that Mayhew, unlike so many other commentators on the mercantile marine, was in no way connected with the business of shipping, hence charges of vested interest can hardly be levelled. A second special feature becomes apparent when we enquire, given the context in which he was writing, why Mayhew chose to write on seamen, and to write so extensively? This is a question worth posing, given that so many writers, both past and present, writing about the labour force have chosen, consciously or unconsciously, to exclude seamen. "Histories of the working class" or "studies of labour organisation" which contain nothing on seamen are very much the rule rather than the exception. In a sense this is understandable – when writers think of the labour force they tend to think of workers in agriculture, industry, in internal trades: of workers living and working in approximately the same location, and certainly workers labouring within the country. The seaman, whose work occurs in a wholly different environment and outside the kingdom, seems hardly to conform with the typical worker. Thus alongside the weavers, tailors, boot- and shoe-makers, carpenters and joiners, casual labourers, dockers, market men, cabinet makers, dressmakers and milliners, hatters, tanners and curriers, coopers, etc. who are the subjects of Mayhew's attention, the seaman sits somewhat strangely with high potential to be regarded as the odd one out. And yet Mayhew chose to include him and to devote six letters to him; indeed, no other worker gained a fuller coverage. Why? Primarily because Mayhew recognised that however different the seaman's lifestyle, work and location pattern, he was an integral element of the working masses. Mayhew appreciated that the seaman was a part of, as well as part from, the labour force. Mayhew's understanding of the position of the seaman revealed a perception denied to many others. Could this, one is tempted to ask, stem from his one-year in the merchant service, the only occasion in his life when he was directly in contact with the lower orders in a genuine work situation?

If Mayhew's perception of the sailor's lot enhances his study, so too does his form of research and presentation. The focus of Mayhew's investigation was workers, and to learn of their position he enquired not, as so many other contemporaries did, of their employers or of middle class observers – clergymen, doctors, poor-law officials, etc. – or, in this context, masters and shipowners; rather he approached the workers themselves and gained his information from direct personal interviews with workers. Mayhew made contact with his informants by various means: sometimes by making enquiry of "persons involved in the trade" he acquired the names of workers who subsequently attended at his office or were met elsewhere. In other cases Mayhew simply visited locations where particular workers were known to congregate, for example, in this instance, the docks or the Sailors' Home, and spontaneously engaged in conversation with those he encountered. There is nothing to suggest that the individuals interviewed were in any way "specially selected" or unrepresentative, although the nature of Mayhew's enquiry led him to seek out experienced and therefore presumably older workers. Mayhew was genuinely concerned to be objective; in another of his letters he wrote, "I seek for no extreme cases...If anything is to come of this hereafter, I am well aware that the end can be gained only by laying bare the sufferings of a *class*, and not of any particular individuals belonging thereto."[16]

In making direct contact with seamen Mayhew is very important, as he provides the views of a class not normally heard from. Seamen may have been the most numerous element of the merchant service, yet their voice was seldom heard in the nineteenth century, let alone listened to. Mayhew not merely spoke with seamen and listened to them sympathetically, but his reports of his conversations enable the reader as well to listen to the mid-nineteenth century seaman. This is because of Mayhew's technique of reporting his interviews which makes them so much more alive and real. Unlike the stilted interrogations on a question and answer basis in the evidence of official commissions and committees, or even the modern tape-recorded interview where the promptings of the interviewer, however discreet, are always present, Mayhew cleverly removed himself from the report, excluding the questions he had asked though they were clearly deducible and were often incorporated into the interviewee's answers.

---

[16]Letter VII, 9 November 1848.

Consequently, Mayhew's letters read as a series of personal autobiographical statements rather than as impersonal formal interviews. This is not to say that those seamen Mayhew spoke with were allowed to ramble and reminisce at will. Far from it; Mayhew had a set number of issues and questions concerning wages, conditions, attitudes to legislation, changes over time, and so on, and each witness was skilfully directed along such lines. Thus, while each letter contains a series of interviews, in each of which the interviewee is allowed to express himself, the whole has a purpose and coherence.

One further feature which makes Mayhew's work of special interest, and additionally may explain why Mayhew treated seamen so generously in terms of space, is that of the letters' topicality in terms of official consideration of the shipping industry. Mayhew certainly appreciated the special position of the seaman vis à vis legislation, as a remark in his opening letter makes abundantly clear: "the reckless and improvident character of sailors, and the peculiar nature of their service, coupled with a consideration of their vast importance to our national welfare, have long induced both the legislature and Courts of Justice to treat them differently from other labourers."[17] Both the shipping industry and sailors were very much a matter of public and legislative interest in 1849-50. The debate over the Navigation Laws was still fresh, and at the time when Mayhew was writing on seamen in the spring of 1850 the Merchant Shipping Bill was before the House of Commons. Mayhew cited the Bill's principal provisions and stated that one reason for his enquiry into the state of merchant seamen was to ascertain the views of seamen, or as he put it, "the men mainly interest" on the proposals before Parliament.

Mayhew's letters on seamen provide the reader with information on two levels; the specific accounts and comments of each individual interview, and the more general overview gained from looking at a number of letters or the study as a whole. The sheer volume of the letters presents a daunting and well-nigh impossible task to any would-be summariser. In a brief survey all that can be done is to indicate the fields in which information is provided and to try at the same time to give a flavour of Mayhew's vivid style of reporting.

---

[17]Letter XL, 7 March 1850.

Mayhew commenced his letters on seamen with a somewhat bizarre opening sentence, remarking that he was "obliged to defer for a few days my investigation...of prison labour. In the meantime [he proposed] to enquire into the condition, earnings and treatment of the men belonging to the Mercantile Marine."[18] Whether the reader was expected to infer that the latter was a reasonable substitute for the former is unclear. However, Mayhew, without more ado, plunged into a statistical survey of the expansion of British merchant shipping over the previous fifteen years, detailing figures of men, vessels, tonnages, clearances and trade. Mayhew stressed the beneficial employment effects of the increased demand for seamen which he observed "must be drafted from the overstocked handicrafts and manufactures of the country."[19] He then drew attention to maritime legislation under consideration at that time. Thus justifying the importance and relevance of his subject, Mayhew then indicated his approach – "I propose directing my attention to the state of the seaman *afloat* – after which I propose following him *ashore* and describing the impositions which are practised upon him."[20] Having then divided his seamen afloat into foreign and coastal trades, Mayhew embarked on his interviews. He opened with a bosun and a carpenter of an emigrant vessel in the Australian trade.[21] Their lengthy tale was a sorry one of vessels under-crewed in able seamen, with the deficiency made up with supernumeraries - "no sailors at all...not able to go aloft...couldn't put their feet above the shearpole;" of unfit vessels, "a man has often to carry emigrant ship in his arms...for the hands are always at the pumps;" crowded conditions for emigrants, with little segregation of the sexes – in consequence "scarcely a single woman who emigrates who keeps her character on board ship;" and provisions so bad "that the biscuits are so full of maggots that the sailors say they're rich as Welch rabbits when toasted." The bosun concluded that emigrant ships, for both men and passengers, were "a system of robbery from beginning to end." An account of a voyage in the South American trade followed with a valuable description

---

[18]*Ibid.*

[19]*Ibid.*

[20]*Ibid.*

[21]*Ibid.*

of the techniques of loading guano in the Chinqua islands, and thereafter came an account of the African trade with a seaman fresh back from the Gold Coast with a palm oil cargo.[22] He described lying off that coast, and visits from natives, "some had a few words of English, all that knew any English could swear; they soon pick that up; it's like their ABC among sailors." The health hazards of the white man's grave were graphically described – "if a man be ashore a day or two he generally has the fever when he gets on board again. Masters go off the quickest, as they are most ashore...the mortality there is great...I heard a Captain say out of twenty clerks he had taken out there seventeen had died." Not surprisingly the interviewee observed, "there's very little desertion on the African coast." He concluded with a description of the one perk of the African trade – that of crew members purchasing parrots for re-sale in England – "I have known 200 parrots on board; they made a precious noise, but half the birds die before they get to England."

The West India trade came next, with an interview with "a very fine looking fellow, as red as a hot climate could make him, fresh back from Kingston, Jamaica."[23] Outward bound most of the crew were foreigners – "I have often sailed with foreign seamen, but never with a Jew seaman...I see *them* only in the bum boats in England." The captain was unappreciative of the crew's efforts and kept calling all hands a "parcel of damned soldiers" – the ultimate insult? – and he swore terribly. He didn't read prayers, "swearing captains do though oft enough – by way of a set off they say." In Kingston, the interviewee described "thousands of blacks seeking for work and can't get it...I've heard hundreds of them say – and many a hundred times – for I've been on four voyages to the West Indies – that they were far better off when they were slaves, but I never heard them say they wished they were slaves again." In a further reminiscence, the informant, seeking to describe conditions, recounted a previous voyage where a dispute led to the Captain ("he was not drunk"), appearing with a brace of pistols and shooting two men, one dead.

Further interviews included a ship's carpenter fresh from a four-year voyage in the "whale fishery of the South seas," and then came two contrasting respondents – a Scotsman in the American mercantile service and an American seaman who had served in both British and American

---

[22]Letter XLI, 11 March 1850.

[23]*Ibid.*

vessels. Two further seamen then spoke of the East India trade. One, newly returned from a voyage to Aden, Ceylon and India complained bitterly of wages and provisions, though there was a "sweethearts and wives" every Saturday night. He made pertinent comments concerning the stowage of provisions. Far more favourable comments were made by an elderly seaman, at sea for about "four or five and thirty years," the last ten years in the East India trade in vessels of the London shipowner, Green.[24] Seamen in Green's vessels, he said, were well berthed, fed and treated; "I can say that if all men were like Mr. Green, our merchant service would be the envy of the world." Far less satisfied was a seaman in the Baltic trade, similarly at sea for over thirty years, who described appalling conditions and the seaman as "robbed on all sides;" while in the North Atlantic timber trade a seaman fresh from Quebec provided a useful account of the trade, recounted desertions in Quebec, and told of a drunken captain who though bound for North America almost made Portugal, and on the return voyage consumed 3½ gallons of brandy and was then reduced to drinking vitrol for nine days, till off Dungeness he gave £1 for a gallon of spirit to a pilot cutter.[25] Statements relating to the Brazilian, Portuguese and Mediterranean trades followed, the last mentioned being delivered by a chief mate returned from a Black Sea voyage who was highly sympathetic to low wages and conditions in the forecastle and equally constructive about officers and their training. A seaman employed in Hudson Bay ships who supplied a splendid account of that company's trading policy and a fine description of sailing in the Polar icefield, completed Mayhew's survey of sail in foreign trades.

From sail, Mayhew moved on to steam in foreign trades, commencing with a statistical review indicating the growing importance of steam vessels, before proceeding to interview two men of long experience aboard steam vessels, a fireman with twenty years in steam and another "sailor" with seventeen years in steam, mostly as a seaman but latterly as mate and master.[26] The fireman graphically described working conditions, "constant fire and steam about," noting how in such a situation "salt provisions were terribly trying." He was critical too of accommoda-

---

[24]Letter XLII, 14 March 1850.

[25]*Ibid.*

[26]Letter XLVI, 3 April 1850.

tion in iron vessels which were cold and wet particularly in their berths, and to go from them to the heat of the engine room "a man to stand it should have the constitution of a negro by day, and an Esquimeaux by night." There was much also on the technological aspects of working steam vessels and a useful comparison of practice, wages and conditions in different steam trades. From steam Mayhew moved to coastal trades, looking in turn at the Newcastle coal trade, and the Scots, Irish and Welsh trades. Two seamen spoke on the coal trade, providing details of loading and discharging practice and wages and conditions.[27] While emphasizing the quality of seamen in the trade, they made pertinent comments on the lack of fixed status amongst men in the trade. "One half are captains one voyage, cooks the next, then mates – then before the mast – and then may be, round to the captains again." There were comments too on the absence of formal navigation skills. Newcastle sailors knew every set of tides and channels down to London and recognised each stretch of coast. If lost they simply steered west or hailed a passing ship to ask where the land bears. "They never ask about latitude or longitude; that's no use to them." Fortunately, no such rule of thumb practice existed in the Scots trade where a seaman spoke of "masters better educated than in the coal trade," and observed how masters and men stuck together with little crew turnover. His account included a splendid description of Scottish clippers – their build, hull design and rapid voyage times. A seaman in the Welsh trade provided a glimpse of popular culture when describing his enthusiasm for visits to the theatre whenever his vessel docked in London. "I'm noways backwards in going to a play," he remarked, and he spoke of T.P. Cooke, a music hall comedian, whose act included a parody of a sailor. He described the act as a regular "good 'un," but as portraying the sailor "for what he was, and not what he is. We don't hitch our trousers so much now, nor shiver our timbers, nor 'd...n our eyes and gallant eyebrows' as much as we used to do. The sailor's hornpipe is much the same as in T.P Cooke's day. But we don't fling about money and grog as he does on stage, because we haven't got it to fling."[28]

From the seaman afloat Mayhew moved on to the seaman ashore: the very fact that Mayhew gave such serious attention to the seaman ashore is indicative of his perception. Mayhew understood that the labour

---

[27]*Ibid.*

[28]*Ibid.*

force of any port, at any time, contained seamen between voyages, whose position was in no way to be compared with that of the unoccupied, unemployed or casual workers, for the seaman's turn ashore was an integral element of his work pattern. Moreover, Mayhew appreciated the unique position of the freshly discharged seaman compared with other workers – that of possessing relative wealth through the accumulation of months or years of wages, but probably lacking a home or family to go to and anxious for the creature comforts denied him during his time afloat. All such features made the sailor the potential "prey of the crimp, slop seller, and a host of harpies who enriched themselves on the systematised ruin and degradation of the thoughtless and improvident mariner."[29] Mayhew's examination of accommodation for seamen was thorough and extensive. He visited the Sailors' Home, a charitable institution set up on the site of the old Brunswick Theatre on Well Street, near the London docks. From there he moved to visit the "better class of seaman's lodging houses," and then to Green's Home, an institution built by Green, the East India shipowner, for the accommodation of his own men. Then, proceeding down the scale, Mayhew enquired into the worst class of boarding masters, or "crimps," an account which encompassed dubious houses kept by dockers or the "lower orders of Irish," and reported on even less savoury activities and establishments in "Skinner's Bay," East Smithfield brothels, kidnapping houses in league with brokers' offices, and so on. In the course of such investigations Mayhew communicated with some twenty persons, most sailors, but also with boarding house masters, house runners and so-called "porters for seamen" – a further specie of crimp's operators.

The experiences which Mayhew's informants related were varied indeed. They included crimps' lodging houses in the courts and alleys of Shadwell, Wapping, St. George's and East Smithfield, "where beds are bad. Men, women and children pig together," and where crimps and runners specialised in "green 'uns," men who had not been in London before. "Most of the men lodging in these houses come from North America mainly – New Brunswick, Nova Scotia and Newfoundland." Such sailors were described as having "the character of being soft, [but] think themselves cunning" – a sure recipe for disaster amongst sharp or

---

[29]Letter XLVII, 11 April 1850.

criminal operators.[30] "Men are encouraged to drunkenness and all kinds of debauchery," said one interviewee, who described lodging houses who provided women who acted as wives (sometimes actually participating in marriage ceremonies) during Jack's stay ashore. Tales of drunken seamen being encouraged to stand treats, being short changed, and being robbed abounded, and there were extreme cases of kidnapping of seamen to supply them to unscrupulous captains, and even of seamen of Russian and Prussian ships being encouraged to desert through the inducement of better berths in British vessels; a practice involving the use of interpreters, the smuggling of belongings ashore, reception houses with secret panels and the connivance of the river police.[31] In this catalogue of the fleecing of the sailor ashore one interview will serve for many, the old story, familiar the world over. "I came [docked in] to London last Wednesday and was on my way to Mr. B...s, a respectable boarding master, whom I have known for eleven years...Well, I was going along the Highway, with a little drop of drink in my head, sailor like, you know, sir – half seas over, that's about the size of it – ...when I met with a young woman, and she asked me if I was looking out for anybody? I told her I wanted Mr. B...s, and she said, 'You had best come to my house; he's gone away.'" I answered, "Well, I don't mind: short reckonings make long friends." If I hadn't been tipsy I shouldn't have been carried off by such a craft. She took me to a house – I remember it was up a dark passage...and we had something more to drink. Next morning I found myself "skinned – that's about the size of it;...A pair of old canvas trousers were left for my good cloth ones but all the rest of my clothes were gone and the young woman was gone too." The sailor concluded that he hadn't bothered to report the incident, and that "it's no use prosecuting the people, I shan't be any poorer a twelve month off," the last phrase revealing much about the sailor's attitude to life.[32] There is far more that could be said of Mayhew's survey of the disreputable end of the "accommodation market," not least his interviews with runners and seaman's porters which provide an interesting account of crimping from another angle. Again, there is the whole of the more seemly and respectable accommodation sector where seamen appear

---

[30]Letter L, 2 May 1850.

[31]*Ibid.*

[32]*Ibid.*

to have gained a fairer treatment, less exploitation and better value for money. Time and space, however, do not permit a full coverage; consequently one example must suffice, namely Mayhew's examination of the Sailors' Home which is indicative of the investigative journalism aspect of Mayhew's work.[33]

Mayhew commenced his report on the seaman ashore with a visit to the Sailors' Home opened in 1835 as a charitable institution to secure a fair deal for seamen and to protect the sailor. He provided an excellent description of the Home; the spacious hall through the windows of which could be viewed a skittle ground; the saloon with its library shelves – on shelf containing a copy of the scriptures in almost every known language; the museum; the schoolroom where an evening class provided free instruction in navigation; the eight dormitories with their total of 300 beds each in a private cabin, and the apprentice ward, hung around with cards exhorting inmates to prayers, all beginning "My dear young friends."

Mayhew, however, was more interested in activities and attitudes within the house rather than its physical aspects. He praised the accommodation provided, noted the imaginative diet – meals including always watercresses or some other vegetable as an anti-scorbutic, and he quoted figures of the increasing number of sailors being catered for in the Home. In particular he was impressed by the fact that the Home was used by several shipowners as a pay office, thus temporarily staving off the attention of parasites waiting for Jack to come into funds, and the fact that the Home served as a savings bank to seamen. Mayhew described how "every inmate is urged to make the institution his banker," and how monies deposited with the Home were actually paid into a bank but were returned (with savings bank interest) to the seaman on demand at the Home: "and so he is saved any trouble, delay or hindrance, through any informality, that might pester him at the savings bank, and make him unwilling to use it a second time," an observation which shows how Mayhew recognised that seamen might feel uncomfortable in the more formal atmosphere of a savings bank office. Various inmates professed their satisfied use of the "bank" at the Home, and Mayhew heard of one of the oldest boarders who had accumulated £200.

But, while other observers would have concluded their visit to the Sailors' Home with hymns of praise for middle class philanthropy,

---

[33]Letter XLVIII, 19 April 1850.

Mayhew was not the ordinary observer: he looked and enquired more thoroughly, observing the Home to be "an excellent institution" but one requiring "many alterations before it can be said to carry out fully the intentions of its benevolent founders." He was critical on a number of counts. He criticised what he regarded as early closing hours (perhaps unfairly, for doors shut at eleven); the treatment of inmates who through illness or being unable to find a new ship had outstayed their funds; he made unfavourable comparisons between the running costs of the Home compared with other boarding houses – implying over-staffing and over-payment of officials; and, this is perhaps most interesting, he uncovered a system of touting for custom for the Home, carried on by tailors. Mayhew discovered that three tailors/outfitters with premises near the Sailors' Home had some form of agreement with the manager of the Home for exclusive custom; the Home management refusing to allow other tailors entry and being unwilling to settle outside tailors' bills. The three favoured tailors employed runners who boarded ships at Gravesend or Blackwall. The runners' function was twofold: to encourage seamen to stay at the Sailors' Home, and, more so, to advance seamen money, the advance being billed to the Home as payment for over-priced or non-delivered mythical items of clothing. Mayhew obtained this information from a tailor's runner who provided full details of the scale of the abuse, "I have seen 8 tailors' runners (all belonging to the three firms) plying in the Home at once," and the response of tailors to sailors seeking cash, "well I can't let you have *money*, you know it's against the rules, but I can as you're so pressing, let you have what you want and charge it as a garment, and put it down with a percentage." The scale of the abuse was revealed by an informant who stated that "tailors' runners do all the touting for the Home which now has only one agent of its own for that purpose; but *he's* not seen to work more than one tide in a week perhaps." Moreover, it is clear that the tailors' runners were no better than those of the normal crimp, they being expected "to look sharp after the seamen that they've had as customers and get them ships before all their money is done, or they may be troublesome to the tailors when they want money or such like." Further dubious practice stemmed from the allegation that the bulk of the Home's officers were licensed shipping agents, and other corruptions and abuses were described such as the closure of the superintendent and cashier's office so that the doorkeeper could advance money at high interest; payment charged for meals not supplied, and the sale of seamen's belongings, chests and clothes, in cases of financial hardship. An interviewee observed, "Men as so sucked, as I have told you from my own knowledge, by runners and tailors and the servants of the House that I'm satisfied £20 in a sailor's pocket will go further at a boarding master's than at the Home." Such charges against the Sailors' Home together with unfavourable comparisons made with Green's Home (which Mayhew was generous in his praise of) led to an aggrieved letter of complaint from the Chairman of the Sailors' Home, Rear Admiral Hope, to the *Morning Chronicle* denying and rebutting Mayhew's report, though the crucial charge linking the Home with tailoring establishments was not satisfactorily explained.[34] Mayhew was not convinced; nor would be any objective observer.

If Mayhew's letters on seamen looked at letter by letter, piece by piece, interview by interview, provide much that is informative and thought provoking, so too does an overview gained by considering the study as a whole. And it must be said that the present-day reader enjoys an advantage over his contemporary counterpart who was reading the letters in instalments, at intervals over nine weeks between early March and early May 1850. Looked at as a whole, the study reveals many themes, not least the diversity and world-wide character of British commerce and shipping, but the seaman is always the focal point, and on a number of aspects Mayhew's study provides impressions and raises issues pertinent to maritime and social historians certainly warranting serious consideration and further study.

Two such features stand out: one, Mayhew's emphasis on the experiences of seamen ashore; and the other, the impression gained of seamen's attitudes through the many statements and interviews recounted. The second is particularly fascinating, not merely because of its unique quality but because it reveals the seaman as more articulate and conscious of his condition than has often been supposed. To comment first on Mayhew's emphasis on seamen ashore. The exceptional length and detail of the coverage, and Mayhew's obvious understanding of the seaman's position, should serve both to excite and interest and to raise questions of maritime historians. The seaman ashore, lurid generalised accounts apart, has hardly received the attention he merits. True, recent studies by

---

[34]Letter L, 2 May 1850.

Fingard[35] and Dixon[36] are important – though perhaps both are over-generous in their rehabilitation of the crimp, but a host of aspects remain for further consideration; not least the need for a fuller appreciation of the position of the seamen ashore compared with other workers, both when he was fully discharged and rich in funds and later when his resources were reduced. Again, the good boarding house sector, which as Mayhew shows did exist, has generally been ignored in favour of the racier and seamier, and finally, what of the accommodation and facilities for seamen in smaller ports? Past research has concentrated on the great ports – London, Quebec, New York, Liverpool and Cardiff. Did lesser anchorages offer simply a microcosm or were facilities and outlook different?

It is, however, in the area of the attitudes of seamen that Mayhew is most compelling: in this area three inter-related aspects stand out, the sailor's sense of grievance, his greater awareness, and, for want of a better phrase, the United States' dimension. Almost all the sailors interviewed professed dissatisfaction about their conditions, and those few fortunate to have found a satisfactory berth were eager to contrast their good fortune with less congenial conditions previously experienced. Complaints were predictable: food – poor quality, limited in provision and often inedible; wages – low and often cut through fines and over-priced slop chest purchases; accommodation – overcrowded, cramped, invariably ill-ventilated and often wet; tyrannical officers; foul-mouthed and foul-behavioured captains, and masters and owners, in particular "petty owners," "who take every opportunity to rob the seaman," are all graphically catalogued many times over by Mayhew's seamen. And while one world expect protest whenever one solicits the view of ship's crews, and any other workers for that matter, it must be said that Mayhew's complainants spoke with apparent justification. What does emerge is much more than forecastle grumbling. One thing which is clear from this catalogue of bitterness is that the seaman was far more fully aware of his position and what was happening around him than might be imagined from the traditional interpretation of the sailor's character. To be sure, in the

---

[35]Judity Fingard, *Jack in Port: Sailortowns of Eastern Canada* (University of Toronto Press, 1982).

[36]Conrad Dixon, "The Rise and Fall of the Crimp, 1840-1914," in Stephen Fisher, ed., *British Shipping and Seamen, 1630-1690: Some Studies* (University of Exeter Press, 1984), 49-67.

main, Mayhew spoke with older, experienced seamen, more likely to possess a wider and maturer outlook, yet the comment of one sailor, "it ain't the same as it used to be, our fathers and mothers you see give us all a little education, and we are now able to see and feel the wrongs that are put upon us....,"[37] is a reminder that the standard of education amongst English seamen was improving, and with it came a more questioning attitude and a greater awareness. This is certainly apparent in comments about conditions which were couched not simply in terms of demands for better conditions, but often as well in terms of complaints about regulations flouted, for example, the undermanning of emigrant vessels or measures of food short of official standards. Again, there was an awareness that government had the power to intervene and a belief that it should, not merely on conditions but particularly on issues such as examinations for officers. Many sailors had sorry tales of the navigational in expertise of captains and mates, but to quote one example: "from the ignorance I have seen in officers, I am certain it is wrong to let anybody command a ship without his being examined first as to his fitness. Young fellows often get command of a ship through favour, they're relations or the owner, or something.... Our second mate was appointed by the owners, and hardly knew how to knot a yarn."[38] Interestingly, the two mates who Mayhew interviewed suggested quite detailed programmes of government action, including not merely examinations but better log keeping, compulsory chronometers, changes in wages practice including a suggestion for standardisation, and for regulation concerning hygiene and ventilation. This is not to imply socialist or interventionist tendencies amongst sailors. Indeed, one sailor probably spoke for all when he observed that what was really needed was "better usage, better pay and more to eat... You may register and register (i.e. legislate) and go nibbling on, but I tell you it's the only way...good seamanship and good usage – they often go together."[39] Above all there was a sense of "rights," or rather the lack of them: "A man daren't speak for his rights on board ship;" "an Englishman feels he hasn't his just rights;" "it's a shameful

---

[37]Letter XL, 7 March 1850.

[38]Letter XLI, 11 March 1850.

[39]*Ibid.*

thing…we are not treated like men at all."[40] Comparisons with slavery
show how issues of the day impinged on the seaman's view of this
condition: "We're worse off than the black slaves, they are taken care of,
and we are not,"[41] and for a sense of injustice it is hard to imagine a
stronger expression than "we are slaves on salt water and the Captain is
a god." "Britons never shall be slaves" is all stuff now – regular stuff, sir.
I'm disgusted to hear it. Why a Russian is happier in his slavery than is an
Englishman with any feelings, if he's poor."[42]

The most frequent comparison alluded to was one which looked
to better conditions elsewhere, namely the United States. Time and time
again, sailors spoke of the American mercantile marine as "better service
than the English, better wages, better meat, better ships."[43] But comments
went much further than creature comforts, and the sense of "rights" comes
out again. "They know how to behave to a man in America;" "they have
got feeling for seamen there;" "An Englishman is very little thought of in
his own country, but he's well thought of in America! He's a man there;"
"They don't impose on sailors in America:" "People don't enjoy
themselves here, I think, as they do in America: they're distant like, and
haven't the feeling for a working man that there is across the water."[44]
Such statements have implications beyond the basic concern of the seaman
about wages and conditions; they suggest that some seamen at least were
conscious of the hypocrisy and concepts of class which prevailed in mid-
Victorian England, and recognised the greater openness, equality and
opportunity of America. The number of English sailors serving in
American vessels, and desertions in Quebec in pursuit of such ends, are
practical demonstrations of such sentiments. More emotive were a few
replies, no doubt in response to a hypothetical question from Mayhew,

---

[40]Letter XL, 7 March 1850.

[41]*Ibid.*

[42]Letter XLII, 14 March 1850.

[43]Letter XLI, 11 March 1850.

[44]See the statements of sailors in the following trades: Letter XL, 7 March 1850,
Australian; Letter XLI, 11 March 1850, West India, South Sea whale fishery, United
States – comments of a "Scotchman" and an American; Letter XLII, 14 March 1850, East
India, Mediterranean; Letter XLVI, 3 April 1850, London foreign steam, Welsh coasting.

where seamen stated that in time of war they would be unwilling to fight for Britain and certainly not against America. A "Scotchman in the American service" bitterly stated, "I'll not fight for a country that starves and cheats you. I'll never fight for short weight and stinting in everything, not I."[45]

It is clear that Mayhew's study goes beyond being a source of information and evidence, and that its special value lies not merely in Mayhew's acute perception of the British sailor's lot, his focus on the seamen themselves for information, and the genius of his vital life-like style of reporting, but also in its provision of a rare insight into the seaman's attitudes and emotions. In all such respects Mayhew deepens our understanding, but more, and perhaps this is of greater importance, Mayhew widens our horizons, he encourages us to look beyond the obvious focus of the seaman aboard ship to the seaman ashore between contracts, and, more penetratingly, he invites us to consider how the society which the seaman lived in, and trends and changes in that society, impinged on the sailor's view of life. While fully appreciating the many varied special features which make the position of the sailor so different from that of other workers, i.e. a calling apart, at the same time Mayhew, in including seamen in his overall study and in his letters on seamen themselves, reminds us that seamen are nevertheless a part of greater entities – the labour force and society as a whole. Maritime historians, like all historians working in specialist fields, occasionally need reminding of the wider perspective and broader context of their study.

---

[45]Letter XLI, 11 March 1850.

Mid-Victorian Attitudes to Seamen and Maritime Reform: The Society for Improving the Condition of Merchant Seamen, 1867[1]

The 1867 Merchant Shipping Amendment Act is well known as a major nineteenth century statute aimed at improving the health, safety and comfort of British merchants seafarers. But maritime historians are less familiar with the extra-parliamentary committee which paved the way for this reform. Its tactics were not those of self-publicity, such as the flamboyant Samuel Plimsoll was to adopt a few years later, and this may account for its comparative neglect, but the Society for the Improvement of the Condition of Merchant Seamen exercised a timely and critical influence on the development of seafarers' welfare legislation. For this reason alone its work merits wider knowledge. A report issued by the Society in April 1867 stands in its own right as a valuable contemporary statement of mid-Victorian opinion on merchant shipping and seamen.[2] As a programme for reform published shortly before the Merchant Shipping Amendment Bill was drawn up, the report is additionally significant, particularly when measured against the legislation eventually enacted. Furthermore, the Society's existence and activity was very much in keeping with the spirit and practice of the times – for although it concentrated on seamen and safety at sea, the Society's involvement with issues such as diet, health, accommodation, labour contracts and the role of government mirrored the approach and interests of other social reform groups in the mid-nineteenth century. In all these respects an examination of the Society, besides promoting an understanding of attitudes to seamen

---

[1]I am grateful to my colleague, Professor P.L. Cottrell, for his comments on an earlier draft of this paper.

[2]*Report of the Committee of the Society for Improving the Condition of Merchant Seamen* (London, 1867). Henceforth cited as *Report*.

and reform, demonstrates the importance of setting studies of maritime themes in the broader context of economic, political and social change.

The Society was formed at a "meeting of gentlemen interested in the condition of merchant seamen" held on 27 February 1867 in the rooms of the Social Science Association in London.[3] Most of the tewnty-nine participants were professionally conncected with the sea, but otherwise their interests and backgrounds were diverse. All however were united in the belief that an organized society would carry more weight than individual initiatives.[4] Captain Henry Toynbee, a leading light in the Society, was a retired master mariner with thirty-five years sea-going experience and an established reputation as an influential writer on the merchant marine;[5] its chairman, Admiral A.P. Ryder, had served as a commissioner on the Inquiry into the State of the Navigation Schools and was a staunch advocate of better training for seamen.[6] Dr. William Dixon, Medical Inspector of Customs, was the author of a treatise on syphilis in

---

[3]*Ibid.*, 5-6.

[4]The Committee comprised: Capt. H.H. Beamish, R.N.; E. Chadwick; Cmdr. W. Dawson, R.N.; Rev. Greatorex; T. Gray; Capt. G. Grigs; Rear Admiral E.P. Halstead; T. Hanbury, M.P.; W. Henty; T.A. Herbert; Capt. E. Hight; E.D. Kilburn; A. Kinnaird, M.P.; H. Leach; S. Lonsdale; T. Mackay; C.M. Norwood, M.P.;Rear Admiral A.P. Ryder; Rev. J. Scarth; J. Southern; G. Sproat; D. Stone, M.D.; W. Strang; Capt. H. Toynbee; Capt. J. Toynbee; T. Twining; Cmdr. E.H. Verney, R.N.; M. Whitwill; and R. Wigram. Apart from the activities and positions of members detailed in the text, it might be noted that Capt. Joseph Toynbee, probably the brother of Henry Toynbee, was a retired East India master who had corresponded with the Board of Trade on the subject of scurvy; see United Kingdom, Parliament, *Parliamentary Papers (BPP)*, LXIV (1867), 66-67. Cmdr. W. Dawson was the author of "Commander R.N." (pseud.), *Merchant Sailors' Wants* (London, n.d.). Arthur Kinnaird, M.P. had chaired Henry Toynbee's paper at the meeting of the Social Sciences Association on 19 November 1866. Dr. D. Stone had written letters on seaman's health to the *Times* and the Board of Trade; see *BPP*, LXIV (1867), 1-68.

[5]Henry Toynbee, "The Social Condition of Merchant Seamen," in W.L. Clay (ed.), *Social Science, being the Journal and Sessional Proceedings of the National Association for the Promotion of Social Science for the year 1866-7* (London, n.d. [1867?]), 39-51.

[6]See, for example, Alfred P. Ryder and S.R. Graves, *A Letter on the National Dangers Which Result from the Great Deterioration in the Seamen of the Mercantile Marine: With Reasons for the Adoption of an Apprenticeship System* (London, 1860).

the navy,[7] while Dr. Norman Chevers, based in Calcutta, was a prolific writer on tropical health matters.[8] Dr. Harry Leach, Resident Medical Officer of the hospital ship *Dreadnought* in 1865 and later attached to the Board of Trade, had produced works on cholera and the "hygenic condition of the mercantile marine;" he was subsequently to achieve a measure of immortality through his *The Ship Captain's Medical Guide*, first published in 1868 and into its fourteenth edition by the turn of the century.[9] Dixon and Leach were also important figures in the agitation over scurvy in the mid-1860s.[10] G. Sproat, a shipowner, and Commander Verney were joint secretaries of the Society along with Toynbee, while the Reverends Greatorex and Scarth were respectively chaplains of the Sailor's Home and Greenwich Water-Side Mission. Messrs. Henty, Mackay, Whitwell and Wigram were all major shipowners and Hanbury and Norwood were Members of Parliament. Edwin Chadwick, the utilitarian reformer at the Board of Health, and Thomas Gray, the exponent of *laissez-faire* at the Marine Department of the Board of Trade, also participated in the Society. This Committee, with its M.P.s, naval officers, medical men, shipmasters, current and ex-civil servants, clerics and humanitarian reformers represented a wide spectrum of interested opinion. The presence of Chadwick and Gray, master mariners and leading shipowners, left no foundation for any charge that the Committee was one-sided or unbalanced in its composition – though the historian might wryly note the absence of the very subject of enquiry, seamen themselves. However, in the mid-nineteenth century the impetus for

---

[7]William Dixon, *On the Prevention of Syphilis in the Navy* (London, 1865). Some confusion exists over the spelling of Dixon's name; whether it is Dixon or Dickson. The British Library cites him as Dixon.

[8]Norman Chevers, *On the Preservation of the Health of Seamen, Especially Those Frequenting Calcutta and the Other Indian Ports* (Calcutta, 1864).

[9]Harry Leach, *Brief Notes on the Last Epidemic of Cholera in Turkey* (London, 1866); *A Report on the Hygenic Condition of the Mercantile Marine and on the Preventable Diseases of Merchant Seamen* (London, 1867); *The Ship Captain's Medical Guide* (London, 1868). The fourteenth edition of the *Guide* appeared in 1906.

[10]Leach and Dixon were significant contributors to "Correspondence between the Board of Trade and... on the Subject of Survey," *BPP*, L (1865), 275-319; LXIV (1867), 1-123. In particular, Leach and Dixon acted as sole analysts of the purity of lime juice in the 1867 enquiry.

reform in the field of seamen's welfare – and for that matter most other areas of social reform – emanated from humanitarian, middle-class interests. Moreover, these people believed that advances were to be made through compromise rather than confrontation. The instigators of the Society for Improving the Condition of Merchant Seamen were sufficiently acute politically to recognise that the path to progress lay through an accommodatory approach.

The minutes of the Society's first meeting suggest that it was conceived as a short-lived investigative and reporting body. The objectives were specified as the collection of information and the making of recommendations; moreover, it was agreed "that the Society should be dissolved after communicating the results of its investigations to the Board of Trade and the publication of its Report." It would appear that the Society saw itself almost as an extra-parliamentary "Royal Commission," but one in which the recognition of divergent opinion and the desire to produce a body of unanimous recommendations dictated a compromise approach. Its object was to influence and put pressure on the legislature and offices of administration, notably the Board of Trade. In typical Victorian fashion it set about doing so by initiating an enquiry. Almost every conceivable aspect of seamen's lives – afloat and ashore, in health, sickness, old age and death – were considered, and attention, although focussing on the seaman's economic and social well-being, extended also to his moral and spiritual welfare. In each of these areas the Committee made observations on the prevailing situation and proposals for action to be taken. In keeping with its overall approach, recommendations applied to all parties: the legislature, offices of administration, shipowners, masters and seamen themselves. Remarkably the report was produced within five weeks. This was achieved through an expeditious division of labour: sub-committees examined each of five areas – health, accommodation ashore, wages, discipline and the protection of the seaman's life at sea. While the unofficial commissioners were experts in their chosen fields, it would be wrong to infer that the Committee was merely re-working past studies. The Society actively sought comments and suggestions and generated considerable correspondence: over thirty letters together with other statements and extracts appeared in an appendix to its report. The authors included shipowners, masters, naval and Customs officers and medical persons – notably Dr. William Dixon and Florence Nightingale, whose opinion was sought on the matter of hygiene. Also in the appendix were three petitions from seamen in Newcastle, Sunderland

and Seaham, the latter comprising the resolutions of a meeting of 170 seafarers held on 18 February 1867 "on hearing that a Society was to be formed."[11] This suggests that some publicity and groundwork had been undertaken before the actual formation of the Society and that its activities extended over a longer period than the five weeks of its formal existence. Indeed it might be said that the Society's formation owned much to an increasing interest in the conditions of merchants seafarers spanning several decades and to the new momentum of reform following the abolition of the Navigation Laws in 1849. Hence as a preliminary to examining the substance of the Society's report it is necessary to identify the issues which had emerged during fifty years or more of discussion of seafaring labour. Debate on these issues was, as we shall see, directly related to the circumstances of the Society's formation.

A paramount concern from an early period was the supply of seafaring men to the Royal Navy. One of the chief purposes of the Navigation Laws was to ensure a "nursery of seamen." Moreover, the peculiar conditions of work and service of seamen – which placed them in a totally different position than all other workers – had led government from the early eighteenth century to regulate their contractual obligations. Both of these long-term concerns were prominent issues in the post-Napoleonic era.[12] The Navy's desire to ensure a reserve was a prime factor in the creation of a Register of Seamen in 1835 and, through the office of the Registrar, a major campaign to enforce apprenticeship regulations.[13] Concern over the "reserve" issue increased as impressment, though never formally abrogated, ceased to be an acceptable means of meeting wartime manning requirements. Sir Robert Parker headed a Commission "On the Manning of the Navy" in 1852 and a Royal

---

[11]*Report*, 95-97.

[12]On the general issue of manning the Navy, see J.S. Bromley, *The Manning of the Royal Navy: Selected Published Pamphlets 1693-1873* (London, 1974); and Stephen Jones, "Blood Red Roses: The Supply of Merchant Seamen in the Nineteenth Century," Mariner's Mirror, LVIII (1972), 429-444.

[13]Valerie C. Burton, "Apprenticeship Regulation and Maritime Labour in the Nineteenth Century British Merchant Marine," *International Journal of Maritime History*, I, No. 2 (1989), 29-49.

Commission on the same theme reported in 1859.[14] Likewise, the issue of contractual obligations was continually under review and the codification and strengthening of the law relating to seamen was a major element of the Mercantile Marine Act of 1850.[15]

Alongside these traditional aspects, new areas of concern developed in the postwar years. That of safety at sea came to prominence first in the specific area of the passenger trades, where from 1802 a massive body of legislation came onto the statute books,[16] and then more widely as indicated by the significant Select Committees on the subject of shipwrecks in 1836 and 1843.[17] Many of these committees' recommendations were ultimately acted upon – notably in 1850 with the establishment of a Marine Department of the Board of Trade and the compulsory certification of masters and mates. A further fresh consideration was the moral and social welfare of seamen. Here the impetus came from voluntary action, notably with the movement towards the establishment of Seaman's Missions and Homes, which developed from the 1820s.[18] Indeed, philanthropic activity directed towards seamen increased rapidly at this time.[19] Thus, the postwar period saw a growth of public interest in seamen, both in old and new areas of concern. Add to these varied aspects such dramatic issues as the repeal of the Navigation Laws in 1849 and the

---

[14]"Copies of a Correspondence on the Manning of the Royal Navy," *BPP*, LX (1852-1853), 9: "Royal Commission to Inquire into the best means of Manning the Navy," *BPP*, VI (1859), sess. 1, 1.

[15]13 & 14 Vict. c. 93.

[16]Oliver MacDonagh, *A Pattern of Government Growth, 1800-60* (London, 1961).

[17]"Select Committee on Causes of Shipwrecks," *BPP*, XVII (1836), 373; "Select Committee on Shipwrecks," *BPP*, IX (1843), 1.

[18]Roald Kverndal, *Seamen's Missions: Their Origin and Early Growth* (Pasadena, 1986); Alston Kennerly, "Seamen's Missions and Sailors' Homes: Spiritual and Social Welfare Provisions for Seafarers in British Ports in the Nineteenth Century," in Stephen Fisher (ed.), *Studies in British Privateering, Trading Enterprise and Seamen's Welfare, 1770-1900* (Exeter, 1987), 121-165.

[19]Jon Press, "Philanthropy and the British Shipping Industry 1815-60," *International Journal of Maritime History I*, No. 1 (1989), 107-127.

beginnings of the transition from sail to steam – both of which had considerable implications for maritime work – and the high profile of seafaring labour in public debate is clearly apparent.

These concerns over merchant seamen, though specific in focus, were nevertheless part of much wider shifts of opinion and interest. The nation's armed forces, both army and navy, were a matter of constant attention in a period when memories of the prolonged war with France were still very real and were to take on fresh dimensions with the embarrassing experience of the Crimea. Conditions of service, discipline, recruitment, and health and welfare all came to be matters of public discussion.[20] Of even wider debate were such basic social issues as health, accommodation and diet. These increasingly demanded consideration as industrialisation and urbanisation created unprecedented social and environmental problems. Public health, notably through epidemic outbreaks such as cholera – a disease emanating from overseas – became of pressing significance.[21] The emphasis during Sir John Simon's chairmanship of the Board of Health was on occupational and industrial diseases, of which scurvy was a prime example.[22] Venereal disease, a condition common, though not peculiar, to seamen, gained publicity through the controversial Infectious Diseases Acts and the subsequent agitation led by Josephine Butler.[23] Shelter for those lacking the means to purchase their own homes also aroused concern. Shaftesbury's Lodging Houses Act of 1851 was the first official measure recognising the problem and was the forerunner of further official action in the housing field in

---

[20]Eugene L. Rasor, *Reform in the Royal Navy* (Hamden, Conn., 1976); Alan R. Skelley, *The Victorian Army at Home: The Recruitment and Terms and Conditions of the British Regular 1859-1899* (London, 1977).

[21]On cholera, see M. Pelling, *Cholera, Fever and English Medicine 1825-1865* (Oxford, 1978); Norman Longmate, *King Cholera* (London, 1966).

[22]W.M. Frazer, *A History of English Public Health* (Bailliere, 1950); Royston Lambert, *Sir John Simon 1816-1904 and English Social Administration* (London, 1963).

[23]Judith Walkowitz, *Prostitution and Victorian Society* (Cambridge, 1980).

1860 and 1868.[24] Alongside such legislation was the "model dwelling house movement" associated with such luminaries as Ruskin, Peabody and Octavia Hill. An offshoot of this movement was the campaign for accommodation of seamen and their dependents. The issue of diet aroused much interest, as well.[25] Contemporary discussion of diet and food adulteration extended to those in the armed services and through them to the mercantile marine where victuals, particularly on long voyages, had special implications for health.[26]

Such concerns, both particular to seamen and general, form the long-term context of the Society for Improving the Condition of Merchant Seamen. Crucial, however, in the shorter term – given the brief existence of the Society – are the immediate influences on its information. In the 1860s a variety of influences were at work: of direct import was the perennial issue of the manning of the navy, illustrated by the Royal Commission of 1859 and attempts to establish a formal reserve.[27] Associated with this were the consequences of two significant mid-nineteenth century developments – the repeal of the Navigation Laws and the growing presence of steam within the British mercantile marine. The outcome of the former was the increasing employment of foreign as opposed to British seamen; the impact of steam was to raise the issue of skill – for increasingly a growing proportion of maritime labour was employed below deck and as such lacked traditional seamanly skills.[28] Such changes in the composition of the British maritime labour force, annually portrayed in the statistics of the Registrar of Seamen, were highly

---

[24]Stanley D. Chapman (ed.), *The History of Working Class Housing: A Symposium* (Newton Abbott, 1971); J.N. Tarn, *Working Class Housing in 19th-Century Britain* (London, 1971).

[25]J.R. Burnett, *Plenty and Want* (London, 1966).

[26]Conrad Dixon, "Pound and Pint: Diet in the Merchant Service, 1750-1980," in Sarah Palmer and Glyndwr Williams (eds.), *Charted and Uncharted Waters* (London, 1981), 164-180.

[27]R. Taylor, "Manning the Royal Navy: The Reform of the Recruiting System, 1852-62," *Mariner's Mirror*, XLIV (1958), 302-313; XLV (1959), 46-58.

[28]See David M. Williams, "The Quality, Skill and Supply of Maritime Labour: Causes of Concern in Britain 1850-1914," in *Proceedings of the North Sea History Conference* (Stavanger, 1991), forthcoming, see 271-290 of this volume.

disturbing to many contempories.[29] More generally, the fresh outbreak of cholera in 1866 brought matters of health to the forefront. Diet and housing too were prominent issues, with the first legislation to combat food adulteration in 1860 and much action, official and voluntary, on lodging and dwelling houses.

Concern over seamen was manifested in many ways. At an official level there were Commissions and Committees of Enquiry and much Parliamentary activity. Outside of government, there was discussion in learned societies and institutions; such debate gained a wider audience through the publication of proceedings and speeches and a steady flow of books and pamphlets. A further means whereby interested parties could advance their concern was through the creation of pressure groups in the form of societies or associations. In all areas of social reform in mid-century, the trend was very much towards organisation. Within a formal body, the like-minded could exchange information, engage in fund-raising, and coordinate policy and activity aimed at promoting their cause. Such activity took various forms: sometimes its chief aim was simply to generate publicity, at others it involved direct action, such as charitable payments to "worthy recipients," educational programmes or the provision of facilities such as model lodging houses or temperance hostels. Thus various seaman's welfare societies gave donations to injured or aged seamen, distributed bibles and wholesome literature, or established and supported seamen's homes and missions.[30] A further purpose was to influence opinion and promote official action. The Society for Improving the Condition of Merchant Seamen falls squarely into this latter category. To describe the Society as merely a contemporary pressure group would be misleading, however, for in a variety of respects it was by no means typical of a body canvassing its own specific view.

The origins of the Society can be traced to a resolution presented to the 1866 congress of the Social Sciences Association by none other than Edwin Chadwick, who proposed that the Council of the Association appoint a sub-committee to consider the welfare of merchant seamen. The

---

[29]On the statistics available to contemporaries, see N. Cox, "The Records of the Registrar General of Shipping and Seamen," *Maritime History*, II (1972), 168-188; Valerie C. Burton, "Counting Seafarers: The Published Records of the Registry of Merchant Seamen 1849-1913," *Mariner's Mirror*, LXXI (1985), 305-320.

[30]See Press, "Philanthropy," Kennerly, "Seamen's Missions."

Association provided a meeting place and assistance in finding committee members, but the work was carried forward by Captain Toynbee and Admiral Ryder.[31] It will be remembered that Toynbee already had an established reputation as a pamphleteer on seamen's issues, while Ryder represented the continuing interest of the Admiralty in merchant marine matters. The instigators of the Society claimed as their justification for the calling of a meeting and the formation of a society that the "attention of the public had been recently directed to the condition of merchant seamen."[32] As earlier comments have indicated, this was certainly the case. The Society's promoters referred specifically to a variety of publications which had appeared in the previous two years: notably, a lecture by Thomas Gray; four papers by Henry Toynbee; various publications by the medical men, Drs. Dickson, Chevers, Barnes, Ward, and Leach; letters to the *Times* and a *Report* of the Royal United Service Institution. These varied references are worthy of comment for they indicate both the context and character of the Society.

Henry Toynbee's four lectures, all presented at important and influential venues and all subsequently published, were highly sympathetic towards the cause of seaman's welfare and strongly supportive of better accommodation for seamen ashore.[33] A further contemporary work referred to was the report on the loss of life at sea produced in 1866 by a committee of the Royal United Services Institution of which Ryder was a member.[34] This dealt at length with the decline in the quality and supply of British seamen and produced a list of thirty-three recommendations for action. Thomas Gray's activities were also acknowledged as having an important influence on the formation of the Society. Significantly, Gray had used the occasion of a paper at the Society of Arts in 1866 to deliver

---

[31]Toynbee, "The Social Condition of Merchant Seamen," 51.

[32]*Report*, 5.

[33]Toynbee, "The Social Condition of Merchant Seamen;" Toynbee, *On Mercantile Marine Legislation* (London, 1867); Toynbee, *The Social Condition of Seamen: A Paper Read at the Royal United Services Institution* (London, 1866). The fourth paper delivered by Tonybee has proved impossible to trace.

[34]Royal United Services Institution, *The Loss of Life at Sea With the Report of the Committee of the Council to the Vice-President of the Board of Trade* (London, 1866).

a remarkable attack on state intervention.[35] The tenor of his talk was anti-interventionist, not only in the sense of opposing any extension of activity but also in that he condemned as positively damaging many of the safety measures introduced in the previous decade. While conceding that government interference and official supervision were sometimes desirable, in Gray's mind the principle was clear: "there can be no question that Government interference is not only unnecessary, but may really become vicious if it attempts to attain an end by official inspection and supervision that can better be attained by the development of free and healthy competition."[36] Gray reiterated such views on the occasion of the Royal United Services meeting.[37]

At a time when the whole philosophy of the role of government, the freedom of the individual and the duties of the state were subjects of intense debate, Gray's strongly expressed views were widely-reported and keenly-supported in many quarters. Such hostility to state intervention was to say the least disturbing to many interested in maritime reform matters, for most envisaged some extension of regulation in the fulfilment of their aims. Although the absence of documentary evidence inevitably forces an historian to resort to hypothesis, it is reasonable to assume that the more politically-acute maritime reformers recognised that their position was weak on two counts: first, that irrespective of shipowners' antipathy to reforms, there was considerable general opposition to the extension of government involvement; and second, the effectiveness and impact of efforts to advance the position of seamen were weakened by the tendencies of individuals to campaign for reform in specific, narrow areas such as health, diet, accommodation or training. The Society for Improving the Condition of Merchant Seamen represented an attempt by persons genuinely concerned with the welfare of seamen to bring together all parties with an interest in the merchant marine, the aim being to draw up an agenda for action that was practical politically – in the broadest sense. Thus the Society's *Report* stated that "the members of the Committee were selected to represent the views of all the classes who might, it was supposed, take an intelligent interest in the objects of the Society" and it

---

[35]Thomas Gray, *Mercantile Marine Legislation* (London, 1866).

[36]*Ibid.*, 6.

[37]Royal United Service Institution, *The Loss of Life*, 20.

drew attention to the catholic composition of the membership.[38] The *Report* stressed the Society's search for a constructive compromise:

> One of the objects has been to ascertain whether a Committee of gentlemen, who might be expected by some persons to regard the question of improving the condition of merchant seamen from very divergent, if not opposite, points of view, could agree in drawing up a report which should contain really valuable suggestions for the legislator, for the shipowner, and the seamen.[39]

The nature of these suggestions must now be assessed.

The issue of health was examined most fully by the Society, perhaps reflecting the substantial presence of medical men.[40] On the subject of provisions, the committee deplored the incidence of scurvy in British merchant vessels, alleging it to be greater than in the "ships of any other nation." It saw the solution in obliging the owners of foreign-going vessels to provide "sufficient, wholesome and suitable provisions" and recommended fines for any failure to do so. But in deference no doubt to shipowning interests, the committee did not favour a prescribed scale, arguing that "government cannot and ought not to enforce a *scale* of rations, since in such a case the minimum of efficiency becomes the maximum of legal necessity." Instead, it suggested that the Board of Trade should merely list the items to be supplied.[41] If details were eschewed in the case of provisions generally, the issue of measures against scurvy were defined much more closely. Emphasising that lime juice should be considered as a provision and not as a medicine – for it was supplied in lieu of vegetables – the committee stressed the necessity of ensuring its

---

[38]*Report*, 6.

[39]*Ibid.*

[40]*Ibid.*, 8-16.

[41]The Society, however, did draw up a "suggested Scale of Provisions" which Toynbee submitted to the Board of Trade early in March 1867. See "Correspondence between the Board of Trade...on Dietary Scales," *BPP*, LXIII (1867), 20-21.

purity. This it was thought could be achieved by supplying juice from bond, licensing vendors and fixing heavy penalties for adulteration. And lest these pre-shipboard measures be rendered irrelevant by practice afloat, details of dosages, measures and stowage practice were prescribed. Dissent was not to be tolerated; almost on the lines of "they should have it and they shall have it," it was stated that ship's articles should contain a clause enforcing on seamen the use of lime juice and that a refusal to drink should be regarded as "disobedience of orders" and entered in the log. In such cases, if scurvy subsequently occurred, seamen would lose their wages while unfit; however, in instances where seamen had complied with regulations but nevertheless contracted the disease, they were to be given the right of legal redress against owners or master. Finally, to secure enforcement, it was recommended that inspectors be appointed by the Board of Trade to examine lime juice and provisions aboard ship and, a telling afterthought, that weighing scales on ships be periodically checked.

The emphasis on scurvy reflects contemporary concern over the issue and perhaps more so the presence on the committee of Drs. Leach and Stone. Leach's hand was even more visible when the committee turned to the specific issue of health. In communications to the *British Medical Journal*, Leach had stressed two aspects of the health of seamen, namely being ill when joining ship and the lack of facilities and medical knowledge aboard most vessels.[42] The committee took a similar line, observing that seamen often left port ill due to "profligacy and debauch" with the likelihood of vessels becoming dangerously shorthanded, especially in the absence of any provision afloat. The committee saw the remedy in measures ashore and aboard ship. Ashore, it advocated giving employers or their agents the right to require a medical inspection of prospective crew members. Again, reflecting the contemporary obsession with venereal disease, it suggested extending the terms of the recent Contagious Diseases Act to the "waterside parishes of the chief mercantile ports." To improve provisions afloat the committee recommended that Board of Trade examinations for masters and mates should test basic medical knowledge; that a guidebook on hygiene and personal cleanliness should be written; and that merchant vessels should carry adequate

---

[42]Leach's "Report on the Hygenic Condition of the Mercantile Marine" appeared in instalments in the *British Medical Journal* of 1867.

medicine chests and special food stores for the sick and convalescent. All these proposals had already been advanced by Leach, whose subsequent *Medical Guide* proved that most ideal of books – bringing benefit to both its public and its author. In one extreme aspect of health, or rather the lack of it, the committee did go beyond Leach's earlier study. For deaths afloat, it recommended report on arrival; coroner-type inquests; arrangements for wages and effects to go to next of kin; and public display of statements concerning the fatality in the appropriate shipping office.

The final element considered under the heading of health was that of accommodation. Again it was the wider contemporary concern with the relationship between living conditions, sanitation and disease which underlay this focus. The committee observed that in many cases crew accommodation was "inexcusably bad, deficient in light, ventilation, space and every sort of comfort." Pertinently, it noted as well that although regulations existed concerning headroom and cubic feet of air for convicts, emigrants, soldiers in transports, invalided servicemen and sailors in the Royal Navy, merchant seamen enjoyed no such minimum standards. In pursuit of better conditions, the committee made proposals for legislation ensuring twelve superficial feet (i.e., seventy-two cubic feet) per crew member on foreign-going ships; recommended various measures concerning ventilation; and stressed the advantages of deck houses compared with forecastles. In keeping with the spirit of an age which sought private solutions to public problems, it suggested a competition with a prize for the best plan or model of a properly-fitted and ventilated forecastle or deck house. To promote good accommodation it suggested that such space should be exempt from tonnage dues. In a strict sanitary vein, partly with a typical Victorian emphasis on "decency," it recommended measures for privies, urinals and disinfectant. Finally, so that all, but especially seamen, would be aware of such provisions, it advocated the public display of a placard detailing the rules.

If the environmental consequences of accommodation aboard ship prompted concern, so too did the moral aspects of accommodation ashore, the subject of the Society's second sub-committee.[43] Throughout the nineteenth century there was a strong belief that a lack of suitable lodgings and the exploitable position of newly paid-off seamen combined to lead to his degradation. To counter this, the Sailor's Home movement had

---

[43]*Report*, 17-20.

developed, with the first home established in London in 1829.[44] The committee praised such efforts but regretted that such residences had not proved self-supporting. It felt that seamen's homes should be on a sound commercial footing and, recognising that such establishments catered only for the unwed, advocated new provision for married seamen. This was Henry Toynbee's particular interest and, with specific reference to the contemporary lodging and dwelling house movement and the fashionable concept of "five percent philanthropy,"[45] the committee advocated that a "Society for Promoting the Erection of Seamen's Family Lodging Houses" should be formed. Indicative of Toynbee's special interest and position in the Society, the committee went into immense detail, listing priorities for accommodation and suggesting negotiations with the newly-formed charitable Improved Industrial Dwelling Company.[46] Nor was this the extent of the committee's, or Toynbee's, optimistic vision. Further advocated, hopefully with government assistance, were the establishment of Sailor's clubs, institutes and playgrounds. In conclusion, recognising that purpose-built accommodation might not always be available, the committee recommended the licensing of boardinghouse masters by the Board of Trade.

Wages and pensions were the concern of a further sub-committee.[47] The idea of pensions, connoting both thrift and provision for the future, was accorded universal commendation at a time when "self-help" was viewed as a prime virtue. And such plans were essential, especially given the termination of the Merchant Seamen's Fund in 1851. The committee strongly recommended that the government establish a pension and life insurance scheme and its detailed proposals covered almost every eventuality, including transfers and early retirement. While the issue of pensions was unlikely to be controversial, wages were a very

---

[44]Kennerly, "Seamen's Missions;" Sarah B. Palmer, "Seamen Ashore in Late Nineteenth Century London: Protection from the Crimps" in Paul Adam (ed.), *Seamen in Society* (Bucharest, 1980), 55-76.

[45]On the general theme of mid-nineteenth century philanthrophy, see B. Harrison, "Philanthropy and the Victorians," *Victorial Studies*, IX (1965-1966), 353-374.

[46]J.N. Tarn, *Five Per Cent Philanthropy: An Account of Housing in Urban Areas, 1840-1914* (London, 1974).

[47]*Report*, 21-24.

different matter. The compromise nature of the Society is evident here, for wage levels were never considered by the sub-committee. However, much attention was directed to forms of wage payment. Both the practice of advance notes and delays in the payment of accumulated wages on arrival in the home port were criticised as leading to abuse. The operation of the Royal Navy system of monthly note payments to dependents, shipping office provision and pay clerk services for the forwarding of wages, were seen as solutions to these problems.

The fourth sub-committee was concerned with discipline.[48] It interpreted its brief broadly, concerning itself also with the quality of labour and the moral and spiritual well-being of seamen. In the mid-nineteenth century, two aspects of discipline were of particular concern. One was the relationship in law between the seaman and his employer; changes in 1835 and from 1850, consequent on the creation of the Marine Department of the Board of Trade, had enormously complicated the seaman's contract.[49] As the committee observed, "the imperfectly defined power of masters and frequent ignorance as to the extent of authority causes extremes of leniency and tyranny." A solution was seen in better information, with "authority" recommended to produce a handbook and a public display aboard all ships of a placard listing "rights and duties."[50] Naval courts were also to be given extended powers. The second aspect of disciplinary concern was desertion, a growing problem from mid-century. In part, the clarification of contractual obligations would assist in the matter, but the committee also recommended tightening regulations on the discharge of men abroad, especially in those cases where masters encouraged desertion to lessen expenses – a recognition that the problem could reflect management as well as labour. Even so, the committee clearly took the view that disciplinary problems in part stemmed from moral failings. Improvement was sought by means of efforts to protect seamen from evil influence and bad company through excluding crimps and prostitutes from docks; the licensing of lodging house runners, seamen's porters and boatmen; and the prevention of unauthorised persons

---

[48]*Ibid.*, 24-29.

[49]Conrad Dixon, "Legislation and the Sailors' Lot, 1660-1914," in Adam (ed.), *Seamen in Society*, 96-106.

[50]*Report*, 21-24.

boarding incoming vessels. Less negatively, moral advance was to be attained by the encouragement of religious services and libraries aboard ship and the inspection of men's belongings to ensure adequate kit – though the latter would also serve to check for smuggled spirits.

The sub-committee on discipline saw problems of contract, desertion and moral weakness as elements of the wider issue of the quality of labour. The "deterioration" of the British seaman was an idea that obsessed contemporaries and almost all members of the Society had written or participated in this debate.[51] The alleged decline was viewed not merely in terms of discipline and character but also in the area of skill. Of course, in an age of technological change, with the wider dispersion of iron and steam, the requirements of the seaman were changing, but a belief that seamen no longer possessed traditional skills was widely held. To arrest this decline the committee proposed that the rating "able-bodied" should be more tightly defined and less casually granted. Prospective "able-bodied" seamen were to be examined by their officers, with a possible test being the standards required by the Royal Navy Reserve. And in order that good and bad seamen might be more easily distinguished, discharge certificates should be more specific in content and more reliably completed by masters – an observation reflecting on the contemporary practice of habitually recording "very good."[52]

The matter of "deterioration" gained a further and fuller coverage from the fifth sub-committee, which was charged with considering the protection of the seaman's life afloat.[53] Arguing that the attraction of sufficient seamen and the maintenance of quality labour were crucial to safeguarding the lives of those afloat, the committee dwelt at length on the subject of recruitment. This was a favoured theme of the Society's Chairman, Admiral Ryder, who as early as 1860 had been the joint author of *A Letter on the National Dangers Which Result from the Great*

---

[51]Some indication of the extent and scope of the "deterioration" debate can be gained from the opening chapter of Thomas Brassey, *British Seamen* (London, 1877), 1-34.

[52]*Ibid.*, 281-282.

[53]*Report*, 29-34.

Deterioration in the Seamen of the Mercantile Marine.[54] Echoing Ryder's long-held views and drawing on figures assembled for the 1866 United Services' enquiry, the sub-committee bewailed the growing presence of foreigners and the declining percentage of ABs within the labour force.[55] Young British entrants were urgently required, and they could best be encouraged by the support of existing, and the creation of new, training and reformatory ships and legislative support for shipowners taking boys as apprentices from such establishments. Both these remedies had long been advocated by Ryder. If the issue of recruitment saw positive, although hardly fresh, recommendations, the same could not be said of the committee's deliberations on the issue of safety at sea. Here the Society was at its least decisive, for after opening with the pertinent comment that a high percentage of "ships lost" was comprised of vessels insured for total loss, subsequent recommendations failed to face up to this disturbing observation. A load line was considered – but rejected on the feeble grounds that no single line was appropriate given different cargoes. Instead, safety recommendations were confined to piecemeal measures concerning compasses, lifeboats and buoys, charts, and additional elements in examinations for masters and mates. Here the interest of shipowners is apparent. Even more obvious is the influence of Thomas Gray, for this inconsequential programme was in keeping with the views he had evinced in his polemic before the Society of Arts and his subsequent conduct over regulation in the bulk trades and the Plimsoll agitation.[56]

Although the deliberations of the final sub-committee may have concluded on a less than positive note, this low key finish should not obscure the fact that as a whole the Society's *Report* was wide-ranging and penetrating in both its deliberations and recommendations. True, in neither respect was much fresh ground broken; indeed, the Committee itself noted that it did "not lay claim to any originality in the various recommenda-

---

[54]See note 6.

[55]Royal United Services Institution, *The Loss of Life*, 48-55.

[56]Geoffrey Alderman, "Samuel Plimsoll and the Shipping Interest," *Maritime Hisotry*, I (1970), 78-79; David M. Williams, "State Regulation of Merchant Shipping, 1839-1914: The Bulk Carrying Trades," in Palmer and Williams (eds.), *Charted and Uncharted Waters*, 55-80.

tions."[57] Much emphasis was placed, however, on the breadth of the enquiry which "had considered every suggestion, various recent publications...and many submissions."[58] Evidently, the Society conceived its role as one of drawing together the varied strands of the contemporary debate in a succinct synthesis – all these recommendations were compressed into a mere thirty-five pages. Toynbee, Ryder and other activists recognised the merits of brevity, if the report were to stand any chance of making a practical political impact.

In compiling its report the Society had fulfilled the major part of its stated objectives. It remained only to communicate the results to the Board of Trade. Here the Society's officers demonstrated again an appreciation of the realities of trying to influence the authorities. Conscious that submissions to government were often the products of blatant vested interests and thus likely to be discounted, they were at pains to point out in a preface that their submission was both unanimous and balanced; in other words, representative of all interests. Aware too that government's most effective weapon was procrastination, the *Report* stressed the need for immediate action. It noted that:

> the Committee is satisfied at being able to state, that although members have differed on certain measures, yet the clauses in their present shape have been adopted without protest, which proves what is most important to point out, viz., that it is the general opinion of the committee, that measures not less stringent, reforms not less radical than those pointed out, should be adopted, and adopted promptly.[59]

And should authority resort to the fall-back position of suggesting that proposed reforms, though worthy, were too extensive and ambitious, the Committee stressed that in presenting the *Report*, it proposed "to draw attention to the fact that direct legislative interference is only recommended in certain cases. The remainder of the clauses are merely

---

[57]*Report*, 6.

[58]*Ibid.*

[59]*Ibid.*, 7.

suggestions to shipowners and others."[60] Thus qualified, and hopefully
countering in advance possible official objections, the *Report* was prepared
for presentation. On 30 March 1867, within three days of its completion,
Ryder presented it to the President of the Board of Trade, the Duke of
Richmond. With this final act the work of the Society was completed and
in accordance with the terms of its foundation, it was automatically
dissolved.

The Society for Improving the Condition of Merchant Seamen thus
had a life span of little more than five weeks. What significance can be
attached to such a short-lived body? Answering this question requires
consideration from various standpoints: the immediate short-term impact
of the *Report*, its longer-term relevance as a pointer to maritime reform
and its value to the historian as an example of mid-Victorian attitudes and
practice.

On the immediate impact, it can be claimed that the *Report* had
some effect in two respects. First, the formation and activities of the
Society stirred the Board of Trade into action. It was hardly coincidence
that early in 1867 Gray embarked on enquiries into seaman's accommodation and diet and revived the Board's correspondence on scurvy.[61]
Second, the Duke of Richmond, in acknowledging the *Report*, replied that
he intended shortly to introduce an amendment to the Merchant Shipping
Act based on proposals drafted by his predecessor.[62] A three-month delay
followed – his bill was not presented to the Lords until early July.[63] When
introduced, its contents mirrored the Society's recommendations,
particularly in the area of seamen's health. This suggests that in the
interim Richmond took careful account of the *Report*.[64] All its detailed
recommendations concerning scurvy – the safeguarding of food purity,
rates of rations, penalties for non-compliance by owners and seamen –
were in the Act. So too were clauses relating to medical stores, a Board

---

[60]*Ibid.*, 35.

[61]"Copies of Applications Made to the Board of Trade on...Accommodation of
Seamen," *BPP*, LXIII (1867), 337; *BPP*, LXIII (1867), 403; *BPP*, LXIV (1867), 49.

[62]*Report*, 35.

[63]*Hansard's Parliamentary Debates*, Third series, CLXXXVII (1867), 850-851.

[64]30 & 31 Vict. c. 124.

of Trade authorised handbook, and provision for seamen's medical inspections (though the latter was permissive and not obligatory). Likewise on accommodation, the Act met the Society's suggestions on size and conditions, surveys, tonnage dues deductions, privies and the public display of certification of official standards. Clearly, the *Report* had served as a draft and perhaps a blueprint.

Official action in the field of health represented the greatest success of the *Report*. None of its other recommendations gained such immediate attention and action. Some were over-ambitious and a few too idealistic, but the *Report* nevertheless identified those areas which were to be the focus of attention over the next four decades or so. And in the main, when progress ultimately was made in these fields, the course of action followed was often along the lines it had envisaged, even if there was no direct debt. The only significant area of future reform not foreshadowed in the *Report* was that of load line legislation – that apart, the Society's deliberations displayed remarkable vision.

To say that the establishment of the Society is indicative of a concern over seaman is not so much to state the obvious as to highlight the level of interest in this question in the 1860s. The publicity accorded to the load line debate and Plimsoll's high profile role was such that the early 1870s have tended to be viewed as the beginning – and by some, as the epitomy – of concern over "Our Seamen."[65] Yet the wave of support which ensured Plimsoll's success was the outcome not of a sudden swell but a long-running tide which had its origins at least thirty or forty years earlier.[66] It is certainly possible to trace concern over the safety of seamen back to the Select Committee on Shipwrecks of 1836.[67] Between that Select Committee and the Society there are certain parallels: both owed their existence to the initiative and energy of genuine reformers and in

---

[65]Samuel Plimsoll, *Our Seamen: An Appeal* (London, 1873).

[66]For example, the action taken in the specific area of timber laden vessels which dates from 1839. See Williams, "State Regulation of Merchant Shipping."

[67]"Select Committee on the Causes of Shipwrecks," *BPP*, XVI (1836); on the circumstances of the committee, see David M. Williams, "James Silk Buckingham: Sailor, Explorer and Maritime Reformer," in Fisher (ed.), *Studies in British Privateering*, 99-120.

both cases their reports were compiled very rapidly.[68] Again, it might be said that each enquiry took place at a time when the general atmosphere was one of social and economic reform. Yet there was a difference in their contexts. By the 1860s there was a greater awareness of the whole spectrum of society's problems and some appreciation of how such issues impinged on each other. In consequence, although reformers in the 1860s still tended to focus on particular issues, their approach had a greater breadth and drew on the current knowledge, experience and approaches of other contemporary social concerns. Thus the Society not only interpreted its theme of the condition of merchant seamen in very broad terms but also in a way that related it to other pressing, current problems, such as endemic and epidemic disease, sanitation, housing, provision for old age, labour relations and so on. And if the Society in its examination of the position of merchant seamen drew on the wider social experience, it did so too in the way it envisaged reform.

In mid-Victorian England the means by which social progress might be attained were seen as many and varied; the advance of knowledge, self-help, philanthropy and state intervention could all contribute. Better knowledge and the fuller dissemination of such wisdom were looked upon as sources of real improvement: hence the emphasis in the Society's *Report* on fuller certificate examinations for masters and mates; technical advances in navigational and safety aids; the provision of handbooks and the stress on placards and notices. Self-help and personal effort offered another path to improvement, especially if such moral qualities could be assisted and encouraged: hence clubs and institutes ashore; libraries and spiritual provision afloat; and above all the promotion of the great virtue of thrift through better systems of wage payment and insurance. All were to be fostered to enable seamen themselves to improve the quality of their lives. None of this was to deny that more responsible and more fortunate classes had a role to play. Charity and voluntary effort, efficiently organised, could provide the leadership, means and structure for progress. Thus in the matter of accommodation ashore Toynbee saw private charitable endeavour as the way forward, an attitude wholly in keeping with the prevailing spirit of five percent philanthropy. And where problems could not be met by such approaches, it was recognised that

---

[68]The Select Committee of 1836 was agreed to on 14 June. Its report and evidence were presented to Parliament on 15 August. The great bulk of its activity occurred between 1 July and 5 August. See Williams, "James Silk Buckingham," 108-109.

government had some obligation to act. In the programme presented in the *Report*, the state had a significant role to play. Although each of the five sub-committees saw a function for the state in its field, strict *laissez-faire* adherents were reassured by a statement that "direct legislative interference is only recommended in certain areas."[69] The Society's proposals cast government as simply an encourager – in the matter of pensions or the employment of apprentices – or as a "policeman," restricting entry to docks and inbound vessels and licensing boatmen and boardinghouse keepers. Other recommendations merely requested extending the provisions of existing action, as in the cases of training and reformatory ships and the Infectious Diseases Act. The only sphere where real intervention, regulation and inspection were advocated was that of the "health of the seaman afloat," with its constituent elements of provisions, health and accommodation. Here there was a precedent: state intervention, albeit imprecise and ineffective, had been a feature of the 1854 Merchant Shipping Act.[70] Thus the Committee's recommendations in the sphere of government action were limited, being constrained by the attitudes of the day, political reality and the Society's own compromise constituency. In sum, the *Report* provides an outstanding summary of the varied dimensions of the seaman's condition. Moreover, it shows how proposed solutions to perceived problems were framed to receive general acceptance in the confused context of a society recognising the virtue of business freedom, ambivalent towards government intervention and disturbed by a humanitarian conscience.

The Committee's terms of reference and its ultimate recommendations also reveal much about attitudes to the subject of its concern, and not merely in the mid-Victorian era, for the debate over the seaman from the late eighteenth to the twentieth century was constantly beset by the dilemma of how he should be regarded. The very fact of the Society's existence, and that of literally hundreds of other maritime societies and charities,[71] is indicative of a recognition of the special position of the seaman within the labour force: his peculiar location, dangers and terms of employment; his role in the economy's vital overseas trading sector;

---

[69]*Report*, 35.

[70]17 & 18 Vic. c. 104.

[71]Kennerly, "Seamen's Missions," 121.

and his potential as a reserve in time of war. But for all these special features – fully appreciated by the Society – the seaman was still an element in the overall workforce and hence affected by, and requiring consideration in the context of, any features bearing on the position of labour generally.[72] It was this dichotomy which gave rise to very real differences of approach on how the seaman should be regarded. Was he to be viewed simply as a unit of labour, albeit working in special circumstances? Or, in the light of these special circumstances, was he to be viewed as more than just a pair of hands – rather as a personality, and if so, what sort of person? While some owners and masters perhaps saw their crews purely as hands, most observers regarded the seaman in human terms. But views varied between the extremes of seeing him as a simple innocent exposed to temptation and exploitation or, perhaps ultimately in consequence, as a degenerate, brutalised misfit. Such conflicting interpretations of the seaman's character explain the strange mixture of protective paternalism and rigid, sometimes harsh, supervision so evident in the maritime legislation of the nineteenth century. At all times the concerns of welfare and discipline exerted an influence.[73] Down to mid-century, discipline exercised a greater weight; from the 1860s, and certainly from the 1870s, the balance swung more towards welfare. Underlying this shift was a greater knowledge and understanding of the seaman's position. Of this new awareness, the Society for Improving the Condition of Merchant Seamen was both a product and a part.

---

[72]Some aspects of the seaman's peculiar position in society are discussed in a collection of essays, the title of which embodies one interpretation: Rosemary Ommer and Gerald Panting (eds.), *Working Men Who Got Wet* (St. John's, 1980).

[73]Dixon, "Legislation and the Sailor's Lot," 96-103.

"Advance Notes" and the Recruitment of Maritime Labour in Britain in the Nineteenth Century

That wage levels are a crucial factors in any labour market is obvious enough. What is less evident is the impact of how wages are paid. Yet the nature and supply of labour are clearly influenced by the form of payment, whether by time (hour, day, week or longer) or the piece, following the completion of agreed tasks or services in small or large units. Forms of payment depend on many elements, notably the character and context of the labour involved and the customary practice that evolved over time. In the age of sail, seafaring labour was paid in various ways, with differences arising from the specific character of the work undertaken.[1] In whaling and some fisheries, labour was paid by the "lay," receiving a share in the returns of a voyage; a similar form of remuneration prevailed on privateers. Payment by the piece, in this instance the voyage, was the usual practice on other fishing vessels and in short-sea trades – in the case of Britain, for instance, coastal shipping (especially the coal trade from the northeast to London) and on nearby European routes.[2] But many seafarers in the merchant service were paid by the month at a rate (which often varied according to destination) agreed at the time of enlistment. Still, many merchant seamen, particularly those engaged for long overseas voyages, were in a sense piece workers, paid on completion based on the duration of the voyage at the agreed rate.

---

[1]On the payment of seamen, see Ralph Davis, *The Rise of the English Shipping Industry in the Seventeenth and Eighteenth Centuries* (2nd ed., Newton Abbott, 1972), 133-158; Jon Press, "Wages in the Merchant Navy, 1815-54," *Journal of Transport History*, 3rd series, II (1981), 37-52.

[2]While payment by the voyage was usually confined to relatively short trades, there are examples from the 1860s of seamen in some North Atlantic trades being paid this was. See Judith Fingard, "'Those Crimps of Hell and Goblins Damned:' The Image and Reality of Quebec's Sailortown Bosses," in Rosemary Ommer and Gerald Panting (eds.), *Working Men Who Got Wet* (St. John's, 1980), 328-329.

While the level and form of returns to labour were clearly crucial influences on the labour market, the timing of the payment was also significant. Seamen, compared with most types of labour, were exceptional in that many were paid irregularly, at the completion of voyages afer months or even years of service. But while such recompense came at the termination of employment, seamen were also often paid in advance for part of their labour. Such payments might be in cash or in the form of an "advance note." In Scandinavia and the Baltic advances were in cash, while in France, Belgium, the Netherlands and Germany notes were more common.[3] In Britain, advances were invariable in the form of notes.

The advance note is the subject of this study. The approach is to consider first the nature and function of advance notes. Second, we will examine the consequences of the system. Third, we will see why notes became a subject of increasing concern in the nineteenth century and how government came to investigate and act on the matter. Finally, we will consider the significance of advance notes in the context of "mariners and markets" in the second half of the nineteenth century.

At the outset it is appropriate to explain the function of the advance note. A statement by J. O'Dowd, Assistant Solicitor of the Board of Customs, before the Royal Commission on Unseaworthy Ships in 1874 described notes as follows:

> The shipowners at the several ports of the United King-
> dom have felt it necessary to give seamen engaged for
> their ships an advance for every voyage of not less than
> a month's wage, to enable them to pay debts contracted
> for board and lodging ashore while waiting employment,
> and for the purchase of clothes and outfit requisite for the
> voyage. This is done, not by a money payment, but by an
> advance note...delivered to the seamen generally signed
> by the shipping master at the port at the time the seamen
> sign the ship's articles in the presence of that officer.[4]

---

[3]*Nautical Magazine*, August 1875, quoted in ThomasBrassey, *British Seamen* (London, 1877), 201.

[4]Great Britain, Parliament, House of Commons, *Parliamentary Papers (BPP)*, "Royal Commission on Unseaworthy Ships," 1873 [853], XXXVI, appendix XXX.

O'Dowd's statement is an admirable starting point but it contains implications which require qualification. First, his comments suggest that advance notes were peculiar to Britain; as well, they convey the notion that notes were of relatively recent origin. Neither is correct. Advance notes were a feature found throughout the world wherever there was a significant demand for seamen. They were used in other European and North American ports, and particularly in Québec, Australia, and India.[5] Hence, although my focus is on Britain, many facets have a significance for international maritime labour markets. Moreover, the practice of granting advances was long-standing. Ralph Davis provides evidence of them in certain trades from the mid-seventeenth century, and a 1744 statement by Bristol merchants reveals established practice:

> It has been always a custom to advance a month's wages
> to all the men intended to be ship (except the chief mate)
> either to discharge the debt contracted to the landlord with
> whom they lodge or to fit themselves with cloths and
> necessary for the voyage.[6]

A further qualification to O'Dowd's submission is the reference to "an advance for every voyage." This was not the case: advances were only given to seamen signing-on for a voyage likely to be of considerable duration. The coastal, Irish and short-sea trades, where voyages lasted at most a few weeks, did not follow the practice. Notes were reserved for the most part for trades outside European waters, although they were also found in the Baltic and Mediterranean trades.[7] It was thus deep-water trades where the advance note was most common. It follows that certain

---

[5]Québec was notorious in this respect because its pattern of trade and the need for crews for newly constructed vessels led to a pressing demand. High wages and generous advances were the result, with the latter used to lure seamen from other vessels. See Judith Fingard, *Jack in Port: Sailortowns of Eastern Canada* (Toronto, 1982).

[6]Walter E. Minchinton (eds.), *The Trade of Bristol in the Eighteenth Century* (Bristol, 1957), 153, quoted in David, *English Shipping Industry*, 143.

[7]Davis, *English Shipping Industry*, 133, writing on the seventeenth and eighteenth centuries, includes Baltic, Russian, Iberian and Mediterranean routes among the "longer voyages." The growing frequency of deep-water trades and possibly some reduction in voyage times provided a new perspective on "long distance trades."

ports – depending on their trading patterns – were more likely to use advance notes. London and west coast ports, such as Glasgow, Liverpool and Cardiff, used notes far more widely than east coast ports, where established coastal routes and close European connections characterized trade. Advance notes were generally confined to large ports with sizeable local markets for maritime labour that had a significant involvement in long-distance trades. In Liverpool, for example, the note was so customary that a witness before an 1878 Select Committee observed that "the thing has got to be so much as custom that whether he [the seamen] wants it or not, I believe he takes it."[8] Still, just as the note was rare in some trades and ports, only some owners issued notes. It is important to remember when considering comments and criticisms that shipowners' views reflected their particular situations.

It is clear then that the advance note was extensively used in long-distance trades and most fully developed in major ports.[9] Perhaps the clearest evidence of its widespread employment – although this anticipated future discussion – is that, following abolition by government, notes had to be offered to secure labour for long-distance sail trades and were eventually legalized anew. The system dated at least to the seventeenth century but, despite such long-standing origins, the bulk of evidence on advance notes is to be found in the second half of the nineteenth century, particularly from the 1860s, when they became a matter of considerable debate.[10] The timing is not without significance, for in the mid-nineteenth century discussion of any aspect of shipping embodied the sail/steam dimension. Many who commented on advance notes observed that they were confined largely to sail because steam voyages were of relatively short duration and steam liners employed seamen on a much more regular

---

[8]*BPP*, "Select Committee on Merchant Seamen Bill," 1878 [205], XVI, qq. 748, 1786-1798.

[9]It is hoped that access to the Atlantic Canada Shipping Project's one percent sample of non-Canadian British Empire crew agreements will, in due course, permit a more precise indication of the extent of usage and changes over time.

[10]Not all those who commented on notes in the mid-nineteenth century appreciated the longevity of the practice. For example, E.A. Arthur, a surveyor with American Lloyds, was of the view that notes had been in existence "at least thirty years;" see *BPP*, "Royal Commission on Unseaworthy Ships," 1874-[1027-I], XXXIV, qq. 15, 370-15, 371.

basis.[11] Such observations underscore the traditional purpose and context of advance notes and emphasise that they were peculiar to the age of sail.

Having established this, it is now pertinent to enquire how the system worked in practice and what is consequences were. An example provided by O'Dowd in 1874 illustrates the form and practice.

> Ten days after the departure of the ship...from the last port or place in the River or Firth of Clyde, in which from any cause she may be before finally leaving for the voyage for which this note is issued, pay to the order of (seamen's name) the sum of £3.17.s.6d., provided the said seamen sails in and continues in the said vessel and daily earns his wages according to agreement.

> (Signed) ROBERT DOUGLAS, Master.
> To Messrs. Henderson and Co.
> Hope Street, Glasgow[12]

The above case reveals a number of features that deserve emphasis, including the fact that advance payment was made not in money but in the form of a promissory note to be paid only if the seamen sailed in the vessel and after such time as the voyage could be said to have properly begun. So there could be no doubt about the "proper" commencement of a voyage, the note defined the term.[13] Moreover, to take account of eventualities, such as seamen who managed to desert soon after sailing or vessels forced to return to port after a few days at sea, payment was not made until ten days after departure, although the precise conditions varied from port to port. For example, London notes were payable three days after the ship cleared Deal, while Cardiff notes were

---

[11]*BPP*, "Royal Commission on Unseaworthy Ships," 1874, [1027-I], XXXIV, qq. 10, 589-10, 590; *BPP*, "Select Committee on the Merchant Seamen Bill," 1878 [205], XVI, qq. 680, 753, 1740-1746, 4292, 4404-4410; *BPP*, "Royal Commission on Loss of Life at Sea," 1884-1885 [4577], XXXV, qq. 20, 647-20, 662.

[12]*BPP*, "Royal Commission on Unseaworthy Ships," 1873, [853], XXXVI, appendix XXX.

[13]The instance quoted included both the "River" and "Firth" of Forth – so there could be no legal quibbling over geographic terms by shrewd Scots lawyers!

payable three days after leaving the docks.[14] Although this became rarer toward the end of the nineteenth century, notes were sometimes given for an advance of two months pay.[15]

While in theory notes were sensible, recognising the peculiar features of seafaring labour and providing a legal safeguard for the risks incurred by shipowners, in reality they embodied significant dangers. These lay in the fact that for a note to be used by a seaman to acquire goods or services, he had to include someone to advance money or credit on it. Moreover, any party who advanced money against an advance note – and thereby incurred a risk – had an obvious interest in ensuring that the promise of service was kept. From these two basic features a host of potential abuses could follow. The cashing of a note put cash or credit in the hands of seamen who were free to use it for any purpose and not necessarily to cover outfitting, lodging debts or family provision. Drink and riotous living were held to be (and probably were) the chief items of expenditure. A more obvious and real abuse was that a seaman, having cashed hit note, might not sail and hence the note would be dishonoured. Such action would represent a breach of contract between the seamen and his employer and a fraud against whoever had advanced money or goods against it. Such risks ensured that money would be advanced only at a discount of anywhere from five or forty percent.[16] Persons who advanced money were generally associated with the avowed purpose of notes: suppliers of kit – usually referred to as tailors or outfitters – and boarding

---

[14]On London, see *BPP*, "Royal Commission on Unseaworthy Ships," 1874, [1027-I], XXXIV, qq. 13, 370-13, 371. On Cardiff, see *Ibid.*, qq. 1764-1769, especially q. 1766, where Thomas Snow Miller, Collector of Customs in Cardiff, described attempts to get the customary period extended to ten days but, no doubt due to the influence of crimps, "masters could not get hands on these terms."

[15]It has been suggested that notes were customarily given for two months pay and in some instances for three months. See Conrad Dixon. "The Rise and Fall of the Crimp, 1840-1914," in Stephen Fisher (ed.), *British Shipping and Seamen, 1630-1960: Some Studies* (Exeter, 1984), 49-67. My own reading of the evidence for the mid-nineteenth century suggests that one month's pay was the standard advance.

[16]Ten percent was the most commonly admitted rate of discount but this has a notional, nominal character about it; invariably, the supply of over-priced goods and services raised the real rate far higher. A rate of fifty percent was suggested by the MP, Henry Labouchere in a Commons debate in 1850. *Hansard's Parliamentary Debates*, 11 February 1850.

house keepers who specialised in catering for seafarers (crimps). Sailors' Homes, following their establishment from the 1830s also discounted notes – at much lower rates – but crimps were the principal handlers.[17] Invariably, outfitters and boarding house keepers worked together and sometimes the functions were combined. Often such individual were actively involved in the supply of seamen to outgoing vessels and were likely to have found the seamen his new berth. Parties who made an advance against a note had a very obvious interest in making sure, by any means possible, that the seaman joined his ship. Hence, these individuals endeavoured to keep control of the seamen until such time as he could be delivered to his vessel. Providing drink and low company were the best means to ensure this and an escort of the crimp's associates – together with some "ladies of the town" to lighten proceedings – served to guarantee it, thereby safeguarding the investment.

Such were the inherent features of the advance note that opened the door to abuse and corruption. Malpractice arising from the notes was the order of the day, according to nineteenth-century commentators. Contemporaries also noted a flood of further deplorable features.[18] Notes, it was said, encouraged seamen to be feckless, recklessly getting through all the earnings of a previous voyage in the knowledge that they could fall back on an advance. Again, dishonest seamen could acquire notes with no intention of sailing. Above all, notes were seen as a factor determining the pattern of labour recruitment for long-distance voyages. Effectively, notes – or rather their discounting, which was what gave rise to profit – encouraged certain parties to seek berths on behalf of seamen. Crimps and boarding house keepers gained the "permission" of seamen to secure contracts on their behalf through providing facilities for drink and "a good time," thereby encouraging debt. Seamen naturally responded to such

---

[17]On sailors' homes, see Alston Kennerly, "Seamen's Missions and Sailor's Homes: Spiritual and Social Welfare Provisions in British Ports in the Nineteenth Century," in Stephen Fisher (eds.), *Studies in British Privateering, Trading Enterprises and Seamen's Welfare, 1770-1900* (Exeter, 1987), 121-165. On rates, see Sarah B. Palmer, "Seamen Ashore in Late Nineteenth Century London: Protection from the Crimps," in Paul Adam (ed.), *Seamen in Society* (Paris, 1980), 62-63. Sailors' homes sometimes discounted notes to their cost. See *BPP*, "Select Committee on the Merchant Seamen Bill," 1878 [205], XVI, qq. 3336-3344.

[18]This paragraph draws on arguments repeated regularly in all the various official enquiries and contemporary literature cited throughout this paper.

incentives, in the process promoting an unhealthy recruitment system as well as access to drink, which allegedly led to debauchery and moral weakness. In short, notes placed seamen in the hands of dubious and often criminal operators and rendered them open to corruption and exploitation. The unscrupulous behaviour of crimps, desirous of ensuring that their "investments" boarded ship, often led to seamen joining vessels in an unfit condition. There were safety implications in this and even more so on those occasions when crimps endeavoured to safeguard their investment by providing "substitutes" who might have no seafaring skills or experience and might literally be picked up on the street. Crew discipline and morale were also jeopardized by disgruntled seamen who knew that their first, and sometimes second, month of labour (referred to by seamen as "the dead horse") was effectively without reward.[19] There was a danger too that seamen, in the opening months of an engagement when they had no accumulated wages to lose, might desert. This was common when vessels called at ports in the early stages of a voyage or visited New York, Québec, San Francisco and other high wage ports. These observations need to be viewed in their context, but while the extent of abuse may be in question, there can be no doubt that it occurred, probably on a wide scale.

Advance notes appear to have been of no concern until the second quarter of the nineteenth century. This may have been because the practice became more widespread from around 1800, as long-distance trades, where notes were given, grew rapidly. North Atlantic trades expanded greatly due to the growth of the Anglo-USA connection, particularly in cotton, and the expansion of the emigrant and British North American timber trades. Further developments included the growth of South American routes, new opportunities in the east following the abolition of the East India Company's monopoly, and the beginnings of commerce with Australasia. Yet while such expansion promoted the use of advance notes, other factors brought them under public scrutiny. From the 1830s, shipping assumed a much wider profile in political, economic and social debate in Britain.[20] Issues such as the strength of the British mercantile

---

[19]Dixon, "The Rise and Fall," 56.

[20]On these general issues, see Sarah Palmer, *Politics, Shipping and the Repeal of the Navigation Laws* (Manchester, 1990); Conrad Dixon, "Legislation and the Sailors' Lot," in Adam (ed.), *Seamen in Society*, 96-106; David M. Williams, "The Quality, Skill

marine and the repeal of the Navigation Laws; safety at sea; the discipline, morals and welfare of seafarers; and the quality and supply of seamen all commanded attention. In each area the advance note emerged as a relevant feature. The first such official instance was probably the 1835 investigation by the Select Committee on the Causes of Shipwrecks, which touched on abuses of "advances of wages."[21] Fifteen years later, the Mercantile Marine Act of 1850 included clauses dealing with advances.[22]

In the 1860s and 1870s, for a variety of reasons maritime issues assumed even greater prominence. First, there was a heightening of the long-standing interest in the condition and welfare of seamen, as witnessed by the activities of reformers such as Toynbee, Ryder, Leach and Dixon, and the Society for Improving the Condition of Merchant Seamen, which prompted a spate of publications and much debate.[23] In addition, the safety issue gained huge prominence because of Plimsoll's campaign against "unseaworthy ships;" while the focus of that crusade was the loading and condition of vessels, the nature and quality of seamen also came up. At the same time, the late 1860s and early 1870s were significant in the more general relations between workers and employers. Laws such as the Master and Servant Act of 1867 and the Criminal Law Amendment Act of 1871 – both hostile to labour in the matter of contracts – and, following the agitation that these provoked, the more equitable Employer and Workman Act and the Conspiracy and Protection of Property Act, both of 1875, encouraged consideration of the special circumstances that

---

and Supply of Maritime Labour: Causes of Concern in Britain, 1850-1914," in Lewis R. Fischer, *et al.* (eds.), *The North Sea. Twelve Essays on the Social History of Maritime Labour* (Stavanger, 1992), 41-58.

[21]*BPP*, "Select Committee into the Causes of Shipwrecks," 1836 [567], XVII, ix.

[22]13 and 14 Victoria, c. 93, c. 60. The act aimed to regulate advance notes by requiring them to be made before a shipping master on prescribed forms. This did not work and was repealed in 1854 in the Merchant Shipping Act, 17 and 18 Vict., c. 104.

[23]On campaigns over seamen's welfare in the mid-nineteenth century, see David M. Williams, "Mid-Victorian Attitudes to Seamen and Maritime Reform: The Society for Improving the Condition of Merchant Seamen, 1867," *International Journal of Maritime History*, III (1991), 101-126.

surrounded contracts between seamen and shipowners.[24] The consequence
of these varied forces was a veritable flood of enquiries, publications and
debate, both public and private. Merely to mention official investigations
in the decade of the 1870s illustrates the high level of concern. In 1873
there was the Report of the Assistant Secretary, Marine Department, with
reference to the supply of merchant seamen; sitting in the same year and
in 1874 was the Royal Commission on Unseaworthy Ships and in 1878
came the Select Committee on the Merchant Seamen's Bill. In addition
there were a series of Consular reports on British seamen. In all such
inquiries and reports the issue of advances loomed large.

Such was the extent of the debate that any attempt to recount it in
full is beyond the scope of this paper. But the gist can be conveyed
relatively succinctly.[25] Almost to a man, those who considered advance
notes condemned them. "The advance note is the root of all evil amongst
sailors," argued the President of the Cardiff Chamber of Commerce.[26]
James O'Dowd claimed that "of all the evils connected with merchant
shipping, the very worst is the advance note."[27] "One great cause of the
deterioration of our sailors appears to me to be the system now prevalent
of giving advances to men," Thomas Brassey observed, continuing that
"the issue of advance notes to seamen on engagement is a matter of
general complaint."[28] One witness before the Select Committee on the
Merchant Seamen Bill even asserted that notes were "mischievous in every
respect."[29] Underlying such condemnations were the basic arguments: that
notes "encouraged drunkenness and debauchery" and "placed seamen in

---

[24]On labour legislation generally, see R.Y. Hedges and A. Winterbottom, *The Legal History of Trade Unionism* (London, 1930).

[25]The best summary of contemporary views is Brassey, *British Seamen*, 178-211. This study, as the author acknowledged, was based almost exclusively on "Recent parliamentary and official documents."

[26]*BPP*, "Royal Commission on Unseaworthy Ships," 1873 [853], XXXVI, qq. 8285 and 8449, evidence of Colonel E.S. Hill.

[27]*Ibid*, q. 8570.

[28]Brassey, *British Seamen*, 187-188.

[29]*BPP*, "Select Committee on the Merchant Seamen Bill," 1878 [205], XVI, qq. 1786-1798.

the hands of crimps," who "put them aboard intoxicated" thereby endangering safety; led to "the defraudment of seamen;" "encouraged the recruitment of a 'lower class' of seamen;" were responsible for "demoralisation;" and provided an incentive to desert in foreign ports. In addition to such long-standing criticisms, there were newer diatribes contending that recent provisions that permitted seamen (who might have received advances) to protest against serving in allegedly "unseaworthy ships" could give rise to fraudulent and false claims. There were also legal questions associated with the commencement of a contract, clearly vital where advance notes were concerned. Did a contract commence when the seaman signed-on; when he received an advance note; when the note was cashed; or when he "joined the ship," a concept which provides its own definitional problems?

Many of these issues came to the fore in the proceedings of the Select Committee on the Merchant Seamen Bill of 1878. The complexities are revealed in an answer by Courtenay Peregrine Ilbert, the civil servant responsible for drafting the bill. In response to a question on a particular clause, Ilbert replied that:

> under existing law, if a seaman obtains an advance...and then breaks his contract and does not join ship, he may be punished; he may be sent to prison for neglecting or refusing to join; but the Bill proposes to repeal so much of the existing law as impose penalties for refusing to join. The consequences would be that, with regard to a seamen who obtained an advance, and then absconded, although he would be subject to a civil liability for breach of contract, yet it would be difficult to hit him under any provision of criminal law. I speak with some diffidence...but it appears...that there is no provision of the criminal law...which would clearly apply...The offence would not be embezzlement, it would not be larceny, and it would hardly be obtaining money under false pretences. Therefore, it was thought advisable to impose a penalty for breach of contract committed under these circumstances, which, in fact, amount to fraud.[30]

---

[30]*Ibid*, XVI, q. 7.

The above reveals clearly the legal niceties associated with the advance note and the failure to meet its obligations. If we add that under the Merchant Shipping Act of 1854 a seamen "neglecting or refusing without reasonable cause to join his ship" was liable to a forfeit of wages and imprisonment, with or without hard labour, while the terms of the 1878 Bill left "neglecting to join" (however that might be defined) as liable to civil remedy, the complexities of the legal position and the wisdom of pursuing them no further here is only too apparent.[31]

For such reasons, opinion was firmly against the advance note. No one really argued for it, although there were those who stressed its original purpose of financing outfits. There were others who, while sharing in the condemnation, argued that it was not a matter for official action since the practice was freely negotiated between employers and workers and shipowners had the power to end the system if they chose.[32] The vast majority of people – and the official reports of 1874 and 1878 – believed that advance notes should be abolished. Yet there were a host of reservations. Many shipowners claimed that advances were crucial to the recruitment of seamen for long-distance voyages in sail and that without them seamen would not be forthcoming. Again it was suggested that some seamen did use advances for their avowed purpose of purchasing necessary kit (and the special cases of the shipwrecked sailors and foreign seamen arriving in Britain seeking work were sometimes advanced), while other mariners, even more virtuous, availed themselves of advances to make provision for dependants.[33] In response, opponents argued that if

---

[31]The 1854 act can be found in 17 and 18 Vict., c 104, while the 1878 bill is formally titled "Bill to amend the Law relating to Merchant Seamen," *BPP*, 1878 [79], V, 125.

[32]Significantly, such views were held by Thomas Gray and Thomas Farrer, long-serving Board of Trade officials who were strong supporters of free markets. See David M. Williams, "State Regulation of Merchant Shipping 1839-1894: The Bulk Carrying Trades," in Sarah B. Palmer and Glynwr Williams (eds.), *Charted and Uncharted Waters* (London, 1982), 55-80; Dixon, "The Rise and Fall," 58-59. Gray recommended to the 1885 Royal Commission that advance notes be legalised again; *BPP*, "Royal Commission on Loss of Life at Sea," 1884-1885 [4577], XXXV, qq. 20, 693-20, 718.

[33]William Tulley, shipowner of Hull, quoted the case of penniless Scandinavian seamen arriving in the port seeking employment. See *BPP*, "Select Committee on the Merchant Seamen Bill," 1878 [205], XVI, qq. 2513-2516.

advances were necessary for recruitment, why not then make them in case which in theory would remove seamen from the clutches of crimps? Alternatively, some suggested that all ships should carry "slop chests" to enable mariners to purchase necessary kit abroad. To cater for dependants, why not provide allotment notes at regular intervals? Yet none of these suggestions really solved the problems. Cash advances hardly guaranteed to protect seamen from crimps; indeed, cash was even more attractive to them and riskier for shipowners. Slop chests imposed additional obligations on masters and owners and were open to malpractice; guarding against such abuse through official regulation was too interventionist for many. As for allotment notes for dependants, these were rightly viewed as confusing the issue.

Thus, for much of the 1860s and 1870s there was general agreement that advance notes were an evil that should be eliminated. Most favoured governmental prohibition. But abolition was not as straightforward as might appear. The Royal Commission of 1873-1874, which concluded that "the system of advance notes is one great obstacle to the amelioration of the condition of merchant seamen" and recommended that they be declared illegal, recognised that there would be "some inconvenience from the abolition of the existing system" and that there might be "considerable opposition to the change in the ports."[34] Above all there was the view of many shipowners that notes were essential to recruitment in long-haul sail.

This impasse led to much wringing of hands but no action. This was due not only to the complexities of the issue but also to the fact that themes such as unseaworthy ships, overloading and marine insurance aroused even fiercer controversy.[35] On such topics, the interests of

---

[34]*BPP*, "Royal Commission on Unseaworthy Ships," 1874 [1027-I], XXXIV, "Final Report," 11.

[35]As Brassey (*British Seamen*, 211-212) observed, "It may be that the abuses, arising from the practice of giving advance notes, are of secondary consequence, when compared with the greater issues raised by Mr. Plimsoll. Many, who now feel a passing, through earnest, interest in our shipping legislation, have been drawn to the subject solely by the desire to lessen the loss of life at sea; and they may view with indifference any proposals for reforms, which do not directly tend to promote the security of life." One might add that according to Geoffrey Adlerman, "Joseph Chamberlain's Attempted Reform of the British Mercantile Marine," *Journal of Transport History*, New series, I (1972), 171, "Plimsoll's voice had been strangely muted on the issue of their [advance notes]

shipowners and reformers clashed and real passions were aroused. The concern over advance notes has to be seen against the backdrop of this greater struggle. Indeed, it was in this context that action was finally taken. The reforming campaigns of Plimsoll and Joseph Chamberlain are not our direct concern here – and have been fully recounted elsewhere – but the evidence suggests that both were increasingly frustrated by the lack of real progress at the end of the 1870s. It seems that Chamberlain felt it was time for decisive action and that when Plimsoll on 19 May 1880 announced his intention to resign, he had been promised that an act would be passed about grain cargoes. Two days later Plimsoll gained a more tangible reward when the government appointed a Senate Committee on the losses of British ships. Simultaneously, Chamberlain introduced a bill to make the advance note illegal. This was duly passed and took effect from 1 August 1881.[36] After more than a decade positive action came in a swift and somewhat unexpected fashion. But abolition – though seemingly a milestone – did not end the matter.

Thus far, we have focussed on the nature, consequences and campaign to abolish advance notes. But it is also useful to consider their role in terms of "mariners and markets." Abundant contemporary evidence suggests that notes were significant in two respects. First, they influenced the way labour was recruited by placing labour in the hands of crimps who arranged and "cashed in" on their engagement. Second, advances were an essential element in the hiring of labour. A further, though subsidiary, issue is whether advance notes had any impact on wage levels. We will consider these matters in turn.

There is no doubt that advance notes influenced the way labour was recruited. Crimping was a complex business that exploited the accumulated earnings of seamen paid off after long voyages. Seamen in such circumstances remained vulnerable because they were not paid

---

abolition."

[36]David Master, *The Plimsoll Mark* (London, 1955); Geoffrey Alderman, "Samuel Plimsoll and the Shipping Interest," *Maritime History*, I (1970), 73-95; Alderman, "Joseph Chamberlain's Attempted Reform," 169-184; Williams, "State Regulation," 55-80; *BPP*, "Bill to Amend the Law relating to the Payment of Wages and Rating of Merchant Seamen," 1880 [119], CCIII; *BPP*, "Report on the Supply of British Seamen, the Number of Foreigners serving on Board British Merchant Ships, and the Reasons Given for their Employment, and on Crimping and other Matters bearing on those Subjects," 1886 [4709], LIX, 14-16.

immediately and thus remained susceptible to inducements of lodgings and "jolly" company "on account."[37] In this sense, crimps accommodated (or preyed upon) seamen who had accumulated "past income." Nonetheless, seamen also had future income in the form of an advance note. Hence crimps, having provided seamen with value – genuine or otherwise – for past earnings, were anxious to get liabilities off their hands by procuring new engagement for them. Advances, with their heavy discounts and the opportunity to supply over-priced goods and services, were a further incentive. "Inward-bound" crimping, the opportunity to grab the accumulated earnings of seamen arriving, was clearly the most important element of the equation, but "outward-bound" aspects, through handling notes, also brought their share of income. Many deep-sea seamen were thus accommodated on arrival by crimps who acted as go-betweens for their charges' further employment. In practice, while seeking berths for seamen who had exhausted past earnings, crimps supplied labour to masters and shipowners. In this sense they became labour agents who could be contacted if men were required. As such, crimps played an important intermediary role that was intimately intertwined with the practice of advances. In this way, notes shaped the very form of recruitment, since an intermediary was in no way essential. As a Board of Trade report of 1886 observed:

> There is no need for such an agent anywhere in this country, as every seamen wanting employment can go of himself to the Mercantile Marine office, or direct to any ship in need of hands. The crimp exists...in the interests of himself...and the shipowner finds the services of the crimp useful.[38]

Advance notes were a more direct influence on the labour market as an inducement to recruitment. Many contemporaries even claimed they were essential to the hiring process. Seamen, it was said, regarded notes as one of the prerequisites to join a long voyage and would not enlist without them. Was this the case? One of the problems of researching

---

[37]For a succinct amount of the business of crimping, see Dixon, "The Rise and Fall," 49-67.

[38]*BPP*, "Report on the Supply of British Seamen," 1886 [4709], LIX, 9-10.

maritime labour is that evidence of the direct voice and feelings of seamen are not readily available. This is certainly the case here, for in the great wealth of material consulted for this paper none emanates from seamen themselves. From these, it would appear that they favoured advances throughout the period. When abolition was threatened, there were demonstrations and strikes, although some observers suggested that such protests were instigated by crimping interests.[39] But whatever the strength of labour's view, shipowners invariably testified to official enquiries that seamen were committed to advances. When reading such claims, it is easy to infer that these were simply the comments of men who preferred to continue with the existing system of recruitment rather than suffer the inconvenience of change. After all, the prevailing system worked; while it was recognised to have abuses, the dissolute habits of seamen or their defrauding by crimps were not matters that caused most shipowners to sleep uneasily. Yet in this instance such cynical interpretations may be unfair because there is strong evidence that notes were an *essential* part of the market. This was especially clear in the 1880s. Despite the fact that the 1880 act abolished notes, advances continued to be made legally, since the law only prohibited any "document authorising or promising...the future payment of money on account of a seaman's wages conditionally on his going to sea...and made before those wages have been earned."[40] In other words, while the act aimed to abolish advances, it simply outlawed notes. Hence, as an 1886 report observed, owners were "free to make cash advances or to give the man a promisory note for any sum, and so long as payment of that note is not conditional on the man going to sea in the ship, it is not void under the statute."[41] The law could be, and was, evaded by making advances under another guise, the so-called "bonus note." The Royal Commission on the Loss of Life at Sea of 1887 reported that:

---

[39]Alderman, "Joseph Chamberlain's Attempted Reform," 174. The *St. Andrew's Waterside Mission Annual Report, 1880*, referred to the "strenuous opposition" of sailors; quoted in Palmer, "Seamen Ashore," note 76.

[40]43 & 44 Vict., c. 16.

[41]*BPP*, "Report on the Supply of British Seamen," 1886 [4709], LIX, 14-16.

A system has been devised under which the seamen engage at nominal wages at 1s. per month for one or two months after the commencement of the voyage, and a note is given by the shipowner for the difference between the nominal and the real wages, which is payable a few days after the ship has sailed if the seamen has really shipped...It is doubtful whether these notes are legal. The shipowner, however, does not in practice dispute the note if the seamen performs his engagement and ships in the vessel. There is no practical distinction, therefore, between these "bonus notes" and the old advance notes.[42]

The response to abolition thus was evasion; the practice persisted in another form. This surely says something about the nature of the market. Seamen continued to expect advances, and although shipowners could justifiably respond that advance notes were not permitted, it proved necessary to meet seamen's demands through subterfuge. As early as August 1882, Chamberlain's privately admitted doubts about "the wisdom of our legislation on advance notes."[43] The 1887 Commission not only recognised that abolition had been "quite ineffectual" but also noted that far from improving and protecting the position of seamen, it had made them even more vulnerable since discounters of bonus notes – who were more at risk because of the dubious legal status of such instruments – demanded even greater margins than in the past. Moreover, while it had been required to enter details about the advance note on crew agreements, no record of the new form of advances was kept.[44] The Royal Commission concluded that:

...the growth of this new practice shows that it is almost impossible to dispense altogether with a system, under

---

[42]*BPP*, "Royal Commission on Loss of Life at Sea," 1887 [5227], XLIII, "Final Report," 28-29.

[43]Quoted in Alderman, "Joseph Chamberlain's Attempted Reform," 174.

[44]*BPP*, "Report on the Supply of British Seamen," 1886 [4709], LIX, 15-16. Clauses to remedy this and to ensure the keeping of a record were included in an 1884 bill which, however, was subsequently dropped.

> which seamen can obtain some advance of their wages
> before proceeding to sea, and out of which they can
> procure new kits and other necessaries. We believe it will
> be the wisest course to recognise this necessity, and to
> legalise advance notes, limiting them in all cases to the
> amount of one month's wages.[45]

This recommendation was accepted and in 1889 advance notes for up to one month's wages were legalised. It would appear then that advance notes were essential for recruitment. Seamen expected them and, after 1881, owners felt it necessary to devise new means of payment advances.

Apart from men and masters, the further element in the labour market was the crimp who for obvious reasons wished to see the practice continue. And herein is the heart of the matter. While seamen demanded advances, were such demands irresistible? The willingness of owners to continue the practice may lie in the fact that, however much they disliked notes, they gained some benefits from the involvement of crimps who acted as labour agents but, far more crucially, could deliver. Owners and masters could hire crews in other ways, but could they ensure that the men turned up at the time of sailing? The crimp could and would do so because of his pecuniary interest.[46] The "essential" quality of advances in recruitment was perhaps more subtle than might first appear.

A final issue to consider is whether advances had any effect on wages. There were suggestions that they served as inducements and thus enabled owners to pay lower wages. Brassey believed that "with many shipowners, their attachment to the system of the advance note arises from a well-founded apprehension that some increase in the rate of wages would follow upon the abolition of advances."[47] Still, the evidence for advances affecting wages is limited. True, a Commander Bevis in 1852 supplied

---

[45]*BPP*, "Royal Commission on Loss of Life at Sea," 1887 [5227], XLIII, 29.

[46]Before 1880, when notes had legal standing, crimps were among the most active in encouraging court action against seamen who "failed to join." They provided information and gave evidence not so much in the hope of regaining advances but rather to discourage others. For examples of such behaviour, see *BPP*, "Select Committee on the Merchant Seamen Bill," 1878 [205], XVI, qq. 165-170, 448-454, 693-704, and 1563-1581.

[47]Brassey, *British Seamen*, 180.

details of wages in Liverpool which included rates of £3 to North America with no advance or £2 10s with one month's advance, and to China of £2 5s with one month's advance or £2 with two months' advance.[48] Twenty years later, Robert Rankin, a leading figure in the North American timber trade, claimed that he hired good men without advances but had to pay fifteen shillings or £1 per month above current rates.[49] Responses to an enquiry on whether advances were accompanied by lower wages, contained in a questionnaire sent to Superintendents of twenty-nine Mercantile Marine Officers in 1886, were varied, but most reported that advances were still widely given and that wage rates were not affected other than where bonus notes led to the nominal wage of 1s for the first month.[50] Indeed, given the volume of material on advances, references to any negative effect on wages were minimal. Rankin's claims may simply reflect that an owner had to pay a considerable premium if, contrary to custom, he did not provide the prerequisite, rather than any general lower wage rates associated with advances.[51] Overall, the impact of advance notes on the market lay in organisation and the strength of customary practice.

The advance note then was a form of payment peculiar to shipping in the age of sail. Its origins lay in the special needs of seamen to equip themselves for long-distance voyages. Though designed for a useful function, its operation led to abuses and from the mid-nineteenth century provoked criticism. Despite repeated demands, it was not abolished until 1880. Even then notes persisted through evasion until officially legalised in 1889. Such resilience stemmed from the role of the advance note in determining the pattern of labour supply and recruitment.

---

[48]*BPP*, "Correspondence on Manning of the Royal Navy," 1852-1853 [1628], LX.

[49]*BPP*, "Royal Commission on Unseaworthy Ships," 1873, [853], XXXVI, qq. 6756-6759.

[50]*BPP*, "Report on the Supply of British Seamen," 1886 [4709], LIX, 34-41.

[51]The emphasis here is on a "considerable premium." Contemporaries of Rankin reported that offers of an additional five or ten shillings per month without an advance had not been taken up by seamen. See *BPP*, "Royal Commission on Unseaworthy Ships," 1874, [1027-I], XXXIV, qq. 16, 260-16, 261; *BPP*, "Select Committee on the Merchant Seamen Bill," 1878 [205], XVI, qq. 1683-1687.

What became of the advance note after 1889? Ironically, given all the controversy engendered, the answer is not a great deal. Notes continued to be issued and the Superintendents of Mercantile Marine offices in London, Greenock, Hull and Barry testified to this in 1897. Yet the London Superintendent observed "but I may mention that now when the proportion of steamers is 537 to 87 sailing vessels, men are more continued from voyage to voyage." Likewise, the veteran campaigner for seamen's welfare, Commander Dawson, noted the decline of crimping other than in ports with a large number of long-distance sail trades.[52] The implication is that advance notes persisted but withered under competition from steam and the decline of sail within British shipping. The shift to steam, and the development of a new maritime labour market that did not feature pre-payment of wages, made notes of declining consequence. Advances soon ceased to be a concern in Britain. A Board of Trade Committee on the Manning of British Merchant Ships in 1896 ignored the subject, and an official 1897 report looked at the engagement and discharge of British seamen at continental rather than home ports.[53] By the early twentieth century the practice was effectively an anachronism. But the rapidity of its demise should not obscure its importance of the market for labour in the age of sail.

---

[52]*BPP*, "Report of the Committee to consider the Engagement and Discharge of British Seamen at Continental Ports," 1897 [8577], LXXXVIII, qq. 100-127, 140-206, 360-416, 465-473 and 2119-2121.

[53]The 1896 study is *BPP*, "Report of the Committee appointed by the Board of Trade to inquire into the Manning of British Merchant Ships," 1886 [8129], XL and XLI.

The Quality, Skill and Supply of Maritime Labour: Causes of Concern in Britain, 1850-1914

In a letter to the *Times*, Captain Robert Methven bemoaned in 1854 that "we have neither seamen or seamanship."[1] There could be no more succinct summary of both the issues and the prevailing opinion in the debate which was to obsess contemporaries for the next sixty years. From mid-century to the First World War, there was widespread concern over the quality, skill and supply of seamen in the British mercantile marine. Shipping interests – owners and masters – M.P.s and government officials all devoted much attention to the issue. So too did Royal Navy officers and parties interested in Imperial defence, for the merchant navy was seen as a source for recruitment and a wartime reserve.

The growth of concern was first visible in the late 1840s; thereafter the matter became a regular subject for discussion, investigation and the advocacy of remedial proposals. Because the issue was regarded as central to the operation and progress of British shipping, it featured in almost every official enquiry into the mercantile marine, but a list of those which addressed themselves particularly to the quality and supply of seamen illustrates the extent, regularity and high level of concern with what came to be known as the "manning question."[2] Commencing with a set of consular reports on seamen published in 1847-1848 (an exercise repeated in 1869-1870), government considered the matter again in two Commissions on manning the Royal Navy in 1852 and 1859. The Board of Trade reviewed labour in the mercantile marine in 1872 and produced a special report on the supply of British seamen in 1886. A Select Committee of 1878 examined the Merchant Seamen's Bill then before

---

[1] *The Mercantile Magazine* (July 1854), quoting a letter of Capt. Robert Methven to *The Times*.

[2] On the general issue of manning, see Eugene L. Rasor, *Reform in the Royal Navy* (Hamden, Conn., 1976); Stephen Jones. "Blood Red Roses: The Supply of Merchant Seamen in the Nineteenth Century," *Mariner's Mirror*, LVIII (1972), 429-444.

parliament. The Royal Commission on Unseaworthy Ships featured seamen in its reports of 1873 and 1874 as did the Select Committee on Saving Life at Sea of 1887. In 1894 the Royal Commission on Labour included seamen in its purview and Board of Trade Committees in 1896, 1903 and 1907, respectively, enquired into manning levels, the mercantile marine and the supply and training of boy seamen.[3] Alongside these official enquiries, such august bodies as the Royal Society of Arts, the National Association for the Promotion of Social Science and the Royal United Services Institution debated the matter and published their findings,[4] as did associations of shipowners and masters, humanitarian and religious bodies,[5] navy pressure groups (notably the Navy League from the

---

[3]Great Britain, House of Commons, *Parliamentary Papers* (henceforth *PP*), Papers relating to the Commercial Marine of Great Britain, 1847-48 (913) LIX, 141; Correspondence on Manning of the Royal Navy, 1852-53 (1628), LX, 9; Royal Commission into the Best Means of Manning the Navy, 1859 (Sess. 1, 2469), VI, 1; Replies by Certain of Her Majesty's Consuls, 1872, C. 630, LIII, 201; Report of the Assistant Secretary, Marine Department, with reference to the supply of merchant seamen, 1873, C. 752, LIX, 225; Royal Commission on Unseaworthy Ships, 1873, C. 853, XXXVI; 1874, C. 1027, XXXIV; Select Committee on Merchant Seamen's Bill, 1878 (205), XVI; Select Committee on Saving Life at Sea, 1887 (249) XII; Royal Commission on Labour, 1892, C. 6708-II, XXXIV: Committee of Board of Trade on Manning of British Merchant Ships, 1896, C. 8127-9, XL, XLI; Committee of Board of Trade on certain questions affecting the Mercantile Marine, 1903, Cds. 1607-9, LXII, 15; Committee of Board of Trade on supply and training of Boy Seamen, 1907, Cds. 3722-3, LXXV, 167.

[4]See, for example, Thomas Gray. *Mercantile Marine Legislation: A Paper Read to the Society of Arts* (London, 1866); J.L. Clifford Smith, National Association for the Promotion of Social Science. Twenty Fifth Anniversary. A Manual for the Congress with a Narrative of Past Labours and Results (London, 1882); Royal United Services Institution, The Loss of Life at Sea with a Report of the Committee of the Council to the Vice-President of the Board of Trade (London, 1866); J. Reddie, "Manning the Navy," Journal of the Royal United Services Institution, XI (1868), 279-360; J.C. Wilson. "Is Our Merchant Service Any Longer a Feeder to the Royal Navy." Ibid., XX, (1877), 61-84; Thomas Brassey, "How Best to Keep Up and Improve the Seamen of the Country," Ibid. XX (1870), 110-156.

[5]See, for example, Report of the Society for Improving the Condition of Merchant Seamen (London, 1867); Anon., "The Deterioration of our Merchant Seamen," *The Life-Boat*, VI (1868), 707-712; Liverpool Steam Ship Owners Association, Annual Report, 1911 (Liverpool, 1912).

1890s) and, once they were organised in later years, seamen themselves.[6] The tide of information produced was swelled further by books, pamphlets and coverage in papers, particularly the periodical press.[7]

To chart the patterns of such a long-running debate and to examine the circumstances and deliberations of individual enquiries is beyond the scope of a short study. But though debate took place over sixty years, and though the impetus of concern varied and some shifts of emphasis occurred, the central issues and the verdict essentially remained the same on every occasion. The weight of opinion, whether in the 1850s, 1870s or 1900s, held that British seamen were deficient in skill and supply. The aim of this paper is to explain and evaluate these persistent pessimistic assessments of labour in the British mercantile marine.[8]

The paper comprises three sections. The first examines the concern over skill, or more specifically, seamanship. It considers the criticisms made, the explanations advanced and then endeavours to explain why contemporary interpretations took the form they did. It then poses the question; was there a decline in seamanship? The second section undertakes a similar exercise on the supply aspect, reviewing contemporary opinions of the scale, nature and causes of the alleged shortfall of seamen,

---

[6]From the 1890s the Navy League assumed the leading role in the debate. *The Navy League* (London, 1896) summarises the League's aims and tactics.

[7]See for example, A Commander, R.N. [William Dawson], *Merchant Sailors' Wants* (London, 1866): Henry Toynbee. *The Social Condition of Merchant Seamen* (London, 1866): *A Retired Captain, R.N., Suggestions for Forming a New Reserve of Seamen* (London, 1871); Thomas Brassey, *Our Reserves of Seamen* (London, 1872); Frederick W. Grey, *Suggestions for Improving the Character of our Merchant Seamen and For Providing an Efficient Naval Reserve* (London, 1873); James Malley, *Our Merchant Ships and Sailors* (London, 1876); William S. Lindsay, *Manning the Royal Navy and Mercantile Marine* (London, 1877); and G. Holden Pike, *Among the Sailors* (London, 1897), A notable exception from this list is Samuel Plimsoll, *Our Seamen, An Appeal* (London, 1873), which despite its emotional title focussed on vessels rather than men.

[8]Because this paper represents an overview of a sixty year-long debate which gave rise to a prodigious volume of material, footnoting presents some problems, for every contemporary criticism, explanation and suggested remedial measure could be supported by a body of references spanning over half a century. For this reason, the basic, ever-present features of the debate are not specifically footnoted: supporting evidence in abundance is to be found in the official papers, and other works listed in notes 2, 3, and 4, though even these are merely representative of the vast literature. In the case of more specialised points and quotations, sources are fully-cited.

before considering whether supply presented real problems. The third section assesses the response to the widely-held view of the decline of seamen and seamanship. Here the remedial measures proposed and undertaken are examined, together with an assessment of why action fell so short of the level of spoken and written concern. This final question raises some important broader issues, notably about the attitudes of shipowners, government, labour, and society to the shifting role of the seaman in an era of technological change.

Since this study is very much concerned with judgements and attitudes, before proceeding to the body of the paper two general observations might usefully be made. First, as Sir Phillip Francis, Consul General at Constantinople in 1869, replied when asked to comment on masters and crews, "many people are inclined to magnify the merits of days gone by and the men of former generations."[9] Similarly, Thomas Brassey, in his seminal *British Seamen*, noted that "old captains and shipowners are equally prone, with all aged persons in other walks of life, to indulge in the *laus temporis acti*; to extol the men and things of the past, and to disparage their later contemporaries."[10] Secondly, it must be stressed that if gilded memories can detract from objectivity, so too can self-interest. This is a crucial point, for almost all who expressed an opinion on the British seaman were directly or indirectly involved with their subject. Many had motive to add urgency to their case but those who succumbed probably sinned through exaggeration rather than falsehood.

From the mid-century, the quality of labour in the mercantile marine, or to use the contemporary phrase, "the deterioration of the British seaman," became a focus of attention. Deterioration was seen in a variety of aspects[11] – skill, subordination, physical condition, moral behaviour – but above all it was skill – seamanship – which was highlighted as the principal and most worrying feature. Contemporaries saw this decline in seamanship as evident in two way: First, in that the proportion of seamen within the maritime labour force was contracting;

---

[9]*PP*, 1872 (C. 630), LIII, 148-151.

[10]Thomas Brassey, *British Seamen* (London, 1877), 27.

[11]The Liverpool Committee of Shipowners in 1870 focussed its enquiry on the issues of seamanship, subordination and physical condition.

and second, in what they believed was a decline in the skills of the individual seaman.

In the former instance, observers from mid-century had recourse to the material issued by the newly-appointed Registrar of Seamen.[12] This regular availability of figures was significant in fuelling the debate, for the Victorians were almost obsessed with statistics. The Registrar's tables revealed a progressive decline in the proportion of men described as "seamen" within the labour force, falling from a predominance at mid-century to around a quarter of all men employed on U.K. - registered vessels by 1911.[13] From the historian's standpoint this development was simply the outcome of the technological transformation of the mercantile marine and consequent changes in the composition of the maritime labour force. This being the case, why did the shift in employment patterns occasion such alarm?

To understand contemporary concern it is necessary to appreciate the constituency and outlook of those making judgements. At mid-century in particular - but also well beyond that date - critics had come of age familiar with sail and their conception of the maritime labour force was based on such an era. Traditionally, that force had effectively comprised solely seamen; anything else represented a departure from all that was regarded as normal and required considerable mental adjustment. Exacerbating this were the facts that the transition to steam was a gradual process, and that no one at mid-century could have visualised the ultimate superseding of sail. There could be no clearer example of these tendencies than the oft-quoted investigation of the Liverpool Committee of Shipowners into the deterioration of seamen in 1870. Of 111 respondents to the Committee's questionnaire, only twenty had any involvement in

---

[12]N. Cox, "The Records of the Registrar General of Shipping and Seamen," *Maritime History*, II (1972), 168-188; Valerie C. Burton, "Counting Seafarers: The Published Records of the Registry of Merchant Seamen," *Mariner's Mirror*, LXXI (1985), 305-320; M.J. Cullen, *The Statistical Movement in Early Victorian Britain* (New York, 1975).

[13]Burton, "Counting Seafarers," 315.

steam.[14] Opinion gathered from such a cross-section was likely to be rooted in the past.

Of course, as the nineteenth century progressed, the increasing steam orientation of the British merchant fleet became apparent to all, but even then concern over the declining proportion of seamen persisted. Seamen were still regarded as the essential element. It was argued that seamen were vital if vessels got into difficulty; less convincingly, ignoring the changed basis of the Navy, it was claimed that only seaman represented real reserve potential. The concern over British seamanship as perceived in the reduced proportion of seamen within the labour force was viewed with even greater concern as a disproportionate number of the foreigners in British service were ABs. Essentially, the problem of the decline in seamanship in its collective sense arose from an inability to come to terms with a new maritime environment in which labour was both more diffuse and specialised. A nationalistic dimension added to this lack of understanding.

Even more disturbing to contemporaries was the belief that seamen were lacking in traditional skills. A report in 1866 of a Committee of the Royal United Services Institution concluded "that not only are the separate crews less able to perform properly the seaman's work required in their ships, owning to the smaller proportion of ABs...but also the seamanlike ability of the individual AB is becoming less and less."[15] This view of a decline in seaman-like ability echoes throughout the second half of the nineteenth century. When the decline commenced and whether it was progressive and continuous were questions seldom if ever addressed, but there appeared to be some general agreement on a degeneration of pre-1850 standards. Often assessments of deterioration were vague – "deficient...to an extent quite startling to old salts"[16] or "of such a quality as was unknown formerly"[17] – but opinion was virtually unanimous. Of

---

[14]Brassey, *British Seamen*, 2. Liverpool as a port was relatively slow in moving from sail to steam, see P.L. Cottrell "The Steamship on the Mersey," in Phillip L. Cottrell and Derek H. Aldcroft (eds.), *Commerce, Trade and Shipping* (Leicester, 1981), 137-164.

[15]Royal United Service Institution, *The Loss of Life*, 50.

[16]William Walker, *Facts for Factories, Being Letters on Practical Subjects Suggested by Experiences in Bombay* (Bombay, 1857), 24-27.

[17]Capt. Murray, P. & O., to Thomas Brassey; see Brassey, *British Seamen*, 10.

the 111 respondents to the Liverpool Committee's questionnaire, eighty-nine percent affirmed that "seamen had deteriorated as seamen."[18]

Although observers were convinced of deterioration, their views were arrived at subjectively, rather than through any objective assessment of seamen against an agreed definition of seamanship. Contemporaries did, however, find themselves having to address the issue of a definition of seamanship, not because they felt any need to test their view of decline, but rather to indicate the qualities and attainments which should be aimed at. Defining seamanship presented something of a dilemma, for in the past there had seemed no need for a definition; in the age of sail, the duties and role of the seaman appeared obvious enough. Definitions, often comprehensive and complex, invariably backward-looking and sail-oriented, were drawn up for future guidance rather than retrospective analysis.[19] In no way were they – or could they be – used to test the contemporary view of declining seamanship.

Because they had no criteria for assessment contemporaries sought to explain what they regarded as a decline in seamanship in terms of failings in the areas of training and assessment. Above all the decline of apprenticeship was held to be a major influence. An apprenticeship system introduced in 1835, and made binding on British vessels in 1844, had been repealed in 1849; thereafter apprentices rapidly dwindled. Although the system had serious failings and had been disliked by shipping interests, mid-century observers claimed the ending of apprenticeship led to a serious fall in boy entrants who would have been trained in seamanship. The failure to re-establish apprenticeship, or to make adequate alternative provision through training ships and schools in the second half of the century, was seen to perpetuate a crucial failing.

The decline of apprenticeship was also held to contribute to the devaluation of the rating of Able Seaman, which was viewed both as a cause and a symptom of the decline in seamanship. The competition of an apprenticeship had served as a yardstick for the rating; without it, rating practice became indiscriminate. AB status was claimed by men of low proficiency and was accepted or granted by shipping masters and captains

---

[18]Brassey, *British Seamen*, 2.

[19]See for example, the criteria listed in the "Proposed Form of Certificate for Rating of AB," in *Report of the Society for Improving the Condition of Merchant Seamen*, 63.

either through ignorance or irresponsibility as standards were sacrificed in pursuit of speedy crew assembly. Resistance to statutory rating and genuine certification by both shipowners and Board of Trade officials for much of the century meant that the AB rating remained a debased currency, almost worthless as an indication of seamanship and as a status of proficiency to which men could aspire or take pride. If contemporaries saw defects at the AB level, even more so the rating of OS – Ordinary Seaman. This was regarded as being utterly meaningless in skill terms and allowed landsmen to assume falsely an immediate status. Moreover, OS wages, being higher than those paid to boys and apprentices, discouraged youngsters from completing any course of on-ship training. These weaknesses in the rating of seaman were seen to be compounded by the irresponsible practice of many masters, who to avoid trouble, always gave their crew on discharge, V.G. (very good) characters.[20] So standard did this become that references became meaningless and incentives for good, efficient seamen were lost.

Inadequacies in training, the system of grading, and assessment practice were held up as the chief causes of the deterioration in seamanship. All probably had some validity, as may have had the one other cause sometimes cited: the failure to recruit the "better class of men," which will be considered in the context of supply. The outcome of all these weaknesses was that those designated as seamen lacked the proficiency normally ascribed to that nomenclature. Thus, seamen lacked seamanship; however, the implication of the contemporary explanations is that, if the failings of training, assessment and recruitment were resolved, then "seamanly seamen," with all their traditional skills would be restored. But would this have been the case; were certain skills inexorably in the process of decline? Probably yes, due to technological advance, increasing vessel size and changing work practice. The opportunity to acquire basic sailing skills, only readily gained in small vessels, was shrinking as such vessels gave way to steamers, the northeast coal trade, the traditional "nursery of seaman" being the outstanding and most frequently-quoted example.[21] For much the same reason, boat-handling skills, less relevant and neglected on large vessels, fell into disuse, a fact often disastrously in evidence in

---

[20]A widely-quoted abuse. See *PP*, 1886, C. 4709, LIX, 4-5.

[21]*PP*, Report from the Select Committee on Merchant Shipping, 1860 (530), XIII, Qs. 818, 3742-5, 3981-4.

emergencies.[22] The almost standard practice from mid-century of shore-based men setting up and rigging vessels prior to departure again removed valuable expertise from the seaman's repertoire.[23] The same may have been true of changes in rig, such as the abandonment of studding sails and royals, the introduction of double-topsail yards and the use of patent windlasses.[24] Besides changed practices, new materials, such as steel and wire instead of wood and hemp, had an impact on some of the oldest elements of the sailor's craft. Technology, in the form of donkey engines and the steam winch (ironically described as the "best man on the ship"),[25] though easing physical labour, embodied a loss of practical knowledge and facility. Thus, irrespective and independent of the quality of its practitioners, aspects of seamanship were on the wane.

How then should we assess the contemporary view of a decline of seamanship. The evidence would appear clear: in quantitative terms, seamen were both absolutely, and relative to the maritime labour force as a whole, a declining group. And because of the absence of suitable training and assessment schemes and the disappearance of certain traditional work practices they may have been less capable than in the past. Such a verdict, though, depends on the definition of seamanship and skill. It is in this context that the historian can use the retrospective overview denied to contemporaries. From a late twentieth century perspective, it is clear that between 1850 and 1914 the British mercantile marine underwent revolutionary change and that with this transformation came a change in the composition of its labour force and the type of tasks and work required of it. Old skills and practices were less in demand; new abilities were needed. It might be said that these new abilities were not seamanship as it had been understood for centuries, but perhaps "old seamanship" was no longer an appropriate means of assessment. The means of traversing the seas was changing but the old definition of the human abilities required to do so had remained the same. The *Encyclo-*

---

[22]A matter discussed at some length in *PP*, 1887 (249), XII, Qs. 202, 293-303, 360-364, 396-400, 1683-1688, 1969-1973.

[23]Royal United Services Institutions, *Loss of Life*, 48-49.

[24]*PP*, 1896, C. 8127-8129, XLI, 11.

[25]*Quarterly Review*, CXLI (April 1876), 263.

pedia Britannica of 1910-1911 noted that "the name of 'seamanship' still continues to be applied to the art of handling ships under sail, and has never been made the subject of a treatise in so far as it means the management of a steamer. Perhaps it can never be."[26] This may well be so, and given the emotional connotations of sail and the scope for subjectivity in all definitions, perhaps the argument cannot fruitfully be pursued further. It would be wrong, however, to regard seamanship and skill as synonymous or to regard seamanship as the sole form of maritime skill. Some of the new tasks required of labour in the age of steam may have made less call on versatility and initiative, but seamen and below-deck workers in steam and even seamen on many sailing vessels developed skills, albeit different from those of their forebears. Old-fashioned seamen and seamanship may have been in short supply in 1914 but skill of a different order was very much in evidence.

While the debate over skill emerged in the mid-nineteenth century, the controversy over supply had a far longer pedigree. The commercial and strategic importance of the mercantile marine meant that its manning was a long-standing issue. But traditional concern was given added impetus at mid-century for three reasons. First, the growth of Britain's trade and mercantile marine demanded more men. Second, the Royal Navy's informal abrogation of impressment, placed additional emphasis on the mercantile marine. Although the Navy had largely solved its manning problem by 1870, lobbyists repeatedly pressed for a Reserve drawn from the merchant arm. Third, the removal in the course of the repeal of the Navigation Laws of any restraints on the employment of foreign labour led to a steadily growing non-British presence in the labour force. On strategic and nationalistic grounds, this commanded much attention, and to many the employment of foreigners was the clearest evidence of a supply problem. To these general concerns over supply was added the more specific fear of a shortfall of skilled seamen.

Estimates of the actual dimensions of the supply problem varied enormously over time and according to the working definitions, interests and motives of those considering the issue. A contributor to the *Nautical Magazine* in the 1870s suggested a need to recruit 10,000 new seamen a year to cope with annual wastage, while the Liverpool Committee's figure

---

[26]*Encyclopedia Britannica* (Eleventh ed., 1910-11), XXIV, 544.

for 1873, later adopted by the Board of Trade, was 16,000.[27] Forty years later, the Liverpool Committee claimed an annual intake of 9000 boys for sea training was necessary to maintain numbers,[28] although official estimates, influenced by financial reality, were somewhat smaller.[29]

Whereas dimensions and terms of reference might vary, general agreement prevailed that there was a supply problem. A legion of factors were put forward in explanation but essentially they were all contributing to two basic arguments; the lack of an adequate young intake and the increasingly residual character of maritime employment. On the former, because contemporaries viewed the supply problem partly in skill terms, the decline of apprenticeship and insufficiency in the provision of training establishments were also cited in this context. The residual nature of sea service, however, requires fuller consideration.

In the main, aside from those lured by, as Adam Smith described it, "the dangers and hair-breadth escapes of a life of adventures," seafaring is not a way of life likely to appeal to the majority. The hard work involved, the exposure to all weathers, the requirement to accept a constraining discipline and, as one authority has put it, the need to live like "an involuntary monk" for months on end, exercises limited appeal.[30] The Liverpool shipowner William Lamport observed in 1860 that "we can only find a certain portion of the population who are willing to go to sea. A seafaring life is not a desirable life."[31] Such comment merely reiterated what had always been the case and hardly explained the alleged growing supply problem. What was significant, however, was that it was increasingly felt that seafaring was becoming less attractive than ever. Various reasons were suggested in explanation. Some commentators claimed that limited prospects, lack of credit for skill and having to serve with

---

[27]Brassey, *British Seamen*, 35-39.

[28]Liverpool Steam Ship Owners Association, *Annual Report 1911* (Liverpool, 1912).

[29]*PP*, 1907, Cd. 3722, LXXV, 167.

[30]Conrad Dixon, "The Rise and Fall of the Crimp," in Stephen Fisher (ed.), *British Shipping and Seamen 1630-1960: Some Studies* (Exeter, 1984), 50.

[31]*PP*, 1860 (530), XIII, Q. 2585.

foreigners – all contemporary developments – discouraged good men.[32] Much more emphasis was laid on the notion that prevailing standards, practices and conditions, though no worse or different than in the past, had ceased to be acceptable. Food, accommodation, general conditions afloat, and terms of service were all seen to be crude and unattractive in an age of reform and advancing standards. And if seamen were pushed from the sea, contemporaries believed that they were pulled by better employment possibilities ashore which offered improved remuneration, prospects and lifestyle – in Frank Bullen's words, "the rise in the standard of comfort in England had diminished the number of British seamen."[33] Although most of these points merit analysis beyond the scope of this paper, some broad observations can be made. It is clear that with the possible exception of deep-water sail, the seafarers' lot improved, particularly in the later years. Accommodation, provisions and safety were all better; with steam, voyages were shorter and technology made work less onerous. Ironically, because standards of shore-based employment improved even more and because attitudes and social values changed, seafaring may have become less attractive and more residual than ever before. Contemporary assessments and fears may have been well-grounded.

Yet whether there actually was a supply problem or whether seafaring had become so unattractive that labour could not readily be obtained is another matter. All the evidence suggests that there was no difficulty in meeting the labour requirements of the British mercantile marine. Had there been, it might be presumed that a significant increase in wages would have occurred. In fact wages, though obviously fluctuating over time, and higher in steam than sail, showed no tendency to increase during the period and relative to wage earners in other major sectors of the economy, the returns to seafarers fell considerably.[34] Nor at a general

---

[32]The presence of foreigners was sometimes advanced as a cause rather than a consequence of poor recruitment. This point was stressed in the Report of the Committee on Manning of 1896; *PP*, 1896, C. 8127-9, XL, 11-13.

[33]*PP*, 1903, Cd. 1607, LXII, Q. 20,050.

[34]On wages in sail, see Lewis R. Fischer, "Seamen in a Space Economy: International Regional Patterns of Maritime wages on Sailing Vessels, 1863-1900," in Stephen Fisher (ed.), *Lisbon as a Port Town, the British Seaman and Other Maritime Themes* (Exeter, 1988), 57-92. On steam, such detailed analysis has yet to be undertaken but figures for the late nineteenth and early twentieth century suggest no increase in wage

level is there any sign of enhanced wages being paid to "better" men. Labour was available, and though the contribution of foreigners was increasing, British vessels were still predominantly manned by nationals. If there were any tightening of supply in Britain, which is extremely doubtful, it was offset by the ready access to labour from elsewhere.

Whatever conclusions retrospective analysis may come to about problems of seamanship and supply, the fact remains that contemporaries were firmly convinced of both deterioration and recruitment difficulties. Such claims were by no means simply carping criticisms: as we have seen, observers sought explanations and they proposed remedial action. Approaches and emphases varied widely, but in general the measures suggested fell into four main areas: young intake improvement through apprenticeship and training establishments: the certification of seamen; restrictions on the employment of foreigners; and improvements in conditions and prospects for seamen. A telling omission from these prescriptions was the incentive of higher wages, which was seldom advanced as a solution. To examine fully the practical response to these varied proposals is beyond the compass of this paper; moreover many aspects, such as training and the broad issue of conditions and welfare, have been assessed elsewhere. In this context, a brief survey must suffice to indicate the tone and level of response.

Most widely canvassed of all remedial proposals were those aimed at increasing the numbers and quality of young entrants. Apprenticeships and training ships or schools were the favoured means; these were supported, often with complex and detailed plans, by almost every writer and official enquiry throughout the period. The regularity of such proposals is a commentary on the lack of progress. Calls for increased apprenticeships, evident within years of the abolition of the compulsory requirement, met with little response.[35] Steam shipowners in particular pleaded costs and competitiveness in rejecting both voluntary and

---

levels. See *PP*, Report on Changes in Rates of Wages, Cd. 5324, LXXXIV, 535.

[35]An early example of campaigning for apprenticeships is Alfred P. Ryder and S.R. Graves, *A Letter on the National Dangers which result from the Great Deterioration in the Seamen of the mercantile marine: with reasons for the Adoption of an Apprenticeship System* (London, 1860).

compulsory schemes.[36] Government for its part foreswore compulsion and steadfastly refused financial support, other than between 1897 and 1903 when a bizarre experiment linked carrying apprentices with the remission of light duties.[37] Finance was similarly the stumbling block in the establishment of training ships. A number were founded, but their bias was towards supplying the Royal Navy and their annual product of boy seamen was limited – only two thousand were trained in 1914.[38] Again, the association of many with a reformatory or "destitute boy" intake hardly enhanced the image of the sea as a respectable career. Government took the stance that it was not the state's duty to finance the education of merchant seamen; in 1912, under pressure from the Navy League and the *Titanic* disaster, it did concede a modest grant, which was "too little and too late."[39]

The certification of seaman was seen as a means of restoring some validity to the rating of AB and thus promoting seamanship and recruitment. Though quite widely advocated from the 1860s, opinion differed on the form, who should administer it and whether it should be statutory. By legislation in 1880 no person was entitled to the rating of AB unless he could prove four years service before the mast, but this was largely cosmetic, as it did not provide for actual certificates and there was nothing to prevent inexperienced men being paid AB wages.[40] No progress came from the 1896 Manning Committee's recommendations on manning schedules and on the rating of ABs, OSs and firemen. Though supported by the new seamen's unions, shipowner fears that such measures would

---

[36]Later proposals for the carrying of apprentices and boys had quite significant cost implications, as it was advocated that boys have supervision, instruction and special accommodation. See *PP*, 1907, Cd. 3722, LXXXV, Report 1-7.

[37]On the Ritchie Act, see Coghlan McL. McHardy, *British Seamen. Boy Seamen and Light Dues* (London, 1899).

[38]Contemporary accounts of the pre-war manning campaign are to be found in Clement Jones, *British Merchant Shipping* (London, 1922), 128-139; *The Times*, Shipowning Number, 13 December 1912. This was later reprinted as a book (London, 1913).

[39]Jones, *British Merchant Shipping*, 135.

[40]*PP*, 1892, C. 6708-11, XXXIV, Qs. 9336-40; 9353-8; 9873-95.

restrain their freedom and increase labour's bargaining strength ensured rejection. Three years later, for the negative reason of checking desertion a system of Continuous Discharge Certificates was introduced.[41] These served as an identity book and work record and thus provided some form of check on competence. Their operation, which was much praised, and greater objectivity in masters' assessments, seems to have removed the impetus from the certification campaign, though ironically, cooks were certificated in an 1910 Act.[42] Certification might well have had some impact on the employment of foreigners, another area of possible action. In the 1890s, when the proportion of foreign seamen became significant, there were demands, notably from seamen's representatives, for the re-enactment of portions of the Navigation Laws to limit the foreign element within crews, and later there were calls to exclude non-English speakers.[43] Nothing came of them; shipowners resisted any interference with their right to hire, reportedly declaring that the "foreign element was an advantage and regulated the market."[44]

A much more positive approach was to improve the seaman's lot. From mid-century, squalid, deprived and dangerous conditions afloat, exploitation ashore, and no safeguards against ill-health, injury or old age were all seen as deterring "decent" men from a sea career. It followed that improved conditions, protection and prospects would strengthen intake and commitment. Such motives, together with genuine humanitarianism and concern over social and moral welfare, prompted a range of measures from the 1860s. Unseaworthy ships and load line legislation in 1871 and 1876 improved safety, although not until the 1890s could protection be deemed satisfactory.[45] Shore-based dangers were also tackled with

---

[41]Dixon, "The Rise and Fall of the Crimp," 62-64.

[42]6 Edw. 7 C. 48.

[43]*PP*, 1896, C. 8127-9, XL, Report; Cd. 1607, LXII, Report.

[44]*PP*, 1892, C. 6708-11, XXXIV, Qs. 10, 706-15.

[45]David Masters, *The Plimsoll Mark* (London, 1955); Neville Upham. *The Load Line - A Hallmark of Safety* (London, 1978); Geoffrey Alderman, "Samuel Plimsoll and the Shipping Interests," *Maritime History*, I (1971) 78-79; Alderman, "Joseph Chamberlain's Attempted Reform of the British Mercantile Marine," *Journal of Transport History*, New Series, I (1972), 169-184.

successful moves against crimping from 1878[46] and the praiseworthy Seaman's Home Movement inspired by temperance and evangelicalism.[47] Problems of health, diet and accommodation were first legislated on in the 1860s but only took on real meaning with acts in 1905 and 1906.[48] All in all, the impressive entries in the statute books are somewhat deceptive: action was usually belated and its scope, effectiveness and enforcement was often limited, with shipowners generally only grudgingly accepting the minimum of responsibility. Though improved, the seaman's lot fell progressively further behind other workers and certain problems such as advance notes, insurance and pensions saw scant progress.

In seeking to explain the contrast of widespread and vociferous complaint with but limited action in some areas and no action in others, three factors are worthy of consideration. Of prime importance is the attitude of shipowners and the political dimension; of lesser substance is the Royal Navy's concern over manning. Any reference to the attitude of shipowners embodies a generalisation about a group which, like any other body, embraced wide differences. The shipowner with a good reputation for fair conditions and treatment seldom encountered labour problems; as Consul Brown at Genoa noted, "Good masters...have invariably well-conducted crew."[49] Far-sighted employers often made individual responses through training schemes, extra payments to long-serving ABs and superior provisions and accommodation.[50] Still, such owners were the exception; the majority, though protesting about labour were not prepared

---

[46]Dixon, "The Rise and Fall of the Crimp," 49-67; Sarah B. Palmer, "Seamen Ashore in Late Nineteenth Century London: Protection from the Crimps," in Paul Adam (ed.), *Seamen in Society* (Bucharest, 1980), 55-76.

[47]Doris Gulliver, *Dame Agnes Weston* (London, 1971); Alston Kennerly, "Seamen's Missions and Sailors' Homes: Spiritual and Social Welfare Provisions in British Ports in the Nineteenth Century," in Stephen Fisher (ed.), *Studies in British Privateering, Trading Enterprises and Seamen's Welfare, 1770-1900* (Exeter, 1987), 121-165.

[48]Conrad Dixon, "Pound and Pint: Diet in the Merchant Service 1750-1980," in Sarah B. Palmer and Glyndwr Williams (eds.), *Charted and Uncharted Waters* (London, 1982), 164-180.

[49]*PP*, 1847-48 (913), LIX, 81.

[50]*British Merchant Service Journal*, 11 (1880), 194; *The Times Shipping Number*, 143.

to undertake anything which would increase cost or inconvenience. Training establishments and apprenticeships were admirable, if supported from the public purse; conditions afloat could no doubt be improved but competition was intense and margins tenuous; and official action was desirable but only to strengthen discipline and to check desertion. This view prevailed because no matter how much they deplored the quality and supply of labour, sufficient men able to do the job came forward at a price which owners were prepared to pay. Moreover, manning ratios were constantly being reduced, betokening greater efficiency and making labour a diminishing element of overall costs.[51] The Committee on Manning of 1896 assessed the situation quite admirably: "it is impossible to conceive any state of things more favourable to the British shipowner in so far as concerns a cheap and a perfectly open market for the labour which he has to employ. The shipowner may select his employees from all nationalities, at any rate of wages, and may also (as the law now stands) at his discretion or caprice, either require or dispense with proofs of qualification."[52]

Likewise, for all the strategic desirability of a merchant navy comprised of British seaman of sound ability and decent character, the Royal Navy felt no need to press the matter. The most serious problems of manning had been solved by the Continuous Service scheme which by the 1870s was proving highly effective.[53] Again, the Royal Naval Reserve, established in 1859, had a strength of 19,000 by 1885, and though influential observers such as Thomas Brassey regularly kept the issue in the public eye with proposals to link the reserve with certification and sea training, the system appeared to work well. Nor did any crisis arise to put the Navy's manning arrangements to the test.

Finally, in explaining the contrast between levels of concern and action, it must be said that the political dimension was hardly likely to promote any initiative. Throughout the period government was ideologically committed to the market and jealous of expenditure. Moreover, it

---

[51]Manning ratios per ton fell dramatically. In sail, they fell from 4.17 per 100 tons in 1854 to 2.57 in 1899. In steam, figures for the same dates were 7.47 and 2.66. See "Tables on the Progress of British Merchant Shipping." *PP*, 1900, Cd. 218, LXXVII, I.

[52]*PP*, 1896, C. 8127-9, XL, 12.

[53]A summary of these developments is to be found in Rasor, *Reform*, 26-37.

only slowly adjusted its role with regard to seamen which traditionally had focussed on contractual and disciplinary aspects and much less on training, standards and welfare.[54] Again, for all the importance of seamen and seamanship, there were other maritime problems which may have been seen as more pressing and commanding priority – the impact of Navigation Law Repeal, the Passenger Acts, the quality of officers, problems associated with new technology, and the ever-present issue of safety at sea which so obsessed the Victorians. In some of these areas like safety, the obstructive role of Board of Trade officials is well-documented. Thomas Farrar, the Board's permanent secretary, and Thomas Gray of the Marine Department, both free market fanatics, adopted similar postures in matters relating to seamen, eschewing involvement, intervention and inspection. To such ends they unscrupulously shifted ground, were economical with the truth, and inevitably concluded that action was uncalled for or inadvisable.[55] The influence of such dogmatic officials extended until late in the century, but though office then passed to less extreme personnel, they too regarded cost competitiveness, the security of capital, and above all the maintenance of the free market as their articles of faith.[56] This creed was apparently successful, as the British mercantile marine continued to dominate world shipping. Politically, therefore, neither government and administration nor ideology and the perceived outcome of policy were likely sources of a positive response.

The surveys in this paper of nineteenth century concern over seamanship and supply both emerged with similar conclusions: that the deterioration and deficiency visualised as so serious and pressing by contemporaries in reality presented no major problems for the British mercantile marine. And this was borne out by the very limited action

---

[54]Conrad Dixon, "Legislation and the Sailors' Lot 1660-1914," in Adam (ed.). *Seamen in Society*, 96-106.

[55]For examples of the negative and obstructive attitude of senior officials at the Board of Trade, see D.M. Williams. "State Regulation of Merchant Shipping, 1839-1914: The Bulk Carrying Trades," in Palmer and Williams (eds.), *Charted and Uncharted Waters*, 55-80; Alderman, "Samuel Plimsoll;" Alderman, "Joseph Chamberlain." Even Brassey felt obliged to note that the Board in its attitude to seamen "has not always been consistent;" *British Seamen*, 22.

[56]R. Davidson, "The Board of Trade and Industrial Relations," *Historical Journal*, XXI (1978), 571-591.

which was undertaken in response to the alleged problems. At the end of the day, pragmatism prevailed and none of the interested parties saw the situation as so serious, or felt strongly enough, to warrant the financial cost and the sacrifice of ideological principles involved. Much agitation, for no great reason and to no great purpose, could be regarded as a general, if somewhat cynical, conclusion.

Yet such a major, long-running debate which produced such a volume of material cannot be dismissed so tritely. How could issues which were not problems, and which led to the minimal response, be the subject of such agitation? The explanation lies in the fact that the concerns were not without foundation. Old-style seamen and traditional seamanship were in decline; in Britain, the sea was tending to become even more of a residual occupation, certainly for good quality labour and perhaps for labour generally. Because technological change and the international character of the maritime labour market which gave rise to the problem also partially solved them, the trends which so obsessed contemporaries may have been of no practical consequence. Nevertheless, as the Report of the Committee on Manning in 1903 perceptively commented, they gave rise to a "feeling of regret not the less real even if it be based on patriotic and even sentimental rather than on strictly economic grounds."[57]

Such a comment goes right to the heart of the matter. The changes occurring were emotionally quite shattering; centuries old views of the seaman and his craft were no longer applicable, and an long-established order where personnel and functions were clearly defined was being totally overthrown. And if emotions were stirred by the demise of the seaman, they were even more agitated over the issue of recruitment. That British vessels should be manned by "a heterogeneous mixture of foreigners,"[58] with some vessels alleged to resemble "Noah's Ark"[59] in their crew composition, and that British boys should be reluctant to go to sea, seemed outrageous and unacceptable. "It is impossible to regard such a change with acquiescence of equanimity" observed the Committee of

---

[57]*PP*, 1903, Cd. 1607, LXII, Report, vii.

[58]This is a much used phrase; see Gray, *Mercantile Marine*; *PP*, 1896, Cd. 8127-9, XL, Report, 13.

[59]*Journal of Commerce*, 15 April 1899.

1903.[60] Did not Britannia rule the waves? The national culture embodied "Hearts of Oak," Trafalgar Day and the Empire across the seas; indeed it was from this that the myriad of seafaring charities and pressure groups such as the Navy League drew their support. Tradition, an increasingly romanticised view of sail, and Britain's maritime heritage were thus all embodied in the concern over seamen and seamanship.[61] In the harsh world of reality, however, emotion weighed lightly in the balance against the economics of the market, and nostalgia had no place in an era of expansion and technological advance.[62]

---

[60]*PP*, 1903, Cd. 1607, LXII, Report, vii.

[61]Some indication of the contrast between reality and the literary image of the seaman is to be found in R.D. Foulke, "Life in the Dying World of Sail," *Journal of British Studies*, III (1963), 105-136.

[62]I am indebted to my colleague Dr. P.L. Cottrell for his comments on an earlier draft of this paper, and the Research Board. University of Leicester, for a grant in aid of research.

David M. Williams: A Bibliography

Compiled by Lars U. Scholl

Books

A Select Bibliography of British and Irish University Theses about Maritime History. St: John's: International Maritime Economic History Association, 1991. Research in Maritime History No. 1. (Compiled with Andrew P. White).

Management, Finance and Industrial Relations in Maritime Industries: Essays in International Maritime and Business History. St. John's: International Maritime Economic History Association, 1994. Research in Maritime History No. 6. (Edited with Simon P. Ville).

Management, Finance and Industrial Relations in Maritime Industry. Milan: Eleventh International Economic History Congress, 1994. (Edited with Simon P. Ville).

Shipping, Technology and Imperialism. Aldershot: Scolar Press, 1996. (Edited with Gordon Jackson).

The North Sea: Resources and Sea Way. Aberdeen: North Sea Society and Aberdeen City Council, 1996. (Editor of Section 1, "Seaway," with introduction).

The World of Shipping. Aldershot: Scolar Press, 1997. (Editor).

Frutta di Mare: Evolution and Revolution in the Maritime World in the 19th and 20th Centuries. Amsterdam: Batavian Lion, 1998. (Edited with Paul C. van Royen and Lewis R. Fischer).

Chapters in Books

"Liverpool Merchants and the Cotton Trade, 1820-50." In J.R. Harris (ed.). *Liverpool and Merseyside*. London: Frank Cass, 1969, pp. 182-211.

"A Select Bibliography of Studies Published between 1953 and 1969." In Judith Blow Williams. *British Commercial Policy and Trade Expansion*. Oxford: Clarendon Press, 1972, pp. 461-487.

"The Shipping of the North Atlantic Cotton Trade in the Mid-Nineteenth Century." In David Alexander and Rosemary Ommer (eds.). *Volumes Not Values: Canadian Sailing Ships and World Trades*. St. John's: Maritime History Group, 1979, pp. 303-329.

"Customs Evasion, Colonial Preference and the British Tariff, 1829-1842." In P.L.Cottrell and D.H. Aldcroft (eds.). *Shipping Trade and Commerce*. Leicester: Leicester University Press, 1981, pp. 99-116.

"Crew Size in Trans-Atlantic Trades in the Mid-Nineteenth Century." In Rosemary Ommer and Gerald Panting (eds.). *Working Men Who Got Wet*. St. John's: Maritime History Group, 1980, pp. 107-153.

"State Regulation of Merchant Shipping 1839-1914: The Bulk Carrying Trades." In Sarah Palmer and Glyn Williams (eds.). *Charted and Uncharted Waters*. London: National Maritime Museum, 1982, pp. 55-80.

"James Silk Buckingham, 1786-1855: Sailor, Explorer, Reformer." In H.E.S. Fisher (ed.). *Studies in British Privateering, Trading Enterprise and Seaman's Welfare*. Exeter: Exeter University Press, 1987, pp. 99-119.

"Pamphleteering and the Timber Duties, 1809-51: A Bibliographical Essay." In Lewis R. Fischer, Helge W. Nordvik and Walter Minchinton (eds.). *Shipping and Trade in the Northern Seas, 1600-1939*. Bergen: Norwegian School of Economics for the Association for the History of the Northern Seas, 1988, pp. 36-59.

"Henry Mayhew and the British Seamen." In H.E.S. Fisher (ed.). *Lisbon as a Port Town, TheBritish Seaman and Other Maritime Themes*. Exeter: Exeter University Press, 1988, pp. 111-128.

"The Rise of United States Merchant Shipping on the North Atlantic, 1800-1850s: The British Perception and Response." In Clark G. Reynolds (ed.). *Global Crossroads and the American Seas*. Missoula, MT: Missoula Publishing Company, 1988, pp. 67-84.

"An Illustrated Source for Maritime History." In H.E.S. Fisher (ed.). *Innovation in Shipping and Trade*. Exeter: Exeter University Press, 1989, pp. 145-176.

"Bulk Trades and the Development of Liverpool in the First Half of the Nineteenth Century." In Valerie Burton (ed.). *Liverpool Shipping, Trade and Industry: Essays on the Maritime History of Merseyside 1780-1860*. Liverpool: Merseyside Maritime Museum, 1989, pp. 8-24.

"The British Government and Merchant Seamen: Efficiency and Welfare, 1870-1914." In W.B. Cogar (ed.). *New Interpretations in Naval History: Selected Papers from the Eighth Naval History Symposium*. Annapolis: United States Naval Institute Press, 1989, pp. 85-101.

"Bulk Passenger Freight Trades, 1750-1870." In Lewis R. Fischer and Helge W. Nordvik (eds.). *Shipping and Trade (1750-1950)*. Leuven: Leuven University Press, 1990, pp. 38-46.

"The Citrus Trade to Britain in the Nineteenth Century." In C. Koninckx (ed.). *El Comercio y Transporte Maritime Mundial de Alimentos*. Brussels: International Commission for Maritime History, 1990, pp. 522-545.

"Bulk Passenger Freight Trades in the Eighteenth and Nineteenth Centuries." In Lewis R. Fischer and Helge W. Nordvik (eds.). *Shipping and Trade, 1750-1950: Essays in International Maritime Economic History*. Pontefract: Lofthouse Publications, pp. 43-62.

"'A Period of Transition:' Personnel in the British Mercantile Marine in the First Half of the Nineteenth Century." In J.R. Bruijn and W.F.J. Mörzer Bruyns (eds.). *Anglo-Dutch Mercantile Marine Relations 1700-1850*. Amsterdam: Nederlands Scheepvaart-museum, 1991, pp. 115-125.

"The Quality, Skill and Supply of Maritime Labour: Causes of Concern in Britain, 1850-1914." In Lewis R. Fischer, *et al.* (eds.). *The North Sea: Twelve Essays on the Social History of Maritime Labour*. Stavanger: Association of North Sea Societies, 1992, pp. 41-58.

"Peter Neville Davies – A Tribute." In Lewis R. Fischer (ed.). *From Wheel House to Counting House: Essays in Maritime Business History in Honour of Professor Peter Neville Davies*. St. John's: International Maritime Economic History Association, 1992, pp. 5-16.

"Shipowners and Iron Sailing Ships: The First Twenty Years, 1838-1857." In Lewis R. Fischer and Walter E. Minchinton (eds.). *People of the Northern Seas*. St. John's: International Maritime Economic History Association, 1992, pp. 115-133. (with Jonathan M. Hutchings).

"Ports and Harbours: Adaptations to Change – A Summary." In Poul Holm and John Edwards (eds.). *North Sea Ports and Harbours – Adaptations to Change*. Esbjerg: Fiskeri-og Søfartsmuseet, 1992, pp. 225-235.

"Business Ethics and Victorian Shipowners: Contexts for Research." In Adrian Jarvis (ed.). *Nineteenth Century Business Ethics*. Liverpool: Merseyside Maritime Museum, 1992, pp. 52-65.

"Laivanvarustajat ja Rautaiset Purjelaivat: Ensimmaiset Kaksikym-Menta Vuotta, 1838-1857." In E. Karppinen (ed.). *Meren Kansaa: IX Itameri-seminaaari Kotkassa 1992*. Kotka: Provincial Museum of Kylemasko, 1994, pp. 225-242.

"Growth, Market Shifts and Technological Change –The Citrus Trade to Britain in the Nineteenth Century." In Klaus Friedland (ed.). *Maritime Food Transport*. Köln: Böhlau-Verlag, 1994, pp. 325-348.

"'Advance Notes' and the Recruitment of Maritime Labour in Britain in the Nineteenth Century." In Lewis R. Fischer (ed.). *The Market for Seamen in the Age of Sail*. St. John's: International Maritime Economic History Association, 1994, pp. 81-100.

"British Sailors." In P.C. van Royen, J.R. Bruijn and J. Lucassen (eds.). *"Those Emblems of Hell"? European Sailors and the Maritime Labour Market, 1570-1870*. St. John's: International Maritime Economic History Association, 1997, pp. 93-118. (with Sarah Palmer).

Articles

"Merchanting in the First Half of the Nineteenth Century: The Liverpool Timber Trade." *Business History*, VIII (1966), 103-121.

"Bulk Carriers and Timber Imports: The British North American Timber Trade and the Shipping Boom of 1824-5." *Mariner's Mirror*, LIV (1968), 372-382.

"Henry Warburton and the Free Trade Movement." *Proceedings of the Dorset Natural History and Archaeological Society*, XC (1969), 285-294.

"Abolition and the Re-deployment of the Slave Fleet, 1807-11." *Journal of Transport History*, New Series, II (1973), 103-115.

"The Shipping and Organization of the Atlantic Slave Trade: A Review Article." *Journal of Transport History*, New Series, IV (1978), 179-184.

"A New Medium for Advertising: The Postcard 1890-1920." *Journal of Advertising History*, XI (1988), 17-34. Published simultaneously in *Journal of European Marketing*, XXII (1988), 17-34.

"Mid-Victorian Attitudes to Seamen and Maritime Reform: The Society for Improving the Condition of Merchant Seamen, 1867." *International Journal of Maritime History*, III (1991), 101-126.

"Industrialization, Technological Change and the Maritime Labour Force: The British Experience 1800-1914." *Collectanea Maritima*, V (1991), 317-330.

"The Progress of Maritime History, 1953-93." *Journal of Transport History*, Third Series, XIV, No. 2 (1993), 127-141.

"Samuel Plimsoll and the Safety of International Shipping: An Appraisal." *Mariners' Museum Journal* (1996), 10-19.

Printed and bound by CPI Group (UK) Ltd, Croydon, CR0 4YY

16/04/2025

14658576-0005